Wes Craven

Wes Craven

The Art of Horror

by
John Kenneth Muir

McFarland & Company, Inc., Publishers
Jefferson, North Carolina, and London

The present work is a reprint of the library bound edition of Wes Craven: The Art of Horror, *first published in 1998 by McFarland.*

Frontispiece: Director Wes Craven faces his audience while a gallery of his most famous film horrors look on. Artwork by Mindy Easler.

LIBRARY OF CONGRESS CATALOGUING-IN-PUBLICATION DATA

Muir, John Kenneth, 1969–
 Wes Craven : the art of horror / by John Kenneth Muir.
  p. cm.
 Includes bibliographical references and index.

 ISBN 0-7864-1923-7 (softcover : 50# alkaline paper) ∞

 1. Craven, Wes — Criticism and interpretation.   I. Title.
PN1998.3.C72M85   2004
791.43'0233'092 — dc21   98-28223

British Library cataloguing data are available

©1998 John Kenneth Muir. All rights reserved

No part of this book may be reproduced or transmitted in any form or by any means, electronic or mechanical, including photocopying or recording, or by any information storage and retrieval system, without permission in writing from the publisher.

On the cover: Wes Craven on the set of the 1997 film *Scream 2* (Photofest)

Manufactured in the United States of America

McFarland & Company, Inc., Publishers
  Box 611, Jefferson, North Carolina 28640
   www.mcfarlandpub.com

For Lara,
who introduced me to Freddy Krueger,
and who is still haunted by him

Acknowledgments

This author would like to thank Frances Leftwich and Karen Toombs for their diligent efforts to locate and procure Wes Craven films on videotape and laserdisc, as well as John and Mindy Easler for their ongoing interest in and commentary on the project. Special thanks also to Kathryn Muir for watching *The Hills Have Eyes*, *Wes Craven's New Nightmare* and *Scream* repeatedly with the author and offering her two cents' worth. Most of all, the author would like to gratefully acknowledge the hard work of Wes Craven and his continuing cohorts Tony Cecere, Marianne Maddalena and Robert Englund for their legacy of screen terror, without which there would be no book.

Contents

Acknowledgments vii

Introduction 1

1. Career Overview 7

2. The Feature Films 39

    The Last House on the Left (1972) 39
    The Hills Have Eyes (1977) 58
    Deadly Blessing (1981) 74
    Swamp Thing (1982) 85
    The Hills Have Eyes Part II (1983) 95
    A Nightmare on Elm Street (1984) 105
    Deadly Friend (1986) 120
    The Serpent and the Rainbow (1987) 131
    Shocker (1989) 145
    The People Under the Stairs (1991) 159
    Wes Craven's New Nightmare (1994) 171
    A Vampire in Brooklyn (1995) 186
    Scream (1996) 196
    Scream 2 (1997) 210

3. The Television Movies 221

    A Stranger in Our House (1978) 221
    Invitation to Hell (1984) 228
    Chiller (1985) 238
    Night Visions (1990) 246

4. Craven as Executive Producer 247

    A Nightmare on Elm Street Part III: Dream Warriors (1987) 247
    Wes Craven Presents Mind Ripper (1995) 256
    Wes Craven Presents Wishmaster (1997) 266

5. The Television Series 275

    The Twilight Zone (1985) 275
    Nightmare Cafe (1992) 279

6. The Battle Over Censorship   291

Epilogue   295

Appendix A: Movie References in *Scream*   297
Appendix B: The Family in Craven's Films   299
Appendix C: Recurring Imagery   301
Appendix D: Rating the Films   303

Notes   305
Bibliography   309
Index   311

Introduction

It may be naive or even worshipful to spotlight the career of a single film director and boast that he is the savior of an entire genre. Yet if one considers that writer/director Wes Craven has thrice pulled cinematic horror up from the flames of self-annihilation during his quarter-century career, the evidence in favor of such an assertion is compelling. It is hard *not* to look at Craven's accomplishments in a flattering light, considering his unique contributions to film, telemovies and even regular series television.

Craven broke into the progressive New York film industry and the horror genre in the early 1970s when the British Hammer Studios' *Dracula* and *Frankenstein* pictures, starring Christopher Lee and Peter Cushing, were winding down into inane repetition (*Frankenstein Must Be Destroyed* [1970] and *Frankenstein and the Monster from Hell* [1973]). Not surprisingly, horror's future looked unpromising in those days. Those few so-called scary movies that did not revolve around the "big" cinematic ghouls such as Dracula and the Frankenstein Monster — familiar creatures who had lost much of their bite after knocking around on the silver screen since the Universal films of the '30s and '40s — they were usually low-brow, out-of-focus Sasquatch efforts such as *Bigfoot* (1969) and *The Legend of Boggy Creek* (1972).

Then, two years before the unswerving brutality of Tobe Hooper's *The Texas Chainsaw Massacre* (1974) and one year before William Friedkin's watershed film *The Exorcist* (1973), Wes Craven presented America with an unflinching look into the heart of human darkness with *The Last House on the Left* (1972), a low-budget, high-impact variation on Ingmar Bergman's classic *The Virgin Spring* (1958).

Craven's first horror picture presented violent subject matter (rape, revenge, substance abuse) in such realistic fashion that audiences were, in the words of film critic Roger Ebert, "rocked back on their psychic heels,"[1] and to this day a more potent horror film has not been produced. Although *The Last House on the Left* was reviled by critics at the time (except for Ebert), audiences responded more positively, and *The Last House on the Left* became a cult classic, the standard-bearer of a new horror subgenre called "rape and revenge." In one fashion or another, films such as *The Texas Chainsaw Massacre* (1974), *I Spit on Your Grave* (1979), *Three on a Meathook* (1973), *My Friend Needs Killing* (1977), *The Little*

Girl Who Lived Down the Lane (1976) and even popular mainstream pictures such as *Death Wish* (1974) owe a great deal of their vitality to Craven's early exploitation classic. Craven demonstrated that horror need not be tied to a star such as Peter Cushing or Vincent Price nor necessarily feature a supernatural or extraterrestrial theme. A trademark of Craven's earliest work is that horror erupts full-blown from the innate brutality of man, not from an outside monstrosity or supernatural force.

After a second hit of equal intensity, *The Hills Have Eyes* (1977), Craven survived the '70s intact if not wealthy. Proving his adaptability, he pulled his first miraculous reinvention and sent horror in a bold new direction in the early '80s. By 1984, audiences had tired of the infinite variations on John Carpenter's seminal stalker film *Halloween* (1978) — variations that included *Terror Train* (1980), *Friday the 13th* (1980), *Prom Night* (1980), *He Knows You're Alone* (1980), *Happy Birthday to Me* (1981), *My Bloody Valentine* (1981) and *Hell Night* (1982), to name but a few. The "stalker" subgenre and the "invincible killer" theme had finally run their course. Most major Hollywood studios went so far as to pronounce the genre dead. At least, that is, until *A Nightmare on Elm Street* premiered in 1984 and took the world by storm.

With *Elm Street*, Craven created a visionary film about a fiendish killer who inhabited the dreams of his victims. Suddenly, baby-sitters, masked killers and machetes were passé, and horror had a more fantastic prototype to follow. "Rubber reality" was the rage, and for the first time since the heyday of Price, Cushing and Lee, horror had a new icon: Robert Englund as the dream-killer, Freddy Krueger. *A Nightmare on Elm Street* was followed by five official sequels from New Line Cinema and numerous unofficial imitators such as *Bad Dreams* (1988), *Dream Demons* (1988), *Dreamaniac* (1986) and *Paperhouse* (1987), all of which partially or totally inhabited the world of hallucinations and dream sequences rather than the typical, reality-based "stalker" world. Effortlessly shifting from the bluntness of documentary-like, reality-based horror to the strange highs of hallucinations, nightmares and alternate realities, Craven marvelously reinvented his own film technique and ideology. *The Last House on the Left* and *The Hills Have Eyes* were nihilistic, existential films that afforded no belief in a better world beyond the violent one their characters inhabited, but *A Nightmare on Elm Street* was a gateway to another dimension, a plane of twisted spirituality where characters might suffer at the hand (or glove) of a maniac or just as easily discover their own inner strength and make use of personality traits that had gone unexplored in mundane reality.

Realizing perhaps that he had changed the future of the horror film, Craven's trajectory remained steady in the '80s. Every film he made in the decade after *A Nightmare on Elm Street*, including *Deadly Friend* (1986), *The Serpent and the Rainbow* (1988) and *Shocker* (1989), featured hallucinatory sequences that took place in the world of nightmares and dreamscapes. By 1989 and *Shocker*, the "dream" template was exhausted through excessive repetition. The once-fresh concept was no longer exciting to audiences who had been exposed to *A Nightmare on Elm Street II: Freddy's Revenge* (1985), *A Nightmare on Elm Street III: Dream Warriors* (1987), *A Nightmare on Elm Street IV: The Dream Master* (1988), *A Nightmare on Elm Street V: The Dream Child* (1989) and even an *Elm Street* TV spin-off called *Freddy's Nightmares* (1988–90). Though the technique had successfully guided the horror genre through the tumultuous waters of the 1980s, the domination of Wes Craven's "fantasy horror" was over.

After returning briefly to the style of *The Last House on the Left* and *The Hills Have Eyes* with *The People Under the Stairs* (1991) and then wavering back to "nightmare" horror with a short-lived TV series called *Nightmare Cafe*, Craven reinvented himself and the genre yet again. At first blush, *Wes Craven's New Nightmare* seems like a retreat to *A Nightmare on Elm Street* horror and the world of its popular villain, Freddy Krueger. However, the film is profoundly self-referential, taking place not inside Krueger's fictional world, but inside the "making of" Krueger's world, the world of filmmaking itself. Craven, Heather Langenkamp, Bob Shaye of New Line and Robert Englund played themselves, and the film emerged as a wry commentary on sequels and horror film fans. Although the film was not a huge success with audiences, Craven received the best reviews of his career for his witty work on that project. *New Nightmare* was described by enthusiastic reviewers as part Robert Altman and part Pirandello. The seeds were thus planted for Craven's new direction, and after a brief stumble with an Eddie Murphy horror/comedy vehicle called *Vampire in Brooklyn* (1995), Craven again rescued horror films in 1996.

By that year, fans and filmmakers around the world were mourning the loss of horror as a viable genre. Freddy Krueger had died in 1991's *Freddy's Dead: The Final Nightmare*, and Jason Voorhees had been finished off in 1993's *Jason Goes to Hell: The Final Friday*. Following the demise of the big '80s franchises, Hollywood returned to classical horror antecedents, and audiences were treated to glorious, big-budget remakes of the literary adventures imagined by Mary Shelley, Bram Stoker, John Wyndham and Anne Rice. Kenneth Branagh's *Mary Shelley's Frankenstein* (1994), Francis Ford Coppola's *Bram Stoker's Dracula* (1991), John Carpenter's *Village of the Damned* (1995) and Neil Jordan's *Interview With the Vampire* (1994) were all sumptuous, well-performed ... and spectacularly *un*scary. In addition to these revisionist visions (*Dracula* was now a love story that stretched across "oceans of time" rather than a horror movie!), endless variations of the popular "cop versus serial killer" theme also dominated cineplexes in the early '90s.

Serial killers also fascinated audiences in the Academy Award–winning Jonathan Demme film *The Silence of the Lambs* (1991), so it seemed natural that every subsequent thriller should concern a serial killer, including *Slaughter of the Innocent* (1993), *Seven* (1995) and the ironically titled *Copycat* (1995). But Craven struck back with *Scream* (1996), a funny, clever and affectionate nod to horror films of the '80s. It was fast-paced, unpredictable, and most importantly, scary.

Craven had never directed a more technically accomplished film, and audiences applauded. Costing only $14 million and grossing more than $100 million, *Scream* was a blockbuster. It was also smart in its twisted approach to time-honored horror film clichés, which when trotted out were overturned, observed or acknowledged with throwaway one-liners. Like *Wes Craven's New Nightmare*, *Scream* was about itself, about the genre and about filmmaking as a whole. At the same time, it was a scary movie...something audiences hungered for. Following the success of *Scream*, horror was back in vogue, and there was a promise of more to come with *Mimic* (1997), *Event Horizon* (1997) and the Kevin Williamson-penned *I Know What You Did Last Summer* (1997). Craven had once again made theaters safe for horror.

Although film purists may argue that well-schooled *wunderkinder* such as Brian DePalma, Francis Ford Coppola or John Carpenter are more accomplished technicians than the self-taught Craven because in a pinch they may paint a more complex composition, few can legitimately deny the combined visceral and intellectual punch of Craven's best film work. More to the point, no other director working in contemporary Hollywood has so successfully and so artfully reinvented himself, his style and his *genre* in a span of two and a half decades. What other modern auteur boasts a résumé that lists films as stylistically diverse as the blunt, brutal *The Last House on the Left*, the hallucinatory, mind-bending *A Nightmare on Elm Street* and the accomplished, self-referential *Scream*? Not George Romero, a gifted director who seems lost somewhere in the twilight of the living dead. Not John Carpenter, a brilliant filmmaker who has not directed a satisfactory genre film since 1990 because of studio interference. Not even the talented David Cronenberg can legitimately assume the title of the genre's last hope, because he has forsaken the horror milieu and crossed over into David Lynch–style oddball terrain like *Crash* (1997). Also missing in action are Sam Raimi, a director who once thrilled horror fans with the *Evil Dead* trilogy and *Darkman* (1990), and Tobe Hooper, whose genre credits (including *The Texas Chainsaw Massacre*, *Poltergeist* [1982], *Eaten Alive* [1976], *Lifeforce* [1985] and *Invaders from Mars* [1986]) are unimpeachable.

On the eve of the millennium, Craven stands head and shoulders above other players in the horror field. In fact, he has become a highly marketable brand name in the 1990s. *Wes Craven's New Nightmare* (1994), *Wes Craven Presents Mind Ripper* (1995) and *Wes Craven Presents Wishmaster* (1997) are three "products" that boast his name not just above the main title, but actually *in* it. These films are sold not by traditional movie star power but by their association with a man who has consistently and imaginatively scared audiences senseless since the early 1970s.

Perhaps Craven's success in the genre results from the fact that unlike Carpenter, Cronenberg, DePalma or Coppola, he has never been afforded a huge budget or the opportunity to run rampant in a mainstream genre. To the contrary, he has been pigeonholed by the entertainment industry as a "hardcore" horror director. So while John Carpenter directs a $50 million action retread of a past glory (1996's *Escape from L.A.*, his sequel to 1981's *Escape from New York*) and DePalma directs the stylish but muddled spy thriller *Mission: Impossible* (1996), Craven instead relieves his ennui with the genre by prodding at its limits. Since he has not yet been permitted to play outside the horror arena, he consistently reinvents the game, thus challenging himself and his audience. Not surprisingly, Craven films incorporate thematic elements uncommon in horror, elements of human experience that are fascinating to the director. To wit: *Shocker* (1989) is a no-holds-barred pop culture horror satire attesting to the power of television, complete with cameos by John Tesh and Timothy Leary. *The People Under the Stairs* takes the '80s, the Reagan Revolution, yuppie-ism and racial divisiveness to task with pointed social commentary. *Wes Craven's New Nightmare* is an Altmanesque nightmare that knowingly unfolds behind the scenes of moviemaking and makes the relevant point that horror is a legitimate outlet for a child's fears. And the popular *Scream* is a loving tribute to the genre efforts of the '80s as well as an overturning of the most overused horror clichés of that era. So while Craven may yearn for the mega-budget mainstream studio picture and the chance to branch out beyond horror, his long stay in an industry-imposed purgatory has resulted in many of the most consistently interesting, funny, frightening and thought-provoking visions in recent American cinema.

After a quarter century navigating the darkest corners of creation, Craven has given modern audiences not only jumps and jolts, but a rollicking tour through the domains of comedy, fantasy, documentary-style filmmaking, dream landscapes and even religion. While many movies in Hollywood are about nothing but explosions, car crashes and CGI natural disasters, Craven's motion pictures invariably harken back to one overriding human theme: the hypocrisy of the modern American family. At the 1979 Toronto Film Festival, Craven eloquently stated what could be the ideological basis of his film career:

> The family is the best microcosm to work with.... It's very much where most of our strong emotions or gut feelings come from.... I grew up in a white working class family that was very religious. There was an enormous amount of secrecy in the general commerce of our getting along.... If there was an argument, it was immediately denied. If there was a feeling, it was repressed.... I began to see that as a nation we were doing the same things.[2]

Considering these comments, it is not surprising that various motion pictures written and directed by Craven reveal the dark side of middle-class families. *The Last House on the Left* and *The Hills Have Eyes* contrast openly violent familial units with so-called civilized ones only to find there is little difference between them. *Deadly Friend* and *The People Under the Stairs* tackle issues of physical and sexual abuse. *A Nightmare on Elm Street* and *Shocker* explore the gulf of understanding separating parents from their children. Even *Scream* with its knowing but dysfunctional teens illuminates a facet of modern suburban life.

Craven's television work similarly revolves around issues in the family. *A

Stranger in Our House (1978) is a dark fantasy about an outsider breaking family protocols; *Chiller* (1984) focuses on a mother's blind acceptance of a deviant son; and *Invitation to Hell* (1984) concerns a wife's misguided quest to get her "piece of the pie," a hunt that leads her and her innocent children straight to a Satanic country club.

When considered in the context of this "family" (or anti-family) theme, Craven's 27-year career in Hollywood can readily be viewed as a consistent whole despite the shifts in style and medium. So even were his repeated efforts to resuscitate the horror genre not reason enough to make a scholarly study of his work, then certainly his career-spanning, consistent obsession with the nature of family offers a backdrop worth analyzing. From barren hills to suburban nightmares, from the cemeteries of Haiti to the wasteland of television pop culture, Craven has been scaring, illuminating and entertaining audiences for a quarter of a century. Those who approach his films with an open mind (and a strong stomach) may discover a liberating honesty in Craven's work. It is an honesty uncommon in the vapid, big-budget pictures regularly cranked out by Hollywood. It is an honesty that can only come from the perspective of an outsider — from a vantage point under the stairs.

Chapter 1

Career Overview

On August 2, 1939, Wesley Earl Craven was born in Cleveland, Ohio, a very long way from Hollywood, California. The son of strict fundamentalist Baptists, young Craven was not permitted to play card games, dance, participate in events where there would be "mixed sex bathing" (i.e., swimming) or even go to the theater to see a motion picture. His childhood years were filled not only with strict rules and regulations, courtesy of the rigid Baptists, but also with genuine pain and tragedy. His parents' marriage failed while he was still a toddler and Craven's father died when Wes was five. The strict rules, the broken household and the death of a loved one were to have an indelible impact on Craven's philosophical outlook, and these early events would one day impact his art heavily. A 57-year-old Craven expressed the lessons he intuited from his troubled youth in *The New York Times* in January 1997, at the height of his power and success as a horror director:

> By my fifth birthday, I'd been exposed to a lot of anger and death. It's never quite left me, that perception that under the surface there's potential for violence and chaos and things that are not accounted for by rational thought.[1]

Perhaps further cementing young Wesley's notion that the world was an unsafe place where God was wrathful, parents were divided and death close-at-hand, a strange event occurred while Craven was 11 years old and in the sixth grade. One night he awoke from a sound slumber to a loud scuffling noise outside his window. When he left his bed and looked down into the street, he saw a stranger standing on the sidewalk there. Somehow, the man sensed that Craven's young eyes were upon him and he looked up to meet the boy's gaze. Terrified, Craven jumped away from the window and hid in a corner of his room for several moments. As he returned to the window, he was confident that the stranger must have moved on but strangely the man was still standing in exactly the same spot, still staring up into the window. Then, even more horrifyingly, this ghoulish figure entered Craven's apartment building and ascended the staircase, rapidly approaching the Craven apartment! Wesley awoke his family, including his older brother, but after the hustle and bustle the stranger mysteriously vanished into the darkness of the night. For Craven, this was a seminal incident in his life, a close encounter with the dark side of humanity:

> As an adult I can look back and say that that was one of the most profoundly frightening experiences I have ever had. That guy has never left my mind, nor has the feeling of how frightening an adult stranger can be. He was not only frightening, but he was amused by the fact that he was frightening and able to anticipate my inner thoughts.[2]

This strange night caller never reappeared, but an adult Craven recalled the terrifying man and the bizarre incident while he was preparing *A Nightmare on Elm Street* in 1984. That stranger, so amused at his own ability to easily frighten the young and impressionable, would form the foundation of the *Elm Street* antagonist, child-murderer Freddy Krueger.

Craven graduated from high school and left Ohio far behind him (although the main characters in *The Hills Have Eyes*, a dysfunctional family, identified themselves as being from Cleveland). Craven relocated to Illinois and attended Wheaton College for four years. Since Wheaton was a conservative religious school, Craven had yet to escape from the rigid rules which dominated his early family life. As he pursued a Bachelor of Arts degree, with majors in Psychology and English, Craven became obsessed with dreams and their origins. While writing a research paper on the subject, he honed his own ability to recall and record his dreams. This was a requirement of the project and so Craven became an expert at waking himself up, recalling his dreams and writing them down before they receded into the netherworld of lost or half-remembered images. At one point, Craven grew so skilled in dream recollection that he was able to write down four to six dreams a night. This influence, like the nightmare man he had glimpsed outside his window in the sixth grade, shaped the future of Craven's artistry. He credits dreams for being the basis of *The Hills Have Eyes* and *A Nightmare on Elm Street* as well as of scenes in *Deadly Blessing* and *The Serpent and the Rainbow*.[3] For Craven, the blending of dreams and film seem a perfect match:

> Cinema lends itself to dreaming. It is in a sense a dream itself. People go into a dark room very much like a bedroom. They see phantasmic images on the screen that aren't really there. It's part and parcel of dreams.[4]

At the same time that Craven was recalling his psyche's own "inner movies" through dream recollection, he went to the theater and for the first time in his life saw a motion picture: *To Kill a Mockingbird* (1962). He was not aware of it as he sat in that theater watching Gregory Peck and Robert Duvall on the big screen, but one day he would hold movie audiences enraptured with his own compelling stories and stylish explorations of darkness.

Following his graduation from Wheaton, Craven pursued an M.A. in Philosophy and Writing at Johns Hopkins University in Baltimore, Maryland. After completion of his Masters, he became a teacher at a nearby engineering college and was married. After a few short years, Craven saw two additions to his family, son Jonathan and daughter Jessica. Later, Craven found that he was not completely satisfied with his teaching career. He felt pressure from his department chair to conform to academic traditions and was instructed several times in no uncertain terms to complete work on his Ph.D. At this point in his career, Craven was not interested in further schooling. He saw himself as a kind of inhibited artist and was a writer of poetry and short stories. He had submitted his first novel for publication, only to have it rejected repeatedly. Looking for an outlet for his artistic yearnings, Craven accepted the offer of a group for students to help assemble an amateur college film. It was a decision that significantly changed Craven's life:

Director Wes Craven in the 1994 film *Wes Craven's New Nightmare.*

> I advised on this film and had so much fun doing it. It was a 45-minute rip-off of *Mission: Impossible*. We shot it in the college town so everyone came to see themselves in it. I then realized I was not particularly happy teaching.... The whole thrust seemed to be not teaching, not learning anything ... just keeping the wheels running smoothly. So I ... went to New York to break into the film business.[5]

At age 30, Craven broke the bonds that held him in Baltimore and traveled to the Lower East Side of Manhattan, where he joined a commune and earned a marginal living driving a taxi cab. Through his singer-friend Harry Chapin (*Heads and Tales*, Elektra Records, 1972), Craven was put in touch with a local film editor and he served as an apprentice for some time. Under the tutelage of a professional, Craven learned film editing, cutting and synching.[6] He soon discovered he had a natural gift for this most technical of arts and the ability to manipulate film images to better tell a story, more powerfully reveal the essence of the character, or move the plot more rapidly. His talent did not go unnoticed for long and in 1971 Craven joined director Peter Locke, later his producer on

The Hills Have Eyes, for the production of *You've Got to Walk It Like You Talk It Or You'll Lose That Beat*, an 85-minute quest for the meaning of life set in Central Park. Serving as editor of the picture, Craven did an exemplary job, and the assignment earned him recognition among the circle of struggling filmmakers with whom he was associated in Manhattan.

First Steps

In early 1972, Craven was off and running on a new project, this time serving as assistant producer on *Together*, a sex education "documentary" which spotlighted a nude swan dive into a swimming pool by future porn superstar Marilyn Chambers (*Behind the Green Door* [1972], *The Resurrection of Eve* [1973], *Insatiable* [1980]). Craven not only served as associate producer on this 70-minute feature, he also edited much of the footage and lensed some additional sequences required for the final cut. *Together* was directed and produced by Sean Cunningham (*Friday the 13th* [1980]), a savvy businessman and filmmaker who took notice of Craven's abilities and would work with him again during the making of Craven's first directorial venture: *The Last House on the Left*.

Together was a regional box office hit. It played in mainstream theaters around New York City and generated ample profits for its financial backers, the Esquire Theater chain. Because of its low-budget earthiness and voyeuristic "documentary" style, *Together* was not hard-core porn but it was more "hard" than the recent soft porn ventures of Zalman King such as *Wild Orchid* (1989). To some film students, Craven's brief participation in the world of soft/hard porn may be difficult to fathom but it is important to remember that he arrived in New York City during an incredibly open time. Societal and Hollywood taboos and barriers were being broken or ignored by ambitious filmmakers with inspired personal visions. The sky really was the limit and, at the same time that major studios were releasing quirky films like *Easy Rider* (1969) and *Five Easy Pieces* (1970), the artistic porn film was also gaining national acceptance with landmark productions such as the aforementioned *Behind the Green Door*, Gerard Damiano's *Deep Throat* and *The Devil in Miss Jones* (1973), and the Swedish *I Am Curious (Yellow)* (1970). All these hard-core epics played to enthusiastic mainstream audiences in urban America just as *Together* and Craven's later jaunt into hard-core porn, *It Happened in Hollywood* (1974), did. Most indicative of America's acceptance of films with sexual themes and featuring explicit sexual acts was Columbia Pictures' nationwide release of Just Jaeckin's exploration of one woman's sexuality, *Emmanuelle* (1974). In all, it was a far more progressive and experimental era than today's rigidly censored film world, where Adrian Lyne's *Lolita* (1996) still cannot find a major distributor in the United States.

Considering the openness of the times, Craven was participating in the most inventive, exciting and personal era in American film history. *Together* and *It*

Happened in Hollywood capitalized on the porn mainstream fad which saw respectable middle-class couples attending porno films together. In regards to this unusual movie trend in general and *Deep Throat* in specific, Danny Peary, author of *Cult Movies* wrote:

> Major critics reviewed it. A few even liked it. Everyone saw it. Children discussed it. Star Linda Lovelace became a household name ... it was not uncommon for there to be long lines in front of showcase theaters where it played, and the men and women in those lines came from every socioeconomic group.[7]

Buoyed by the success of *Together*, Sean Cunningham's investors requested another film from the team of Cunningham and Craven but this time they suggested a genre switch. Instead of pushing the boundaries of sex in cinema, they wanted an ultra-violent exploitation flick that would do essentially the same thing for the floundering horror genre.[8] A 33-year-old Wes Craven went home and over a long weekend wrote a compelling script based on the Ingmar Bergman film *The Virgin Spring* (1958). Craven's screenplay was almost hypnotic in its power. It told the story of two teenage girls of the "peace generation" and their brutal rape and murder at the hands of a gang of sexual deviants. The screenplay followed Bergman's template almost perfectly and ended not with the death of the innocent youths but with a strange twist of fate: The family of killers ended up at the home of one of the murdered girl's parents! In short order, the parents discovered the grisly crime and exacted brutal, final retribution on the criminals. Although various titles were considered, including *Krug and Company*, *Sex Crime of the Century* and *Night of Vengeance*,[9] the 1972 film became known forever after in the United States as *The Last House on the Left*.

Craven's first horror movie was shot in Westport, New York, and it cost under $100,000. It starred unknowns Lucy Grantham, Sandra Cassell and Martin Kove (*Cagney and Lacey*). David Alexander Hess, who had written the popular Elvis Presley tune *All Shook Up* in the 1950s,[10] made a powerful impression as the villainous Krug, leader of the sadistic rapists. He not only acted in the film, he also wrote the musical score, which included a haunting folk melody entitled "The Road Leads to Nowhere." This song was repeated throughout *The Last House on the Left* many times and it perfectly captured the feelings of waste and emptiness generated by the violence portrayed within.

Even with a sparse running time of 82 minutes, *The Last House on the Left* afforded Craven ample opportunity to demonstrate his skill with actors and film technique. He opened the film with crisp cross-cutting, captured the beautiful "natural" surroundings of a forest and river where all the hideous events would soon take place, and (best of all) knew when *not* to be flashy at all. The controversial rape scene, the centerpiece of this powerful film, was purposely edited not with over-the-top "horror" film lingo (extreme high and low angles, crazy close-ups and Wagnerian music pumping on the soundtrack). Instead it was photographed and cut together from the perspective of an observer watching the events in medium and long shots. The rape was determinedly *not* stylish and Craven never backed away from the intrinsic horror of the events. From the stabbings to the rape, to the final burst of gunfire, everything was captured head-on by Craven's camera. Instead of flinching and cutting away to reaction shots or a scene more palatable, Craven let audience members fully experience the events as if they were indeed participants. As a result, the film simultaneously caused feelings of voyeurism, shame and rage in its viewers.

The Last House on the Left was a provocative film from start to finish and it challenged everyone's perception of a what a horror movie should be about and what one could accomplish. Accordingly, various advertising lines for the movie stressed its graphic, unflinching nature. "Can a Movie Go Too Far?"[11] one ad asked. Another ad line offered this helpful mantra for the squeamish in the audience: "To Avoid Fainting, Keep Telling Yourself 'It's Only A Movie. It's Only a Movie, It's Only A Movie...'"

Predictably, the critical establishment reacted to *The Last House on the Left* with moral indignation and outrage. For the most part, the reviewers were seemingly unaware that they had seen a virtuoso debut, a film that challenged them and made them face human ugliness that no film before (or since) has. *The New York Times* critic Howard Thompson even walked out of *The Last House on the Left* with 35 minutes of the film remaining. The lone voice of reason among the naysayers was Chicago critic Roger Ebert, who recognized *The Last House on the Left* as a powerful and well-executed exploitation film. He gave the film three-and-a-half stars and championed it many times against those who argued it should be banned or destroyed. Adding insult to injury, the foreign movie critics, usually suckers for American product vaguely different and/or moderately challenging, vilified the film too! On its original release, it was banned from Great Britain. A decade later, the home video version of *The Last House on the Left*, what the Brits term a "video nasty," was also banned.

Despite the brickbats and state-mandated censorship in the rigid U.K., *The Last House on the Left* generated strong word of mouth among American audiences and the film became a runaway hit. By 1982, ten years after its release, *The Last House on the Left* had grossed over $18 million.[12] The final box office tally said it all: The film was a smash success.

Unfortunately, the "take no prisoners" approach of *The Last House on the Left* proved such a point of contention with critics that Craven was still being reviewed for *Last House* in major periodicals as late as 1984, 12 years after the low-budget film's release. While reviewing *A Nightmare on Elm Street*, various critics harkened back to the "unsavory" and "loathsome" nature of Craven's first directorial effort. For a film that so many reviewers insisted was so bad, it certainly struck an emotional chord with them. After all, they were recalling it with vitriolic clarity a dozen years later, presumably after a single viewing and after Craven had made four other films. A question that was never asked of these reviewers was this: If *The Last House on the Left* spawned such powerful feelings, even after years, how could it be garbage? At the very least, critics should have admitted that Craven had shown remarkable skill in making such a powerful film even if they found its subject matter distasteful.

What the hostile responses to *The Last House on the Left* proved was not only that critics have long memories, but that Craven was to find himself forever trapped by his past success. The visceral, gut-wrenching nature of *The Last House on the Left* assured that even if he had other plans, Craven would be forever known as a horror movie director.

While *The Last House on the Left* made its powerful mark, Craven edited another film for his friend Peter Locke in 1973. It was an X-rated, hardcore production entitled *It Happened in Hollywood*. The film concerned a sort of "pornographic" Academy Awards and ran for a scant 74 minutes. As Craven struggled to get another picture off the drawing boards, an Italian exploitation picture made in 1971 was re-named *The Last House on the Left II* and imported to America to cash in on the box office success of Craven's first film. It is important to note that neither Craven nor any of the cast members of the original *Last House* had anything to do with this low-quality "sequel."

In 1985, it was widely announced that an official *The Last House on the Left II* would soon go into production under the auspices of Sean Cunningham. Although a director was attached to this project (Danny Steinmann, who would later direct *Friday The 13th Part V: A New Beginning*), the film was never made.

Off and Running

Craven struggled for several years to further his cinematic ambitions but was not afforded the opportunity to direct a second feature film until nearly a half-decade after *The Last House on the Left*. In 1976, Craven hooked up again with producer Peter Locke and wrote a horror screenplay entitled *The Hills Have Eyes*. By now Craven had relocated to California, and his grisly story of a cannibalistic family was set in the Yucca flats, where *The Beast of Yucca Flats* (1961) starring cult icon and Swedish wrestler Tor Johnson was filmed years earlier. In writing his story of a civilized and savage family in deadly opposition, Craven utilized not only facets of his dreams but a historical footnote that caught his eye during his days in the halls of academie. The point of interest was a 15th century Scottish legend about a vicious cannibal called "Sawney Bean." Bean was an outcast from a nearby Scot city called Galloway, and he and his common-law wife lived outside the bounds of civilization for almost 25 years. They had many children together and then their children sired children. Before long, a wild cult of three dozen Beans was roving the countryside, capturing and torturing any passersby. The unfortunates apprehended by these crazed monsters were robbed of their belongings and then eaten. Finally, the law caught up with the Bean family and the men were mutilated and bled to death and the women were burned alive.[13]

What fascinated Craven about this arcane bit of history was the fact that it occurred in Scotland during what was supposedly a "civilized" time. Most incidences of cannibalism occurred not in the heart of Western civilization but in areas such as the West Indies, Africa or South America, where cultural isolation or primitive social conditions led to desperation. Craven realized that by updating the Sawney Bean story to 20th century California, he would have the opportunity not only to comment on a cult society dwelling inside modern civilization, but also the chance to comment on that civilization's less-than-civilized retribution against the cannibals. Like *The Last House on the Left*, the combatants in *The Hills Have Eyes* would be two families, one representing savagery and one representing contemporary society. Of course, by the end of the film, the distinctions between families would be negligible ... just as in *The Last House on the Left*.

The Hills Have Eyes was shot in spurts over a span of many months, whenever there was enough money available to continue shooting. The picture starred Dee Wallace, who would achieve genre stardom in Joe Dante's *The Howling* (1981), Steven Spielberg's *E.T.* (1982) and Peter Jackson's *The Frighteners* (1996). Also present in the cast was a striking bald man with the look of a savage himself, actor Michael Berryman. Berryman proved to be such an effective menace in *The Hills Have Eyes* that he returned for the sequel *The Hills Have Eyes II* (1984) and also worked for Craven in *Deadly Blessing* (1981) and briefly in *Invitation To Hell* (1984). After his years with Craven, Berryman also appeared in other films (including *Star Trek IV: The Voyage Home* [1986] as well as a guest spot on a first season episode of *Star Trek: The Next Generation* entitled "Conspiracy."

The Hills Have Eyes was an even bigger box office success than *The Last House on the Left* and it was met with greater appreciation from many critics, particularly those familiar with the horror genre. *Fangoria* magazine recently listed it as one of the top 13 horror movies of the seventies. It was also the first Craven film to successfully incorporate dark humor into the grisly proceedings and so did not feature the grim and oppressive air of his premiere picture. Still, by shooting *The Hills Have Eyes* after *The Last House on the Left*, Craven would be even further connected with the horror genre and grisly subject matter. The similarity in plots between the two films (two families in deadly opposition) did not help matters, and Craven was forever branded a horror maven — perhaps a skilled one, but a horror maven nonetheless.

Importantly, *The Hills Have Eyes* preceded the slasher trend of the late '70s and early '80s and was seen as a turning point in the horror genre. It was visceral and savage like *The Last House on the Left* but it was funnier and more accomplished technically. This was the path that films such as *Halloween*, *Friday the 13th* and *Prom Night* would soon follow.

Because *The Hills Have Eyes* was widely recognized as an effective if grisly horror film, Hollywood finally opened its doors just wide enough for Craven to squeak in. He took advantage of the opening and won an assignment: the directorial reins of a TV movie entitled *A Stranger in Our House* (1978). It was a great break for Craven because the telefilm was to be shown on NBC and therefore his name and work could be easily accessed by millions more than the faithful who had been brave enough to venture to *The Last House on the Left* and *The Hills Have Eyes* in theaters. Based on Lois Duncan's 1976 teen novel *Summer of Fear*, *A Stranger in Our House* also offered other opportunities for Craven. For the first time, he worked with the 35mm film format as well as established rather than unknown performers such as Macdonald Carey and horror celebrity Linda Blair. *A Stranger in Our House* was also perfect terrain for Craven artistically since it concerned a villainous interloper intent on destroying a family by encouraging infidelity in the formerly meek patriarch.

A Stranger in Our House premiered on NBC-TV on October 31, 1978, Halloween night, and performed exceptionally well in the all-important Nielsen ratings. It did two important things for Craven's career. First, it further established him as a stylish director with an eye for horror because it featured dream sequences, escalating suspense and genre standards such as slow-motion photography and ghoulish makeup. More importantly, it introduced Craven to the universe of television production, a domain he would return to in his lean years even though it was more artistically restrictive than the venue of the feature film.

Mixed Blessings

August 1981 brought the release of *Deadly Blessing*, Craven's third full-length feature. Distributed by United Artists, *Deadly Blessing* was directed with remarkable skill by Craven. Like elements in *The Hills Have Eyes*, *The Last House on the Left* and later in *A Nightmare on Elm Street*, many of the film's most harrowing sequences were based on Craven's own nightmares and dreams. *Deadly Blessing* also owed a measure of debt to the slasher genre popular at the time.

The slasher subgenre was at its peak in 1981, still riding high from Sean Cunningham's smash *Friday the 13th* (1980), Brian DePalma's *Dressed to Kill* (1980), Abel Ferrera's *The Driller Killer* (1979), *Prom Night* (1980), *Fade to Black* (1980), *Hell Night* (1981, with Linda Blair), and Richard Franklin's *Road Games* (1981, starring the ubiquitous Jamie Lee Curtis). Accordingly, *Deadly Blessing*'s plot structure was in much the same vein as the prototypical slasher film: An unknown killer slices and dices innocent victims, usually women, as punishment for some past sin that has gone unprosecuted. What was different about the film was its location in Amish-like country, the presence of a repressive religious sect called the Hittites, and the maturity of the protagonists, who were well over 18. Even more surprisingly, the suspenseful and well-orchestrated killings were perpetrated by not one psychopath, but two (foreshadowing *Scream*).

Reflecting Craven's ability to keep an audience off-guard, *Blessing*'s surprising climax introduced a third antagonist, a supernatural one! The provocative "dawn of the incubus" epilogue, which was the pay-off for all the "supernatural" animal attacks, was subsequently excised from British prints of the film, making *Deadly Blessing* a less than satisfying experience for overseas audiences.

Of special note in *Deadly Blessing* was the sensitively handled subplot about a young Hittite, John (Jeff East), and his decision to abandon his restrictive religious upbringing and discover, among other earthly pleasures, the joys of movies. John's situation obviously echoed Craven's own alienation from organized religion. Interestingly, John was killed midway through *Deadly Blessing* for his transgressions against God and his community, indicating perhaps that deep down Craven still feared the wrath of an unforgiving deity.

Cast members in *Deadly Blessing* included future star Sharon Stone in her first speaking role, Ernest Borgnine (a graduate of *The Devil's Rain*), *The Hills Have Eyes* alumnus Michael Berryman (in his best role) and the lovely Maren Jensen of TV's *Battlestar Galactica* (1978). Despite positive reviews from prominent critics such as Janet Maslin of *The New York Times* and the fact that it was a well-crafted horror vehicle, *Deadly Blessing* failed to find a sizable audience in theaters when pitted against more traditional "stalker" competition. It is a much better film than even Craven gives it credit for being. Consisting of many layers and surprises (again like *Scream*), *Deadly Blessing* is well worth seeking out.

In early 1982, Craven jumped to the big time with a brief side-step into the ancillary world of monster films. *Swamp Thing*, a film based on DC Comics' character of the same name, was written and directed by Craven and produced for Avco-Embassy by Michael Uslan and Benjamin Melnicker, a former vice president at MGM. Still fresh in the minds of all concerned were the blockbusters *Superman* (1978) and *Superman II* (1981). Uslan and Melnicker had hoped to mount a film version of *Batman* but because of budgetary concerns they finally opted for their second superhero on the short list: *Swamp Thing*.

Begun in DC Comics in 1972 (the same year Craven directed *The Last House on the Left*) by writer Len Wein and illustrator Berni Wrightson, *Swamp Thing* was a forerunner of today's "dark" superheroes. True to the comic's somber origins, Craven penned a melancholy script about a man transformed into a noble beast. Although the film was also witty, full of crackling one-liners (delivered with considerable flair by Adrienne Barbeau), the ending was unhappy and the overall tenor was dark. Craven's faithful interpretation of the contemporary superhero ethos was light years from the cartoonish world of Richard Donner's *Superman*, or the popular 1960s *Batman* TV series.

Location shooting in swamps near Charleston, South Carolina, was plagued with problems. Cypress Gardens and Magnolia Plantation were beautiful, but they were populated with poisonous snakes and alligators. Poison ivy also proved to be a very real safety hazard, and the rubber "Swamp Thing" suit was difficult to manage. Dick Durock told *Starlog* about his unpleasant experiences on the set:

It wasn't because of design factors... It was the brutal heat. Also, being in the swamp absorbs water. It would sag just from the weight. I don't know if there's any way to prevent that, because if you did, you'd prevent your body from breathing... The eyes were too low on the first suit. All I had to act with was mainly the eyes.[14]

Despite hardships, Craven brought the film in on time and on budget at $2.5 million. *Swamp Thing* was Craven's highest budgeted film yet and had the largest crew of his career (over 125 people and multiple vehicles). There was much dangerous stunt work too, including boat crashes and men set afire. The stunts were coordinated and performed ably by a frequent future Craven team member, Tony Cecere (pronounced like Caesar). After *Swamp Thing*, Cecere would work with Craven on virtually every film up through *Scream 2*.

Swamp Thing was good for Craven personally even if the shoot was dangerous. He was married to Mimi Meyer, who portrayed Arcane's assistant. The beautiful Mimi Meyer appeared in many Craven productions including *Chiller* and an episode of the new *Twilight Zone* directed by her husband.

Like *Deadly Blessing*, *Swamp Thing* did not fare well at the box office when it was released in July 1982. Competing with Steven Spielberg's *E.T.*, Tobe Hooper's *Poltergeist*, Nicholas Meyer's *Star Trek II: The Wrath of Khan*, Clint Eastwood's *Firefox*, John Carpenter's *The Thing* and Ridley Scott's *Blade Runner*, *Swamp Thing* simply drowned. Not helping matters any, most critics disliked the film and criticized it for its obvious low-budget origins. An exception was, again, Roger Ebert, who gave *Swamp Thing* three stars and found considerable beauty and humor in it.

In this case, Craven was ahead of his time. His *Swamp Thing*, complete with its doomed love affair, melancholy hero and extreme violence, arrived seven years before Tim Burton's similarly styled "noir" *Batman* became a blockbuster in 1989. That film made superheroes with depression disorders and schizophrenia popular. Sam Raimi's *Darkman* (1990) certainly owes *Swamp Thing* some tribute too. *The Crow* (1994), starring the ill-fated Brandon Lee, and Tod McFarlane's New Line release *Spawn* (1997), also hit many of the same marks as Craven's early entry.

After *Swamp Thing*'s failure at the box office, something interesting happened. The film became profitable thanks to the burgeoning home video market. Apparently, people who had avoided *Swamp Thing* in theaters were willing to spend a few bucks to view it in their living room. In the end, *Swamp Thing* made back its investment and much, much more.

Craven's film spawned a sequel: 1989's *Return of the Swamp Thing*, directed by Jim Wynorski for Lightyear Entertainment and shot just outside Savannah, Georgia. It saw the return of Jourdan as Dr. Arcane and Durock as Swamp Thing. But Craven, reportedly offered the directorial reins, was nowhere to be found.

Even the lukewarm audience response to the campy *Return of the Swamp Thing* was not enough to kill the regenerating superhero. He returned in a 1990 TV series of 30-minute episodes made for the USA network. Craven's film was the tentpole of a giant franchise!

Following the release of *Swamp Thing*, Craven experienced the worst "dry spell" of his career. With no directing offers on the table and rejections for his dream script (*A Nightmare on Elm Street*) coming in left and right, Craven was sorely in need of funds and at one point had to borrow cash from friends just to pay his taxes. The studios that rejected *A Nightmare on Elm Street* informed Craven that the horror fad of the '80s was over. Since Craven had been pigeonholed as a genre director for ten years, he knew his options were truly limited.

Salvation arrived not in a hot new property or a startling opportunity but in an earlier film that producers felt could become a franchise along the lines of *Friday the 13th* or *Halloween*. That property was *The Hills Have Eyes*. A sequel offered Wes Craven the chance to direct again, as well as write the screenplay.

The Hills Have Eyes II (written and directed by Craven) was made on the cheap in 1983 and, after a short shooting schedule, production ceased for lack of monetary backing. The unfinished film was held on the shelf until 1985. When it finally premiered (after *Elm Street*), it was padded with multiple flashbacks from the first *Hills*, one of which originated from the family dog, the Beast! Although certain portions of the follow-up film were mildly suspenseful, especially those involving a likable blind teen (Tamara Stafford) being menaced by the savage family, the film as a whole was probably Craven's worst film venture. He expressed his reaction to *The Hills Have Eyes II* when it was released on the heels of his *Nightmare on Elm Street* success in 1984-85:

> It was released before it was finished. I'm not happy with it, so I avoid talking about it. We ran out of time and money on the initial shoot... But when the footage was cut together, they went straight to answer print... The whole thing needs work. Shots are missing. Some scenes aren't right.[15]

A Dream Come True on Elm Street

In 1984, Craven directed a picture that many would soon call his masterpiece. *A Nightmare on Elm Street* was produced at New Line Cinema with executives Robert Shaye and Sara Risher overseeing production. At a meager $1.8 million, the film was a budgetary step downwards for Craven after *Swamp Thing*. The shooting schedule was so tight that Craven asked his friend and longtime associate Sean Cunningham to direct second unit work on a crucial alley chase scene, for which Cunningham was thanked in the credits. The picture was a taut thriller about a killer named Fred (*The Hills Have Eyes*) Krueger (*The Last House on the Left*) who, after his own murder, returned to stalk innocent teens in their dreams. Krueger punished the young for the sins of their parents, forecasting the results of the Reagan revolution: a generation of youngsters paying for their parents' excesses and ill-gotten wealth.

In a stand-out performance of uncommon subtlety and power, Heather Langenkamp portrayed the lead teenager, Nancy Thompson. The film featured exciting newcomers such as Langenkamp and Johnny Depp (*Ed Wood* [1994]) as well as B-movie favorite John Saxon (*Enter the Dragon* [1973], *The Bees* [1978], *Blood Beach* [1980], *Cannibals Are in the Streets* [1980], and *From Dusk Till Dawn* [1995]). Cast as the dream killer was Robert Englund, a veteran of Tobe Hooper's lost masterpiece *Eaten Alive* (1976), Roger Corman's *Galaxy of Terror* (1981) and the hit TV series *V* (1985). As Krueger, Englund attained screen immortality. He described his first meeting with Craven in a *Fangoria* interview:

> I didn't know exactly what the Fred Krueger character was supposed to be so I went to the interview looking as punk-rocked, psychoed-out as I could with a four-day beard growth and expecting Wes Craven to look like Charles Manson. And there is Wes, sitting impeccably attired, a preppy humanities professor with sandy red-hair. A true gentleman. I let Wes do all the talking while I stared at him with my Lee Harvey Oswald stare, and I got the part.[16]

Englund, Depp and Langenkamp were not the only people to emerge as stars from *A Nightmare on Elm Street*. Craven also became a favorite of genre aficionados for his direction of this shocking film. Much of the film's reputation came from the manner in which Craven delivered a particular scene of startling ferocity. Just 15 minutes into *A Nightmare on Elm Street*, this death scene went far beyond anything seen in horror films up to that point, even *The Last House on the Left* or George Romero's splatter epic *Dawn of the Dead* (1979). Teenager Tina (Amanda Wyss), whom the audience had cleverly been led to believe would be the film's star (*à la* Janet Leigh in *Psycho* [1960]), was slashed down her naked torso by invisible razors, propelled into mid-air, dragged across her bedroom ceiling and then viciously slaughtered. The scene culminated with gallons of dark red blood splashing on both a bed and Tina's lover (Nick Corri). The sequence was unexpected, horrific and perfectly executed thanks to a locked-down camera and a spinning room. Amazingly, the rest of the film was equally terrifying.

A Nightmare on Elm Street was an artful blending of hallucination, teenage paranoia, nightmares and grim reality. Simply put, it was the best and most frightening horror film since Carpenter's *Halloween* (1978), and audiences responded with crazed enthusiasm. *A Nightmare on Elm Street* grossed an amazing $26 million in U.S. theaters alone. Robert Englund became a star, New Line Cinema (which is still known in the film industry as "The House that Freddy Built") had itself a franchise and America found a favorite new monster who could stand shoulder-to-shoulder with Frankenstein, Dracula and the Wolf Man. Even better, Craven finally received some critical accolades. *A Nightmare on Elm Street* won the Critics Prize at the 1985 Avoriaz Festival of Fantastic Films.

Despite the overwhelming success of *A Nightmare on Elm Street*, Craven was still not satisfied artistically because he had been overruled about the specifics of the film's conclusion. He felt that Bob Shaye's suggestion to have Freddy drive the teens away in a speeding car was a cheap shot indicating that evil was triumphant. Craven wanted "good" to triumph in an ending which suggested that the events of the entire film were a dream. Shaye demanded a final jolt and a hook for a sequel and Craven was obligated to listen to the man who had given his film a chance after other studios had rejected it outright. Although various endings were printed, the one finally used showed Nancy's mother being pulled to her death by Freddy while Nancy and her friends were driven away in an out-of-control car bearing the green and red stripes of Freddy's sweater. It was a compromise but one that Craven was never happy with. The battle over *A Nightmare on Elm Street*'s ending caused many years of animosity between Craven and Shaye, but New Line hardly suffered from Craven's alienation.

In 1985, New Line released *A Nightmare on Elm Street II: Freddy's Revenge*. After reading the uninspired script, Craven turned down the opportunity to direct the film and that chore went to Jack Sholder (*Alone in the Dark* [1981] and *The Hidden* [1987]). The sequel made mincemeat of *Elm Street* continuity by staging its finale inside Freddy's "real" boiler room, even though Ronee Blakeley had clearly stated in the first film that she burned the boiler room to the ground. Also ludicrous was a scene in which Freddy appeared and disappeared in the real world with no rhyme or reason and managed to slaughter a bevy of teens relaxing poolside. Despite these odd moments, *Freddy's Revenge* managed to win popular and critical acclaim and some fans even asserted it was better than the original. The sequel grossed $29 million, $3 million more than the original film.

A Nightmare on Elm Street III: Dream Warriors followed in 1987. It featured the return of Langenkamp and Saxon and a screenplay penned by Wes Craven. These touches made all the difference and the picture, though weak in spots, seemed a legitimate continuation of the "rubber reality" defined by the now seminal original. Directed by Chuck Russell (*The Blob* [1988]), *Elm Street III* generated an amazing $44 million in revenue. Renny Harlin's *A Nightmare on Elm Street IV: The Dream Master* fared even better at the box office, almost topping $50 million in August 1988. Attesting to the power of Freddy, the box office gross of *The Dream Master* far exceeded the profits generated by Harlin's later high-profile films like *Cutthroat Island* [1995] and *The Long Kiss Goodnight* [1996]). Next came *Elm Street 5: The Dream Child* (1989), perhaps the best of all the sequels. It was stylishly directed by Stephen Hopkins (*Predator 2* [1991]) but this darker sequel died against hits like *Batman, Lethal Weapon II, Indiana Jones and the Last Crusade* and *Dead Poets Society* and grossed only $22 million. Still, Freddy's franchise was not mortally wounded. The same summer that saw Freddy fumble the ball also nearly wiped out a whole host of sequels. *Star Trek V: The Final Frontier, Karate Kid III, Licence to Kill* (the 16th big screen adventure of James Bond) and *Friday the 13th Part VIII: Jason Takes Manhattan* all bit the dust.

While Freddy tore up the big screen in the *Elm Street* sequels, New Line Cinema also offered a syndicated TV series co-produced by Lorimar (home of *Tales from the Darkside*) entitled *Freddy's Nightmares* (1988-90). The show ran for two full seasons and featured episodes directed by Tobe Hooper and Robert Englund. The final film in the Freddy "canon" was probably the weakest, a lame 3-D excursion called *Freddy's Dead: The Final Nightmare* (1991). Indicative of New Line's silly approach, the final Freddy film featured Roseanne Barr and Tom Arnold in an extended comic cameo but otherwise had few genuine scares. Still, *Freddy's Dead* grossed a whopping $34 million at the box office, $8 million more than Wes Craven's 1991 horror entry, *The People Under the Stairs*. Amazingly, at the height of the "Freddy" phenomenon, the National Coalition on TV Violence found that 60 percent of children ages 10-13 recognized Freddy Krueger. Only 33 percent recognized Abraham Lincoln![17] Certainly, that was proof that Craven had launched not only a franchise (his third if one includes *The Hills Have Eyes* and *Swamp Thing*) but a media superstar.

Despite the popularity of his ghoul, Craven himself was horrified by the fact that the monster he had created to represent pure evil had been transformed into a joke-spewing, pizza-faced James Bond for the late '80s. Still, it would not be until 1994's *Wes Craven's New Nightmare* that he was able to express on film his disbelief/anger/irritation with all the watering down required to feed and nourish a sequel-generating franchise.

Invitations, Chillers and Detours to The Twilight Zone

Following production on *A Nightmare on Elm Street*, Craven returned to television for the first time since 1978. In 1984-85, he directed two superlative telemovies, *Chiller* and *Invitation to Hell*, both of which centered on Craven's favorite theme: the problems of the modern American family. Both shows could be interpreted as Craven's reaction against what he perceived as encroaching yuppie values. While the cinema would not officially revile yuppies and their upwardly mobile generation until *Tin Cup* (1996) and *Jerry Maguire* (1996) — two films which extolled the virtue of good character over money — TV drama was far ahead of the game. Craven found a relevant theme he could sink his teeth into as he worked with excellent performers such as Joanna Cassidy (*A Vampire in Brooklyn* [1995]) and Michael Beck (*The Warriors* [1976]) while movies were still offering yuppie fantasies such as *The Secret of My Success* (1988).

After directing twin "anti-yuppie" horror telepictures, Craven segued for the first occasion into weekly television series work. At the behest of his old friend Phil DeGuere, Craven directed the opening installments of 1985's CBS revival of Rod Serling's *The Twilight Zone*. For reasons known only to programming executives, 1985 was the year of anthologies and viewers were treated not only to the new *Twilight Zone* but also to Steven Spielberg's less-than-*Amazing Sto-*

ries and a remake of the classic series *Alfred Hitchcock Presents* featuring colorized introductions by the late great master himself. Spielberg had the clout not only to secure a two-season commitment for his anthology from NBC exec Brandon Tartikoff, but also the services of directors Clint Eastwood, Peter Hyams, Martin Scorsese and Tobe Hooper. Still, most of these fine directors were lost in a sea of hopelessly juvenile stories which Spielberg had once confessed was his "elephant burial ground for new ideas that will never make it to the big screen."[18]

By contrast, *The Twilight Zone* revival put strong directors such as Craven, Peter Medak (*The Changeling* [1981], *Space: 1999* [1975-77]), Joe Dante (*Piranha* [1978], *Gremlins* [1984], *Explorers* [1985]), Gerd Oswald (*Star Trek* [1966-69], *The Outer Limits* [1962-64]), Jeannot Szwarc (*Bug* [1975], *Jaws II* [1979], *Somewhere in Time* [1981]), and William Friedkin (*The Exorcist* [1973]) in charge of fascinating stories penned by accomplished scribes such as Harlan Ellison, David Gerrold, Alan Brennert and others, adapted from the works of Arthur C. Clarke, Ray Bradbury, Stephen King, Richard Matheson and even legendary *Twilight Zone* creator Rod Serling.

Craven directed both of the half-hour segments of the premiere *Twilight Zone* episode which aired September 27, 1985. His stories were "Shatterday" (written by Harlan Ellison and starring then-unknown Bruce Willis) and "A Little Peace and Quiet" (starring Melinda Dillon of *Close Encounters of the Third Kind*). Craven returned the following week with "Wordplay" starring Robert Klein and Joseph Whipp (*A Nightmare on Elm Street*, *Chiller*, *Scream*) and the outer space drama "Chameleon." Other *Zone* stories directed by Craven included "Dealer's Choice" and "The Road Less Traveled."

His best effort by far was "Her Pilgrim Soul." Written by Alan Brennert, "Her Pilgrim Soul" was a tender drama about an eternal love affair which crossed time and space via a computer-generated hologram. It was a beautiful piece starring successful Broadway actress Anne Twomey as the mysterious hologram "Nola." Twomey, who would soon act for Craven again in *Deadly Friend* (1986), was a revelation in "Her Pilgrim Soul" and this show might have been the best hour of television in 1985. Other Craven alumni also appeared on the series, including Adrienne Barbeau (*Swamp Thing*) in "Teacher's Aide" and Martin Kove (*The Last House on the Left*) in "Opening Day."

After Craven left *The Twilight Zone* behind, it continued to delight audiences for a couple of years ... the only survivor of the anthology swarm. *Alfred Hitchcock Presents* folded after one season and *Amazing Stories* died the instant its two-season guarantee was up, but *The Twilight Zone* stayed on Friday nights for two years before airing a season's worth of new episodes in syndication under the direction of J. Michael Straczynski (*Babylon 5*). Craven can be proud for giving this re-working of a TV legend a fresh start. Many years after his work on *The Twilight Zone*, Craven was referred to by friend Robert Englund as Rod Serling's "heir apparent," not only for his fine work on *The Twilight Zone* but because of *Nightmare Cafe*, a semi-anthology genre series created by Craven in the early '90s.

Deadly Success

Following his notable excursions into *The Twilight Zone*, Craven discovered that Hollywood was finally ready to embrace him ... or at least cash in on his success. *A Nightmare on Elm Street* was the envy of every major studio in town: both a blockbuster and the foundation of a new franchise. At this juncture, several possible Craven projects were bandied about in the genre press including a *Frankenstein* update for Roger Corman, *Haunted*, a ghoulish love story in which one of the lovers was dead, and *Old Fears* about childhood nightmares come to life.[19] The most interesting project with which Craven was associated during this period was *Flowers in the Attic*, an adaptation of V.C. Andrews' best-selling gothic novel. Although it is disappointing that none of these projects ever became films directed by Craven, the biggest tragedy was undoubtedly the failure of *Flowers in the Attic* to bloom in Craven's directorial garden. Andrews' book provided compelling "domestic" material that only a director with Craven's background in "family" could effectively tackle. Since *Flowers* concerned the dysfunctional Dahl family, a group riddled with incest, children in denial, infanticide, a neglectful mother and a Bible-thumping grandmother, it seemed tailor-made for Craven. The twisted sexuality and interpersonal relationships of *Flowers in the Attic* would have been perfect fodder for his typically insightful commentary and it would also have allowed him to chart completely the terrain of the failed family home: from *Flowers in the Attic* to *The People Under the Stairs*!

New Line eventually made the film in 1987, but without Craven's leadership it devolved into melodrama. Even with impressive talents such as Louise Fletcher (*One Flew Over the Cuckoo's Nest* [1975], *Invaders from Mars* [1985]), Victoria Tennant, and Kristy Swanson (*Deadly Friend* [1986], *Buffy the Vampire Slayer* [1991]), the film was tedious and less than scary. While many Internet sources indicate that Craven wrote the screenplay, his name is not in the credits. It was written and directed by Jeffrey Bloom, not by Craven.

The year 1986 saw Craven direct *Deadly Friend* for Warner Bros. The screenplay by Bruce Joel Rubin (*Ghost* [1990] and *Jacob's Ladder* [1991]) was an adaptation of Diana Henstell's 1985 novel *Friend*. Known alternately as *A.I.*, *Artificial Intelligence* and *Friend* before finally becoming *Deadly Friend*, the novel and screenplay told essentially the same story of a teenage genius who loved his robot and his girlfriend but ended up losing both to tragic circumstances. Unable to cope with these losses, the genius brought his girlfriend back to life utilizing the robot's artificial intelligence chip.

Conceived as a lightweight updating of Mary Shelley's *Frankenstein*, Craven's *Deadly Friend* featured a fully operational robot known as "BB." This automation was actually fully capable of performing lawn and kitchen work and even playing basketball. Designed by Robotics 21 in California to be the perfect "best friend,"[20] BB was also reminiscent of the "real life" robots seen in *Short Circuit* (1986) and *SpaceCamp* (1986), two films with which *Deadly Friend* would compete at the box office. With its emphasis on a teenage genius and harmless science-based pranks, the film also fell into the same subgenre as *Real Genius* (1985), *Weird Science* (1985) and *My Science Project* (1985).

Despite the story's derivative nature, *Deadly Friend* was an opportunity for Craven to make his first "big" Hollywood picture outside the hardcore horror genre. According to *Deadly Friend* star Matthew Laborteaux, it was a project Craven intended to make the best of:

> Wes said that the one thing he didn't want to do was make this a horror movie because it's one of his first large-budget movies which isn't from New Line Cinema or Joe Blow Pictures... That gave me a little sense of security knowing he wanted to do a nice picture.[21]

True to his promise, Craven delivered to Warner Bros. a teenage film filled with charm, wit and solid performances by likable teens Swanson and Laborteaux. It was definitely a mainstream, PG film all the way, similar in tone to a *Real Genius* or a *Short Circuit*, but the point was made that Craven could direct something other than double-barreled horror. However, Craven's final cut of *Deadly Friend* was not at all what Warner Bros. intended or audiences wanted! The teenage fun and games and the touch of *I Was a Teenage Frankenstein* (1957) left bloodthirsty preview audiences weaned on *A Nightmare on Elm Street* feeling disappointed. They had been promised a *Wes Craven* film, not something as inoffensive and relatively tame as *Deadly Friend*.

As a result of disastrous preview screenings, Warner Bros. executives instructed Craven to go back and shoot some "gory stuff." Craven reluctantly implemented the instructions of his employers and added horrific nightmare sequences, punched-up death scenes which included more grotesque special effects and even a ludicrous horror tag that ruined much of the film's intelligence and humor. Do not blame Craven, however, for the substance of these changes. As Bruce Joel Rubin confided in 1990, the director was not the culprit:

> The studio told me to give them six more scenes, each bloodier than the last. ...That really destroyed our love story, and everyone still blames me for the ending! That robot coming out of the girl's head belongs solely to Mark Tapin, and you don't tell the president of Warner Bros. that his idea stinks! But as far as the production went, *Deadly Friend* was one of the happiest experiences I've ever had ... I loved Wes...[22]

As it was released, *Deadly Friend* was a schizophrenic jumble of genres and even Craven said he did not know "what the hell kind of film it was."[23] Audiences agreed with the director's assessment and the film grossed less than $9 million. It was not the *Nightmare on Elm Street* bonanza that Warner Bros. had hoped for and the film's two disparate halves kept it from being embraced either as good horror or as clean fun in the vein of *Real Genius* or *Short Circuit*.

With *Deadly Friend*, Wes Craven learned a powerful lesson: With a bigger budget and a Hollywood studio also came less control over the final direction of his art. *Deadly Friend* was one of Craven's least satisfying films, despite the solid work he oversaw with his young actors. He was undermined by a studio "marketing" approach to filmmaking and built-in audience expectations.

Haiti, by Way of Elm Street

Following *Deadly Friend*, Craven returned to New Line Cinema to join Robert Shaye and Sara Risher in the second sequel to *Elm Street*. Craven was given an executive producer credit on the finished film, *Dream Warriors*, and he and writing partner Bruce Wagner shared screenplay credit with director Chuck Russell and writer Frank Darabont (*Mary Shelley's Frankenstein* [1994]). The script went through numerous revisions but the central concept of "dream warriors" was one created by Craven. The film was budgeted at $4.7 million, more than double the budget of the original *A Nightmare on Elm Street*, and Craven found that his input on creative matters, casting and the like were not being considered or even solicited. The relationship between New Line and Craven, rocky at best since the argument over the finale of the original *Elm Street*, intensified when a battle erupted over creative ownership of *Dream Warriors*. In a *Cinefantastique* interview, Craven argued that *Dream Warriors* was basically his script but with new character names and a few changed sequences so writers Darabont and Russell could get equal billing and equal points in the profits.[24] This assertion angered New Line and Darabont, and Sara Risher was blunt in her response:

> I don't understand why he [Craven] doesn't give credit where credit is due. Chuck Russell made the script [for *Part III*] work. I give Wes complete credit for the terrific idea of these kids — the dream warriors — I'm not faulting that. But Chuck Russell and Frank Darabont turned that script around... They rewrote 70 percent of it.[25]

Risher also revealed that Craven had been given the opportunity to direct the film but had turned the assignment down in favor of pursuing *Superman IV*, an assignment Craven did not win (it went to Sidney J. Furie). Frank Darabont also responded to Craven's charges in the letters page of *Fangoria*. He claimed that if he and Russell had merely changed a few character names, the Writers Guild would not have awarded them screen credit. To buttress his case, he quoted the Writers Guild Credits Manual.[26]

The bottom line about *Elm Street* in-fighting is that the originator of Freddy Krueger and the *Elm Street* universe was pushed aside or ignored while New Line businessmen vigorously pursued their cash cow, their *own* vision of the franchise. Though New Line executives claim the Chuck Russell/Frank Darabont script was "better" than Craven's and Wagner's, what they really meant was that it better fit New Line's specific criteria for an ongoing film series: with a mainstream emphasis on humor and spectacular special effects instead of real terror. It is hardly surprising then that Craven opted not to direct what could easily have been just another toothless sequel like *Freddy's Revenge*. If New Line had been at all serious about offering Craven the directorial assignment, it would have satisfied his need as originator of *Elm Street* to exert some level of artistic control over the final content of the film and the universe Craven created.

A Nightmare on Elm Street III: Dream Warriors was a monster hit for New Line and Craven did share in the profits. The film succeeded not only because of the great special effects but also because it saw the return of actors Langenkamp, Saxon and Englund in their original roles. Additionally, Craven's extension of "dream skills" into team combat against Freddy made the film's plot unique. The film also revealed more of Freddy's back-history, including his origin as "the bastard son of a hundred maniacs." Unfortunately, director Russell's final cut also revealed more than that. Freddy's face was out of the shadows and squarely in the light. As a result of this exposure, *Dream Warriors* was much less scary than either of its predecessors. Although Freddy's jokes were funny, the impact of all the humor in the later sequels was that by 1996 and *Scream*, the film series was universally regarded in the derogatory manner actress Drew Barrymore described in Kevin Williamson's script: "The first one was scary, but the rest sucked!"

Deciding that *A Nightmare on Elm Street* and its sequels were best left behind, Craven turned his attention in 1987 to another project that many admirers insist is an unqualified masterpiece and perhaps even superior in quality to *Elm Street*. *The Serpent and the Rainbow* was based on a book of the same name by author Wade Davis, a Harvard graduate and ethnobiologist/anthropologist/photographer/adventurer who traveled to Haiti in 1982 to seek out "zombie powder," a powerful native anesthetic which contained the poison tetrodotoxin and was capable of producing a death-like state. Davis, author also of *Passage of Darkness: The Ethnobiology of the Haitian Zombie*, served as an advisor to Craven during the shoot of the Universal film to assure that the spirit of his work would be respected.

Budgeted at $10 million, Craven's largest budget ever, *The Serpent and the Rainbow* was a fictionalized account of Davis' journey into the land of voodoo. It was shot over a period of three months, with eight weeks spent in the Dominican Republic and another month in Haiti. It was even more difficult than the arduous *Swamp Thing* shoot of 1982 because Craven and his crew were constantly sick from bad food or incapacitated because of extreme heat. The film was shot under the auspices of the Haitian government, specifically the Department of Culture, and in a few hair-raising incidents the Haitian Army had to provide armed security for Craven's endangered production crew! Thousands of Haitian nationals also appeared in the film and at one point many began to riot. It was reported that Craven was nearly forced to drink pig's blood in an authentic voodoo ceremony to appease his unhappy extras! Many such bizarre stories came off the shooting of *The Serpent and the Rainbow*; several cast and crew members also reported strange visions, nightmares and hallucinations.

The Richard Maxwell screenplay was basically faithful to Davis' non-fiction book, but Craven added his own unique touches: a tense political angle and a powerful voodoo villain. In addition, he brought to the film his trademark nightmare sequences. At the end of a very long and stressful shoot, Craven also saw the finished film as an opportunity to fulfill a promise:

> I promised the people of Haiti that this film was going to be a fair representation of their country, and that the film would look at voodoo as a well-rounded thing with both a dark and a light side. I truly believe I have accomplished that.[27]

The Serpent and the Rainbow does boast a strong documentary-like feel. In one beautifully captured sequence, Craven's camera tracked thousands of Haitians on a religious pilgrimage through an almost primeval forest, their candles burning bright and forming a living, breathing line of light stretching to the horizon. It was a powerful moment, as were those in which lead actress Cathy Tyson clinically described how Haitians viewed their religion. To the Haitians, their unique blend of voodoo and Catholicism was not only spiritual but physical as well. They felt that God inhabited or "possessed" their physical bodies through lesser deities. With incredible locations, profound religious epiphanies and nightmarish hallucinations, *The Serpent and the Rainbow* was a well-done film that starred not only Tyson but Bill Pullman (*Spaceballs* [1987], *Malice* [1993], *Independence Day* [1996], *Lost Highway* [1997]) and Zakes Mokae (*Dust Devil* [1993]) *A Vampire in Brooklyn* and *The X-Files* episode "Teliko").

The film was originally scheduled for national release on January 15, 1988, but it was delayed by Universal until February 5. Unfortunately, it arrived in cinemas during the same season as the similarly themed *Angel Heart* and *The Believers*, and some skeptics accused *The Serpent and the Rainbow* of being a part of the trendy "voodoo" pack rather than an artistic original that could stand on its own.

At the time of its release, *The Serpent and the Rainbow* was accompanied with the frightening advertising line "Don't bury me ... I'm not dead!" and the trick paid off handsomely; the film was anything but buried when viewers were finished with it. *The Serpent and the Rainbow* was an unqualified hit for Universal and Craven (more than $20 million). It was also well received by the majority of critics, with Roger Ebert again leading the pack. Above all, *The Serpent and the Rainbow* proved that Craven could paint on the big canvas, capture exotic locations and rituals, and shepherd good performances to the screen even under the most trying (and life-threatening) circumstances. Moreover, he was able to make the film seem like a documentary and *still* be scary, which was no mean feat.

No More Mr. Nice Guy!

After *The Serpent and the Rainbow*, Wes Craven signed a two-picture deal with Alive Films and executives Shep Gordon and Andre Blay, the group which John Carpenter had labored with on *Prince of Darkness* (1987) and *They Live* (1988). When this arrangement was made, it was rumored that *The Hills Have Eyes III*, a screenplay by Bruce Wagner which Craven described as a "very bizarre sort of near-future near-outer space horror film,"[28] would be one of the pictures in the deal. Unfortunately, that interesting-sounding project never materialized. The first motion picture in Craven's Alive deal was 1989's *Shocker*, originally titled *No More Mr. Nice Guy*. Ironically, that very title "No More Mr. Nice Guy," was also the title of the *Freddy's Nightmares* pilot in 1988.

Shocker began principal production in February 1989 and it boasted a heavy metal title song by Alice Cooper (*Prince of Darkness* [1987]). *Shocker* was basically Craven's response to the Freddy Krueger film series and to Universal Studios, which informed him they wanted their very own horror franchise *à la A Nightmare on Elm Street*. Accordingly, moments in *Shocker* echo Craven's earlier milestone film. Both films open with grisly serial killers working in their den of evil, both feature non-believing parents who also happen to serve on the local police force (in *Shocker*, Michael Murphy played the John Saxon role), and both films also dramatize the now-expected "rubber reality" dream sequences. Further enhancing the connection between the world of Fred Krueger and Horace Pinker, the villain of *Shocker*, was the fact that Pinker's first victim in the film was Heather Langenkamp, the actress who had so ably defeated Freddy in 1984.

Craven also made *Shocker* very different from *Elm Street* in some significant ways. It was less grim, and at times it was downright funny. The media played an important role in *Shocker* and so *Entertainment Tonight*'s John Tesh had a small role. When lead Peter Berg chased Mitch Pileggi through the "universe of television" at the film's finale, *Shocker* really took off. Berg ended up not inside a boiler room hell, but in an episode of *Leave It to Beaver* and the film *Frankenstein*! With Pileggi and Berg jumping in and out of television sets at random, confronting couch potatoes who believed they were witnessing "the ultimate in audience participation television" and even meeting Timothy Leary as a cheesy TV evangelist, the final sequence of the film is hilarious. *Shocker*'s final 20 minutes are a stylistic special effects *tour de force* and well worth the price of admission.

Despite the fact that many critics liked *Shocker*, the film grossed only $16 million after it premiered just days short of Halloween in 1989. Although there was some talk of a *Shocker* sequel, Universal begged off, perhaps feeling that, with its special effects requirements, a *Shocker* franchise would be too costly to develop.

At the same time *Shocker* was in production, Craven oversaw a TV sitcom called *The People Next Door*. It starred Jeffrey Jones (*Howard the Duck* [1986], *Beetlejuice* [1988], *Mom and Dad Save the World* [1991]) and Mary Gross. The non-horror comedy series ran briefly on CBS Monday nights before being abruptly canceled. Craven was not able to supervise the series because of his responsibilities on *Shocker* and he has always regretted the series' untimely passing.

Dark Visions and People Beneath the Stairs

Craven again returned to TV in 1990 to helm *Night Vision*, his first telefilm since 1984's *Chiller*. This two-hour production was co-written by Craven and Thomas Baum (*Nightmare Cafe*) and it was intended to be a "back door" pilot for a TV series. The show aired on NBC on November 30, 1990, and was squarely in the "cop versus serial killer" venue but with a significant twist. Actor James Remar, as the cop, was paired with Loryn Locklyn as a woman with the psychic abilities to gain impressions about the killer they were pursuing. With its nightmare visions and "get inside the head of a killer" approach, *Night Vision* was a variation on the same theme developed in *Eyes of Laura Mars* (1978), Chris Carter's TV series *Millennium* (1996-?) and NBC's *Profiler*. *Night Vision* did not go to series for NBC, but Craven was busier than ever. Not only was he intent on developing new TV properties, he was also hard at work on a new feature film: *The People Under The Stairs*.

The People Under the Stairs was the second feature in Craven's two-picture deal with Alive Films and it too would be distributed by Universal. This time Craven dug deep into his files and pulled out some newspaper clippings he had saved from 1978 to form the basis of his plot. The news articles were about two crazed parents in Santa Monica who had tortured their children for a long period of time, never allowing them to leave their home. Craven was fascinated with the concept of a world within a world, and *The People Under the Stairs* became his first film since *The Hills Have Eyes* not to feature his trademark dream sequences.

The People Under the Stairs told the story of an inner city African American boy (Brandon Adams) who became trapped in a house of horrors at the mercy of a demented, incestuous white couple (Everett McGill and Wendy Robie of *Twin Peaks* [1990]). For Craven, this film was an opportunity to return to the kind of work he had done early in his career:

> This is much closer to *The Hills Have Eyes*... It's a raw film with no dreams in it whatsoever... This isn't *Shocker* or *A Nightmare on Elm Street*. I've sort of played out the whole dream thing. With this film, I'm getting back to basics.[29]

However, the final film also revealed something else that had been evident only sporadically through his career: Craven had an incredible sense of humor. *Shocker* was a mixed bag of thrills and chills with laughs one minute and horror the next, but in *People Under the Stairs* Craven was able to weave a consistently horrific atmosphere while also generating appropriate laughs from within the parameters of the scenario. It was a revelation for his fans and critics who remembered that the *Nightmare on Elm Street* series *stopped* being scary once the humor was added to the mix. *The People Under the Stairs* remained frightening until the bitter end, despite the presence of some wicked satirical material. Even Craven realized he had managed to articulate his humorous side clearly in *The People Under the Stairs*:

> I've always felt that horror films are a form of humor, a dark humor, but still a way of laughing at the darkest aspects of life and human nature. They use a great deal of the tool kit of humor as far as timing and surprise and they deal in a way that somehow is oddly liberating and exhilarating with things that would in any other way be painful and frightening.[30]

The People Under the Stairs was released near Halloween of 1991 and it made a killing at the box office ($24 million). It also fared especially well with critics, who found that Craven was exploring new territory and not merely relying on the dream shtick that in one way or another had dominated *A Nightmare on Elm Street*, *Deadly Friend*, *The Serpent and the Rainbow* and *Shocker*.

While Craven was finishing with *The People Under the Stairs*, he was also developing a new "horror" property for NBC with his co-writer from *Night Vision*, Thomas Baum. Craven was still interested in "rubber reality" but he promised that his new series would explore many alternate realities, not just dreams or nightmares. *Nightmare Cafe*, described by Craven as "*The Twilight Zone* meets *Cheers*," was produced by MGM/UA and the pilot episode was directed by Philip Noyce (*Dead Calm* [1989], *Sliver* [1992], *Patriot Games* [1993]) from a teleplay by Craven and Baum. The series starred Jack Coleman and Lindsay Frost as down-and-out loners who stumbled upon a strange cafe and its enigmatic owner, Blackie (Robert Englund). Craven described the series concept in this manner:

> Two people ... inherit a cafe that's somewhere between life and death; they serve as moderators and participate in the stories. People in the real world come to experience their worst nightmares, their turning point, their comeuppance, or their breakthrough; they see their life on television and disappear into the stories. The people in the cafe make bets on how it's going to come out and go into the story to influence it.[31]

Nightmare Cafe landed on NBC on Friday nights. The show was not without interest and Robert Englund was able to stretch his acting muscles by playing a variety of characters in each episode. The series also offered good guest appearances from friendly faces such as Brandon Adams (*The People Under the Stairs*) and Angela Bassett (*A Vampire in Brooklyn*). Despite these plusses and the fact that Craven himself co-wrote two episodes and directed the installment,

"Aliens Ate My Lunch," the short-lived series had its final new broadcast on April 31, 1992. *Nightmare Cafe* was dead after just six hour-long episodes, a victim of network indifference. In 1994-95, the series was frequently rerun in prime time on The Sci-Fi Channel's Series Collection, an "umbrella" gathering of genre productions which had died on network television but had not been forgotten by genre die-hards. *Nightmare Cafe* thus rotated with *The Fantastic Journey* (1977), *Planet of the Apes* (1974), *The Amazing Spiderman* (1978), *Darkroom* (1981), *Automan* (1983), *The New Dark Shadows* (1990), *Mann and Machine* (1992) and other series that failed because of insufficient network support.

Starring Wes Craven!

Following the failure of *Nightmare Cafe*, Craven joined fellow horror director John Carpenter for a cameo role in *John Carpenter's Body Bags*, a horror movie for Showtime produced by Sandy King and Dan Angel and written by Angel and Billy Brown. Carpenter and Craven were in good company in *Body Bags* since the genre-heavy cast also boasted contemporary horror directors Tobe Hooper, Roger Corman and Sam Raimi. The actors populating the three-story anthology were also significant ones in the genre: George "Buck" Flower (*They Live* [1988], *Wes Craven Presents Wishmaster* [1997]), Tom Arnold (*Freddy's Dead* [1991]), David Naughton (*An American Werewolf in London* [1981]), David Warner (*Time After Time* [1979], *Time Bandits* [1981], *Waxworks* [1988]), Stacy Keach (*Road Games* [1981], *The Class of 1999* [1990]), Deborah Harry (*Videodrome* [1983]), John Agar (*Revenge of the Creature* [1955], *The Mole People* [1956]) and Mark Hamill (*Star Wars* [1977], *Black Magic Woman* [1990], *Sleepwalkers* [1991], *The Guyver* [1991]). Also along for the ride were celebrities Sheena Easton, Charles Napier and Twiggy!

Craven appeared in "The Gas Station," the first of three stories. He portrayed "The Pasty-Faced Man" a Haddonfield resident who purchased cigarettes from night attendant Alex Datcher. With his hair windblown and his clothes wrinkled, a wild-eyed Craven attempted to lure the beautiful Datcher (*Passenger 57* [1993]) back to his car with the promise of free booze. Craven's moment of stardom was a funny one and he added to the spirit of ghoulish horror/comedy generated by Carpenter. Craven also shared his insight into horror's status as a "lesser" film genre with his fellow horror icon John Carpenter, who later said,

> Wes Craven did a part for me, and we've all been through ... the exact same thing. Wes told me that part of the reason is that people think of horror like pornography sometimes....and they tend to look down on you so if you do any serious work, you often don't get taken as seriously as you want to be.[32]

Freddy's Resurrection!

On the tenth anniversary of *A Nightmare on Elm Street*, Craven, Robert Shaye and New Line cast aside their differences to create *Wes Craven's New Nightmare*, a self-referential horror movie which found Freddy Krueger terrorizing the makers of the first *Elm Street* film instead of a new group of teens. John Saxon, Heather Langenkamp, Robert Englund, Robert Shaye, Sara Risher, Wes Craven and even Freddy Krueger all played themselves but Langenkamp was again the standout in the cast. Also particularly strong was child actor Miko Hughes (*Spawn* [1997]), who portrayed Langenkamp's disturbed son.

Wes Craven's New Nightmare arrived in theaters in mid-October 1994 with the ad line "This Time the Terror Doesn't Stop at the Screen!" Although that promise was all too true, *New Nightmare* had to contend with its own screen-bound terrors. It premiered in a season of blockbusters which included *Stargate* and *Star Trek: Generations* and high-profile "horror" such as *Mary Shelley's Frankenstein* and *Interview With the Vampire*. Despite the heavy competition, *New Nightmare* emerged as the best-reviewed genre production of the season. It won raves from most critics (including Craven's old supporter Roger Ebert) and was nominated for Best Feature at the Independent Feature Project West's 1995 Spirit Awards. *New Nightmare* was praised highly because it was intelligent and scary, a feat which *Interview* and *Frankenstein* never quite managed despite bigger stars, glossier production values and much higher budgets. Craven's film ended the *Elm Street* series on a high note and is this author's favorite Craven film.

Strangely, *New Nightmare* has never found a large audience; even when it was released on home video during March 1995, it did not fare well. It premiered in twentieth place on *Billboard*'s list of new videos, well below losers like *Camp Nowhere*, *The Specialist* and *Angels in the Outfield*. Dauntingly, *New Nightmare* never rose above 14th position. Freddy really was dead.

In the same year that Krueger last stalked the silver screen, his creator made another rare appearance in front of the camera as an actor. In the low-budget feature *The Fear*, directed by Vince Edwards, appearances by Craven as psychologist "Dr. Arnold" book-ended the film. At the urging of Craven's character, a young graduate student pursues his thesis, which involves setting loose the fears of a group of dysfunctional young adults at an isolated mountain house. The film is remarkable not only for Craven's performance and off-screen presence (his voice can be heard taunting the hero with the word "diametric," an anagram for "matricide," in a nightmare sequence near the start of the film) but also for a frightening little set-piece which occurs midway through the picture at an eerie Christmas-theme amusement park. This strange village, ostensibly a place of joy, is grotesque and disturbing because it seems constructed of non-human proportions. It is also inhabited by the spirit of Black Peter and a horrifying living wooden doll called "Morty." Craven does a good job in the film and even gets to quote his favorite psychologist, Sigmund Freud.

Beverly Hills Craven?

In 1995, Craven teamed with Paramount Pictures and Eddie Murphy for the $20 million production *A Vampire in Brooklyn*. Most critics found it neither funny nor scary and audiences stayed away from it after a strong opening near Halloween. The film grossed only a dismal $19.8 million in general release but it should be remembered that 1995 was not a good time for horror anyway. Craven's latest opus was not the only one to suffer from indifferent audience reaction and other genre products also took it on the chin. *Candyman II: Farewell to the Flesh* earned only $13 million, as did Clive Barker's *Lord of Illusions*. *Halloween VI: The Curse of Michael Myers* did slightly better at $14.7 million but Dean Koontz's *Hideaway*, Spike Lee's *Tales from the Hood* and John Carpenter's *In the Mouth of Madness* and *Village of the Damned* all fared far worse than *A Vampire in Brooklyn*, making only between $6 and $12 million apiece.[33] Most commentators saw *A Vampire in Brooklyn*'s failure to find an audience as a sign of Eddie Murphy's waning box office appeal rather than a reflection on Craven's directorial abilities.

In 1995, Craven introduced his first "Wes Craven as brand name" productions: *Wes Craven Presents Mind Ripper*, also known as *Outpost*. The film was produced and co-written (with Phil Mittleman) by Craven's son Jonathan and only executive-produced by the elder Craven. Much of the film was shot in post-Communist Bulgaria inside an atomic packaging center. Directed by Joe Gayton, *Mind Ripper* starred Dan Blom (*Body Bags*) as a genetically enhanced supersoldier called "Thor" and Lance Henriksen (*Aliens* [1986], *Near Dark* [1987], *Pumpkinhead* [1988]) as the scientist responsible for his creation. Although written by the younger Craven, the film carried a theme common to Wes' work: the reconciling/destruction of a middle class American family. The final product had a low-budget energy but was not a strong enough film to merit a theatrical release. In 1995 and 1996, *Mind Ripper* was shown on HBO and it was released on video in 1997 following the success of *Scream*.

The Dream Scream

Although *A Vampire in Brooklyn* bombed out in 1995, Eddie Murphy and Wes Craven were vindicated on a blockbuster scale in 1996. Murphy made millions in the delightful remake of *The Nutty Professor* and Wes Craven directed *Scream*, the sleeper of the year. *Scream*, originally titled *Scary Movie*, was written by North Carolinian Kevin Williamson, a graduate of East Carolina University, as an homage to the stalker films of the late '70s and early '80s. His script prompted a bidding war in Hollywood; Miramax emerged the victor and *Scream* was produced under the banner of Miramax's Dimension Films. After lengthy contract negotiations, Craven ceased work on his remake of the Robert Wise classic *The Haunting* (1963) and took the reins of the $14 million production. The project was shot in and around Santa Rosa, California, and — despite problems from a puritanical local school board which felt that *Scream* was morally degenerate — the shooting forged ahead on schedule. The film featured a great cast which included Drew Barrymore, Neve Campbell, David Arquette, Courteney Cox, Rose McGowan, Matthew Lillard, Jamie Kennedy and Skeet Ulrich, as well as wonderful direction from Craven. Although it was released on December 13, 1996, against such heavy hitters as Tom Cruise's *Jerry Maguire*, Tim Burton's *Mars Attacks* and Denzel Washington's *The Preacher's Wife*, *Scream* went on to become the surprise hit of the year.

Six months after its release, *Scream* had earned $102.6 million. As of June 1997, it was still playing in 400 theaters across the United States even though the videotape version was released on June 24![34] Most critics loved *Scream* but, more importantly, audiences went wild for it. The film proved so popular that it won the MTV Movie of the Year Award, beating out both *Jerry Maguire* and *Independence Day* in the process. The success of *Scream* also saw Craven elevated to the status of media superstar. In 1997, he was interviewed on MSNBC's *Edgewise* about *Scream* and *A Nightmare on Elm Street* and he was a celebrity guest on the Comedy Channel's *The Daily Show* starring Brian Unger. On the latter program, he successfully answered five out of six of Unger's game show questions but missed the lyrics to the song *Monster Mash*.

Rumors soon spread that Craven would soon be the auteur of a new CD-ROM game entitled *Wes Craven's Principles of Fear* and, even more rewardingly, he would finally see his long-held dream of becoming a published novelist fulfilled. The *Los Angeles Times* reported in June 1997 that Craven was paid a $1 million dollar advance from Simon and Schuster to write a novel, a scientific/medical thriller called *The Fountain Society*.[35]

The only bad news for Craven in his post–*Scream* phase was that the release of his blockbuster in Japan was delayed because of a serial killer's rampage there. Although Japanese authorities were quick to point out that there were no similarities between *Scream* and the brutal decapitation of an 11-year-old boy in Kobe, they nonetheless felt that the release of a horror film was ill-timed. *Scream* finally premiered in Japan on August 23, 1997, two months after the scheduled June 21 premiere.

Scream proved to be such a popular film that Craven found himself shooting the sequel (known alternately as *Scream 2*, *Scream the Sequel*, and *Scream Again*) in Atlanta by June 16, 1997. Although Craven's work on the *Scream* sequel meant that his highly anticipated werewolf opus *Bad Moon Rising* was off the boards, it also meant that he had the opportunity to escape the confines of the horror genre. His contract with Miramax dictated that after two horror films, *Scream* and *Scream 2*, Craven would have the opportunity to helm a film of his choosing. His choice was *Fiddlefest*, a story based on an Academy Award-winning documentary short about an inner city music teacher imparting life lessons to her violin students.³⁶ Rumors flew hot and heavy through Hollywood that Madonna was interested in playing the East Harlem teacher in a story that one critic disparagingly described as "*Dangerous Minds* meets *Mr. Holland's Opus.*" The film was budgeted at a measly $7 million, but to Craven the budget was not the point. He would at last have the chance to escape from his horror "purgatory" and show the world that Craven could direct any kind of film. Although production on *Fiddlefest* had not commenced as of this book's writing, all indications were that following *Scream 2*, Craven would leap out of horror and into mainstream filmmaking.

From a Whisper to Scream 2

Gossip about *Scream 2* flooded the Internet, entertainment magazines and evening movie programs during late 1997. Word was that Jada Pinkett would play the "Drew Barrymore role" in the sequel as the big-name star killed off in the first sequence. It was confirmed that Neve Campbell, Courteney Cox, David Arquette, Liev Schrieber and Jamie Kennedy would be back for more slicing and dicing along with newcomers Jerry O'Connell (*Joe's Apartment* [1995]) and Sarah Michelle Gellar (*I Know What You Did Last Summer* [1997]). There was even news that Cox and Arquette were involved in a torrid love affair and that there had in fact been a mysterious third killer in the original *Scream* who would make himself/herself known in the sequel.

The plot of *Scream 2* was rumored to involve not only Sidney's arrival at a College in Atlanta, but the making of a film called *Stab*, based on the events seen in *Scream*. Most interesting of all was the rumor that Johnny Depp would apparently be playing the *Stab* version of Skeet Ulrich's Billy Loomis (not true!) and that Tori Spelling, the butt of a wicked joke in *Scream*, would be playing Sidney (true)! Indeed, one of the funniest and most talked-about moments from *Scream* involved Sidney's guess that she would probably be played by "Tori Spelling" if a movie were ever made about her life. How did Spelling react to this joke when she finally met Craven?

> Tori was very sweet about it. I said, "Look, we made fun of you, but we made fun of everybody. You're part of a charmed circle."³⁷

Scream 2 lensed for 52 days, with a good portion of the shooting schedule spent at Agnes Scott College in Georgia, a beautiful Gothic campus. When shooting on *Scream 2* was complete, the only thing that remained uncertain was its release date. Miramax had originally intended to open their sequel opposite the new James Bond flick *Tomorrow Never Dies* and James Cameron's *Titanic* on December 12, 1997, less than a year after *Scream*'s release. By late summer, however, the Miramax release board on the Internet indicated that *Scream 2* would not premiere until January 8, 1998. Then, by early fall, the release date was back to December 12, 1997. Ironically, *Scream 2* was considered such a box office contender that both *Tomorrow Never Dies* and *Titanic* were scared off by it. Their releases were moved to December 19, leaving *Scream* as the only blockbuster contender on December 12.

Be Careful What You Wish For...

On other fronts, the second "Wes Craven as brand name" picture was released on September 19, 1997. *Wes Craven Presents Wishmaster* was directed by Robert Kurtzman, the talented special effects genius who had worked for Craven since *The People Under the Stairs* in 1991. The screenplay for *Wishmaster* was by Tony Atkins, the writer of *Hellbound: Hellraiser II* (1988) and *Hellraiser III: Hell on Earth* (1992), and Craven was involved only as executive producer. *Wishmaster* played very much like a late-'80s *Elm Street* sequel with an evil force, this time a Djinn, stacking up a massive count by exploiting the psychological weaknesses of his victims. *Wishmaster* featured extended cameos by four modern horror giants: Robert Englund of *A Nightmare on Elm Street*, Tony Todd of the *Candyman* series, Reggie Bannister of the *Phantasm* series and Kane Hodder of the *Friday the 13th* series. None of these modern icons had significant duties in the film and their presence, like Craven's name over the title, had more to do with marquee attraction than film content. During its first week in major release, *Wishmaster* grossed $6 million and finished well behind the gay comedy *In and Out* starring Kevin Kline. By the second week *Wishmaster*'s grosses were cut by nearly 50 percent (it was now up against *The Peacemaker* starring George Clooney and Nicole Kidman); the film earned slightly over $3 million. What money *Wishmaster* did make was probably partly due to Craven's association with it. Still, a sequel has been announced.

Scream opened the doorway for many new quality horror films. On October 17, 1997, *I Know What You Did Last Summer* blew away the competition (including *The Devil's Advocate* with Al Pacino and Keanu Reeves and *Playing God* with David Duchovny). It earned $16.3 million in its opening week, $12.5 million the following week and $10 million the weekend of Halloween. In many theaters, the picture was preceded by a preview of *Scream 2* which featured footage of David Arquette (Dewey) and Jamie Kennedy (Randy) discussing the "rules" of sequels. This same preview was played during the season premiere of *The X-Files* on November 2, 1997.

On October 31, 1997, Craven branched out in another direction. At seven a.m. on ABC, *Wes Craven Presents Good Morning America* (or *Ghoul Mourning America*) bowed. Proclaimed by host Charles Gibson to be "the king of horror," Craven led audiences through a two-hour Halloween special which was filled with fun and terror. Early on, the *Good Morning America* camera traveled into Craven's home, where many props from his films were spotlighted (including a model of the dog "Prince" from *The People Under the Stairs*, the sledgehammer which Langenkamp used to bash Freddy in *A Nightmare on Elm Street* and many other "Freddy" toys). When asked what scared him, Craven replied, "My taxes and being on a live TV show." Robert Englund (with Freddy Glove), Jamie Kennedy, Greg Nicoreto of KNB Effects, Kevin Williamson (who talked about his "unconditional love of Jamie Lee Curtis") and Sarah Michelle Gellar (*Scream 2, I Know What You Did Last Summer*) joined friend Craven for this special program which found the set and crew of *Good Morning America* terrorized by an unstoppable killer. This cloaked maniac hanged weatherman Spencer Christian, scared the heck out of film critic Joel Siegel by bursting through an oversize TV screen, unleashed a bevy of hungry leeches on a production assistant and even "killed" a lighting technician with a butcher's knife. At the end of the program, the killer was revealed to be ... actress Susan Lucci, Craven's old friend from *Invitation to Hell* (1984)! Her killing spree, as it turns out, was misdirected. "I thought this was the Emmy judging panel," she explained apologetically.

Ghoul Mourning America was a fun-filled show which included black-and-white photography, a "killer cam" and much discussion about horror films and their impact on American society. Joel Siegel talked about Hansel and Gretel (which Craven had already referenced heavily in *New Nightmare*) and the fact that the "uncharted territory of the inner mind" was the subject of the holiday.

Scream 2 *Hits Theaters*

As December 12, 1997, approached, *Scream*-mania continued and the Sci-Fi Channel was part of it. Airing on successive weeknights at six-thirty and seven p.m. was "The Making of *Scream 2*," hosted by Jerry O'Connell (*Sliders*), executive produced by Bill Margol and produced by Gold Coast Television Entertainment. The half-hour documentary, which featured interviews with all the *Scream 2* performers and Craven, revealed some interesting perspectives on the modern master of horror. Jada Pinkett called Craven "a dream" to work with, Neve Campbell referred to him as "wonderful, balanced and serene," and Courteney Cox called him "funny, funny, funny." O'Connell called his time in the presence of Craven a "phenomenal, awesome experience."

When Craven was interviewed regarding the film, he revealed that *Scream 2* was actually the "middle story" in a horror trilogy. *Scream 3*, anybody? Other *Scream 2* participants could be heard on Asylum's December 9 Online Chat, or read about in the pages of *Rolling Stone*, which devoted its cover to Tori Spelling and "The Girls of *Scream 2*." Kevin Williamson, fresh off signing a $20 million deal with Miramax, also shared the intense publicity. *Time* magazine's Michael Krantz dubbed him "The Bard of Generation Y" in the December 14, 1997, issue.

MTV, which awarded *Scream* its Movie of the Year Award in 1996, also featured a *Making of Scream 2* special at noon on December 13, 1997.

Scream 2 opened big on December 12, its only major competition the Steven Spielberg historical drama *Amistad* and the tired situation comedies *Home Alone 3* and *For Richer or Poorer*. Early box office estimates put the film at a weekend gross of $33.2 million, a good start compared to the opening weekends of *Alien Resurrection*, *Starship Troopers* or *Flubber*. The film richly deserved its success. Unlike the disappointing sequel *Alien Resurrection*, *Scream 2* really delivered the goods. Arguably, it was as scary and as funny as the first *Scream*, and such a strong bond had been forged with characters such as Weathers, Randy, Dewey and Sidney in the first film that the suspense in the sequel was actually palpable. When one or more of these beloved Williamson characters was unexpectedly offed in the sequel, the viewer *felt* the loss. Because of these feelings, the sequel carried considerable dramatic weight, and not surprisingly was met with positive reviews. *Rolling Stone* called it "delicious, diabolical and fun" and *Entertainment Weekly* raved that it was "clever and sophisticated." Also of interest in *Scream 2* was the emergence of the dominating female character. A delightful Jada Pinkett opened the film with an assertive lecture about the role of African-Americans in horror films, Sarah Michelle Gellar (who does not have a good record for surviving these kind of movies!) played a concerned "sober sister" responsible for driving her drunken friends home from a party, and Cox and Campbell became stronger, more determined and more heroic. Even the new villain was a woman, the mother of Billy Loomis! Part of the reason for the preponderance of strong women in *Scream 2* was Miramax data asserting that an estimated 16 percent of women age 25 and under saw *Scream* more than once. In contrast, only 3 percent of boys in the same category returned to see the film again.[38]

The Future

The rest of Craven's career in horror remains unwritten in the closing days of 1997. Will he return to the genre for the inevitable *Scream 3*? Will he be allowed to make *Fiddlefest*? Will *Bad Moon Rising* or *Wes Craven's Millennium* ever see the light of day? Will Craven return to his roots and produce a remake of his seminal *The Last House on the Left*, a film that is just as timely today as it was in 1972? Will he direct a film based on his novel *The Fountain Society*? Will he ever be allowed to play with a budget greater than $25 million? These are the questions his fans mull over on the internet at the many sites and pages devoted to Craven and his films.

Hopefully, Craven will continue his association with horror well into the 21st century and continue to terrify and enlighten new generations of moviegoers. Even if he does not continue, his first 25 years in the genre are a gift to horror lovers. To paraphrase Craven's script from *Swamp Thing*, there's beauty in Wes Craven's films ... if you know where to look for it.

Chapter 2

The Feature Films

The Last House on the Left (1972)

Last House on the Left is a tough, bitter little sleeper of a movie. ...What comes through in *Last House on the Left* is a powerful narrative, told so directly and strongly that the audience ... was rocked back on its psychic heels. ...Craven's direction never lets out from under almost unbearable dramatic tension.... This movie covers the same philosophical territory as Sam Peckinpah's *Straw Dogs*, and is more hardnosed about it.— Roger Ebert, *Roger Ebert's Movie Home Companion, 1993 Edition* (Andrews and McMeel, page 361)

Last House begins by depicting opposites, gradually blurring barriers, until the audience's emotional involvement with violent actions leads not to catharsis but self-disgust and self-awareness.... *Last House* condemns any audience member who complies with excessive violent displays. It is an extremely complex film that unveils an ugly sadistic lust most horror films pander to.— Tony Williams, *Hearths of Darkness: The Family in the American Horror Film* (Associated University Presses, 1996, page 130)

In a thing (as opposed to a film) titled *Last House on the Left*, four slobbering fiends capture and torture two "groovy" young girls who airily explore the bad section of town and more or less ask for trouble. When I walked out, after 50 minutes (with 35 to go), one girl had just been dismembered with a machete. ...The party who wrote this sickening tripe and also directed the inept actors is Wes Craven ... [F]or anyone interested in paying to see repulsive people and human agony.— Howard Thompson, *The New York Times* (December 22, 1972)

Sick, sick, sick gore film about middle-aged parents out to avenge their daughter's death. The old couple must have seen *The Texas Chainsaw Massacre* a few times.— Harry and Michael Medved, *The Golden Turkey Awards* (A Perigee Book, 1980, page 215)

[T]he filmmakers seem to get great pleasure from the torture, sexual humiliation and killing of two truly sweet teenage girls. *The Last House on the Left* ... is a sick sexual fantasy for predators that is indeed an "incitement to violence."— Danny Peary, *Cult Movies* (Delacorte Press, 1981, page 348)

Intense and disturbing watershed movie with an almost documentary feel, which director Craven now considers so grim that it shocks even him.— John McCarty, *The Official Splatter Movie Guide* (St. Martins Press, 1989, page 81)

Pandering effort of producer Sean S. Cunningham and writer-director Wes Craven, made to shock in the grossest manner with its tale of retribution.... And yet this has an unrelenting power that makes it compelling despite crudities.—John Stanley, *Creature Features Strikes Again* (Creatures At Large Press, 1994, page 222)

Until *The Texas Chainsaw Massacre*, *Last House on the Left* was considered the ultimate gore film.... The film has little style and little humor but it is marked by documentary-like intensity.—Darrell Moore, *The Best, Worst, and Most Unusual: Horror Films* (Publications International, Ltd., 1983, page 147)

A particularly unimaginative offshoot of the violent but artful cinema of director Sam Peckinpah. ...[T]he *raison d'etre* of the proceedings is revenge, blunt and simple-minded. The approach was to become standard in the sub genre, and came to characterize a heartless brand of moviemaking that takes no prisoners.—David J. Hogan, *Dark Romance: Sexuality in the Horror Film* (McFarland and Company, Inc., 1986, page 246)

I had seen *Last House on the Left* and was frankly appalled. It was beyond horrific. It was brutal.—New Line President Robert Shaye, in his foreword to *The Nightmare Never Ends* by William Schoell and James Spencer

CAST: Sandra Cassell (Mari Collingwood); Lucy Grantham (Phyllis Stone); David A. Hess (Krug Stillo); Fred Lincoln (Fred "Weasel" Podowski); Marc Sheffler (Junior Stillo); Jeramie Rain (Sadie); Gaylord St. James (John Collingwood); Cynthia Carr (Estelle Collingwood); Ada Washington (Ada); Marshall Anker (Sheriff); Martin Kove (Deputy Harry); Ray Edwards (Postman).

CREDITS: Sean S. Cunningham Films Ltd. The Night Company. *Director of Photography:* Victor Hurwitz. *Original Music:* David Alexander Hess. *Producer:* Sean S. Cunningham. *Writer/Director:* Wes Craven. *Film Editor:* Wes Craven. *Assistant Editor:* Stephen Miner. *Costume Design:* Susan S. Cunningham. *Assistant Director:* Yvonne Hannemann. *Associate Producer:* Katherine D'Amato. *Sound:* Jim Hubbard. *Gaffer:* Dick Donovan. *Production Assistant:* Steve Miner. *Wardrobe and Makeup:* Anne Paul. *Special Effects:* Troy Roberts. *Mix:* R.S.I. *Sound Mixer:* Gary Leibman. *Opticals and Blow Up:* The Optical House. *Title Design:* David Miner. *Unit Production Manager:* Larry Beinhart. From Lobster Enterprises. *MPAA Rating:* R. *Running Time:* 82 minutes

> The events you are about to witness are true. Names and locations have been changed to protect those individuals still living.
> —The opening title card of *The Last House on the Left*

SYNOPSIS: On a sunny day, a mailman arrives at the home of J.H. Collingwood, M.D., and his family. As he delivers their mail, the old mailman wistfully reflects that there is not a more lovely girl in the whole county than young Mari Collingwood, who is turning 17 in just a day.

Inside the house, Mari showers and prepares for her big celebration. Downstairs, her father John and her mother Estelle go about their business in the living room but John is perturbed because the telephone is dead. His mood is worsened further when he spots young Mari, all ready for her night on the town. She is not wearing a bra and Collingwood complains that he can "see her nipples as plain as day!" Estelle is worried because Mari is going to New York City for a concert performed by "Bloodlust," a band which once dismembered a chicken on stage.

Although her parents find her interest in the violent rock band alarming ("I thought you were supposed to be the love generation?"), Mari assures her parents that she will be fine for just one night alone in New York. She and her parents continue to argue briefly about "Bloodlust," breasts, bras and Mari's bad language before the Collingwoods present their daughter with her first birthday present: a beautiful silver necklace adorned with a peace emblem. The final source of discomfort for the Collingwoods is Mari's partner on her night out: Phyllis Stone. Estelle does not approve of Phyllis because she comes from a bad neighborhood in New York City and is reputed to be sexually active.

After introducing Phyllis to her parents, Mari and her friend head into the beautiful woods behind the Collingwood house. They frolic by the lake and talk about life. While drinking champagne, Mari and Phyllis wonder what it would be like to "make it" with members of "Bloodlust." Mari thinks it would be a soft and gentle feeling like making love in "cotton" but Phyllis thinks young Mari has a lot to learn about life. In fact, Mari is eager to learn about almost everything and she is positively thrilled because in the last few months her breasts have "filled out." For the first time in her life, she feels like a woman.

Phyllis and Mari drive to New York City. While they are not paying attention, their car radio reveals that two convicted murderers have escaped from jail. Two prison guards are dead and a German shepherd has been kicked to death by a feral woman. The driver of the getaway car was a boy named Junior Stillo, the illegitimate son of Krug Stillo, who had been serving a life sentence for the killing of two priests and one nun in 1966. Krug Stillo is reported to have hooked his son Junior on heroin. The second escaped convict is Fred "The Weasel" Podowsky, a man accused of child molesting, "peeping tomism" and assault with a deadly weapon. This foursome is on the loose and very dangerous.

Elsewhere in the city, Krug, Fred, Junior and the "feral" woman, Sadie, share an apartment. Junior brings Sadie a beer while she takes a bath. He is upset because he does not get along with his father, Krug. Sadie just wants to be someone ... *any*one ... else. She wants to change her name to "Agatha Greenwood" or some such thing. Junior responds that he wants to be a frog, a solitary creature who is left alone and who has his own lily pad. Krug breaks in on the duo's conversation and shoves Junior face first into Sadie's bathwater. Later, Krug wants to have sex with Sadie but she refuses to "put out" for him or Fred until there are more chicks around. Krug does not understand her reluctance and refers to himself as "the cream of American manhood."

Mari and Phyllis arrive in Manhattan and buy ice cream, then go looking for some decent "grass" before the concert begins. After they walk the streets for a time, the two girls encounter Junior on his front stoop. They approach him and ask if he knows where they can purchase marijuana. Junior tells them that he's got some real good Colombian stuff for only $20. They are excited by the prospect and follow Junior up to his apartment. Once inside Krug's home, they realize they have made a mistake but it is too late. They are locked inside by Fred, who is armed with a pistol. Krug tells the girls he wants "company."

In suburbia, the Collingwoods blissfully prepare for Mari's seventeenth birthday party, unaware of the danger their daughter now faces. John giddily tells Estelle that he "wants to attack" her, making clumsy sexual advances.

Back in Krug's apartment, Fred pulls a knife when Phyllis threatens to scream. Krug unbuttons her shirt and Sadie quickly wraps her hands around Phyllis' breast. As the thugs make the moves on her, Phyllis spits in Fred's eye. He threatens to kill her if she tries that again. Upset, Krug silences Phyllis' resistance by punching her in the gut. Phyllis collapses on the floor and Mari watches as Krug and Fred rape her.

Early the following morning, Krug and his companions carry the unconscious girls out through the back door of the apartment and dump them in the trunk of their 1958 Cadillac convertible. Realizing that it is only a matter of time before the police are onto them, Krug and his companions leave the city.

At the Collingwood home, John and Estelle are worried because Mari never came home from the concert. The phones are working again, so the Collingwoods contact the theater manager. He informs the anxious parents that the "Bloodlust" concert ended at two A.M. Estelle is now convinced that something is very wrong, but John tells her to relax and let Mari have "her fling." He says that this behavior is "classic" in teenage girls and is merely Mari's way of saying she's grown up.

Krug and company travel through the countryside. Junior drives while Krug merrily has intercourse with Sadie in the backseat. When Fred and Junior keep gabbing, Krug grows angry that they are breaking his rhythm. After Krug finishes with Sadie, Fred grows philosophical and asks his friends who has committed the sex crime of the century. Sadie suggests that Sigmund Freud is the greatest criminal in history. Before Freud, a telephone pole was just a telephone pole; now it is a phallus!

The police arrive at the Collingwood house. The sheriff, an overweight, bespectacled man, assures them that Mari will be home before supper, but the Collingwoods are very worried.

Nearby, Krug's car breaks down. Junior tries to fix it but he knows nothing about cars. Deciding that he needs to have more fun, Krug opens the trunk and releases Phyllis and Mari. Mari spots her mailbox and realizes she is just outside her house. Krug wants to take the girls into the woods and have his way with them, even though "Weasel" warns Krug that they must get out of the state. Krug cannot be swayed from his course of action and with Fred, Sadie, and Junior in tow, he leads the girls into the forest where less than 24 hours ago they enjoyed

The road leads to nowhere for Phyllis Stone (Lucy Grantham) and Mari Collingwood (Sandra Cassell) in *The Last House on the Left*.

champagne and talked about life's possibilities. Phyllis bites Krug on the wrist in defiance but it is a useless gesture of resistance.

Soon after the criminals have left their vehicle, the sheriff and Deputy Harry leave the Collingwood house. They spot the broken-down dark-green Cadillac but do not investigate it. Instead, they drive to the police station and wonder where Mari has disappeared to.

Amidst the beauty of nature, Krug and his friends torture Phyllis and Mari. Krug orders Phyllis to follow his instructions lest Mari be stabbed by Fred. Phyllis is reluctant to cooperate, especially when Krug orders her to "piss" her pants, but she has no choice but to do as Krug commands. The thug orders her to take her pants off and Junior grows increasingly uncomfortable. Then Krug orders Phyllis to strike Mari. This is too much for Junior and he finally protests. Krug ignores Junior and orders the girls to disrobe. By now, Mari and Phyllis are both naked and crying. Phyllis attempts to comfort Mari, certain the worst is yet to come.

At the local police station, Deputy Harry and the sheriff sit around uselessly. Harry reads the *Classics Illustrated* comic version of *Captains Courageous* and speculates about a farmer who may be having carnal relations with his pig! The Collingwoods telephone the station and inform the police that they are holding them personally responsible for Mari's safety.

Back in the woods, Krug realizes that it is time to end the fun and get back on the road. Phyllis overhears that he is returning to the car to get something to

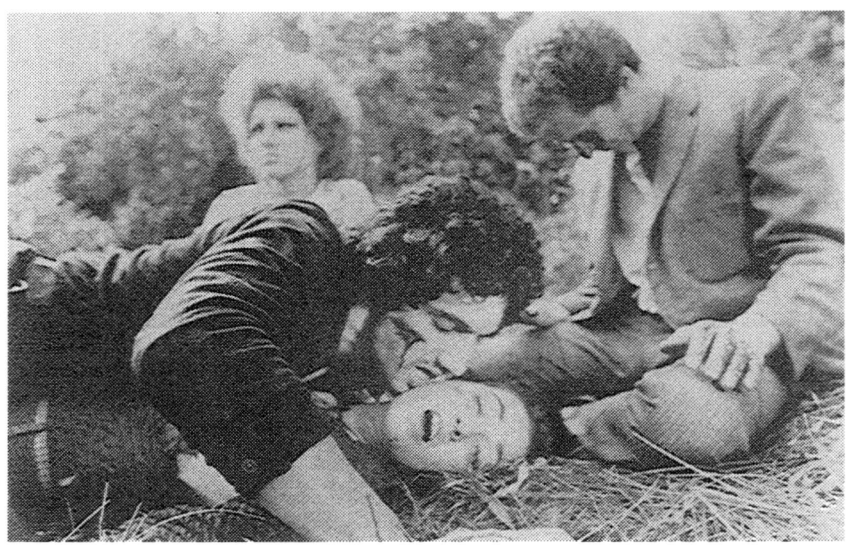

The Last House on the Left: Krug (David Hess) rapes Mari, with Sadie (Jeramie Rain) and Weasel (Fred Lincoln) looking ashamed in the background.

"cut firewood with." She realizes this really means he is going to kill her and Mari. Phyllis whispers to Mari that she is going to make a run for it once Krug has left. All Mari will have to do is run in the opposite direction. Phyllis makes her break and Weasel and Sadie run off after her. Junior stays behind with Mari, who begs him to let her go. Junior, Mari realizes, is a frightened boy who is as much a victim as she is. She renames him "Willow" and appeals to his humanity. She begs him to set her free and then gives him a present: the peace emblem necklace given to her by her parents. Junior is torn but he is too afraid of Krug to take direct action against him. Only when Mari promises Junior that her father can give him the drug fix he needs (methadone) does he agree to go with her to her house.

While Mari and Junior make for the Collingwood home, Phyllis runs through the woods. She encounters Sadie first, who promises to help her. Phyllis cracks Sadie on the head with a rock and calls her "a stupid dyke." Then Fred and Sadie pursue Phyllis into a cemetery. Phyllis realizes she has taken a wrong turn and turns around only to find herself face-to-face with Krug. Armed with a machete, Krug is ready to kill. Phyllis is surrounded and "Weasel" stabs her repeatedly in the back. She falls to the ground, bloodied, and the gang of thugs kick her over and over again.

At the police station, the officers are playing checkers when they hear a bulletin about Krug leaving New York City. The report includes the make of Krug's car and the policemen realize they saw that very car outside the Collingwood house. They race to their car and speed to John and Estelle's home. It is a 45-

minute ride and, after a few minutes of driving, the police car stops unexpectedly ... out of gas! The sheriff and Deputy Harry leave the useless vehicle and walk toward their destination.

In the woods, Phyllis staggers to a tree, her back gushing a river of blood. She spits at Weasel as he approaches and stabs her again. After Phyllis expires, the group returns to find Junior and Mari attempting to escape. When Mari asks if Phyllis has escaped, Krug throws Phyllis' dismembered hand at her. Mari now realizes there is no hope. Krug rips off her clothes and rapes her, drooling on her face throughout the forced intercourse. After the rape, Mari stands and staggers away. She vomits and then prays. Krug and his cohorts watch Mari's ritual and look at each other. They are stained with blood and for a moment they seem ashamed of their actions. Dazed, Mari staggers towards the nearby river. Instead of pursuing her, Krug shoots her three times. Mari, now neck-deep in the river, finally dies. With both girls dead, Krug and his friends go to the river and wash up.

Miles away, the two policemen are still walking to the Collingwood house. They stop an oncoming truck filled with chickens, driven by an elderly black lady named Ada. They order her to drive them to the Collingwood house, but since she has no room for them, they will have to sit on the roof! The police reluctantly agree to this arrangement but when the vehicle starts, they fall off the truck onto the street. The sheriff explains the emergency to Ada and negotiates with her for a better seat.

Krug, Sadie, Junior and Fred have now dressed up in their Sunday finest. With their car broken down, they seek lodging for the night and end up at the Collingwood house. They are invited inside by the gracious Estelle and they explain their vehicular woes. Unfortunately, the telephone is dead again, so the Collingwoods cannot call a repair shop for their guests. They are invited to spend the night, and Krug's brood takes Estelle up on her offer. She shows them to their rooms, and Krug, Sadie, Fred and Junior all sit together on Mari's bed. They see pictures of her on the wall and a mirror and realize whose house they have arrived at. Later, the Collingwoods and Krug's family eat dinner together. John and Estelle note that the group seems very strange. They belch during the meal and Sadie gulps her wine. Mysteriously, there are teeth marks on Krug's wrist. Estelle and John attempt to make polite conversation and Fred claims that he and Krug are in the plumbing insurance business.

While Krug, Sadie and Fred do their best to act with a degree of decorum, Junior suffers. He is going through a painful withdrawal from heroin and is haunted by dreams of Mari. He sees her, beautiful and alive, calling him "Willow." He screams out in agony that he is "sorry." The Collingwoods hear this and Fred explains that Junior recently lost the insurance company a big "account." After dinner, Krug, Sadie and Fred return to their rooms to relax.

Estelle hears Junior vomiting in the bathroom. She tends to him and is shocked to discover that he is wearing the peace emblem that she and John gave to Mari. Estelle opens Krug's suitcase and finds bloodied clothes inside. Together,

John and Estelle run out to the river. They find Mari's corpse and weep over it. They bring her body back to their living room and place it on the sofa. Then, they plot revenge.

That night, Fred has a nightmare. He sees John and Estelle dressed in surgical scrubs, standing over him. They chisel out his teeth with a hammer! He awakes with a start and looks around the house. He finds Estelle standing alone in the living room, drinking whiskey. (Behind her is the sofa and Mari's body, but Fred has not seen it yet.) Estelle leads him outside, informing Fred that she finds him a sexy man. She tells him that her husband is afraid of her sexuality and that she has always dreamed of a man who could "take her" with his hands tied behind his back. Fred takes this as a challenge and says that he is the man Estelle has been awaiting. Estelle binds Fred's hands with his necktie. Then she performs fellatio on him after "accidentally" zipping his penis up in his pants. Just short of bringing Fred to orgasmic climax, Estelle goes wild. She bites off his penis and spits it out.

Weasel's dying screams awaken Krug and Sadie, but John Collingwood is ready for them. After shooting Krug in the shoulder with a shotgun, the two men duke it out in the living room. Krug beats John badly but Junior stops his father, shooting at him with Fred's pistol. Krug is enraged by his son's betrayal and he orders the impressionable youngster to turn the weapon on himself and blow his brains out. Junior does just that, ending his agony at last.

Junior has distracted Krug just long enough for John to come after the criminal with a chainsaw. Instead of helping Krug, Sadie runs out of the house and is attacked by Estelle. Outside, the two women fight to the death. Estelle cuts Sadie's throat with Fred's switchblade and throws her into the pool. Inside, John Collingwood carves up Krug Stillo just as the police arrive. Blood-spattered and exhausted, John and Estelle fall into each other's arms. Horrified, the policemen take the bloodied chainsaw away from Dr. Collingwood.

COMMENTARY: Written over a period of four days, the screenplay for *The Last House on the Left* was designed by Craven to serve as a loose re-interpretation of the 1958 Ingmar Bergman film *The Virgin Spring* (*Jungfrukallan* in Swedish), which premiered in the United States in February of 1960 and which many, especially critic Vernon Young, felt was a modern cinematic masterpiece. However, the origins of *The Last House on the Left* go back even further than that film. *The Virgin Spring*, an Academy Award winner for best foreign film, was itself modeled on an earlier work, a medieval German ballad (twelfth–fourteenth century) called *Tore's Daughter*.

While researching the long history of that ballad, Bergman's screenwriter Ulla Isaksson reportedly found more than 25 variations of the basic story. One such variation suggested that Dr. Tore had seven daughters and that *all* of them were raped and murdered by a gang of seven herdsman! That fact was changed in both the Bergman and Craven versions for obvious dramatic reasons. One brutal rape allowed audiences to "personally" feel the pain of a single, well-developed character. It would have been quite difficult to write a screenplay that adequately developed seven characters so that all seven rapes would come across as powerfully and individually as just one would. And besides, at least in Craven's case, there was a limited budget to consider. Seven girls and seven rapists (14 performers!) represented an unnecessary financial burden on a $40,000–$50,000 motion picture!

Another acknowledged influence on Bergman's film version of *Tore's Daughter* was the Japanese film *Rashomon* (1951), directed by Akira Kurosawa. That picture recounted the story of a rape and murder as well, but the gimmick of *Rashomon* was that the events were told from four varying perspectives (which demonstrated that "objective" truth was impossible to ascertain). Although Bergman later referred disparagingly to his *The Virgin Spring* as a wretched imitation of that classic Kurosawa film, many critics feel that Bergman's work is superior even although it makes no such comment on the subjectivity of eyewitness accounts. Its concern instead is mostly religious.

There are many parallels between Craven's modern adaptation of the material and Bergman's *The Virgin Spring*. Both films are sparse in length, running under 90 minutes, and both tell (in vastly different settings) the story of *Tore's Daughter*. Dr. Tore, a medieval physician, is played in *The Virgin Spring* by Max Von Sydow (*The Exorcist* [1973], *Flash Gordon* [1980], *Dune* [1984]), and by Gaylord St. James in *The Last House on the Left* as the re-named "Dr. Collingwood." In *The Virgin Spring*, Tore's beloved and much-indulged daughter Karin is raped and beheaded by a trio of unwashed herdsmen while she is on the way to church to light candles for the Virgin Mary. In *The Last House on the Left*, it is Mari Collingwood who is murdered by thugs on her way to, of all things, a rock concert. In *The Virgin Spring*, Dr. Tore and his wife Mareta commit brutal revenge upon the herdsmen, who by a strange twist of fate have ended up staying at their home for the evening. The revenge angle is also carried over in Craven's film but with John Collingwood brandishing a chainsaw against his enemies instead of a butcher's knife. The innocent youth tortured by the images of the dead girl is also translated in the Craven film. In *The Virgin Spring* he is a ten-year-old child (Tore kills him anyway!), but in *The Last House on the Left* he is Junior, a young adult, who kills himself because of his anguish. Mareta's hatred for the servant girl Ingeri is also carried over in *The Last House on the Left* with Estelle Collingwood's severe disapproval of Phyllis, a girl of a different social class than Mari. Where the two plotlines differ most is not in specific detail or characters but in religious conviction and overtones.

In *The Virgin Spring*, Dr. Tore's wife Mareta blames herself for the death of her daughter because she loved Karin more than she loved God. For Dr. Tore, the matter is more basic. He wonders how God can allow such monstrosities to occur in the world. ("You see it and you allow it. The innocent child's death and my revenge, you allowed it! I don't understand you!" he cries at one point.) In his confusion, Tore swears to erect a church in the wild where Karin's corpse lies cold. As if in response, God causes a spring to bubble there. In a high angle shot focusing on the dead Karin, Bergman's camera captures the birth of this beautiful spring and Tore's awe. With the questioning of God and the final miracle of the virgin spring, Bergman's film ultimately confirms the existence of a Christian God who does watch over man even if he does not intervene when horrible events occur.

The film could also be interpreted in another, more disturbing way. Perhaps Tore and his wife actually *caused* the incident by caring more for their daughter than they did for Jesus Christ! If this interpretation were to be considered, mankind has much to worry about because God is a selfish, demanding and wrathful creature with an inferiority complex. Either way, *The Virgin Spring* views the world in a religious context and the characters are overtly religious, praying before every meal. Mareta is so devout, in fact, that she burns her wrists with the fire of a candle every Friday, Christ's day of agony. Most importantly, the protagonists of *The Virgin Spring* question God and their own faith, and in the climax God gives them a miracle so their faith in Him is restored. By contrast, in *The Last House on the Left* there is no suggestion at all of an afterlife or of God. The film's theme song, repeated time and again, is appropriately titled "The Road Leads To Nowhere," which implies that life is a trip that has only one destination: death. Since there is no God, only a road going nowhere, *The Last House on the Left* is squarely existentialist, even nihilistic in its assertion that life will end in horror and violence.

Terrible things happen to innocent people in *The Last House on the Left* with regularity and even so-called "good people" such as the Collingwoods easily resort to brutal violence and bloodlust. Although Mari prays to God before she is murdered, in a scene staged in almost identical fashion to Karin's rape and murder in *The Virgin Spring*, there is no salvation for her or redemption for her fallen parents. Unlike the Tores in *The Virgin Spring*, the Collingwoods are not enlightened in the finale by the existence of God or an awareness of divine method. They are left totally isolated in a shattered living room filled only with the blood of villains. The camera does not swoop heavenward to give the impression God is watching because in Craven's film, God is dead.

A standard flaw of most film remakes is that they slavishly attempt to recreate the original film. *The Last House on the Left* is successful because Craven has removed the theological context of *The Virgin Spring* and substituted an equally provocative secular philosophy. *The Last House on the Left* takes place in a completely Godless world, a perfect reflection of the early 1970s when atheism was finding more adherents and many, including *Time* magazine, asked the very question "Is God Dead?" Unlike Bergman, Craven does not treat Karin, Dr. Tore, Mareta and the servant girl Ingeri (Phyllis Stone in *The Last House on the Left*) as game pieces to be manipulated in God's master plan, but as realistic people caught in a terrible situation. Mari's death is a horrible moment, and after her rape the audience members thirst for the death of Krug and his deviant cohorts. Yet when Craven finally grants his viewers these murders, there is no joy in the film or in the audience, only a deep-seated sense of shame and anger. Importantly, *The Last House on the Left*'s final moment is not a reaffirmation of faith or even a celebration of violence but an opportunity for grim reflection. The Collingwoods have been as ruthlessly violent as Mari's attackers, and yet what has been gained by their spilling of blood? Nothing. Mari is still dead and, for the Collingwoods anyway, the road still leads to nowhere. The final shot of *The Last House on the Left* indicates that John and Mari have lost much more than their child. They appear shell-shocked. It is evident by their battered faces that they have lost themselves and the life of "goodness" and morality they thought they had built. They have committed murder and for what? Their house is still empty; as the film's soundtrack asserts, "the castle stays the same."

By freeze-framing on the shattered Collingwoods, the final shot of *The Last House on the Left* reveals the futility of bloodshed and retribution in a way the uplifting finale of *The Virgin Spring* does not. The final image of twisted agony lingers and is therefore forced down the throats of theatergoers. There is no triumphant music on the soundtrack, no heroic overture indicating "justice," only a still-life picture of people in pain. By ending on this downcast note, by freezing on tortured faces, the film serves as an argument against violence and revenge, not an incitement to violence as some blind critics have asserted. It is clear that it is not so much the death of their beloved daughter that has taken its toll on the Collingwoods but rather the realization that they are no better than the people who murdered her so casually. In some ways, *The Last House on the Left* is actually a more responsible or moral film than *The Virgin Spring* because of its thorough condemnation of violence. The final image of Craven's effort is not a beautiful bubbling spring which blithely puts aside the violence of the past and suggests the existence of God, but rather the frozen portrait of two shattered human beings. *The Last House on the Left* finds no validation for revenge whereas *The Virgin Spring* suggests that horrible acts of violence will be forgiven by God and that there is redemption if only one asks. Erecting a church in God's name, it seems, will wash one's hands forever of blood. This is a dangerous argument, especially in a society where (in the name of God) people bomb clinics or kill doctors who perform abortions. Where *The Virgin Spring* takes Dr. Tore and his wife off-the-hook for their violence by allowing God to forgive their violent trespasses, *The Last House of the Left* makes the Collingwoods responsible for their actions. Because *The Last House on the Left* so daringly re-interprets the context of *The Virgin Spring* and makes Bergman's story a tale about man's violent nature instead of one wherein "God moves in mysterious ways," it is also much more meaningful to a society where retribution, via capital punishment, is legally mandated.

If the final frame of *The Last House on the Left*, that of the broken Collingwoods presiding over a fractured castle, is considered the film's destination, it is illuminating to see how writer-director Craven artfully arrives at that powerful apex. The two families (Krugs and Collingwoods) are nicely paralleled through the entire film to suggest that perhaps they have more in common than meets the eye. Since Craven believes the families are identical, and the final freeze frame acknowledges that even the Collingwoods have become aware of this fact, the details of the parallels are important. First, both families are seen in roughly the same circumstances. As the film opens, John Collingwood sits in the living room of his home and reads the newspaper, blissfully ignoring his wife until she rips the paper out of his hands. The camera later finds the Krugs in their home, where the mother figure, Sadie, is also ignored by the men of the household. "Weasel" sits in his living room fiddling with a gun and listening to the radio (mirroring Collingwood with the paper) and Krug steadfastly ignores Sadie's comments about being a more "liberated" woman.

Importantly, the families resemble each other in another way: they both have a family pet. Like most Craven film protagonists, the Collingwoods have a dog, and the Krugs own a black cat, traditionally a symbol of evil in the cinema. But both castles are the same in more ways than they are different. Krug and John Collingwood both complain about their children, albeit in different modes of expression. Collingwood expresses his irritation with Mari's revealing clothing, and Krug curses angrily and hits his son when the boy disappoints him. Mari and Junior are alike in other ways. They are both aware that they are "growing up." Mari longs to experience life and her recently found womanhood and Junior yearns to be free of his father. He wants to be a frog and live alone on his lily pad where no one will bother him. The connections between family units are established not just through character similarities and dialogue, but through Craven's most potent cinematic tool: cross-cutting.

After the initial scenes indicating similar family circumstances and a segment wherein Sadie yearns to be a lady with the noble-sounding name Agatha Green*wood*, not unlike Estelle Colling*wood*, Craven cross-cuts between the activities of the two families with regularity. In the Collingwood home, husband and wife frolic in their kitchen as Estelle spreads a creamy icing over Mari's birthday cake. After cross-cutting to the Krug household, Krug declares to Sadie that he is the "cream" of American manhood and makes similar if more blunt advances on the matriarch of his family. After Mari and Phyllis are captured, Craven again cuts back to the Collingwoods. John declares lasciviously to his wife "I want to attack you," and then the scene switches back yet again to Mari and Phyllis being physically assaulted by Krug and Weasel.

The cross-cuts forge a spiritual connection between the Krugs and the Collingwoods even before the two families have intersected. John expresses his will to attack, and Krug actually does just that. This bond will blossom throughout the film and the final connection between the two families is that both stoop to physical violence and commit heinous acts before the film has ended. The final freeze-frame on the Collingwoods is not unlike the earlier shot of Sadie, "Weasel" and Krug at the lake after Mari's rape. The killers realize what they have done and they stand in the composition looking uncomfortable and ashamed, much as John and Estelle feel after dispatching their opponents in the finale.

Craven utilizes an arsenal of film techniques, not just cross-cutting, to make the point that violence is never justified. Since he wants to inspire in audiences disgust for violence, he must first draw them into the story. To accomplish this, Craven is purposely teasing. Early in the film, his camera finds Mari showering. The sequence is edited so that no details of Mari's young body are revealed. Although the camera focuses on her as she showers, there is a translucent wall between the camera and Mari. Only a flesh-colored silhouette can be seen, not a beautiful nude girl. Then Mari steps out of the shower and approaches a mirror. Again, the viewer's voyeuristic impulse to see Mari naked is foiled because there is steam on the mirror impeding a clear view. As she wipes away the steam, Mari's towel on the mirror then obstructs a clear glimpse of her breasts and nipples. Undoubtedly, this obfuscation of details is Craven's method of roping in the audience. He sets up a deliberately provocative situation (a beautiful woman showering) and then purposely frustrates his viewers by revealing almost no details. Voyeuristic impulses are aroused.

Similarly, while Phyllis is raped in Krug's apartment, the camera reveals no specifics. On the soundtrack there are sounds of clothes ripping and of Phyllis crying "no!", but the camera zooms in instead on Mari's shocked face. The audiences watches Mari watching a rape, but again is denied access to the main event. Just as in the shower scene, curiosity is aroused as to exactly what is happening, further reeling in the audience. Because there is no on-screen brutality and because Phyllis's soft moans of "no" are erotic, this scene serves only to stimulate audience interest, not to disgust or shock.

By the time Krug and his companions drag the girls to the lake, nothing particularly graphic or explicit has been shown in *The Last House on the Left*, so audiences are thoroughly unprepared when Craven abruptly reverses technique and focuses on every grisly detail. The audience watches as Phyllis is forced to "piss her pants." They stare as the two girls disrobe and are forced to kiss one another in humiliating fashion. Now Craven's camera spares the audience nothing: Phyllis' stabbing and brutal murder, as well as Mari's rape by Krug, are shown in sickening detail. Craven has really pulled a fast one on his audience here. He has teased them throughout the film with brief glimpses of nudity and off-screen acts of carnal lust, creating in them the desire to see more. Then, suddenly, he shows everything and the impact is gut-wrenching. The rape is not sexy or erotic. Instead, it is heart-wrenching. The audience watches as two lovely girls, well-developed by Craven as sweet people by this time, are tortured. The result? The audience feels sickened by their earlier voyeuristic impulse to see more.

By the time Mari is finally shot dead, it seems to many audience members to be a mercy killing. The events preceding her death are so harrowing that the viewer cannot endure any more. Violence is welcomed because it ends the suffering

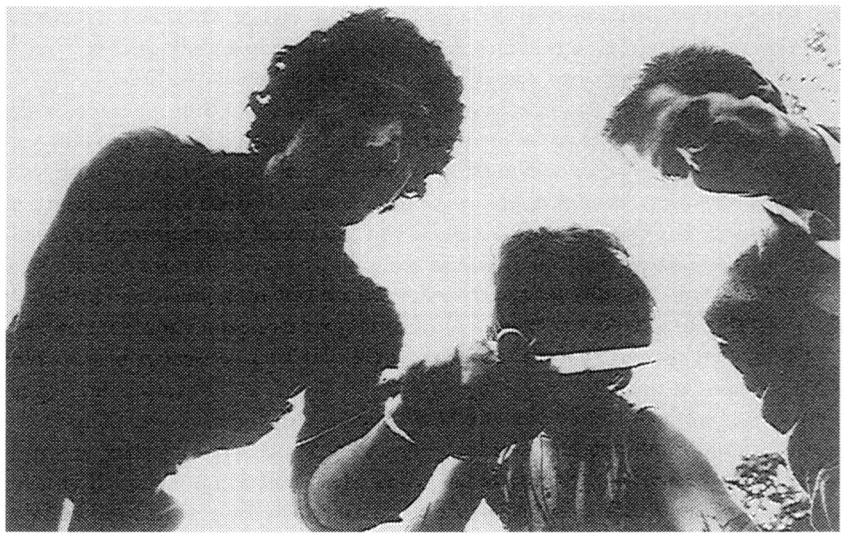

The three killers finish the job in a disturbing point-of-view still from *The Last House on the Left*.

of an innocent. Craven's clever manipulation of audience expectations and desires is a master stroke of directorial technique and it makes his point about the abhorrent nature of violence and revenge all the more powerful. People leave *The Last House on the Left* shocked and horrified as much by their early complicity in the events as by the traumas that have unfolded on the screen.

Craven's technique of creating parallels through cross-cutting and his unique method of drawing audiences in and then shocking them are certainly paramount factors in his first film's success. There are also other elements that make the film memorable, particularly the writing and the performances of the actors. Early on, the screenplay establishes the sweet nature of Mari and Phyllis' friendship. With Mari's musings about making love to "Bloodlust" and preoccupation with her breasts, it is clear that she is the more naive and open of the duo. Phyllis is tolerant and amused by Mari but she also seems to admire her innocence. They are not just victims as in the *Friday the 13th* films, but real people who love each other. It is a heart-wrenching moment when they are forced to take off their clothes and perform for Krug. Out of control, Mari weeps and leaves Phyllis in the role of protector. She tells Mari that they are "alone" out there and she does everything to make the torture more bearable for her friend. Finally, Phyllis gives up her life to save Mari. She sacrifices herself and breaks free from the thugs so Mari can escape. This is especially ironic since Mari's parents have made a point about how uncomfortable they are with Phyllis. She is from the wrong side of town and Estelle thinks that Phyllis is worthless because rumors have floated around town that she is sexually active. The Collingwoods never learn that this girl does everything possible to save their daughter's life.

The remainder of the *dramatis personae* are painted successfully in *The Last House on the Left* as well. Craven's literate script boldly pinpoints the hypocrisy of many lead characters while still making them sympathetic people. The Collingwoods argue with Mari not only about Phyllis, but about Mari's lack of a bra. Mari points out her parent's hypocrisy by noting that people of Estelle's generation wear pointed bras that make their breasts "stand out like torpedoes." In other words, Mari asserts that she is only showing what nature has given her as opposed to her mother, who wears bras which *exaggerate* her attributes and foster desire in the opposite sex.

Even Mari shows signs of hypocrisy. Her father asks how she feels about "Bloodlust" after a band member dismembered a chicken on stage. Mari replies sarcastically that she has lost a lot of sleep over that chicken. When Estelle replies that Mari is supposed to be of the "love generation," Craven's point is made. Even people who are supposedly "peaceniks" thrive on violence when it is inflicted on others. Mari has no sympathy for the chicken because she lives a sheltered life and has never been the victim of violence. Though she in no way deserves to be raped and murdered, it is ironic that Mari should end up being essentially the sacrificial "chicken" in an act of brutality.

Other characters are developed with equal care. Although Sadie is seen having sex with Krug in the back of their convertible, it is obvious from many lines of dialogue that she is by preference a lesbian. When Sadie first spies Phyllis and Mari, she stares at them and comments pointedly that she "wants something to eat," indicating her lust for the young girls. Later, she protectively puts her hands over Phyllis' bare breasts and argues with Krug that she "had her first!" When Phyllis is forced to disrobe at the lake, Sadie declares admiringly that she has a "good-looking ass." Finally, when Phyllis strikes back at Sadie afterwards, she calls Krug's woman "a stupid dyke." Sadie's status as a lesbian is important because it establishes her as a sexual predator equal to Krug or "Weasel." She is just as much a rapist as her male friends and is therefore an equal danger to Mari and Phyllis.

In a strange way, Sadie's sexual preference is also important because of what it reveals of Krug's family. Sadie is never ridiculed or taunted for her preference but wholeheartedly accepted (even fulfilling the role of mother to Junior). This is ironic since the supposedly "heroic" Collingwoods have been dramatized as judgmental people unable to accept someone (Phyllis) who is not of an acceptable social class. Unlike the Collingwoods, the Krugs do not pass judgment. But then how could they? Krug is a murderer, "Weasel" is a peeping Tom and Junior is a heroin addict. In this group, Sadie's so-called "perversion" marks her as part of the family rather than an outsider. Whatever the implications, Sadie's complicated nature (as mother, lover, social climber and lesbian) elevates her above caricature status. Jeramie Rain does a remarkable job in creating a "complete" person rather than a black-and-white rapist.

Of all the performers in *The Last House on the Left*, it is undoubtedly David Hess who dominates the film. Hess portrays Krug as a charismatic bully, the perfect leader for a group of misfits. Krug is such a monster that he causes his own son to commit suicide, yet Hess does not play the man as an out-and-out villain. On the contrary, Krug at times seems to have a high degree of self-awareness. He knows that he is a terrible person responsible for horrid things. After he has raped Mari and killed Phyllis, Krug knows he has finally gone too far. Ashamed, he shoots Mari in the head not so much for the joy of killing but to end the girl's misery. Craven has often referred to this moment as the most disturbing in the film, and in a sense it is. As horrible as he is, Krug remains *human*. When he kills Mari, one feels it is out of shame as much as necessity. Any critic who claims that *The Last House on the Left* is condoning violence has missed the point. Even a scum of the Earth like Krug shows the capacity to be ashamed of his behavior, indicating that he knows right from wrong even if he cannot tread the line of right.

Hess also deserves kudos for composing and performing the soundtrack for *The Last House on the Left*. The music of the film is in a large way responsible for the success of the movie's many themes, as it too operates on various levels. "The Road Leads to Nowhere" is a haunting melody which perfectly captures the film's nihilism, but there is much more involved than that. The folksy rhythm which plays as Mari and Phyllis relax by the lake captures the progressive and free-wheeling mood of the early '70s and the "anything is possible" attitude of the naive youngsters. The song speaks of changes in seasons and nicely matches the dialogue wherein Mari declares that she "changed this winter too": her breasts have filled out. Already then, the soundtrack mirrors the events on screen.

Later, Hess's music signals a mood change in the film. Once Mari and Phyllis are in the car, they turn on the radio and hear the final bars of "The Road Leads to Nowhere" just as the audience sees a road stretching before the girls. The last word of the song, "nowhere," echoes suddenly and the music stops dead. It is replaced by a news report about Krug Stillo's escape from jail. This transition makes the connection between the girls and their future captors.

Perhaps the reason *The Last House on the Left* has so repeatedly been criticized by angry reviewers is that late in the film the music changes perspective abruptly. After Phyllis and Mari are captured and thrown in the trunk of Krug's car, the music turns light and humorous. It is a total contrast to the dark mood of the film. The girls are in mortal danger, yet the music joyfully suggests a romp and fun and games. There is even a kazoo underlying the silliness! Many critics interpret this "romp" music to suggest that the movie feels the girl's predicament is humorous and light. On the contrary, the music here is utilized in a completely ironic fashion. It is *Krug's* music, the music that suits the mood of his family. It *is* giddy because Krug and the others are giddy. The song is sung by Hess and makes pointed mention of Krug, Sadie, Junior and "Weasel" by name. The song notes that they are "out for the day for some fresh air and sun" and that they're going to "off 'em [the girls] as soon as *we're* done." It is written in the first person, which is not surprising since Hess is not only songwriter, but the actor playing Krug. The playful music perfectly expresses the tenor of the villains, not the director's moral standpoint. Many critics made an identical complaint about *Bonnie and Clyde* (1968), which put fun honky-tonk music over car chases and violent scenes and was therefore also accused of "glorifying violence." The music in that situation, as in *The Last House on the Left*, was an ironic comment on the mood of the central characters, not an expression of the film's overall viewpoint.

As the two girls are tortured, the music is anything but fun. It turns sour and thoughtful and the lyrics then reflect the mindset of Mari and Phyllis. It declares that in such a situation, you "feel the world close in on you ... and you're looking for someone to hold your hand, someone who'll understand." There is no fun in the music at that juncture, only sorrow. Hess' music is also effective when it tunes down to a fevered heartbeat as Phyllis flees her captors and is finally killed.

Hess's music is also an evolution of the compositions heard in *The Virgin Spring*. In the Bergman film (music by Erik Nordgren), a wandering forest dweller sings a medieval ballad about the beauty of nature and the changing of seasons. It ends with a repetition of "in the springtime, in the springtime." As Karin rides to her doom, blissfully unaware of her fate, she sings the refrain again. Likewise, Hess's score speaks of a change of seasons and the beauty of nature, and both films use their music ironically. Each ballad about nature's wonders contrasts with the horrible events that actually occur against the bucolic backdrop.

The Last House on the Left is also successful because it reverses in a savage fashion the central conceit of Jean Renoir's classic film *A Day in the Country* (1936). Based on a story by Guy de Maupassant and filmed at the beautiful Bords du Loing in Montigny, France, *A Day in the Country* tells the story of the Du Four family as it vacations near a beautiful lake. The women of the family are unexpectedly seduced by two farmhands who live nearby, and the sudden outburst of passion culminates in an unexpected thunderstorm. It is a film that makes an explicit connection between man and nature and suggests that nature provokes man (and woman) to commit irrational acts. Similarly, Craven's first picture makes a tacit connection between nature and the events which unfold at the Collingwood lake. However, the connection is exactly the reverse of that in the Renoir picture. The spirit of *Last House* characters seems to infect nature, not vice versa.

The Last House on the Left opens with a pan across a still lake of incredible beauty. The soothing twitter of birds is heard and ducks are seen moving through glassy waters. An old postman pulls up to the Collingwood mailbox wearing a cowboy hat and the feeling of a placid, middle-class American existence is established. The film seems peaceful and happy and there exists a tender harmony with nature. Later, Mari and Phyllis sit on a rocky outcropping above the serene lake and there are many beautiful closeups of the peaceful water, tree branches and golden leaves. The music refers specifically to the changes of season and again nature seems deceptively calm. That perspective changes when Phyllis and Mari are trapped in the trunk of Krug's car on their way back to the very same lake. As if in response to Krug's proximity, nature has suddenly grown violent and the water of the lake is no longer placid but harsh, bubbly and turbulent. Editor Craven quickly cuts to several shots which feature water racing faster and faster downstream in an orgiastic frenzy. Ironically, the crescendo of this montage is not a shot of tempestuous waters crashing against the shore, but one of Krug's car racing down the highway. Nature has suddenly become hostile, the flowing water chaotic, and the cause of these stormy feelings is Krug's approaching vehicle. He has turned the lake sour.

Late in the film, Phyllis seeks escape in the lake but it is not the tranquil body of water she encountered the evening before. It is white with foam and virtually untraversable. The environment has reared up and prevented Phyllis's safe escape, as if the very presence of Krug nearby has stirred it to violence. Finally, Mari staggers into the same lake after being raped. As she does so, she is dazed and completely defeated, and the lake again reflects the shift in mood. Its violent needs sated by Krug, the lake is glassy again and it offers comfort to the traumatized Mari. She sinks into the cleansing water and all but disappears. After her blood has mingled with the water of the lake, the Krug family cleanses themselves in it and emerges miraculously transformed. Immersion in Mari's "civilized" blood and the lake's water momentarily gives the thugs a civilized appearance. Thus the lake behind the Collingwoods' house purposefully reflects the moods of the various characters and the intense events of the film. The characters shape the landscape with both their calmness and their savagery. It is an artistic conceit that elevates the film above the exploitation arena and proves that Craven can create parallels not only between dueling family units but between man and nature.

The most criticized aspect of *The Last House on the Left* is the inclusion of the "cop" subplot. Two police officers are at various points depicted trying to get to the Collingwood house and save the day. The officers are portrayed as buffoons and many critics, even the insightful Roger Ebert, have complained that the dopey humor seems out of place in a serious film about retribution and violence. However, one must realize that Craven's film is a vision that sees hypocrisy in every level of society. The Collingwoods are hypocrites because they believe they are better than people like Phyllis Stone, but they are proven to be less noble and more prone to violence than she is. Mari is shown to be a hypocrite because she worships "Bloodlust" (both the band and emotion) even though she purports to be of the love generation. Similarly, the police officers in *The Last House on the Left* are hypocrites. They arrive at the Collingwood house and calmly assure the family that Mari will be fine and that everything will be taken care of. They project an aura of competence around the Collingwoods but nothing could be further from the truth. They are absolutely incompetent. They fail to investigate a broken-down car just outside the Collingwood home, and when they learn the criminals are close, they fail to catch them because their car runs out of gas! The policemen are essential to the story not only because they continue the hypocrisy motif, but because they represent the failure of society's institutions to prevent violence in virtually every circumstance.

First, Krug and "Weasel" escape from prison, indicating the first failure of society's legal mechanism to keep citizens safe from predators. Secondly, the local sheriff and his deputy fail to investigate a strange vehicle. Instead of showing the least bit of curiosity or deductive reasoning, they go back to their station and sit around. They do not make calls or investigate Mari's disappearance. Supported by the Collingwoods' tax dollars, they read comic books, play chess and gossip about a local who may be having sex with his livestock. When they finally get the call that the Krugs are in town, they rush out to their car and drive off, only to come to a dead stop when the car runs out of gas. Once more, Craven uses cross-cutting to effectively make his point about society. While the cops play their stupid games at the station, Mari and Phyllis are tortured! The cross-cutting plays with expectations too and the audience is given some reason to hope that maybe, just maybe, the cops will get their act together and save the girls before permanent damage is done. That brief hope is destroyed when Phyllis is killed but then the film mercilessly cross-cuts back to the police as they race to the scene. Again, there is brief hope that Mari, the film's protagonist, might still be saved. But then the police car breaks down and Mari is killed. Now the audience is angry and impatient. There is no reason for Mari's death except blatant incompetence on the part of the police. The mechanisms that should have assured Mari's survival have completely failed her. The police station is only 45 minutes away from the Collingwood house, yet the police take all day and part of the night to get there! They not only fail to save Mari and Phyllis, they fail to apprehend the criminals and save the elder Collingwoods from a descent into bloody violence!

The police are very important to *Last House* because they frustrate audiences who are hoping for a happy ending. Craven's *modus operandi* is to pull in the audience so they will be mad as hell and demanding the blood of the rapists. The stupid policemen add immeasurably to these feelings. It is all part of a stacked deck so that Craven can then pull out the carpet, do his quick reverse, and inspire shame in the audience for demanding retribution. This structure is a brilliant one and the cops are crucial to its success. Incidentally, the cops in *The Last House on the Left* underline Craven's anti-establishment bent, a factor which would reappear in virtually all of his films and telemovies.

The Last House on the Left is a stunning debut and a powerful film. It is not an easy film to watch, but the best films never are. *Platoon, Natural Born Killers, A Clockwork Orange, Schindler's List, Do the Right Thing* and *The Virgin Spring* are critically praised films that also face human ugliness, and *The Last House on the Left* has much in common with all of them. However, it is a far less palatable vision to many viewers and critics because there is no "barrier" separating the filmmaker from audience. *Platoon* takes place in Vietnam, *Natural Born Killers* is pointedly a satire that exists outside the confines of the real world, *A Clockwork Orange* takes place in a future society, *Schindler's List* remembers the horror of the Holocaust, *Do the Right Thing* confronts racism in a ghetto neighborhood which is a hotbed for those feelings, and *The Virgin Spring* is a medieval religious story. All of these films have an element of safety to them because they do not confront the audience with horrors in a place and time where the audience dwells on a day-to-day basis. After *Platoon*, a viewer can click off the TV and satisfy himself that Vietnam is halfway around the world. As its title indicates, *The Last House on the Left* could happen right next door to any of us. There is no artifice in the film's structure to protect us, no setting as remote as Vietnam, future England, World War II, Harlem or Medieval Sweden to make the film's message more easily digestible. *The Last House on the Left* makes its points about violence and retribution in our living rooms and our backyards. For that reason it is arguably more powerful than the above-mentioned films, but also much more difficult to accept. Since *The Last House on the Left* does not occur within the safe confines of a specific film "genre," its raw power incites all kinds of feelings, from curiosity and voyeurism to disgust and shame ... but certainly not violence, as some critics have asserted.

Oppositely, *The Last House on the Left* is a film that rails against violence in every frame. It is far less offensive than popular vigilante pictures such as *Death Wish* and its sequels. It makes a succinct statement about the place of violence in our society and our families. More than that, it is a well-written film that is crisply edited and directed with the craft of an artist. Craven's powerful use of cross-cutting, music and directorial voyeurism all convey a message more timely today than in 1972. Perhaps it is for that very reason that rumors of a *Last House on the Left* remake have sprung up in the late '90s. One can only hope that if the film is re made, its raw imagery and forceful film techniques will not be forsaken.

The Hills Have Eyes (1977)

> Wes Craven's simplistic allegory means to say Something About America and ends up on a fairly obvious note about The Savage in All of Us. But as portentous as it is, the movie contains some unsettlingly strong moments: the slow death of the matriarch is particularly harrowing, as is the use to which her corpse is put. And Craven delights in nasty gallows humor....— Glenn Kenny, *Entertainment Weekly* (March 10, 1995, page 74)
>
> In some ways, Wes Craven's *The Hills Have Eyes* is an existentialist's notion of a Saturday matinee...structured to be peak on peak, without much time for human values or even logic, but with the kind of relentlessness that makes these films fun

to watch... Craven makes good use of the desert, perhaps the best use since Jack Arnold... Craven captures the eeriness of vast emptiness and the frantic, furtive way one must live in such conditions to survive... Craven is never showy and knows how to shoot, cut and pace action. *Hills* is a very exciting movie.— Ed Gorman *Horror Writers on Horror Film:* "A Few Hundred Words About Wes Craven" (Berkley Books, 1992, pages 113–115)

Ghoulishly funny (and suitably gross) reworking of the Sawney Bean cannibal-killer case. Not to be missed.— John McCarty, *The Official Splatter Movie Guide* (St. Martin's Press, 1989, page 67)

[F]un and games from Wes Craven, that modern intellectual who gave us *The Last House on the Left*. ...This pandering plunge into depravity and death does, however, have a social comment: When innocent people resort to violence, they become no better than their nemeses.— John Stanley, *Creatures Features Strikes Again* (Creatures At Large Press, 1994, page 180)

CAST: Susan Lanier (Brenda Carter); Robert Houston (Bobby Carter); Martin Speer (Doug Wood); Dee Wallace (Lynn Wood); Russ Grieve (Big Bob Carter); John Steadman (Fred); James Whitworth (Papa Jupiter); Virginia Vincent (Ethel Carter); Lance Gordon (Mars); Michael Berryman (Pluto); Janus Blythe (Ruby); Cordy Clarke (Mama); Brenda Marinoff (Katy); Arthur King (Mercury); Flora (Beauty); Striker (Beast).

CREDITS: Peter Locke Presents a Film by Wes Craven. Blood Relations Company. *Producer:* Peter Locke. *Writer/Editor/Director:* Wes Craven. *Cinematography:* Eric Saarinen. *Music:* Don Peake. *Location Scouting and Coordinator:* Tom Pickette. *Assistant Cameramen:* Tim Wawrzeniak, Bob Eber. *Script Supervisors:* Joanie Blum, Rick Braverman. *Sound Mixer:* Craig Felburg. *Make up:* Karen Grant, Donald Muldenck. *Best Person:* Carolyn Ames. *Production Manager:* Walter Cichy. *Casting:* Gus Schirmer. *Dogs:* Moe Disesso, Tom Morrocco. *Stunt Coordinator:* Ron Stein. *Stunts:* Ron Stein, Alton Jones. *Special Effects:* John Frazier, Greg Auer. *Snakes:* Jim Dannaldson. *Art Director:* Robert Burns. *Assistant Director:* Valley Hoffman. *Assistant Cameraman:* Leslie Otis. *Assistant Editor:* Robert Alsheimer. *Sound Effects:* Doneil Productions, Peter Hitchcock, David Marsh, David Lee Fein, Jill Devin. *Sound Mixer:* Jan Schultze. *Assistant Sound:* D.G. Fisher. *Gaffer:* Dennis Bishop. *Costume Design:* Joanne Jaffe. *Wardrobe Supervisor:* Paula Cain. *Props:* Mary Church. *Special Make up:* Ken Horn, Dave Ayres. *Best Boy:* Ken Wheeland. *Key Grip:* Lynn Rogers. *Grips:* Richard Scheid, Bill Moore, Larry Boyd. *Assistant to Producer:* Rose Marie Yurinko. *Production Assistants:* Rhonda Hopkins, Florence M. Amico. *Set Editor:* J. Larry Carroll. *Still Photographer:* Ray Fischer. *Film Processing:* Movielab Inc. *Re-Recording:* MGM. *Rerecording Engineer:* Hal Watkins, C.S.E. *Prints by:* MGM Laboratories Inc. *Titles:* Freeze Frame. *Running Time:* 89 minutes. *Rating:* R.

SYNOPSIS: Amidst a barren desert landscape stands a small wooden shack. Near the shack, an old man talks incessantly to himself. The old codger's name is Fred and he is packing up his truck and preparing to leave this wasteland for good. He is interrupted by the arrival of Ruby, a beautiful young savage girl who wants to go with him. Fred refuses to help Ruby escape with him and complains that officials from the Air Force have been by twice to question him. Fred blames Ruby since her "family" recently robbed an Air Force PX. Ruby pleads for help, stating that her family is starving and that nobody comes out "there" anymore. Fred will hear none of it. The "family" has been so active lately that the people of Corn Creek want to block off the desert and march the National Guard right through to see what they find. Besides, Fred insists, Ruby is a savage. She smells like a horse and does not even know how to use a knife and fork. How can she possibly survive in civilized surroundings?

Fred and Ruby's conversation is cut short by the arrival of a station wagon and trailer at Fred's gas station. The Carters, a Midwestern suburban family, are headed for Los Angeles but are making a stop in the desert to find a silver mine left to Ethel and "Big" Bob Carter by Ethel's Aunt Mildred on their silver anniversary. Along for the trip are Bobby and Brenda, Bob and Ethel's two youngest children, and Lynn Carter, their oldest daughter, with her husband Doug and their infant Katy. Also in the trailer are two Alsatians: Beauty and the Beast.

Fred takes one look at the "whitebread" family and warns them not to go any further down the dirt road. The Air Force uses areas of the Yucca desert as a bomb testing range, and the people who live out there among the hills and the dust are nobody the Carters would care to meet.

A stubborn racist and hard-headed man, Bob ignores Grandpa Fred. After 25 years on the Cleveland police force, he has retired because of a bad heart and he has no intention of leaving his silver mine unattended. He suspects Fred ripped-off his mine and that is the reason the old coot is pressuring his family not to investigate it. Despite Bob's thick-headedness, Fred fills the station wagon with his last drops of gas and warns the family to stay on the main road. A few minutes after the Carters have departed, Fred's truck explodes. Ruby's family has destroyed it so the old man cannot run away. "There'll be hell to pay now," Fred realizes as he returns to his shack alone.

As the Carters' station wagon and trailer traverse the dirt road, Ruby's family watches from the hills. Inside the car, Brenda complains that the family is going to be nothing but "human French fries" by the time they get to the silver mine. A jet suddenly flies by low overhead and startles Bob. He loses control of the vehicle and crashes the station wagon and trailer. He complains that 25 years in the worst precinct in Cleveland fighting "niggers" and "hillbillies" were never as bad as taking a family vacation. Ethel calms Bob down and the family faces the possibility that they will be stranded in the wasteland for some time. From a nearby mountain, Ruby's family continues to watch. From this vantage point, a bald, misshapen creature called Pluto comments that Brenda is "pretty."

Bob plans to walk back to Fred's gas station and use a phone. He takes with him the pistol that was his retirement gift. Doug will head off in the opposite direction, to the north, because he saw a military installation on a map. Bobby will stay behind with a second gun, the girls and the dogs. Before the family separates, Ethel asks for a moment of prayer. Although the family objects, they agree to humor their mother and Bob voices a prayer. Once they separate, Pluto calls them "easy pickins!"

Brenda, Lynn and Ethel Carter set up a table, fold paper napkins and set places for the family. They joke about becoming human French fries as well as an incident in Miami when the Beast killed a poodle. Things turn grim, however, when Beauty runs off into the desert. Bobby follows her but hears her cry in pain. He climbs a mountain after the dog but finds the animal gutted. Its bloody innards have been devoured by Pluto! After discovering Beauty's corpse, Bobby runs down the mountain. He tells no one what he has seen on the mountaintop.

Night arrives in the desert and Ethel uses the CB radio to call for help. She is surprised when someone answers her plea—someone who only grunts and groans into the receiver. Ethel insists it was only an animal, but Lynn is concerned. She swears in fear and her mother reminds her that she never used language like that before she moved to New York City. Bobby returns to the trailer, visibly shaken by the death of Beauty, but he still keeps the dog's death a secret. To make matters worse, the Beast breaks his chains and runs out into the desert too. Now both dogs are gone.

Bob Carter arrives at the gas station and he finds Grandpa Freddy trying to hang himself! Bob saves Freddy and asks what he was doing. Fred responds that Bob and his family are "trespassing" and then he tells his story. In 1929, Fred recounts, the gas station was brand new. Young Fred and his bride Martha had a beautiful baby girl and their life was perfect. Martha soon became pregnant with a second baby. It was a huge, hairy monstrosity that weighed over 20 pounds. It came out of Martha sideways and nearly ripped her apart. This strange animal-boy was fully grown by ten and fully developed in evil ways. Dogs would disappear down wells and chickens would be found with their heads bitten off. In August 1939, disaster struck. While Fred was in town, his home mysteriously burned down. By the time he returned, his daughter was a cinder but the boy was not even singed. Realizing the boy was responsible, Freddy tried to kill him. He cracked his face apart with a tire iron. Believing that he had killed his devil son, Fred left him in the desert to die. But that was not the end of the boy called Jupiter. Maturing from a Devil Boy to a Devil Man, he stole a whore from town and raised a pack of wild kids. They now haunt the desert together.

While recounting his history, Fred is attacked by the giant Jupiter, who jumps through a window and pulls him into the darkness. Bob watches stunned as Jupiter beats Fred to death with a tire iron and then impales the old man on it. Bob shoots at Jupiter but the strange man disappears into the night. Bob runs back for his trailer, realizing his family is in mortal danger. He has a heart attack and, as he struggles, he hears someone calling him "daddy."

Back at the trailer, Doug has returned. He found no one at the military base, but has brought back coils of thick cord in case the family should need it to get on the road again. Doug is hungry for dinner and hardly notices that Bobby seems upset. He and Lynn then go out to the station wagon to make love.

At the wild family's homestead, Ruby learns that she is eating a dog and spits it out. Her mama, a fat old woman, calls her a "runaway slut" and warns that Papa Jupiter will deal with her. Mama and Ruby hear the Beast barking in the distance and Ruby fears it is the ghost of the dog she was just eating. Mama understands there is another dog out in the wilderness — another meal for the family.

Near the Carter trailer, trouble begins. Pluto siphons the remaining gas from the station wagon while Doug and Lynn make love. Bobby hears the Beast barking outside and investigates. It is not Beast, but the wild family making authentic-sounding animal cries. When Bobby hears dogs, lambs, cows and a wolf, he realizes he has been tricked. He runs back to the trailer but finds the door locked. Bobby thinks he has locked himself out but in fact Pluto is now inside with Ethel, Brenda and baby Katy. Pluto raids the overstocked refrigerator and gathers beef, milk and other items. Outside, Bobby interrupts Lynn and Doug to get their keys. Only then does he finally reveal that Beauty is dead.

There is an explosion in the distance: Bob has been crucified and set aflame with the gasoline from the car. Ethel, Bobby, Lynn and Doug rush to help Bob as he is burned alive. They do not realize they have left Pluto inside the trailer with Brenda. With the family gone, Mars also enters it. He rips the head off the Carters' parakeet and drinks its blood. He then finds Pluto having his way with the horrified Brenda. Mars stops the rape so *he* can have her. While Mars mounts Brenda, Pluto grows enraged and trashes the trailer.

Outside, Bob is brought down from the burning yucca plant and Ethel becomes delirious. "That's not my Bob," she insists, nauseated by the burned figure writhing on the ground. Doug sends Lynn and Ethel back to the trailer for water, whiskey and blankets, unaware he is sending them into danger. When they arrive at the trailer, they confront Mars, who has just raped Brenda. Ethel strikes Mars with a broom and he shoots her in the stomach. Realizing he is planning to steal her baby, Lynn fights Mars, stabbing him in the leg with his own knife. Mars shoots Lynn twice, killing her. He then steals Katy and grimly informs Brenda that he will be back for her.

Bob has died and Doug and Bobby run back to the trailer. They find Lynn dead, Katy missing, Ethel badly wounded and Brenda hysterical. Doug runs after Mars. "Why are you doing this?" he shouts. "What do you want?" There is no answer, and Doug returns to the trailer. Ethel is delusional about Bob and Lynn, so Doug lies to her and tells her everything is fine. Then the lights go out in the trailer and there is a scratching outside. Bobby and Doug brace for another brutal assault but discover that the Beast has returned. Although the wild family does not know it yet, the dog has killed one of the siblings, Mercury, and taken his walkie-talkie to the Carters!

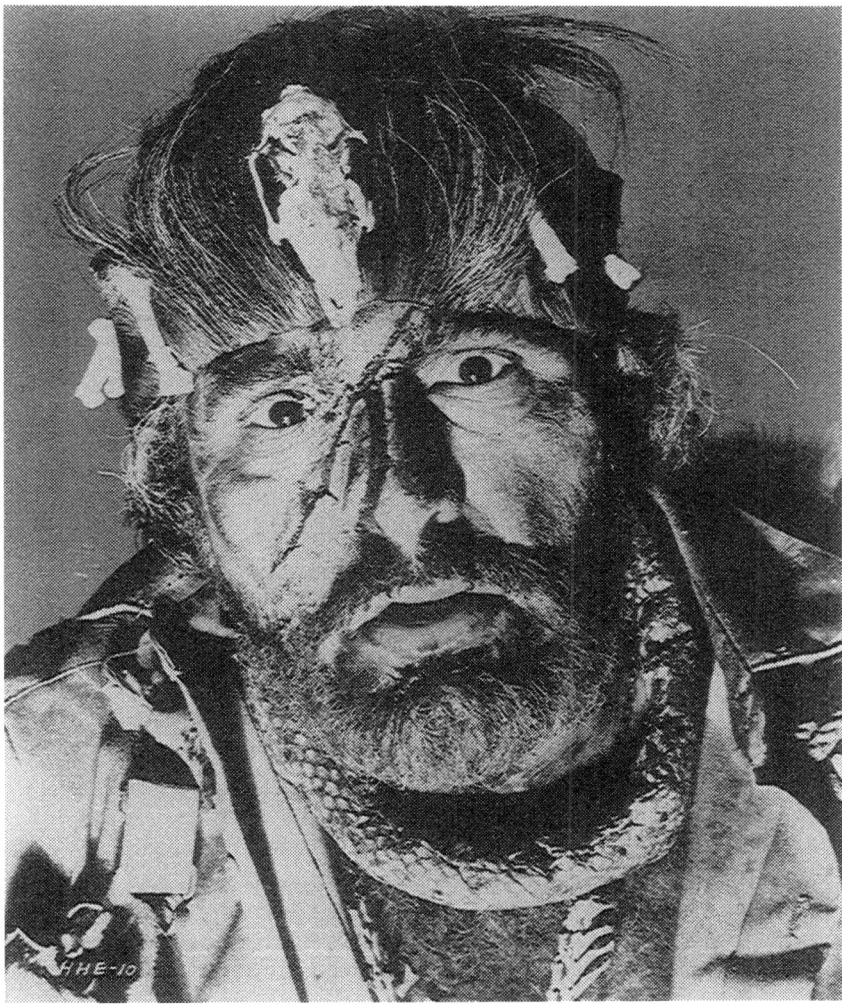

The face of evil: Papa Jupiter (James Whitworth) in *The Hills Have Eyes*.

At the home of the wild family, Pluto and Mars bring the baby, what they call "a young Thanksgiving turkey," to Jupiter and Mama. When Mercury fails to report, they realize there is trouble. As the family feasts on the roasted corpse of Big Bob Carter, Jupiter states his intention to kill the entire family. At daybreak, the attack will begin.

Early the next morning, the Carters plan strategy. Beast and Doug head out into the hills with the walkie-talkie to send information back to Bobby and Brenda in the trailer. Inside the trailer, however, Bobby and Brenda are at each other's throats and Ethel has died. Bobby uses the CB to issue a mayday call. Air Force Rescue responds, asking Bobby his exact location and about their weapons. After revealing that he and his family have only two bullets left and are basically "sitting ducks," Bobby realizes that he has just reported his status not to Air Force Rescue, but Pluto and Jupiter!

From a hilltop, Doug sees two men heading towards the trailer and sends the Beast to defend Bobby and Brenda. Then he proceeds to the wild pack homestead, where he sees Mars.

Tired of Bobby's ineffective strategies, Brenda takes matters into her own hands. She and Bobby tie cord around the tire rim of their station wagon. They loop the other end and set a trap. They now need bait. They decide to use Ethel's corpse as a decoy. They set their dead mother up in a lawn chair and wait.

Not far away, Beast attacks Jupiter and Pluto. The dog rips open Pluto's heel and then tears his jugular once Jupiter has gone on to attack the trailer. Hearing his boy scream in pain, Jupiter returns and shoots at Beast, who scurries away unharmed. Furious, Jupiter gets on the walkie-talkie and orders Mars to kill the baby. Doug hears the order on the radio and rushes into action. Fortunately, he has a new ally: Ruby! The teenage girl saves the baby and runs off into the desert. Mars pursues and the final combat begins.

At the trailer, Jupiter spots Ethel sitting in the chair. Confused, he investigates. Bobby starts the car and Jupiter is tangled in the cord and dragged toward the vehicle. He is yanked brutally through the desert terrain until the cord snaps. Hopping mad, Jupiter chases Bobby and Brenda to the trailer, which they have rigged to explode. Bobby and Brenda watch from safety as their trailer goes up in flames. Still, they are not satisfied the crisis is over. Bobby runs through the debris and is attacked by Jupiter. Brenda jumps into the fray and plants an axe into Jupiter's back several times. As Jupiter claws at the blade in his spine, Bobby uses the last two bullets at close range to kill Papa Jupe.

In the hills, Doug hides in an area where rattlesnake breed and is cornered there by Mars. Ruby arrives just in time to throw dirt at her brother, and Doug escapes. As Doug and Mars fight, Ruby picks up a rattlesnake and throws it on Mars' back. It snaps at his neck and poisons him. As Mars goes down, Doug steals his knife and stabs the dying Mars repeatedly. He becomes more frenzied the more he stabs, and then everything turns red with blood.

COMMENTARY: *The Hills Have Eyes* is an intelligent re-working of the siege film, a genre in which a group of people are isolated in a remote location and attacked from all corners by their enemies. In horror, the "siege" has been handled well by George Romero in *Night of the Living Dead* (1968) and by John Carpenter in *Assault on Precinct 13* (1976). Many critics have suggested that *The Hills Have Eyes* has roots further back than those examples, in Westerns such as *The Alamo*. Not surprisingly, the film can easily be fit into the Western genre mold with a few modern flourishes. A group of pioneers (vacationers) head west in a wagon train (an RV trailer) only to be attacked by a group of savage redskins (inbred cannibals). However, to look at *The Hills Have Eyes* as just another entry in the siege genre does it a great disservice. Just as *The Last House on the Left* is much more than its "rape and revenge" plot, *The Hills Have Eyes* is much more than a rehash of Western film tradition.

The heart of *The Hills Have Eyes* is the duel between two families, one from "civilization" and one from the wild. The battle for survival takes place not on neutral territory but in the home court of the uncivilized clan, in this case the barren landscape of the Yucca desert. The landscape plays a critical role in the film. Craven tied the events of *The Last House on the Left* to the forest and lake behind the Collingwood house; here he defines a landscape of danger that is as much a nemesis of the Carter family as is Jupiter's killer clan.

The Carters stumble upon a vast world of rocky, inhospitable terrain. It is a world where their enemies can come and go as they please and remain hidden because of camouflage. The Carters have no such protection and the hard right angles of their trailer stand out against the random outcroppings of the terrain. The Carters are just as they describe themselves in the finale: sitting ducks.

The desert is even more dangerous at night. The darkness provides a shroud, yet another sort of camouflage, for the activities of the marauding cannibals. Again, the Carters are out of their element. Even in the darkness of night, they constantly have a fire burning outside their trailer and all the lights on inside it. They possess the only light in the entire desert and it serves as a sort of beacon, drawing their opponents ever closer.

Because they are products of modern city life, the Carters are instantly uncomfortable once they are trapped in Craven's forbidding landscape. Brenda repeatedly asserts that dwelling outside gives her the "creeps." The others naively insist clean air is "good" for them, but they do not respect the land. Instead of adapting to their new surroundings, they attempt to tame it. Almost immediately, they set up a dinner table outside of the trailer and begin to picnic. It is a ridiculous scene as the Carters fold their napkins and put out their silverware amidst the vast desert. From this sequence alone, it is clear that they are truly out of touch with their new locale and have no idea how to cope with it. This is the first strike against them in Jupiter's deadly war.

The Carters are out of their element in another manner as well. Although they are in unfamiliar terrain, they continue to rely on technology that has failed them. Their car breaks down and strands them, making them susceptible to attack in the first place. Then their trailer's battery goes dead and they are plunged into darkness and total confusion. Next, the members of the family depend on modern weaponry that they have never used before. At one point, Bobby has a clear shot at Mars with his pistol and he misses *three times*. He has no idea how to harness the technology at his disposal! Brenda is just as lost, asking at one point, "How do you use this thing anyway?" Even Bob Carter, who should know how to use a gun from his years on the police force, cannot effectively make use of his "howitzer" pistol, and Jupiter takes it from him easily.

Other technology proves equally as troubling for the family. Their CB radio, which should help the Carters contact rescuers, ends up being the tool with which they hand over critical defensive information to their enemy. Their car "betrays" them again when the gas is siphoned by Pluto and used to set Bob aflame. Even the chain leash with which the family tethers the Beast breaks apart. The result is that the dog runs off when they need him most. If Beast were present at the right time, Pluto and Mars might not have gained access to the trailer, raped Brenda and killed Mrs. Carter and Lynn.

When the surviving Carters forsake the tools of 20th century man, they begin to succeed in defending themselves. They only defeat Jupiter once they stop seeing their trailer as a shelter, a mobile representation of their suburban safety, and instead use it as a weapon and blow it apart. Similarly, they kill Papa Jupe once they have forsaken Brenda's car axle gimmick for a hatchet (it might as well be a tomahawk). As for Doug, he only beats Mars when he embraces a knife instead of the surplus supplies he has brought back from the abandoned military base. It is only by resorting to basics that the Carter family can compete in a world where their technology is meaningless.

It is not just the landscape and untrustworthy technology which threatens the Carters, it is the meaningless family conventions they cling to as well. Early in the film, the family gathers together and prays. No one wants to do it, and the prayer has a rote, mechanical feeling. Yet the family gathers together like zombies and prays for the Lord to look over them. In the very next shot, a long shot lensed from at least half-a-mile away, their total isolation is revealed. They are in the middle of nowhere, yet they ask the Lord to deliver them. It is hardly a practical solution to the crisis. Craven's long shot also reveals that the Carters are being watched over but not by God ... by Pluto! The Carters cannot grasp the danger of the situation and so they apply pat societal remedies, such as prayer, to a world without civilization or religion.

Secondly, the family is crippled by its own neuroses. They continue to depend on behavior that in the safety of their city would not be fatal, but which in the desert is absolutely deadly. For instance, Bobby reveals to no one that Beauty is dead. He cannot cope with that unpleasant fact and he does not want to worry his family. By withholding this critical information, Bobby delays the Carters from mounting a defense. He is the only one who knows the danger that awaits them in the desert, and yet he represses it and denies it because it is not palatable to him. *The Hills Have Eyes* suggests that repression and denial are a way of life for this confused lad, but in wild nature the Carters *must* depend on each other's honesty. In this regard, Bobby fails his family.

Ethel Carter is even less effective a protagonist. She hears heavy breathing on the radio yet mindlessly declares that it "was nothing." She seems to think that if she blocks out reality, it cannot hurt her family. Instead of handling the big things, like a dangerous communication, she obsesses on tiny details and fusses at Lynn because of her bad language! Denial is Ethel's *modus operandi*, and once Bob is dead she becomes completely useless to her family. She slips into a state of total denial, choosing to believe that Bob and Lynn are alive and everything is okay. Ethel is absolutely unable to cope with reality and she therefore suppresses it from her consciousness. Denial is obviously a habit for her. At home, she denies that her husband treats her as an inferior servant. The result in the wild is that Ethel, like Bobby, fails to be a useful combatant in the war for survival.

The inter-relationships among the Carters cause great damage. Big Bob Carter is an opinionated loudmouth who thinks he knows all the answers, and his family meekly submits to his every whim. He has never been challenged, and the family goes along with his idea to "split up" and find help even though this is the precipitating factor which makes them all "easy pickins" for the Jupiter brood. The Carters are so browbeaten by the aggressive head of their family that they willfully allow Bob to override their better judgment and take them out on the deserted road in the first place. They are a family that has been tyrannized by one of Craven's archetypical bad fathers, and they have responded in various ways.

Ethel takes the route of denial, Brenda is an aggressive whiner and pouter who is "Daddy's little girl," and Bobby meekly obeys his father's instructions in hopes that it will somehow gain him his father's respect ... an impossibility since Bob recognizes no authority other than his own.

When the surviving Carters jointly abandon technology and overcome meaningless societal conventions, they defeat their enemy. The last hurdle to cross, the last moral institution they must destroy before victory, is a deeply ingrained Christian respect for the dead. Bobby and Brenda realize that to survive, they must deploy their mother's body. Bobby has trouble making this final leap from civilized behavior but Brenda, who has been raped, understands that they must depend on their own smarts to defeat their opponents. Ironically, Ethel is more useful in death than she ever was in life. Her corpse lures Jupiter to his doom and saves her children.

Importantly, there is also an undercurrent of violence in the Carter family members all along to suggest that it is possible for them to make their breaks with city life and "go primitive." They keep vicious dogs as pets. When one dog, all teeth, jumps at old Fred, Ethel laughs it off and claims the dog "just wants to play." This is a common refrain for dog owners who do not understand that their beloved pet could easily knock over a person and tear a piece of flesh off without hardly trying! Later, the family jokes about how Beast killed a tiny poodle in Miami. To the Carters, this is an amusing family anecdote. They do not see how destructive behavior within their own family unit has damaged another family unit.

Furthermore, the Carters brandish their guns casually, as if totally unaware of the damage firearms can inflict. Bobby plays with his pistol and jokingly warns the other men that if they're "not back by midnight, we board the submarine without you!" He and his family are trapped in a life-and-death situation and yet he is play-acting a scene from some movie! Perhaps the ultimate indicator that the Carters are not so different from the cannibals is the oversized chunk of raw beef that resides in their refrigerator. The Carters too eat the flesh of the dead.

As a whole, violence is viewed differently by Craven in *The Hills Have Eyes* than it was in *The Last House on the Left*. The violence launched by the Carter family is not so much retribution as it is a matter of survival. The law of the desert is "kill or be killed." There are no societal mechanisms here, failed or otherwise, to protect the family. As Brenda suggests, it is up to them to want to survive. In that way, the film is not so much a lesson about the savage lurking in "us all" as it is about the primacy of survival.

Craven's point is that only by shirking neuroses, giving up technology and breaking the meaningless conventions of society can modern man hope to defeat an enemy who is in touch with the land. This theme raises a question that survivalists frequently contemplate: What do we do if enemies land on our soil? Would we be able to fight and defend our families and homes, or have Americans grown too lazy? The answer delivered by *The Hills Have Eyes* is that the American man can overcome civilization and breeding, and fight back as savagely as his opponent, once he stops thinking of himself as a creature with religion, shelter and technology.

The final freeze frame of *The Hills Have Eyes* shows Doug hovering viciously over Mars' body. It is a shot which suggests man has violent tendencies just beneath the surface, instincts that he can tap even with hundreds of years of civilization behind him. When the frame turns blood-red, the indication is that man is a creature awash in blood and that there really is no difference between civilized people who supposedly have morals and the wild sociopaths who roam the hills. Both will fight and kill to protect their families.

The Hills Have Eyes has often been misinterpreted by critics who suggest that the Carters are actually worse than the barbarians of the desert. In *American Horrors: Essays on the Modern American Horror Film*, Charles Derry (in an essay entitled *More Dark Dreams: Some Notes on the Recent Horror Film*) writes:

> So little is the mother respected that her dead body is set afire and used by her son as a weapon against an attacker. And finally, the most horrifying acts are not committed by the monsters but by members of the American family who give in to the violence with an enthusiasm that is frightening.[1]

Not quite. Mrs. Carter is never set on fire, just dragged out into the desert in a lawn chair and used as bait to lure Jupiter. Secondly, her children are clearly horrified that they must stoop to this level of barbarism. Bobby is virtually paralyzed by the morbidity of it all, but Brenda realizes that to insure survival, society's conventions (including respect for the dead) must be overcome. It is also rather difficult to assert that the most horrifying violence in *The Hills Have Eyes* is committed by the Carters. After all, the barbarians murder Fred, rape Brenda, kill Lynn and Ethel, roast and eat Big Bob after hammering him to a yucca plant, steal a baby, gut a dog and rip the head off of a parakeet and drink its blood. The Carters do commit bloody acts but it is in response to their dilemma. The point is not that the Carters are worse than the barbarians, it is that they must stoop to the level of the barbarians to survive.

Many critics have read very deep Vietnam allegories in *The Hills Have Eyes* because they see a primitive enemy defeating a technologically superior force. Unfortunately, this approach is often taken too zealously as well. In his fine book *Hearths of Darkness*, Tony Williams builds much of his defense of this allegory on a misinterpreted word. He notes that Jupiter is referred to as "Papa Duke" in *The Hills Have Eyes*, reflecting silver screen icon John Wayne (The Duke) and anticipating "Big Duke" (Robert Duvall) in *Apocalypse Now* (1979). The only problem with this interpretation is that Jupiter is not "Papa Duke" at all, he is "Papa Jupe." Jupe is a simple shortening of the word Jupiter, not a reference to *The Green Berets* or *Apocalypse Now*. Still, it is not beyond reason to read the story broadly as a Vietnam allegory. However, America lost in Vietnam and pulled out in disgrace, and in *The Hills Have Eyes* the force representing America (the Carters) wins the war. There is a tremendous cost, but the Carters are still victorious.

The Hills Have Eyes is much more closely related to situations inside America than to any war on foreign soil. To Craven, our enemy is not one residing in another country, but the classes repressed right here at home, classes that have remained down-trodden for so long while the middle class has grown rich. These are the forces in America which will someday claim what they lack and foster a class revolution because of societal inequities. Bob Carter, who angrily rails against "niggers," leads what Craven often calls a "whitebread" family against people who do terrible things but who are, significantly, desperate.

The film opens with a pan across a barren highway and it is immediately apparent that this is a wasteland. Ruby begs Fred for food and says that her family is starving. The Jupiter clan is desperate to survive, and although this in no way justifies their ruthless actions, it does make their "evil" understandable. Like the Carters, they are fighting for survival in a world without resources. Jupe's clan does not have the benefits of refrigerators, vehicles and artificial light. The battle between the clan and the Carters in *The Hills Have Eyes* is not the Viet Cong versus the United States, it is a single house divided: the poor of America versus the wealthy.

Craven has written that the Carters and Jupiter family are two sides of the same coin. Both families possess dominating fathers who rule without question. A sibling dies in each family (Lynn Carter, Mercury) and each family uses that death as an excuse for more hatred and bloodshed. Both families also reveal siblings with strong and unrequited sexual urges. Mars and Pluto attempt to rape Brenda, exploring their desire to sate themselves. Much of the film suggests that Bobby may want to do the same thing to Brenda, but is unable to do so. A strong undercurrent of attraction runs between the siblings in the Carter family and the two youngest share a kind of "flirty" relationship. After the car crash, Bobby pointedly asks Brenda, "Aren't you going to ask how *I* am?" It is part joke and part something else, maybe even jealousy because she has turned her attention to her father. Additionally, Brenda and Bobby constantly have their hands on one another. When Jupiter is finally dead, Brenda enthusiastically jumps on Bobby and wraps her legs tightly around his hips. He grabs her and jumps up and down exuberantly, shaking her against his athletic body in a spasm of joy. If one reads a little into this, it is not difficult to equate their exuberance as a sort of sexual climax.

Furthermore, Bobby seems a repressed person who has trouble dealing with his feelings. When frightened, he comes across as angry, and he is also prone to bursts of crying and pouting. Clearly he is the baby of the family, not Brenda. Fittingly, it is Brenda, not Bobby, who deals Jupiter the death blow; Bobby takes after his Mom and cannot act effectively. Perhaps Bobby Carter is civilization's refined version of Pluto or Mars: the submissive son of an overbearing father who is unable to deal openly with his feelings of lust toward his sister.

Craven weaves all of these themes into a 90-minute motion picture of escalating terror. He brilliantly stages the siege on the Carters in waves. First a spider invades the trailer, signifying what is to come. Then the first dog is killed, the father is lost, the RV is invaded and so forth. Incident builds upon incident until the viewer is overwhelmed, and half the Carter family is already dead. The film maintains this startling pace throughout and is successful at maintaining tension. The gut-wrenching feeling of the rape in *The Last House on the Left* is also back in one central sequence. Mars and Pluto break into the trailer and for ten minutes the action is so horrible, so frightening, that one's heart feels ready to burst. Although *The Hills Have Eyes* is less a "message" picture and more a conventional entertainment than *The Last House on the Left*, it still packs a visceral punch mostly unmatched in modern horror.

The cross-cutting, the "voyeuristic" approach and the ironic musical score which made *The Last House on the Left* stand above the ordinary are missing in *The Hills Have Eyes*. Fortunately, those elements have been replaced with a true sense of "place." In the unbroken opening shot of the film, Craven pans across the hills while strange sounds dominate the soundtrack and the credits roll by. It is an eerie sequence which immediately sets up the desert as a player in the battle that will ensue. Many later scenes find the Carters as tiny specks in a frame surrounded by rocks and yucca plants, tiny lost souls on a vast battlefield.

Other than beautifully capturing his location, Craven maintains pace through a combination of techniques. At appropriate moments, he tracks his

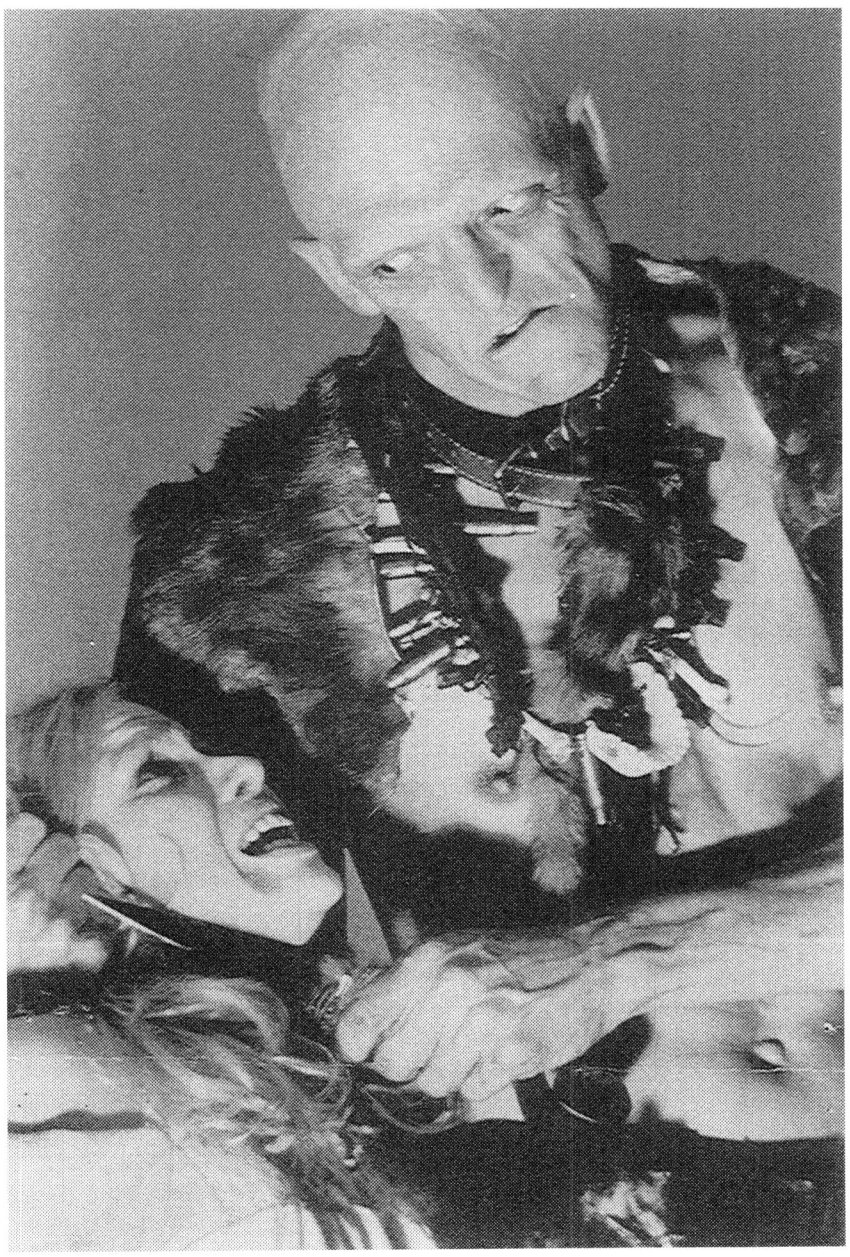

Pluto (Michael Berryman) finds Brenda Carter (Susan Lanier) to be a "juicy" prize in *The Hills Have Eyes*.

protagonists with a moving hand-held camera and the result is an unbound feeling that one is actually running in the desert with them. This creates a frenetic feeling of time speeding by.

Craven occasionally cuts to wild point-of-view subjective shots for scenes following big "scares." After Beauty is killed, there is a rustling in the bushes, and Bobby leaps down the side of the mountain. The camera cuts to his perspective and we race down the hill with him in a near-panic state. Moments like these make the horror intensely personal. It is not just Bobby Carter who is running away, it is the audience.

Also effective is the night photography. Somehow, Craven has managed to film the night sequences so that only the people are visible. Behind the characters remains a cloak of darkness, impossible to see through. When monstrous voices begin to call out or mimic animals, there is a sense of horror and uncertainty because the audience cannot see anything beyond the frightened faces of the Carters.

Rapid-fire editing is also particularly important in selling some of the more difficult-to-dramatize scenes. The dog attack on Pluto is filled with quick cuts but nonetheless emerges as incredibly realistic. With multiple close-ups of the dog's snarling mouth intercut with Berryman's terrified face, groping hands, a bloody neck and the dog's body tugging backwards (as if it is yanking on flesh) the attack is perfectly dramatized. Also well-staged is the Air Force jet fly-by and wreck of the Carter station wagon. Wind blows through the car, a sonic boom is heard, the car weaves crazily, we get a P.O.V. shot from the driver's perspective and it is all over. Economical, but effective.

The Hills Have Eyes is a technically accomplished film with very few gaffes. One minor mistake can be found in the sequence in which Mars jumps off the trailer roof and prepares to enter it. In the door handle, the trailer keys are clearly visible. In the next shot, the keys have disappeared and Mars has not moved (he still has one hand on his walkie-talkie). Other than that very minor continuity glitch, the film holds up amazingly well for a low-budget production filmed in a difficult location.

There is more humor in Craven's *The Hills Have Eyes* than in *The Last House on the Left* and it is most welcome. The early scenes involving Ethel Carter and Big Bob are alive with wit and satire, and it is not hard to determine that Craven is having some fun at the expense of the middle-class family. Michael Berryman's Pluto is also humanized significantly by the fact that he exhibits a sense of humor. He tricks the Carters into revealing their defensive capabilities over the radio and then guffaws at his own skill. It is grim humor, but humor nonetheless.

In *The Last House on the Left*, Craven knew just how to build on audience expectations and fears, and this film shares that insight. Putting a helpless baby in the hands of cannibals may seem a cheap trick to some, but few can deny that it adds urgency to the film's closing passages. Viewers are desperate, along with Doug, to save little Katy after Jupiter has ordered Mars to kill the child. Other moments are equally cunning. Craven's screenplay has the level-headed wife and mother murdered, a difficult scene for anyone to sit through. It is absolutely devastating when Doug discovers his wife dead and his daughter missing. He runs into the darkness and yells (in long shot), "Why? What do you want?" His life has been ruined and he is absolutely incapable of understanding his opponent. This cry of "Why?" also echoes Dr. Tore's questioning of God in *The Virgin Spring*, but (like *The Last House on the Left*) there is no answer from God in *The Hills Have Eyes*. The fact that Bob is the first family member to be killed (not counting Beauty) and that Ethel is more useful in death than in life are also unexpected touches that provide the script with a texture of unpredictability.

Above all, *The Hills Have Eyes* proves that Craven is not a director who presents digestible horror. He goes for the jugular and provides scene after shocking scene of real terror. Few films have captured the feeling of terror as effectively as that central scene in the trailer in *The Hills Have Eyes*.

One interesting common point in *The Hills Have Eyes* and *The Last House on the Left* is that they both feature passing references to Sigmund Freud. In *Last House*, Sadie comments that Freud is the sex criminal of the century, and in *The Hills Have Eyes* Bobby notes that Freud would certainly have something to say about Ethel Carter's rattlesnake fixation. Since Freud is mentioned in both films, it is possible to speculate that writer Craven is himself a fan of Freud's work. (Certainly any film in which a woman bites off a man's penis begs for a Freudian interpretation.) However, what these twin films suggest is that their characters exist in a world where Sigmund Freud's psychology is *not* applied. The characters involved in both plots apparently do not subscribe to Freud's theory: that truths repressed resurface as symptoms rather than vanishing. The Carters, Collingwoods and later the Thompsons in *A Nightmare on Elm Street* are rigidly repressive in terms of sexual mores and the like. Phallic symbols such as rattlesnakes, handguns, knives and even ice cream cones dominate early Craven films. What Craven suggests is that all these characters need therapy they are not getting, so they inappropriately "act out" their desires with the above-listed substitutes.

Considering Freud's importance in Craven's work, it is only right that Craven should end up playing a psychologist who spouts Freudian theories to a graduate student responsible for matricide in Vince Edwards' film *The Fear* (1994).

A joy of Craven's early work such as *The Last House on the Left* and *The Hills Have Eyes* is that Craven himself writes, directs and edits. Since he handles those chores personally, it is easy to assess how much of his personality is involved in the films, something not so easy to do with a film like *Deadly Friend*. These early films are thus significant in defining Craven's ideology as a filmmaker and artist. Nowhere in his career is the family so carefully dissected and so thoroughly examined as in his opening duo. Although later films would also handle the theme, it was without the raw edge of cynicism that defines *The Last House on the Left* and *The Hills Have Eyes*. If one really wants to see how Craven feels about contemporary America without the filter of studio interference, other writers and editors, these films are the place to begin such an exploration. Although *A Nightmare on Elm Street* and *Wes Craven's New Nightmare* also cogently express themes and ideas important to the artist, these films are the best starting point for a student of Craven's career. There is enough provocative material and technique in just these two feature films to fill a book.

Craven forged many friendships during the shooting of *The Hills Have Eyes*, and a high percentage of the performers seen in this picture reappeared in the director's later work. John Steadman (Fred) played a veterinarian in *A Stranger in the House* in 1978, Houston and Blythe returned for *The Hills Have Eyes Part II* in 1983, and Michael Berryman worked for Craven in the *Hills* sequel, *Deadly Blessing* and *Invitation to Hell*. Virginia Vincent, who is quite convincing as Ethel Carter in *The Hills Have Eyes*, also appeared in *Invitation to Hell* as Robert Urich's non-demonic secretary, Grace Henderson.

Deadly Blessing (1981)

> Craven has a flair for scaring his audience and ... talent for making his characters comfortable and believable, even under the weirdest circumstances. The performances here are restrained and plausible... *Deadly Blessing* ought to fascinate students of horror-film morality because its notions of sin and retribution are so out of the ordinary... Its big battle-to-the-death scene takes place entirely among women ... reveals an odd perception of sexual mores.—Janet Maslin (*The New York Times*, August 15, 1981)
>
> A minor miracle. A consummately crafted, small genre movie with more ideas than most big movies you can name. Wes Craven might be the man to bring horror films out of their current dark ages ... remarkable.—Carrie Rickey (*Village Voice*, August 20, 1981)
>
> Wes Craven knows how to manipulate and sustain tension. He keeps your juices flowing... Craven tries to create psychological terror the way Val Lewton's films in the '40s did ... a nihilistic protest against societal and religious oppression.—Linda Gross (*The Los Angeles Times*, August 18, 1981)
>
> It never makes a subatomic particle of melodramatic or psychological sense yet nevertheless provokes an overwhelming proportion of women spectators into screaming fits... Craven establishes a distinctive, malicious rapport with the audience.—Gary Arnold (*The Washington Post*: "The Creepy Crawlies: *Deadly Blessing* Diabolical Nonsense," August 19, 1981)
>
> For a moment there is the surreal feeling of an Ingmar Bergman film as the camera pans the somber figures in fuzzy light, but the artsy mood soon deteriorates into standard, thriller-chiller fare... *Deadly Blessing* offers a few genuine moments of carefully built terror and suspense.—Bill Kaufman (*Newsday*, August 15, 1981)

Good looking but mostly ineffective horror story with a few mild shocks for addicts.— Howard Maxford, *The A-Z of Horror Films* (Indiana University Press, 1997, page 74)

CAST: Maren Jensen (Martha Schmidt); Sharon Stone (Lana); Susan Buckner (Vicky Anderson); Jeff East (John Schmidt); Coleen Riley (Melissa); Douglas Barr (Jim Schmidt); Lisa Hartman (Faith Stohler); Lois Nettleton (Louisa Stohler); Ernest Borgnine (Isaiah Schmidt); Michael Berryman (William Gluntz); Kevin Cooney (Sheriff); Bobby Dark (Theater Manager); Kevin Farr (Fat Boy); Neil Fletcher (Grave Digger); Jonathan Gulla (Tom Schmidt); Chester Kulas, Jr. (Leopold); Lawrence Montaigne (Matthew Gluntz); Lucky Mosley (Sammy); Dan Shackleford (Medic); Annabelle Weenick (Ruth Schmidt); Jenna Worthen (Mrs. Gluntz); Percy Rodrigues (Narrator)

CREDITS: PolyGram Pictures Presents an Inter Planetary Production. A Wes Craven Film. *Editor:* Richard Bracken. *Music:* James Horner. *Associate Producers:* Glenn M. Benest, Matthew Barr. *Production Design:* Jack Marty. *Director of Photography:* Robert Jessup, A.S.C. *Executive in Charge of Production:* Jere Henshaw. *Executive Producer:* William Gilmore. *Story:* Glenn M. Benest, Matthew Barr. *Screenplay:* Glenn M. Benest, Matthew Barr, Wes Craven. *Producers:* Max A. Keller, Micheline H. Keller, Patricia S. Herskovic. *Director:* Wes Craven. *Stunt Coordinator:* Ted Grossman. *Stunt Doubles:* May R. Boss, Kerrie K. Cullen, Stephanie Epper, Donna Garrett. *Unit Production Manager:* Bert Gold. *First Assistant Director:* Jerram Swartz. *Second Assistant Director:* John Eyler. *Script Supervisor:* Martin Kitrosser. *Costume Designer:* Patricia McKiernan. *Makeup Artist:* Jim White. *Hair Stylist:* Lynn Decker. *Casting:* Shari Rhodes, Liz Keigley. *Set Decorator:* Okowita. *Property Master:* Michael Parsons. *Assistant Property Master:* Bob Parsons. *Construction Coordinator:* Bill Bradford. *Sound Mixer:* Bob Ward. *Boom Man:* George Baetz. *Special Effects:* Jack Bennett. *Transportation:* Clifford Yarborough. *Gaffer:* Robert Driskell. *Electrical Best Boy:* Curtis Bingham. *Key Grip:* Tony Poston. *Best Boy:* Kerry Riker. *Camera Operator:* Phil Pfeiffer. *First Assistant Camera Operator:* Robert Horme. *Still Photographer:* Zade Rosenthal. *Production Assistant:* Joan Aldrich. *Production Coordinator:* Betty Buckley. *Production Assistant:* Edward Gold. *Production Secretary:* Zoila De La Pena. *Assistant Film Editor:* Chuck Ellison. *Re-Recording Mixers:* Michael J. Kohut, C.A.S., Jay M. Harding, C.A.S., Bud Grenzbach, C.A.S. *Musical Scoring Mixer:* Dan Wallin. *Sound Effects Editor:* Bill Phillips. *Music Editor:* Ken Karman. *Unit Publicist:* Bob Jennings. *First Aid:* Janet Lawlers. *Panaflex Cameras:* Panavision. *Production Services:* FPS, Inc., Dallas, Texas. *Insurance:* Robert Jellen, Albert G. Ruben and Company, Inc. *Color:* MGM Laboratories. *Title and Optical Effects:* Modern Film Effects. *Special Thanks to:* Texas Film Commission and the people of Texas. *Running Time:* 102 minutes. *MPAA Rating:* R

SYNOPSIS: In the bountiful farmland of the religious community called the Hittites, a young couple, the Schimdts, have moved into a beautiful farm home called "Our Blessing." Jim Schmidt is a former Hittite and the son of the Hittite leader Isaiah. Just a year earlier, Jim rebelled against his father's strict religious beliefs and went away to a secular college. On campus, Jim met the beautiful Martha and married her. On the eve of their first anniversary, the lovers have returned to build a life together on the farm, but the Hittites are never far away with their disapproving glances and stern warnings that "the Incubus" has infiltrated the countryside.

On a beautiful autumn morning, Jim tends diligently to the field. While on his tractor, he spies the Hittite man-child William Gluntz pursuing Faith, a non-Hittite neighbor and daughter of Louisa Stohler. William has ripped up one of Faith's paintings and chased her off her own property. Jim tells William to go home at once, and he protects Faith from the bald, simple-minded Hittite. Faith's mother arrives on the scene shortly thereafter and thanks Jim for looking after her daughter. Jim informs Louisa that she may be able to return the favor soon in her capacity as local midwife: Martha is pregnant and will give birth in the coming spring. Louisa congratulates Jim and says she will be glad to help out. She also tells Jim that she hopes the baby is a girl because "boys are nothing but trouble!"

After Louisa heads home, Jim returns to work and waves to his Hittite brother, John, as he works in an adjacent field. Isaiah witnesses the friendly greeting and punishes the young man. He orders John not to "covet" what Jim has, because Jim is "dead" to the Hittites.

After a long day working on his crops, Jim drives his tractor into the barn and sees the word "INCUBUS" painted on an interior wall in red paint. He paints over the word angrily and heads inside. In the shadows, William Gluntz watches. In another barn, Louisa finds Faith painting a strange picture of Martha's house and barn. Louisa insists that girls should "paint their nails," not strange, impressionist visions. Faith assures her that many girls paint such strange visions.

Back at the "Our Blessing" farmhouse, Martha and Jim celebrate their first wedding anniversary. Martha presents Jim with a special photo album filled with pictures of their life together. Jim is touched, and he and Martha retreat to the bedroom to make love. They are unaware that someone has sneaked into the house and is watching them from the darkness. The voyeur leaves the house after Jim and Martha have fallen asleep. Soon, Jim awakens with a start. He hears a noise and heads out to the barn, only to discover that the tractor is running. He turns it off and examines the barn in detail. The chickens have been released from their coop by an intruder. As Jim considers what has happened, the tractor lights are switched on. Jim cannot see who is controlling the tractor, and it suddenly rolls into him, crushing him against the wall. He screams in agony and dies. Martha hears the screams and runs out to the barn.

At Jim's funeral, Martha stands alone, dressed in black. She remains until the grave digger finishes. In the distance, she spots a Hittite group led by Isaiah. They conduct their own ceremony for the fallen Jim. Martha is then driven home to her farm by Louisa. Further down the road, two of Martha's friends, Vicky and Lana, arrive. They have heard of Jim's death and have come to help their grieving friend get through a difficult time.

At Martha's barn, William Gluntz and a group of Hittite children dare each other to enter the structure. They break in and find trails of Jim's blood. Martha arrives home to find intruders in the barn and goes after the Hittites with a pitchfork. They flee, and William loses a shoe in the process. As Martha pushes out the trespassers, Vicky and Lana arrive. They all go into the house and talk to Martha about Jim, the Hittites and her marriage. Martha tells her friends that Isaiah calls her an "incubus," a demon who can come up from the ground and "take you like a beast." Vicky asks Martha when she plans to return to Los Angeles, but Martha informs her that she is going to remain to manage the farm and raise her child. She asks her friends if they will stay with her for a week, and they agree.

In the Hittite community, William is scolded by his father Matthew for losing his shoe. The old man orders his simpleton son to find the shoe even if it takes all night. William returns to Martha's house and watches as Lana walks on the second-story ledge in her nightgown. She then goes inside and medicates herself with alcohol and pills. As she is falling asleep, she sees a large spider crawling across the ceiling of her bedroom.

Outside, William continues to spy on the inhabitants of the house. He watches Martha undress in her bedroom. He is surprised, however, when he finds a knife sheath on her window ledge. Someone else is watching Martha! Suddenly William is attacked from behind and stabbed to death. After dispatching the Hittite, the killer watches Martha sleep.

Early the next morning, Matthew Gluntz and Isaiah come to "Our Blessing" to ask Martha if she has seen William. Martha has not, but she offers to help find him. Isaiah refuses and says that she is "with incubus." Then Isaiah attempts to pressure Martha into selling her farm back to the Hittites. He offers her what he says is a fair price, and Martha slams the door in his face. "May you be damned in Hell!" he shouts at her. Trying to put the incident out of her memory, Martha joins Lana and Vicky for breakfast. Lana has had a bad nightmare. She dreamed of a man with ashen skin breaking into the house. He called her name like a lover, and Lana tried to kill him with a cannon. It did not work, however, and the man transformed into a spider. Vicky tells Lana not to be so creepy and tries to inject a little levity into the proceedings. She pulls open a blind and is surprised to find Faith staring into the house. She has brought a basket of eggs for Martha. Martha thanks Faith for the gift. On the way out, Faith wanders into Martha's bedroom. She sits on the bed and starts rocking on it provocatively, causing Martha to ask her to leave.

Vicky goes for a jog and encounters a vicious dog. It jumps at her ferociously and she incapacitates it with mace. Then she meets Jim's brother, John Schimdt. The two strike up a friendship. They sit together in a field and share their impressions of life. Vicky feels as if she is in a time warp, and John tells her that the 18th century is a much more peaceful place than the 20th century. Isaiah arrives in a wagon with John's betrothed, cousin Melissa. Isaiah scolds John for abandoning his work in the field and talking with Vicky. He tells John that Melissa is the only woman he should talk with, and that he must shun the rest.

Back on the farm, Martha works the fields on Jim's tractor. It breaks down abruptly and Lana goes to the barn to fetch the toolbox. While she is inside, the barn door slams shut. She opens it and it closes again. Realizing she is trapped, Lana scurries for a window, but all the windows slam shut. Lana senses the presence of "death" inside the barn and climbs a ladder into the loft to escape. From the second floor she sees the front door re-open. As she heads for it, she finds William Gluntz's missing shoe. Then a dark figure jumps up at her. She falls to the first floor and lands on her back. When she looks down at her chest, a huge spider is perched there. She swats the creature away and runs for the open door. As she makes her escape, William's body falls from the roof, a noose around his neck.

Matthew Gluntz and the Hittites arrive to take the corpse away. Matthew accuses Martha of murdering his son, and Isaiah will not allow the police to conduct an autopsy on the boy. The Hittite leader informs the sheriff that police "laws cannot crush the incubus," but Hittite laws can. Once the Hittites have left the property, the sheriff suggests to Martha and the others that they pack and leave at once. Once again, Martha refuses to abandon the home she and Jim built. The officer understands her decision but warns her that he will not be able to arrive in time should something dangerous occur.

Later that night, a shadowy figure approaches Martha's house. While she takes a steaming bath, this mysterious person releases a rattlesnake into the bathtub with her. It slithers into the water and rises between her legs. Martha jumps to safety and kills the snake with a fireplace poker. While Lana, Vicky and Martha recover from the incident, John Schmidt and Melissa join Isaiah at the Hittite chapel. John is having serious doubts about his father's strict leadership, but Melissa does not understand his problem. At William Gluntz's funeral service, Isaiah blames William's death on whomever took the boy to the barn of the incubus. One of the young Hittite boys fingers another, Leopold Smith, as the culprit. Leopold is brought in front of the congregation to be punished. He asks God for forgiveness, but Isaiah beats him viciously on his wrists. John Schmidt hates what he sees.

The next day, Vicky and Martha travel to town to fill Vicky's car with gas. Vicky goes shopping while Martha conducts some secret business, and wanders into the same shop where John Schmidt and Melissa are selecting a dress for their wedding. John spots Vicky and talks with her, apologizing for his father's unfriendly behavior the day before. Sensing there is a connection between them, Vicky asks John out to a movie. Melissa overhears the proposition and runs off, crying. John pursues Melissa and kisses her roughly. She does not understand his urgency and he informs her that it is difficult "waiting." She resists his advances and John and Melissa wrestle in the grass. She finally escapes and runs home. Isaiah learns what has happened and orders John to the barn for immediate punishment. John wants to talk with his father, but Isaiah will not discuss matters. John fights back as Isaiah beats him and Isaiah is stunned. Outraged, he banishes his son from the peace of the Hittite community, informing John that he is a "stench in the nostrils of God."

Back at "Our Blessing," Martha and Vicky practice shooting at paint cans with a newly purchased pistol. Then, Vicky decides to go to see a movie. Just as she leaves, Louisa Stohler stops by to ask Martha if she has seen Faith. She also tells Lana that men are hopeless. Faith's father abandoned her when she was just a baby and Louisa has hated men ever since. She also warns Martha to watch the Hittites.

In town, Vicky leaves a showing of *Summer of Fear* at the Tara Theater and runs into John. They go out together in her car and "make out." Vicky teaches John to drive, and he almost smashes the car into a tree. As they first kiss, the Hittite Melissa suddenly awakens in her house and shouts John's name in anguish. She grabs a knife and runs into the woods. Vicky stops kissing John when she thinks she has heard a noise. John goes to investigate but hears nothing. He returns to Vicky and they continue to caress one another. Suddenly, someone attacks the car. A knife pierces the car top and stabs John repeatedly. Then the attacker pours gasoline on the car and sets it afire. Vicky attempts to escape, but the car explodes with her inside.

At the same time, Lana is experiencing another bad dream. Something gray and monstrous calls her name and puts his hands around her head. He tells her to open her mouth. She obeys and a spider falls from the ceiling into it. She awakens with a start, choking. Martha goes immediately to her side and comforts her. Lana goes to the kitchen to pour herself a glass of milk but the carton is filled with blood. Lana freaks out and believes that death is coming for her. Martha opens the door to her bedroom and a scarecrow dressed like a Hittite pops up. On the scarecrow is the flower Martha placed on Jim's lapel! Realizing that her husband's grave has been tampered with, Martha drives out to the cemetery. She opens his unearthed casket and a swarm of chickens fly out. Martha makes the connection between chickens and Faith, and drives out to the Stohler farm. She enters Louisa's barn and finds Faith's paintings. All of the paintings are idealized versions of Martha! The terror does not end with the paintings, however. Martha also discovers Jim's body strung up in a dark corner.

Led on by a psychic impulse, Melissa has also found her way to the Stohler barn. Louisa spots the young Hittite girl and attacks her. Martha flees the scene but bumps into Faith. The two women wrestle and Martha tears open Faith's shirt. Faith's exposed chest reveals that Faith is not a woman at all, but a man! Faith claims that he was only hurting people who were trying to keep Martha and him apart. Martha is terrified and runs for her farm. Louisa soothes Faith, telling her that Martha must die to preserve Faith's secret.

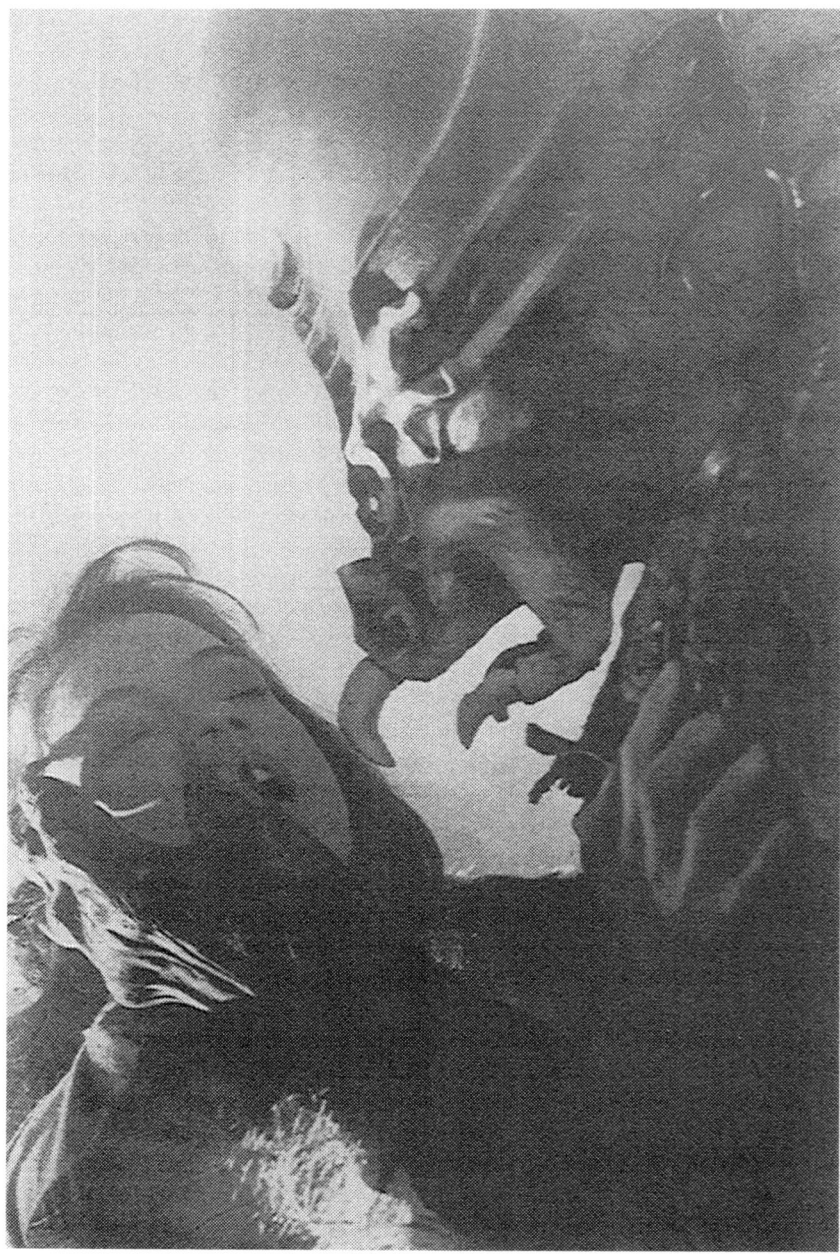

In *Deadly Blessing*'s terrifying climax, an incubus ascends from Hell and abducts Martha (Maren Jensen).

2. The Feature Films
81

Spurred on by insanity, Louisa and her son Faith attack "Our Blessing." Martha shoots Faith in the chest but then must contend with Louisa, who is armed with a shotgun. After spraying mace in Louisa's face, Martha and Louisa battle in the living room and Martha's bedroom. Lana regains her senses and shoots Louisa dead with Martha's gun. Faith suddenly reappears and attacks Martha again. He is stabbed and finally killed by Melissa. Then Isaiah arrives at the home and surveys the damage. He looks down at Faith's body and tells Martha that "the messenger of the incubus is dead."

The next day, the police arrive. Lana decides it is time for her to return to the safety of Los Angeles and she says her goodbyes to Martha. As Lana and the sheriff drive away, Martha enters her home. It darkens suddenly and Martha is confronted with Jim's ghostly apparition. He warns her of the impending arrival of the incubus. The ghost fades away and the house starts to shake. Before Martha can escape, a demon bursts up through the floorboards. It grabs Martha with force and yanks her down to Hell. The room lightens and all becomes quiet again. A spider and its web come abruptly into focus.

COMMENTARY: *Deadly Blessing* is in many ways a more complicated film than either *The Last House on the Left* or *The Hills Have Eyes*. There are more characters, more subplots and more locations to explore. The result is that during certain moments, the film appears to lack the almost ruthless cohesion that marks Craven's two earlier directorial efforts. Still, the film is a strong one that becomes increasingly powerful on repeat viewings.

Craven's directing technique in *Deadly Blessing* is markedly different from his earlier work. On the surface, the film apes the style of Sean Cunningham's *Friday the 13th* or John Carpenter's *Halloween*. Point-of-view shots of intruders entering a darkened home and watching the beautiful protagonist disrobe dominate the film, but rewardingly Craven has pulled another fast one on his viewers and again defied their expectations. The P.O.V. shots represent not one intruder, but three! Louisa, Faith and William Gluntz are all obsessed with Jensen's Martha, and at various times are all stalking her. One of the best scenes in the film involves Gluntz's death. He stands outside the window watching Martha prepare for bed. At this point, the audience believes he is the killer, a belief buttressed by Michael Berryman's role as a lunatic in *The Hills Have Eyes*. Then the camera takes Gluntz's point of view and he spots a knife sheath on the window sill. Gluntz and the audience both puzzle over this development for a moment and then the killer strikes from behind. It is a moment the audience is unprepared for, and Craven's manipulation of it is perfect.

Deadly Blessing overturns viewer expectations in another way as well. Once Martha has discovered the chickens in Jim's grave, she (and the audience) realize that Faith is involved. The tension builds as Martha ventures to Faith's art "studio" in the barn and finds strange paintings of herself and Jim's body. The audience is now convinced that Faith is the killer. Moments later, this perception is overturned when Louisa attacks Melissa. Yet another surprise follows that revelation as Faith is revealed to be a man! These rapid-fire shocks keep the audience totally off-guard and create the realization that they have, for over an hour, witnessed the attempts of not one killer but many! Finally, of course, the ending reveals that there is an even more sinister force at work: the incubus.

Although some critics have suggested that this final supernatural twist is out of place in a psychological thriller, the ascension of the incubus in *Deadly Blessing* has been laboriously set up by Craven. The Hittites constantly refer to the creature as if he walks among them, and the film is punctuated by a series of animal attacks. A rabid dog, several spiders, a swarm of chickens and even a snake go on the offensive against Martha, Lana and Vicki during *Deadly Blessing*. Since animals (or "familiars") are easily controlled by supernatural forces of evil, a fact established in Craven's *A Stranger in the House* (1978), the periodic animal attacks are an indication that something beyond the violent psychoses of Louisa and Faith is at work in Hittite country. *Deadly Blessing* does not make sense without the presence of the incubus since there are so many clues to the true nature of evil sprinkled through the film, including Lana's prophetic nightmares.

Although *Deadly Blessing* offers human and supernatural villainy, and plays with red herrings, diversions and surprises, the most interesting element of the film is perhaps the Hittite culture and the effect it wields on outsiders, particularly family units. As Carol Clover suggests in her text *Men, Women and Chainsaws: Gender in Modern Horror Films*, the repressive atmosphere created by Isaiah's leadership "infantalizes all the younger men and drives the women to lesbianism."[2]

The negative impact of repression is a common theme in Craven's motion pictures. Parents continually deny the reality of situations in *A Nightmare on Elm Street*, *Last House on the Left*, *The Hills Have Eyes* and even *Shocker*. *Deadly Blessing* is the only film that overtly points at religious oppression, but it nonetheless fits the pattern of Craven's career. His fascination with the subject stems from his real-life concern about the conservative direction America is leaning:

> The Christian Fundamentalist-political right is a very powerful force now in America, and they will really target horror films ... under the guise of family values. ...[L]ook at the responses to abortion clinics and people who are willing to go out and murder people and feel completely all right about it, because they think they're acting on the part of God. That gets pretty scary.[3]

Isaiah (Ernest Borgnine) is the character whom Craven sees as the primary hypocrite in *Deadly Blessing*. He claims to be "the kindred of God" yet mercilessly beats his children and the children of others in his flock. He passes judgment on all who do not share his sense of right and wrong, although the Bible specifically states that one should *not* judge lest he or she be judged. Not unlike contemporary judges who post the Ten Commandments in their courtroom and refuse to acknowledge that there are people in America who may not share Christian tenets, Isaiah treats all non-Hittites (read: non-Christian) as immoral, inferior creatures. He is a bigot who uses his position of authority and personal relationship with God to judge the value and morality of other human beings. As a result of his strict adherence to so-called religious principle, he alienates both of his sons and leads Louisa and Faith to hate men. It is his repression of natural human feelings such as desire that causes the human psychoses which abound around him.

Isaiah is directly responsible for Louisa's pathological hatred of men (whom she considers useless authority figures who just want to knock a woman up) and indirectly responsible for Faith's confused sexual identity. Since Louisa hates men so vehemently, she does not allow her son to show masculinity, and the result is a generation twisted by the values of a previous one. Isaiah's control of the Hittites, an extended family, and his domination of local politics is also resented by every major character in the film, even the warm-hearted Martha. Isaiah attempts to run both Martha and the Stohlers off their land, another bit of hypocrisy since material wealth should not be important to a man of God. He also turns a blind eye to William's continued harassment of these "non-believers" since it suits his overall purpose (their removal from his domain).

In a sense, *Deadly Blessing*'s incubus is really Isaiah's id. It strikes out against those he cannot tolerate and it removes the threats to his way of life. At the end of the film, the incubus kills Martha, consequently leaving her house and property available to the Hittites! The incubus, operating through its messengers (Faith or Louisa), also kills the two men who have purposefully flouted Isaiah's authority: sons Jim and John. If the incubus is Isaiah's alter ego, then the point of *Deadly Blessing* is that men who claim to be kindred with God are actually responsible for the greatest evils in the world.

Beyond the theme of religious oppression and its effects on various families, *Deadly Blessing* is important in the context of Craven's career because it is his first film which highlights the dream sequence as a method of conveying theme and subtext. In *Deadly Blessing*, the dream sequences foreshadow the victory of the incubus/Isaiah during the climax as well as the distrust of men among the *dramatis personae*. In one sexually charged dream, two powerful hands pry Lana's mouth wide open as if to forcibly prepare her to perform *fellatio*. Then, a huge spider falls into her gaping mouth and she awakens, choking. She has unwittingly swallowed the instrument of evil (semen?) following an act reminiscent of oral sex.

As Lana recounts another dream, she informs her friends that the nightmare "man" actually became a spider, again equating men with monsters. Lana's dreams not only pinpoint males as the source of evil in *Deadly Blessing* and contribute to the mood of growing horror, but make the viewer aware that evil is invading even the landscape of the mind.

This invasion of evil is suggested not only through dreams exhibiting sexual imagery, but through ongoing animal attacks. Martha is nearly killed in her tub when a slithering snake moves between her legs and toward her vagina. Although the snake is obviously a phallic symbol acting on behalf of the lustful Louisa, the lustful Faith or even the repressed Isaiah, it is also a further symbol of encroaching, *male* evil. In her *New York Times* review, Janet Maslin noted the special role of women in the film, and as usual she hit the nail on the head. The protagonists of the picture are *all* female. Vicki is a smart, resourceful character who serves as instructor to John Schmidt in the ways of the world. Martha is a determined heroine who will "not give up the farm" no matter what. Even Lana with her substance abuse and tender psyche is dramatized in sympathetic terms. She is weaker than her two friends in resilience, but far more sensitive and aware of the supernatural side of life. Significantly, the Hittite Melissa shares these qualities with Lana and for that reason is able to ferret out the evil in the climax. In the end, it is this connection with the supernatural that proves most useful since of all the women only Lana and Melissa survive.

Serving as a surrogate for Wes Craven, John Schmidt is the only truly sympathetic male character in *Deadly Blessing*. The others are either hypocritical authoritarian figures (Isaiah, the sheriff), useless in the conflict against evil (Jim, Mr. Gluntz, Leopold), demented by society (Faith) or just plain stupid (William). Only John Schmidt redeems his sex by rebelling against the dictates of restrictive society and attempting to grow beyond the cycle of tradition which has bred so much repression. Because John is a likable person, the scene in which he is murdered is perhaps the most tragic in the film. It is clear that he was taking the first steps of a journey that would have allowed him to experience the wonders of life away from his father's brutality and hypocrisy. It is sad that he does not escape the wrath of one of Craven's most memorable "bad" fathers.

Deadly Blessing is a rich film that uses surprise, sympathetic characterizations and dreams to tell a story of repression and its widespread ramifications. Despite many strengths, the film did not garner much attention during its release and is not well remembered today by most fans of the genre, perhaps because it expresses its complicated ideas in the worn-out stalker milieu. Thus it is all too easy to look at *Deadly Blessing* in its historical context and dismiss it as another *Prom Night* or *Terror Train*. Considering that Craven knowingly manipulates the *modus operandi* of post-*Psycho* slasher flicks such as P.O.V. shots, surprise antagonists and seemingly facile psychological motivations for killings, it is not difficult to understand this perception.

The final supernatural twist is also off-putting to viewers who, having not picked up on the subtle clues, find the ending dramatically unmotivated and even a cheat. Some small technical flaws also lead to viewer dissatisfaction. The tense nature of the "snake in the tub" sequence, the most harrowing scene in the picture, is severely undercut when Maren Jensen's black bikini bottom is clearly visible for seconds at a time beneath the bath water.

Yet *Deadly Blessing* boasts some surprising strengths. The final 15 minutes, wherein Louisa and Faith Stohler launch their final assault on Martha's farmhouse, match the best of *The Hills Have Eyes* and *The Last House on the Left* for pace, editing and intensity. The sequence in which Jim's ghost appears to Martha in a darkened room is also suitably spine-chilling, and the performances by Jensen, Bruckner and Sharon Stone are all better-than-average for a genre which tends to see women as victims rather than people. If any of Craven's work deserves the title of "diamond in the rough," it is certainly *Deadly Blessing*. *Last House on the Left*, *The Hills Have Eyes*, *A Nightmare on Elm Street* and *Scream* are all better known, almost legendary, but *Deadly Blessing* has undeservedly been overlooked. It is a worthy detour into horror.

Swamp Thing (1982)

An off-the-wall, eccentric, peculiar movie fueled by the demented obsessions of its makers ... [W]ith *Swamp Thing*, [Craven] betrays a certain gentleness and poetry along with the gore... Craven moves confidently through the three related genres he's stealing from (monster movies, mad scientist movies and transformations...).— Roger Ebert, *Roger Ebert's Movie Home Companion, 1993 Edition* (Andrews and McMeel, A Universal Press Syndicate Company, page 640)

A shoddy, camp effort. ...It has so-called performances by Adrienne Barbeau (as Alice Cable) and Louis Jourdan (as — get this — Dr. Arcane) that make the posturing in TV's *Batman* look like profound thespian achievements by contrast. The Charleston swamp locations seem phony, as though director Wes Craven got his camera stuck in the quicksand and had to match shots in the mudbath room at Elizabeth Arden's.— Carrie Rickey (*Village Voice*, August 17, 1982, page 48)

It has an astonishing verisimilitude to the low-budget '50s horror movie. Producers could spend millions and not replicate the flavor — the mediocre camerawork, the poor sound and color, the wooden performances ... *Swamp Thing* is about as scary as a chef's salad.— Alex Keneas (*Newsday*, July 30, 1982)

The cartoony aspects of the film are the best part, but they aren't carried far enough. Too often, *Swamp Thing* looks like a souped-up version of *Starsky and Hutch*. The ending is too moronic even for cartoons, but overall the film is entertaining.— Darrell Moore, *The Best, the Worst, the Most Unusual: Horror Films* (Publications International, 1983, page 69)

Craven adapted the DC Comics character with care and consideration. ...Craven knew that most modern comic books were more sophisticated and poetic. *Swamp Thing* is enthralling until Holland becomes the monster. After that, the picture becomes meandering and indecisive.— Richard Meyers, *The Great Science Fiction Films* (Citadel Press, 1983, page 240)

Despite some campy moments, most of this *Incredible Hulk* rip-off is just plain silly.— Douglas Menville & R. Reginald, *Futurevisions: The New Golden Age of the Science Fiction Film* (Newcastle Publishing Company, 1985, page 133)

CAST: Louis Jourdan (Dr. Arcane); Adrienne Barbeau (Alice Cable); Ray Wise (Dr. Alec Holland); David Hess (Ferret); Nicholas Worth (Bruno); Don Knight (Ritter); Al Ruban (Charlie); Dick Durock (Swamp Thing); Ben Bates (Arcane Monster); Nannette Brown (Dr. Linda Holland); Reggie Bates (Jude); Mimi Meyers (Arcane's Secretary); Karen Price (Arcane's Messenger); Bill Erickson (Young Agent); Dov Gottesfeld (Commando); Tommy Madden (Little Bruno).

CREDITS: An Embassy Pictures Release. *Music:* Harry Manfredini. *Editor:* Richard Bracken. *Art Direction:* David Nichols, Robb Wilson King. *Director of Photography:* Robin Goodwin. *Executive in Charge of Production:* Al Ruban. *Based Upon Characters Appearing in Magazines Published by D.C. Comics. Writer/Director:* Wes Craven. *Producer's:* Benjamin Melniker, Michael E. Uslan. *Unit Production Managers:* Yoram Ben-Ami, Robert Bordiga. *First Assistant Director:* Todd Corman. *Second Assistant Director:* Tony Cecere. *Set Coordinator:* Mary Salter. *Production Office Manager:* Kimberly Myers. *Location Manager:* Jack Briggs. *Production Auditor:* Aviva Gellman. *Stunt Coordinator:* Ted Duncan. *Airboat Stunt Coordinator:* Mickey Gilbert. *Stuntpeople:* Pam Bebermeyer, Bill Erickson, Art Brewer. *Fire Gag Stuntman:* Tony Cecere. *Special Make up Effects Designed and Created by* William Munns. *Make up Effects Crew in Charleston:* Ken Horn, Esther Mercado, Deborah Shankle. *Property Master:* Tom Estridge. *Set Designer:* Robb Wilson King. *Construction Coordinator:* Carl Copeland. *Assistant Editor:* Rick Mitchell. *Script Supervisor:* Charlene Webb. *Make up:* Tonga Knight. *Hair:* Tony Marrero. *Unit Publicist:* Michael Klastorin. *Still Photographer:* Russel Jeffcoat. *Production Aide:* Jeffrey Mandel. *Casting:* Cathy Henderson, Barbara Hanley. *Casting in Charleston:* Michael Wyka. *Costume Designer for Principal Cast:* Patricia Bolomet. *Ms. Barbeau's Evening Gown:* Bennett Choate. *Wardrobe Designer in Charleston:* Paul A Summers. *Post-Production Supervisor:* Paula Hines. *Re-recording:* Gomillion Sound, Inc. *Re-Recording Mixers:* Dave Dockendorf, Bob DesChaine, John Mack. *Sound Effects:* Jay's Meats and Provision Company. *Titles:* Modern Film Effects. *Color:* Technicolor. *Grateful Acknowledgments to:* Radio Shack, Ferneau Buick, S.C. Department of Health and Environmental Control, the City of Charleston, Cypress Gardens, Magnolia Plantations and the American Red Cross. Filmed on location in Charleston. *Running time:* 91 minutes. *MPAA Rating:* PG

> Not long ago, in the unexplored reaches of an unmapped swamp, the creative genius of one man collided with another's evil dream and a monster was born. Too powerful to be destroyed, too intelligent to be captured, this being still pursues its savage dream.
> — Title card of *Swamp Thing*

SYNOPSIS: A helicopter transporting special government agent Alice Cable flies above a fog-ridden swamp to the headquarters of a top secret research project. Far below, armed men in camouflage uniforms hunt one of Cable's compatriots amidst the natural beauty of the swamp. The soldiers are led by the hulking Ferret, the head goon of the villainous Dr. Arcane. Ferret captures his quarry and forces the agent to face a deadly rattlesnake. The snake strikes, and its venomous bite kills the agent.

As her comrade dies, Alice Cable is led from the landing helicopter to a small boat. She is ferried across the bog and informed by Charlie, the project leader, that local fisherman believe this land is haunted by ghosts. The boat travels through the half-sunken gates of an old church that was flooded years ago and stops at a small research compound just off the water. It is in this primitive facility that Dr. Alec Holland's research team has been working for ten weeks. The eccentric genius insisted that his team operate in the swamp because the "life" which interests him exists only there. His top secret project involves plant life, but beyond that vague description Cable knows nothing of the operation. She soon meets Ritter, the head of security, and he is upset to hear from her that Dr. Arcane may be planning something. Cable tells him she is there to evacuate the team to safety immediately.

Cable is introduced to Alec Holland and his sister Linda, whom Cable first mistakes for his wife. Almost immediately, an attraction develops between Cable and Alec, and he offers to take her to Sector 3 to examine some malfunctioning sensor equipment. In a small motorboat, Alec gives Cable a tour of the swamp and flirts with her. She learns quickly that he is not only a man with a libido but a man with vision as well. He believes "half the world could eat off the swamps," and is a true humanitarian. Cable also learns that her predecessor was devoured by an alligator while attempting to repair the same sensor in Sector 3.

When Cable and Holland return to the research compound, Ritter is furious that Cable, a "broad of an agent," has taken Holland outside without security. Cable apologizes and Holland defends her actions. Before the argument can go further, a noise emanates from the lab. Holland and Cable run inside and discover that Holland's new batch of green formula is explosive. Holland writes about this unusual development in his notebook and then explains the details of the project to Cable. It is his goal to combine animal and vegetable matter to build a plant for the 21st century. He wants to develop vegetable cells with an animal nucleus and create a plant with an animal's aggressive power for survival. He believes this development could feed the world: Tomatoes could grow in the desert and corn could flourish in the U.S. in the 21st century when there are 6.5 billion people inhabiting it. This explosive green solution is the final step in the process. Alec and Linda discover that it replicates quickly: On the spot where Linda dropped the liquid, the wood floor-boards have started to grow pine!

Late that night, there is a raid on the research compound. Cable checks the security station and discovers that all defenses have been penetrated. On one monitor, she sees Charlie being killed. Then she is attacked from behind by Ferret and dragged to the lab. Ferret forces her to open the security lock, and Alex

Gung-ho secret agent Alice Cable (Adrienne Barbeau) defends the Holland experiment in *Swamp Thing*.

and Linda are captured. Ritter arrives on the scene and reveals that he is behind the raid. Amazingly, he is not Ritter at all, but Dr. Arcane in disguise. Arcane threatens to kill Linda unless Alec turns over the formula immediately. Alec acquiesces and gives Arcane the solution and his notebooks. Linda attempts to escape and Arcane shoots her in the back. As she falls, she drops the final research notebook. Cable, pretending to be unconscious, grabs it when nobody is watching. Alec breaks loose to help his dying sister but in the ensuing struggle he spills the green formula on himself and catches fire. His body consumed by flames, Alec runs out of the compound and dives into the swamp.

Arcane orders Ferret and his men to kill everyone, burn the research center and leave no witnesses. The soldiers go about this gruesome task and start dumping the dead scientists and agents into the swamp. Ferret takes Cable out into the swamp and starts to drown her.

Just as Cable is about to die, a green hand lunges up from the water and throws Ferret into the swamp. Then a half-man/half-vegetable being rears up and overturns the boat. This creature, "Swamp Thing," rescues Cable and carries her to shore and safety. While the beast fights off Arcane's men, Cable makes her escape.

At the Arcane estate, the evil doctor inspects Holland's data and realizes that the final notebook in the research sequence is missing. He heads to the swamp immediately and meets with Ferret and Bruno, his two top men. He orders them to capture Cable and retrieve the notebook. They tell him of the monster and he orders it captured at all costs.

Cable makes it to a small gas station on a nearby road and asks the teenage boy working there for the use of the phone. Jude agrees to help her, but when Cable reaches her superiors, she is actually communicating with Arcane. She reports her position and that she has acquired the final Holland notebook. Arcane and his men arrive soon and Jude provides Cable with a pistol to defend herself. There is an exchange of gunfire, but Cable's gun misfires and explodes after the first shot. She flees back to the swamps and is pursued by a sports utility vehicle.

Just as she is about to be run down by her pursuers, Swamp Thing appears and rips off the vehicle's roof. He is shot several times, but he barely flinches. He saves Cable again, but she still thinks he is just a monster. She runs away from him and joins up with Jude once more. He takes her to a nearby cabin for a change of clothes and then they head back for the research cabin. Swamp Thing, there surveying the wreckage of the laboratory, finds a locket with Linda's picture in it. Cable watches him from a distance and then leaves when he detects her. Sad, Swamp Thing smells a beautiful flower and mourns his sad life. Then he hears the roar of Arcane's motorboats: soldiers are pursuing Cable. Once again, Swamp Thing intervenes and takes on three boats single-handedly. Ferret attempts to destroy the beast with machine guns and grenades, but Swamp Thing is victorious, destroying all three boats. Ferret and Bruno barely escape with their lives.

Cable gives Jude the research notebook and decides to help Swamp Thing fight Arcane's goons. She stops cold when she hears a gunshot. Jude has been shot! Then Cable herself is ambushed. While she is taken away to Arcane, Swamp Thing goes to the dying Jude and rejuvenates him with his touch. Jude hands Swamp Thing the notebook and thanks the creature for saving his life.

Cable is taken to Arcane's houseboat, where Ferret makes sexual advances and she debilitates him with a knee to his crotch. She jumps overboard and swims for shore, Ferret in hot pursuit. Cable reaches land and is saved by Swamp Thing, who fights Ferret. Brandishing his machete, Ferret chops off one of Swamp Thing's arms. The beast retaliates by grabbing Ferret and breaking his neck.

When Swamp Thing gives Cable a flower and reveals his scientific knowledge of orchids, she realizes that he is a transformed Alec Holland. Cable tells him that she is sorry for what has happened to him and asks if it hurts. Swamp Thing replies, "Only when I laugh." Cable and Swamp Thing share a tender moment together and then Cable bathes in the swamp. Swamp Thing watches her sadly and realizes he can never be with her like a man. He wanders off into the woods and throws his notebook to the ground. His research has only brought him horrible pain.

Arcane arrives in the swamp and captures Cable. He nets and subdues Swamp Thing while Bruno finds the notebook.

That night, Arcane holds a magnificent banquet in his plantation house to celebrate the capture of Swamp Thing and the duplication of the Alec Holland formula. He reveals that he has slipped the formula into the drink of the unwitting Bruno. Before Arcane's eyes, Bruno transforms into a subhuman ape creature of minuscule proportions. Furious, Arcane demands to know from Swamp Thing why Bruno does not share Swamp Thing's strength. Swamp Thing replies that Bruno never had his strength, even as a human. The formula amplifies a person's natural essence. It makes people more of what they already are. Bruno was timid, weak and stupid, so the formula has given him a timid, weak and stupid form.

Arcane is thrilled with this explanation. He realizes that if he takes the formula, he will become even more of a genius. Standing alone on his veranda, Arcane pours himself the formula in a champagne glass and drinks. He starts to change, his fingers elongating and hair growing rapidly.

Trapped in Arcane's prison with Cable, Swamp Thing regenerates his arm. He breaks his bonds and frees Cable. Bruno helps Swamp Thing and Cable escape from the prison by leading them to an underground spring which comes out at the swamp. Cable and Swamp Thing dive in and escape but by now Arcane has changed into a hideous beast that is part ass and part boar: the two main characteristics of Arcane's personality. Infuriated, he picks up a sword and pursues Swamp Thing and Cable. Arriving in the misty bog, Swamp Thing and Cable are unprepared when Arcane attacks. The two beasts fight and Arcane stabs Cable in the chest. Swamp Thing is enraged and beats the Arcane beast into unconsciousness. Then he uses his miraculous healing ability to rejuvenate Cable.

As she returns to consciousness, Arcane attacks again; Swamp Thing finally kills the mad scientist with Arcane's sword. Swamp Thing carries Cable away from the water and then begins to leave, telling her, "It's over." Cable begs him not to go; he can continue his work and she can be his hands. Swamp Thing refuses and asks her instead to tell his story. After assuring her that he will always be with her, Swamp Thing disappears into the mist. Cable watches sadly as he vanishes. She is joined by Jude, who tells her that Swamp Thing will be back.

COMMENTARY: Before earning his own comic book series in 1972, the character Swamp Thing first appeared in D.C.'s *House of Secrets #92* in June of 1971,[4] while Wes Craven was still struggling to find his route to success in the film industry. Since no director has the luxury of exploring his favorite theme on every project, the film *Swamp Thing* is an anomaly in the Craven canon. It does not focus squarely on family or societal issues, but is designed instead as a pure entertainment. The violence is also significantly toned down, as is appropriate for a PG-rated film. Still, the project is of interest because Craven scripted the film as well as directing it.

At first blush, *Swamp Thing* appears to be the most dated of all of Craven's films. It lacks the rich stylistic techniques of *The Last House on the Left*, the pace of *The Hills Have Eyes* and the thematic density of *Deadly Blessing*. Because the film was produced on a low budget, it looks grainy and "old." The sound is poorly recorded as well, making many scenes difficult to comprehend. All of these factors hinder enjoyment of the picture, but it is certainly not without merit. Indeed, *Swamp Thing*'s primary strength is its script, which is dotted with some very witty dialogue.

In perfect comic book style, Adrienne Barbeau snaps off sharp one-liners and Louis Jourdan, in the manner of the best James Bond villains, quotes Friedrich Wilhelm Nietzsche. As in most Craven projects, the film also nicely balances tragic circumstances with a sense of humor. Swamp Thing is, delightfully, a fully-developed personality in Craven's hands. He is able to make jokes and express love at the same time that he mourns the loss of humanity, thereby making audiences aware that he is still Alec Holland inside, not just a brainless "monster." The approach is not an overtly campy one, like *Return of the Swamp Thing*, but one designed to evoke humor out of situations that are incredibly strange and tragic.

Even though Craven works from the template of Len Wein and Berni Wrightson in *Swamp Thing*, there are some distinctly "Craven" thematic touches in the film. Echoing scenes from *The Hills Have Eyes* and *Deadly Blessing*, a snake is again wielded against a human being as a lethal weapon. Recalling *The Last House on the Left*, Arcane's lead thug is essayed by actor David Hess, the man who made Krug Stillo such a memorable cretin. Most interestingly, an entire sequence is repeated from *The Hills Have Eyes*. In that film, Bobby Carter inadvertently communicated the status of his defenses to Pluto, who was masquerading as an Air Force officer. In *Swamp Thing*, Cable also reports her location and defensive capabilities to Arcane, who has disguised his voice to sound like Ritter. In both situations, the scenario is effective. There is nothing much scarier than escaping a deadly situation and seeking help, only to learn that "help" is never coming.

More significantly, Craven repeats a central tenet of *The Hills Have Eyes* and *The Last House on the Left* by pointedly building a connection between the landscape and the main characters. Arcane, like the Carters in *The Hills Have Eyes*, misunderstands the true nature of adaptability. He brings his fully equipped boat into the swamp (a substitute for the fully equipped Carter trailer in the desert in *Hills*) and expects it to serve his purpose. But despite Arcane's boats, land vehicles and weapons, Swamp Thing (who was born of the swamp) is able to defeat him easily because he was born of the landscape.

By contrast, the suave Arcane and his men exploit the landscape. They force snakes and alligators to do their bidding, they steal a valuable secret (Holland's miracle formula) and even conduct a sort of scorched-earth policy by burning all evidence of their tampering. Swamp Thing, the living and breathing extension of the land, has his revenge. *Swamp Thing* is thus a revenge-of-nature film in a very unconventional way. Nature does not attack by flood, tornado, volcano, hurricane or earthquake. Instead it chooses a humanoid champion to defend it ... the vegetable Swamp Thing!

It is only when Arcane forsakes his modern tools and concentrates on Swamp Thing's one weakness, love, that he finally captures the hero. Using Alice Cable as bait for Swamp Thing, Arcane is capitalizing on a human trait he himself does not possess: compassion. Despite the temporary setback, the landscape and Swamp Thing work in unison to defeat Arcane. Having amazing restorative and regenerative powers, Swamp Thing commands all the forces of the swamp to combat his opponent. Conversely, when Arcane transforms into a beast, he becomes only an extension of his own pettiness: a literal jackass.

Unfortunately, the very landscape which Craven uses to such effect in *Swamp Thing* is also a problem for the script. Because Swamp Thing is born of the swamp, the film is limited to the swamp. After the prerequisite boat and land chases, there is very little that can be explored there. Perhaps for that reason, the last third of the film seems monotonous. Once the formula has been discussed and the transformation of Holland explored, all of value that remains is the final conflict between Arcane and Swamp Thing. Instead of proceeding to this inevitable clash, the script bogs down in one rescue and capture after another. Since the locale is the same, the film becomes repetitive instead of innovative. Matters are not helped by the fact that the Arcane super-monster is not very convincing in appearance.

Despite these shortcomings, there are elements of *Swamp Thing* that shine. The central boat chase in the bayou is well staged with three racing boats cornering Swamp Thing. Detonations, blaring machine-gun fire, P.O.V. shots of speeding vehicles and spectacular human stunts make the sequence a memorable set piece worthy of a more expensive franchise.

Stylistically speaking, Craven's choice to dot the film with "comic book"-like wipe transitions, sometimes dripping down the screen like ooze, sometimes blossoming out in cartoon explosions, is one that simultaneously reminds viewers of the source material and provides the production some visual distinction. It was a technique that George Romero also used in 1981's *Creepshow* to link his horror stories.

Swamp Thing also sports some memorable images. The moment when Swamp Thing tenderly pulls a pink flower from a tree and sniffs it longingly harkens back to *Frankenstein*, the 1931 James Whale film referenced again by Wes Craven in *Shocker* (1989) and *Scream* (1996). This scene adroitly establishes that "he [Swamp Thing] is capable of giving and receiving tenderness."[5] The final sequence, which sees a lonely Swamp Thing disappearing into the mist, also successfully paints a tragic picture of the angst-ridden, tragic hero. All of this foreshadows the modern superheroes such as *Spawn* or *Batman* ... creatures who are tortured by inner demons, yet who feel compelled to battle evil.

Adrienne Barbeau adds much to *Swamp Thing*. Although she received some poisonous reviews for her performance, she is the perfect protagonist for the picture. Cable is scripted by Craven as a smart-talking, physically capable government agent, and Barbeau makes the most of every barb and one-liner. This is

Animal or vegetable? The Swamp Thing (Dick Durock) contemplates his humanity.

Heather Locklear (left) joined Louis Jordan for *Return of the Swamp Thing*, a 1989 sequel to Wes Craven's 1982 superhero film.

important because Cable's own feelings of disbelief and shock deflect the audience's similar feelings. She is their surrogate and so appropriately responds to the world of Swamp Thing with wit, cynicism and intelligence.

The only time the script fails the character is, again, in the somewhat slow-paced central section. By that time, it should be perfectly obvious to Cable that Swamp Thing is on her side, yet she continually shoos him away as if he is simply a beast. Alice Cable should be smarter than that. Also delightful in the film is the romance between Barbeau and Ray Wise, who have a genuine chemistry.

Even if *Swamp Thing* is not a great film, or even one of Craven's best, it certainly served as his calling card to the major Hollywood studios. He proved that he was able to handle big action scenes, explosive stunts, experienced actors and the superhero genre with aplomb and wit.

In the Craven continuum, *Swamp Thing* is important for featuring a repeat villainous performance from David Hess and introducing Craven newcomers such as Mimi Meyers and Nicholas Worth. Meyers would soon become Meyers-Craven and play a nurse in *Chiller*, and Nicholas Worth would work with Craven again as a demonic security guard in *Invitation to Hell*.

The Hills Have Eyes Part II (1983)

> Writer-director Craven ... fills the sequel with clips from the first film to help us remember what happened in it... He really didn't have anything new up his sleeve, he was just trying to pad out the running time. The movie is so bad that it was shelved for two years.—John McCarty, *The Official Splatter Movie Guide* (St. Martin's Press, 1989, page 67)

> Wes Craven's sequel to his earlier film lands with a resounding thud... Craven's ludicrous screen play is so bad that even the derogatory laughs aren't there ... Trash.— Dan Scapperotti (*Cinefantastique*, March 1986, page 50)

CAST: Michael Berryman (Pluto); Kevin Blair (Roy); John Blom (The Reaper); Janus Blythe (Rachel/Ruby); Peter Frechette (Harry); Robert Houston (Bobby); Penny Johnson (Sue); John Laughlin (Hulk); Willard Pugh (Foster); Coleen Riley (Jane); Tamara Stafford (Cass); David Nichols (Psychiatrist); Edith Fellows (Mrs. Wilson); Lance Gordon (Mars); Susan Lanier (Brenda); Brenda Marinoff (Katy); Martin Speer (Doug); Virginia Vincent (Ethel); James Whitworth (Jupiter); Arden Meyer (Man With Towel)

CREDITS: Adrienne Fancey in Association with New Realm Entertainments and VTC Present a Film by Wes Craven. *Production Designer:* Dominick Bruno. *Director of Photography:* David Lewis. *Associate Producer:* Jonathan Debin.

Costume Designer: Taryn De Chellis. *Music:* Harry Manfredini. *Editor:* Richard Bracken. *Producers:* Barry Cahn, Peter Locke. *Writer/Director:* Wes Craven. *Unit Production Manager:* John Callas. *First Assistant Director:* John Callas. *Second Assistant Director:* Tony Cecere. *Script Supervisor:* Sharon Hagen. *Casting:* Steve Kolzak Casting, Dennis Cornell. *Make up:* Ken Horn. *Hairdresser:* Ramona Joy. *Sound Mixer:* Arthur Names. *Boom Operator:* Peggy Names. *Camera Assistants:* Bill Dickson, Clint Doughtery, Louis Patrou, Brian Tatsumo. *Grips:* Robert Gray, Kim Kono, Bill Eckert. *Gaffer:* Ben Batzdorff. *Electricians:* Raymond Bilger, Jesse Mather. *Special Effects:* Richard Brownfield. *Assistant Special Effects:* Frank Monroe, Mark Stimpson. *Stunt Coordinator:* Tony Cecere. *Location Manager:* Lisa Shuart. *Location Scout:* Suzanne Benoit. *Production Associate:* Sheri Smith. *Assistant to the Producers:* Barbara Dreyfus. *Bookkeeper:* Karen Locke. *Location Auditor:* Mary P. Zinda. *Assistant Costumer:* Mimi Craven. *Transportation:* Ron Simpson. *Driver:* Mardy Macy. *Set Decorator:* Forrest Chadwick. *Construction Foreman:* Rick Cutler. *Lead Man:* Robert Johnson. *Assistant Prop Master:* Steven Levit. *Assistant Editor:* Margaret Carlton. *Still Photographer:* Carol Westwood. *Dog Wrangler:* Patricia Holland. *Armor:* John Harrington. *Set Design Consultant:* Robb Wilson King. *Production Assistant:* Tim Perovich. *Carpenters:* Michael Norris, Robert Varney. *Extra Labor:* Richard Zink. *Communications:* "Albacore" Joe Addison. *Stunt Players:* Pam Bebermeyer, Clifford Bruce Carson, Shane Dixon, Chris Doyle, Joseph Gilbride, David Goodrich, Kane Hodder, Desiree Ayers Kens, Robert O'King, Rex Pierson, Sharon Shaeffer, Jeff Smolek, Speed Stearns, Cindy Willis. *Post Production Sound:* Gomillion Sound, Inc. *Re-Recording Mixers:* Don MacDougall, Alan Holly, William Gazecki. *Sound Effects:* Anthony Ippolito, Eddie Campbell, David Kulczycki. *Color:* Movielab. *Opticals:* Creative Film Arts. *Insurance:* Bob Jellan/Alber G. Ruben and Company. *Payroll:* Talent Payments, Inc. *Camera Systems:* Clairmont. *Special Thanks to:* Yamaha, Bell Helmets, Malcolm Smith, the Yucca Inn, People of Yucca Valley, Joshua Tree, 29 Palms and Pioneertown, California. Hills Two Corporation, 1984. *Running Time:* 85 minutes. A Thorn EMI/HBO Home Video Release.

> The following film is based on fact. In the mid–1970s, a family of tourists from Cleveland unwisely left the paved highway and drove across the desert on an unmarked dirt road. Soon lost, they wandered onto a vast, deserted bomb range inhabited only by tarantulas, rattlesnakes and a family of cannibals unknown to the civilized world. By nightfall, the innocent vacation had become a brutal battle for survival which left few alive. And for those who did survive, none can forget that far out in the unmapped desert, beyond the towns and roads, the hills still have eyes.
> — Opening scrawl in *The Hills Have Eyes Part II*

SYNOPSIS: It has been eight years since Bobby Carter fought for survival against Papa Jupiter and his family of wild cannibals. Although time has passed, Bobby is still haunted by memories of the desert and the battle that took the life

2. The Feature Films   97

Ruby (Janus Blythe) suffers from amnesia in *The Hills Have Eyes Part II*, until a trip to the desert brings everything back.

of his mother, father and sister. He has tried to put it all behind him with the help of a psychologist, but the doctor is less than sympathetic. He assures Bobby that Jupe and company "were all beatable" and tells him to go thumb his nose at the desert because "the bogeyman's dead." He is pushing Bobby so hard because the young man has a lot at stake today: He has recently invented a revolutionary type of gas fuel for mountain bikes, and he is supposed to show it off to industry pros at a race taking place in the desert. But Bobby cannot bring himself to return to the land where he lost so much of his family. He must fight the urge to warn his team not to go because it is simply too dangerous.

Elsewhere, a man in a pocked mask rides a motorbike up to a beautiful house. He uses a ladder to get inside, and he creeps up on a sleeping blind woman, Cass. She is ready for him, however: He is just her boyfriend Roy, trying to scare her. The young couple make love before driving to Burbank Yamaha. Today is the day they are planning to tests Bobby Carter's super formula at a major dirt bike competition.

A bus soon pulls up at Burbank Yamaha and unloads more people preparing for the trip. Jane and Sue will be going along, as will Harry, Hulk and the team mechanic, Foster. Also present for the ride is lovely young, Rachel. Unfortunately, she has brought bad news about Bobby: He is having a bad day, and has already had one panic attack. Rachel and Roy try to convince Bobby to go to the desert, but he states that he cannot go back, not for any reason. Rachel, Roy and the others board the bus and head out on the highway. Their first stop is a dog "stud" farm where they pick up "The Beast," the dog who survived the first encounter with the wild desert family.

As the group drives out into the desert, Hulk recounts the story of Jupiter and the land where he held sway. The kids on the bus recall the '70s incident and that there was a wild girl named Ruby involved. This comment causes Rachel to recall a repressed memory. In her mind's eye, she sees Mars, Doug, a baby and a rattlesnake. She realizes that she herself is Ruby, the girl who joined civilization after living with Jupiter and his family all her life!

Foster, reading the newspaper, suddenly realizes that today is the start of daylight savings time and the bus is going to be late for the race. Harry suggests a shortcut through the desert. Rachel/Ruby urges her friends not to take a detour onto Furnace Canyon Road, but the group decides they must take the shortcut to get to the competition on time. From a hilltop faraway, the bus is observed by Pluto, who signals to his family members that new prey has arrived.

Rachel/Ruby and the teenagers learn that they are approaching a bomb range. This worries Ruby; she remembers all too well now the location of her old home. The bus stops at a weird welcome sign (spelled "welcum") made out of wood, feathers and bone. This sign proves to Ruby that someone in her family survived the deadly encounter eight years earlier. The teenagers marvel at the sign and the blind Cass smells gasoline. The bus gas tank is leaking and they cannot go much further. The group drives a short distance to a strange old house and mine shaft in hopes of buying some gas from the inhabitants. Inside the house, there is a hodgepodge of stolen furnishings, camping equipment and even a butcher's block filled with dead animals. Ruby realizes it is the home of her wild family. The group of teenagers explore the house, picking up property and playing with it.

Meanwhile, the Beast barks up at a loft. When Roy goes to investigate, he finds only a raccoon. Later, Ruby investigates a large room and is confronted by Pluto. The ex-siblings fight viciously, and Pluto strikes Ruby in the head with a small stick. Pluto runs off and Ruby tells her friends about her real identity. She thinks that her dead brother has returned to life to seek vengeance upon her. Roy and the others are reluctant to believe that Ruby is "the wild child" of Jupiter's clan, but Cass senses the ring of truth in the tale. Meanwhile, Pluto steals a dirt bike out of the bus and drives away.

Furious, Roy and Harry don helmets and racing armor to pursue him. There is a wild chase through the desert until the two city boys encounter devious booby traps laid out by the savage family. While Roy catches up with Pluto, Harry is knocked off his bike by a stretched rope. He hears someone calling out his name and walks into another booby trap. He successfully survives a swinging rock loaded with spikes, only to be killed when a giant boulder is dropped from a hilltop onto his head.

Meanwhile, Pluto warns Roy of another family member called "The Reaper." Roy does not listen and is consequently surprised when "The Reaper" appears on Harry's bike and rescues Pluto. Roy gives chase but is caught up in a giant black net.

Back at the bus, Cass thinks she heard Roy scream but her friends do not believe her. When night falls, Ruby and Huck go out to look for the missing Roy and Harry. Foster and Sue leave the home and enter the bus to have sex. While they make love, Beast guards the bus and Pluto taunts the dog.

Exploring their surroundings, Cass and Jane find a shower inside one of the rooms. Jane takes a shower while Cass continues to explore the butcher's abattoir.

Out in the desert, Ruby and Huck find Roy's motorbike and helmet, which has blood inside it. They realize they are being hunted, and hop on the bike to escape. Ruby falls off the rear of the bike and Hulk is impaled by a giant spear. Pluto taunts Ruby from his hiding place and she runs off. While Ruby faces terror in the desert, Foster and Sue argue after making love. Foster wanders into the shower room and spots Jane nude. Sue sees him ogling Jane and grows angry. After she has run into the desert, Foster drives the bus after her into the darkness. When it finally runs out of gas, he looks for Sue on foot. Instead, he finds Ruby, who orders him back to the bus and safety. As Foster is about to reenter the bus, Pluto kills him with a hatchet and drags him under the vehicle.

Cass searches the strange house and finds that the refrigerator door leads to a mine shaft! In another part of the house, Jane dries off and looks for Cass. She opens a giant wardrobe and Foster's body, hatchet planted in his head, falls out. Terrified, Jane runs right into the arms of the giant monster called "The Reaper." This fat, hairy goliath with a bulging forehead crushes Jane in his arms and then proceeds to kill Sue, slicing her throat with a machete.

Outside the house, Pluto and Ruby fight it out. Pluto reveals to his sister that after Papa Jupe died, his older brother "Reaper" took over the family. He patched Pluto's wounds up and now the pair kills anyone who wanders into the hills and they throw the bodies down mine shafts. That is the unpleasant fate that awaits Ruby until the Beast arrives and attacks his nemesis from eight years earlier. After a chase through the hills, the Beast pushes Pluto off a cliff, sending the crazed savage plummeting to his death. While the Beast finishes off Pluto, Ruby is pursued by the Reaper. He attacks her and knocks her unconscious with Hulk's corpse.

Beast discovers Roy unconscious and awakens him. Together, the two search for Cass. Unfortunately, Reaper has also turned his attention to the blind girl. Cass realizes she is being stalked and climbs into a loft. There she discovers Roy's helmet, on which she inscribed a message of love in Braille. When Reaper jumps down through the roof, Cass runs for her life and finds Jane's corpse. Screaming in terror, Cass hides in the mine shaft and finds a grisly graveyard. Hulk, Sue, a dog and other bodies are hanging on meathooks or strewn about on the ground.

Cass smashes a large bottle of toxic chemicals on Reaper's head and then climbs a rope out of the mine shaft. Reaper pursues but Roy pulls Cass out of the vertical passageway. He then cuts the rope so Reaper cannot climb up after them. Reaper uses another exit and attacks, but Roy and Cass have prepared for him.

Using Bobby's gas formula, they encircle Reaper with flames. Reaper retreats into the bus only to find that it contains the drum of high-powered gasoline. Roy and Cass escape as the bus explodes. On fire, Reaper dashes from the explosion and plunges into the open mine shaft. With Reaper finally gone, Roy, Cass and the Beast set off across the desert together, hoping to find help.

COMMENTARY: It seems almost unfair to review *The Hills Have Eyes Part II* since it was assembled and distributed without Craven's input or consent. Since he was unable to finish principal photography on the motion picture before it was slapped together and marketed, one can hardly fault the director for the film's low quality. Although *The Hills Have Eyes Part II* bears Craven's name, it is by no means representative of his film portfolio. It is the weakest film intrepid viewers will find with his name attached to it, and a sad sequel to a film that is a masterpiece of modern horror.

The Hills Have Eyes Part II opens promisingly with sounds of horror from the first film played over the same pan of the desert which began the first *Hills*. If one listens closely, Brenda shouting "Don't leave me," Doug wondering "Why?" and Papa Jupe threatening to eat the heart of Bob's "stinking memory" are audible on the soundtrack ... but are distorted to sound like cries from a terrible nightmare. The film then finds Bobby Carter recounting the horror in the desert to his therapist. Both performers are seen in tight closeups and there is an intensity and urgency to the scene. So far so good, but then the film shifts immediately into extended "flashbacks," fully excerpted scenes from Craven's first tale of wasteland terror.

From there, the film never recovers. There are four flashbacks in the short film, one told from the dog's perspective(!), and each goes on for several minutes, replaying key events from *The Hills Have Eyes*. Though these are all good scenes, they slow the sequel down. The insertion of lengthy flashbacks interrupt the action and impede the audience's association with and identification of the new characters.

Furthermore, the inclusion of actor Robert Houston as Bobby Carter is somewhat of a mystery, since his character plays a role of virtually no importance in *The Hills Have Eyes Part II*. He opens the film, and it is nice to see a familiar face, but then his therapist encourages him to go to the desert and work out his fears. Theoretically, Carter should have to face and conquer his anguish. But Bobby does not accompany the main characters into the desert, and this plot strand is nothing but a dead end. After 15 short minutes, Bobby and Houston are gone from the picture, never to return. All along, one expects a last-minute rescue from him ... or at least an assertion of some kind that he has overcome his fears.

Pluto stalks new prey in Craven's ill-fated sequel to *The Hills Have Eyes*.

In its central plot, *The Hills Have Eyes Part II* plays as a repetition of the first film but it is lacking in much of the style and verve that made the original so memorable. The teenagers are the heart of the film, and somewhat likable, but no more developed than Jason's innumerable victims in any *Friday the 13th* film. The focus on stereotypical teenagers instead of a believable family also lends a rather clichéd feeling to the goings-on. One teenager is sarcastic, two are black, one is cocky and another is blind. Other than that, they are not differentiated or individualized, and the two-dimensional characters immediately deposit the sequel in a lower stratosphere of quality. Years later, Craven would make fun of these kinds of characters and films in *Scream* (1996).

There are other problems as well. One of the things that made *The Hills Have Eyes* so frightening was the fact that every frame of the film took place in the desert. There was no relief from that environment, just as the Carters had no relief from their terrifying situation. Craven captured the danger of the desert beautifully, and his film was as much about the landscape as it was about the interesting characters. Conversely, *The Hills Have Eyes Part II* opens in modern suburbia and lingers there before finding the desert. It seems a tactical error to start the film outside the "world" of the desert, especially since these early scenes build characters in rudimentary fashion.

The film also re-works all the clichés of the stalker cycle, which the original *The Hills Have Eyes* preceded by more than a year. There are typical "stalking" point-of-view subjective shots, practical jokes played by teens pretending to be the "real" killer, and even a hackneyed scene in which the survivor, typically a woman, uncovers the den of the villain and finds the corpses of all her friends. As far as this "required" scene goes, it is hard to top *Halloween*, in which Jamie Lee Curtis found the corpse of her friend Annie stretched out on a bed with a headstone over the pillow and jack-o'-lanterns grinning devilishly on either side. *Hills 2*'s riff on the convention is to have a blind Cass feel her way through the human detritus, *à la Wait Until Dark*. It's a scary moment but not enough to save the film.

There are also some unbelievable plot developments in *The Hills Have Eyes Part II*. Early on, Roy is caught in a net and captured by the Reaper and Pluto. He disappears from the film for a stretch, but miraculously re-emerges unharmed at the climax. It is not at all likely that these desert scavengers would spare the boy's life, so this is hard to swallow. Equally implausible is the revelation that Reaper is Papa Jupe's big brother. Grandpa Fred revealed the entire story of Jupe and his family in *The Hills Have Eyes* and made no mention of Reaper, who according to this sequel was his first son! Fred had no reason to lie in *The Hills Have Eyes*, so what are audiences to make of the sudden appearance of a heretofore unknown brother? It is an explanation that flies in the face of the original film. This kind of sequel problem is, again, the kind of thing Craven makes fun of in *Scream 2* (1997).

The Hills Have Eyes Part II seems put together in haphazard fashion, indicating that Craven had no hand in post-production. Early in the story, for instance, Cass calls loudly to "Ruby." Unfortunately, at that juncture in the plot the character is still being referred to as "Rachel." Cass and the other teens are not yet aware of her true identity as Ruby, the sister of the wild family! The line was probably dubbed in post-production and no one caught the gaffe.

The worst misfire in the film, however, is Ruby's fate. The last the viewer sees of her, she has hit her head against a rock and been knocked unconscious. She is obviously not dead, but her fate is left completely unresolved when the end credits roll ... a sure sign that the film was not complete. An artist with Craven's skill would never end a film so clumsily. Indeed, both *The Last House on the Left* and *The Hills Have Eyes* end quite decisively. The moment the pertinent action is complete, the films freeze-frame and fade to credits. The confusing and ambivalent conclusion of *The Hills Have Eyes Part II* is an anomaly.

The Hills Have Eyes Part II does have some interesting parallels to the first film that make it worth a single watching. Aboard the bus, Ruby refers to "human French fries," harkening back to Brenda's jokes in the first film. Foster comments on "pythons" while exploring Pluto's house, alluding to Big Bob's joke about snakes to wife Ethel. The "python" reference also reveals Craven's continuing obsession with snakes, which have been seen in or talked about in every Craven film since the first *Hills*. Finally, the primary vehicle of the protagonists is destroyed in the finale of each film, and Pluto is defeated by Beast in both original and sequel. Unfortunately, these elements all seem a bit tired the second time around. Sequels are notoriously dicey because they require loyalty to original product and innovation. *The Hills Have Eyes Part II* has a tough time with that mixture.

Thematically, *The Hills Have Eyes Part II* has little to offer. At one point, one of the teenagers remarks about "alienation from planetary roots caused by too much urbanization," but that is a thread left mostly unexplored. Also, the teens march into the Pluto home as if they own the place. They try on garments, take showers and generally act as if everything is theirs. This selfish attitude could have made for an interesting subtext about teen greed/apathy, but again it is only hinted at and not exploited.

Despite its many shortcomings, *The Hills Have Eyes Part II* features some trademark Wes Craven moments. The villains are defeated by resourceful heroes who have out-thought them and rigged clever booby traps. Heroes who lure villains into a trap are featured in *The Last House on the Left* (the Collingwoods and the notorious castration scene), *The Hills Have Eyes* (the Carters use their dead mother as bait), *A Nightmare on Elm Street* (with Nancy's research and practice on personal self-defense), *Shocker* (when Parker traps Pinker with a TV remote control) and *People Under the Stairs* (with Fool rigging a mausoleum of explosives). In *The Hills Have Eyes Part II*, Cass and Roy surround Reaper within a ring of fire and lure him into the van where explosive "super-fuel" is ignited.

With all these incidents of heroes striking back, Craven films succinctly make the point that survival requires more than good luck or a blending of fortunate circumstances. The director believes that protagonists must play an active role in their victory. They must be clever, resourceful and sturdy enough to execute their plans. This separates him from many other horror directors, such as John Carpenter. Consider *Halloween* and Laurie Strode (Jamie Lee Curtis). She survives her first encounter with Michael Myers not because of any good planning (in fact she traps herself in a closet) but because Dr. Loomis arrives to shoot the serial killer. Similarly, in *The Fog*, Adrienne Barbeau is saved only because the rampaging ghouls have claimed the requisite six victims, not because of her own resourcefulness. In this sense, Craven is unabashedly pro-humanist. In his eyes, human beings can be clever and resourceful, and in a crisis they can be victorious if only they make use of their better qualities.

The Hills Have Eyes Part II is at its most exciting and effective during the finale. Tamara Stafford is credible as the blind Cass, and of all the characters she is the most developed. When she is put in jeopardy and stalked by the Reaper, the film finally comes to life. The charnel house in the mine shaft is appropriately disgusting with severed limbs and hanging corpses everywhere. The leadup to the fiery battle royale is also satisfying, if less intense than the action of *Deadly Blessing* or *The Hills Have Eyes*.

It is also nice to see Michael Berryman back in action as Pluto, even if his effectiveness is somewhat dimmed because viewers are now familiar with him. One of the interesting things about Craven is that he prefers to keep his villains human instead of invincible. The villains of *The People Under the Stairs*, *The Last House on the Left*, *The Hills Have Eyes*, *The Serpent and the Rainbow*, *Scream*, *Scream 2* and even *Shocker* and *A Nightmare on Elm Street* have vulnerabilities that can be exploited by the protagonists. That approach is a commendable one, but it works against the scenario in *The Hills Have Eyes Part II*. The horror in the first film came about because the desert family was depicted as a wild bunch of barbarians. They developed individual personalities as the film went on, but they remained a vivid personification of man's savagery. By the time of *The Hills Have Eyes Part II*, Pluto is human and familiar enough that he does not inspire dread or anxiety. Ruby fends him off twice in the film, seriously diminishing his physical presence. Much of the film simply does not work because the two bad guys are outnumbered by a squad of strapping teenage boys in their imposing, sleeveless muscle shirts. It is only through their total incompetence that the teens are killed. They should have been able to mount a defense against an enemy of lesser number.

Of course, the same ratio works in the *Friday the 13th* films but the villain there is superpowered and indestructible. A whole platoon of marines could go up against Jason at Camp Crystal Lake and still be destroyed. Since the villains of *The Hills Have Eyes Part II* are human and capable of being injured, the failure of the protagonists to succeed for so long leads one to the inescapable conclusion that the majority of the teens, except the resourceful Cass, are idiots.

It is a shame that *The Hills Have Eyes Part II* is such an unremarkable picture because the *Hills* franchise could have dynamite potential. At one point in the late 1980s, Craven contemplated doing an outer space version of the material written by Bruce Wagner, and that sounds like a terrific idea. Outer space, like the desert, is a forbidding terrain and it would make a great setting for a futuristic battle between "haves" and "have nots." Unfortunately, the film has never been made.

In the ongoing horror line up of Wes Craven, *The Hills Have Eyes Part II* does have some distinctions. Penny Johnson, who played Sue in this sequel, worked with Craven again in the 1990 telefilm *Night Vision* and later played Capt. Sisko's girlfriend Casidy Yates in *Star Trek: Deep Space Nine*. *Hills II* stuntman Kane Hodder went on to become a horror icon as Jason Voorhees in the later *Friday the 13th* pictures and he guest-starred in *Wes Craven Presents Wishmaster*. Kevin Blair, the intrepid Roy in this Craven follow-up, would later have his own close encounter with Jason and Hodder in 1988's *Friday the 13th Part VII: The New Blood*.

A Nightmare on Elm Street (1984)

Wes Craven uses many of the conventional tricks of the trade — dark corridors, eerie staircases, long shadows and special effects galore — but he wields them with a verve that makes all those Stephen King movies seem very second-rate. Craven has said that he wanted to prove that horror needn't be synonymous with misogyny, and I think he's succeeded.— Francis Wheen (*The New Statesman*, September 6, 1985)

Gore and sex are kept to a minimum. Imaginative ideas, cinematography and physical special effects are maximized. The teenagers are well-cast. John Saxon is sympathetic. Only Ronee Blakeley's disabled performance, an accumulation of corny lines, and a very iffy double-ending mar a fast, pleasant horror-thriller for a larger mass audience than the genre usually allows.— Roy Frumkes (*Films in Review*, February 1985, page 209)

Craven is something of a generational turncoat. While he is 35, all of his adult characters have the intelligence and courage of cantaloupes. ...Langenkamp is quite impressive; if this were a different movie, her acting ability would probably attract some attention.— Ralph Novak (*People Weekly*, May 27, 1985)

As skillful as it is sickening. Written and directed by maestro of ultragore Wes Craven, it has considerable style, some good performances and clever special effects.— Kevin Thomas (*The Los Angeles Times*, November 10, 1984)

Though not *The Hills Have Eyes* by a long shot, *Nightmare* is one of Craven's better splatter efforts. It boasts an interesting concept (the seamless interweaving of dream states and waking states) plus a number of truly spectacular splatter set pieces.— John McCarty, *The Official Splatter Movie Guide* (St. Martin's Press, 1989, page 95)

CAST: John Saxon (Lt. Donald Thompson); Ronee Blakeley (Marge Thompson); Heather Langenkamp (Nancy Thompson); Amanda Wyss (Tina Gray); Nick Corri (Rod Lane); Johnny Depp (Glen Lantz); Robert Englund (Freddy Krueger); Charles Fleischer (Dr. King); Joseph Whipp (Sgt. Parker); Lin Shaye (The Teacher); Joe Unger (Sgt. Garcia); Mimi Meyer-Craven (Nurse); Jack Shea (Minister); Ed Call (Mr. Lantz); Sandy Lipton (Mrs. Lantz); Dave Andrews (Foreman); Jeffrey Levine (Coroner); Donna Woodrum (Tina's Mom); Shashawnee Hall (Cop #1); Carol Pritikin (Cop #2); Brian Reise (Cop #3); Jason Adams (Surfer #1); Don Hannah (Surfer #2); Leslie Hoffman (Hall Guard); Paul Grenier (Tina's Mom's Boyfriend).

CREDITS: A New Line Cinema Corporation Release. Media Home Entertainment and Smart Egg Presentation of a Robert Shaye Production. *Casting:* Annette Benson. *Director of Photography:* Jacques Haitkin. *Production Designer:* Greg Funseca. *Special Mechanical Effects Designer:* Jim Doyle, Theatrical Engines. *Associate Producer:* John Burrows. *Film Editor:* Rick Shaine. *Music:* Charles Bernstein. *Co-Producer:* Sara Risher. *Executive Producers:* Stanley Dudelson, Joseph Wolf. *Producer:* Robert Shaye. *Director:* Wes Craven. *Production Manager:* John Burrows. *Production Supervisor:* Amy Rabins. *Assistant Production Manager:* Rachel Talalay. *Special Effects Makeup:* David Miller. *Co-Editor:* Pat McMahon. *Production Executive:* Stephen Abramson. *Legal Consultant:* Benjamin Zinkin. *First Assistant Director:* Nick Batchelor. *Script Supervisor:* Kathy Weygard. *First Assistant Camera:* Ann Coffey. *Second Assistant Camera:* Tom Venghele. *Still Photographer:* Joyce Rudolph. *Production Coordinator:* Lisa C. Cook. *Location Manager:* Craig Pointes. *Assistant Accountant:* Sheridan Liu. *Gaffer:* Scott Buttfield. *Electricians:* Zen Electric. *Best Boy Electrical:* Rowdy Herrington. *Second Unit Gaffer:* Steve Crawford. *Electrician:* Toni Semple. *Grip Production Services:* Key Grip Associates. *Best Boy Grip:* Joseph Adolph. *Grips:* Warren Kroeger, Nelson Elwell. *Second Unit Key Grip:* Cindy Logerstrom. *Set Decorator:* Ann Huntley. *Set Dresser:* Dorree Cooper. *Art Department Assistant:* Barbara Metzenbaum, Don Diers. *Swing Gang:* Gavin McCune, Michael E. Listorti. *Construction Coordinator:* John Reinhart. *Set Carpenter:* Mix. *Prop Master:* John Stadelman. *Assistant Property Masters:* Kara Lindstrom, Timaree McCormick. *Costume Designer:* Dana Lyman. *Costume Supervisor:* Lisa Jensen. *Costumer:* Terence McCorry. *Makeup:* Kathy Logan. *Hair:* Ramona. *Sound Mixer:* James LaRue. *Boom Operator:* Greg Nave. *Set Production Assistant:* David Householter. *Transportation Coordinator:* Chuck Clarke. *Transportation Captain:* Brian Delahunty. *Production Assistants:* Steve McAfee, Steve Harris, Steve Cassling, Wally Uchida. *Assistant to Producers:* Anita Lucciani. *Second Assistant Director:* Peter C. Graupner. *Craft Services:* Lillian Fuenters. *Animal Wrangler:* Jim Picciolo. *Casting Assistant:* Lauren Roman. *Animals Provided by* The Animal Consultants. *Storyboard Artist:* Bill Kroyler. *Second Unit Camera:* Henning Schellerup. *Assistant Editor:* Valerie Schwartz. *Apprentice Editors:* Alison Paul, James Flatto. *Editorial Assistant, L.A.:* Kevin Krasny.

Supervising Sound Editor: Jess Soraci, Magnofex. *Sound Editor:* Albert Nahmias. *Assistant Sound Editor:* Abe Nejad. *Looping Editor:* Karen I. Stern. *Re-Recording Mixer:* Jack Cooley. *Re-Recording:* Magno Sound. *Grip and Electronic Equipment:* Leonetti Cine Rentals. *"Nightmare" Performed by* 213. *"Nightmare" Written and produced by* Martin Kent, Steve Karshner, Michael Schurig. *Special Thanks to* Sean Cunningham, Sam Raimi, Jack Sholder. *Color:* Deluxe. *Prints:* Precision. *Production Sound:* Glenn Glenn Sound. *Looping-ADR:* Gomillion Sound, Inc. *Opticals:* Cinema Research, Cinopticals and the Optical House, New York. *Stunt Coordinator:* Tony Cecere. *Makeup Effects Assistant:* Mark Wilson. *Titles Designed by:* Dan Perri. *Stuntpersons:* Jeff Habberstad, Leslie Hoffman, Paul Shaver, Kerrie Cullen, Maggie Foehner, Bruce Carson, Sandy Wilson, Cynthia Brannon, Cindy Wills, Jim Stearns, Don Pike, Tany Lee Russel, Larry Phillips, Tony Cecere, Christina Johnson, Christina Rideout. *Special Effects Assistants:* Lou Carlucci, Larry Lapointe, Charles Belardinelli, Tassilo Baur, Peter Kelly, Christina Rideout, James Upham, Jim Rynning. The Elm Street Venture. *Running time:* 91 minutes. *MPAA Rating:* R

> One, two, Freddy's coming for you.
> Three, four, better lock your door.
> Five, six, grab your crucifix.
> Seven, eight, gonna stay up late.
> Nine, ten, never sleep again.
> —An old jump-rope song sung on Elm Street.

SYNOPSIS: A grizzled, horribly burned man wearing a red and green sweater moves to his work bench and assembles a devastating weapon. He has welded long knives to metal fingertips and then attached them to a glove. He adorns the glove proudly and prepares to use it on his first victim...

Tina Gray finds herself inside a dank basement with water dripping from the ceiling. As she wanders the subterranean labyrinth, she hears a guttural voice whispering her name. A lamb crosses her path sadly, and Tina wanders into a hot boiler room. She pulls a ratty curtain aside and finds herself near the bedroom of the man pursuing her. He finally shows himself, scraping his metal finger-knives across a boiling pipe. Tina runs for her life, but she cannot seem to make headway. Finally, she ducks into an alcove and hides. She hears the sounds of babies crying and animal shrieks, and then there is silence. Suddenly, the evil man pops up behind her and slashes at her with his dangerous glove...

Tina suddenly awakens to find that she has been experiencing a horrible nightmare. The man, the boiler room and the knives were just a dream — or were they? When Tina looks down at her nightgown, it is cut in four vertical slashes, as if the bogeyman's knives had actually struck her. Tina clutches her crucifix tightly and explains to her mother that she had a nightmare. When her mother sees Tina's ripped garment, she comments that Tina has to trim her nails or stop having dreams like that!

The next day at school, Tina tells friends Nancy Thompson, Glen Lantz and Rod Lane about her vivid nightmare. Strangely, Nancy had a real bad dream last night too. Glen will not admit it, but Nancy and Tina suspect that he may also have had a nightmare. Tina suggests that this rash of nightmares might be due to the approach of a big earthquake: "Things get really weird just before," she tells Nancy. Nancy is not convinced, and both she and Glen agree to stay over at Tina's house that night when the worried girl learns that her mother is going to Las Vegas.

Night falls and Glen, Nancy and Tina enjoy their sleepover. Tina talks obsessively about her nightmare and goes into detail about the man who pursued her. She mentions his finger-knives and this strikes a chord with Nancy — she dreamed of the same man. Glen is curious, too, because it seems they have all imagined the same killer: a man in a ratty sweater who wears a beat-up fedora. The teens become increasingly alarmed by this bizarre coincidence and then jump with fright when they hear a scratching sound outside. They investigate, and are startled by Rod, Tina's boyfriend.

Tina and Rod retreat to her mother's bedroom, lock the door and make love loudly all night. After the sex is over, Rod admits that he has also been having nightmares of the same bogeyman.

In another bedroom, Nancy has trouble falling asleep. As she slumbers, a crucifix pops off the wall behind her and lands on the sheets. Later in the night, Tina hears someone bouncing pebbles off her bedroom window. It is the man from her nightmares. She walks downstairs and confronts him outside. She walks down a long dark alley and the nightmare man pursues her, his arms elongated. Tina screams and runs back to her house, but the man catches her on the porch. They wrestle as he attempts to slash her with his knives.

Rod awakes to find Tina writhing in bed. He pulls away the covers to see that she is locked in mortal combat with an invisible foe. It pulls up her nightgown and slashes at her stomach, causing rivers of blood to spurt out of her. Then the invisible assailant picks Tina up and drags her across the ceiling. She screams and begs for help while Rod watches. She falls to the bed and splatters blood all over the room. Rod screams in horror and Nancy and Glen break into the room. They see Tina, a bloody mess, and watch Rod as he escapes through a window.

At the police station, Lt. Donald Thompson, Nancy's father, questions Nancy and her mother Marge. He blames Marge for letting Nancy shack up with a group of teenagers, but the real issue is Rod Lane. Lt. Thompson believes Rod killed Tina and he has his men combing the streets for him.

The next morning, the murder is on the television news. As Nancy walks to school, she is grabbed by Rod and dragged into the bushes. Rod says that he did not kill Tina, but before the situation can go any further, Lt. Thompson and the police arrive to capture Rod. Nancy's own father used her as bait to catch the killer! Rod is hauled away to jail and Nancy proceeds to school.

Nancy's English class is studying Shakespeare, and as one of the students reads a famous speech from *Julius Caesar*, Nancy grows groggy. When she looks out into the hallway, Nancy sees Tina standing inside a bloody body bag. Nancy follows a trail of blood down a long corridor. In the distance, an invisible hand drags Tina away. Nancy follows and runs into a hall monitor, who turns into the nightmare man complete with finger-knives. Nancy continues to pursue Tina until she has arrived in a boiler room. The nightmare man follows Nancy now. Nancy runs for her life, but arrives in a dead end. The monster comes in close, his glove ready to strike, when Nancy accidentally hits a boiling pipe with her arm. The sudden pain awakens her just as the killer is about to attack, and she is back in the classroom. She screams bloody murder, but realizes it was all a dream. Nancy leaves school confused and notices that her arm is burned where she touched the pipe in her dream. What she experiences in her dream is affecting her reality.

When Nancy visits Rod in jail, he says that he saw someone cut her as he watched and that the cuts just "happened all at once." When Rod describes his own nightmares, matching those of Tina, Glen and Nancy, Nancy realizes the nightmare man killed Tina and is coming after her. She runs home and tries to relax. She takes a bath and falls asleep in the tub. As she sleeps, the gloved hand of the monster reaches up between her legs. Mrs. Thompson wakes Nancy up, saving her life, and warns her not to fall asleep in the tub. Nancy ignores the warning and goes back to sleep. Suddenly, she is pulled underwater by her nemesis. She wakes up

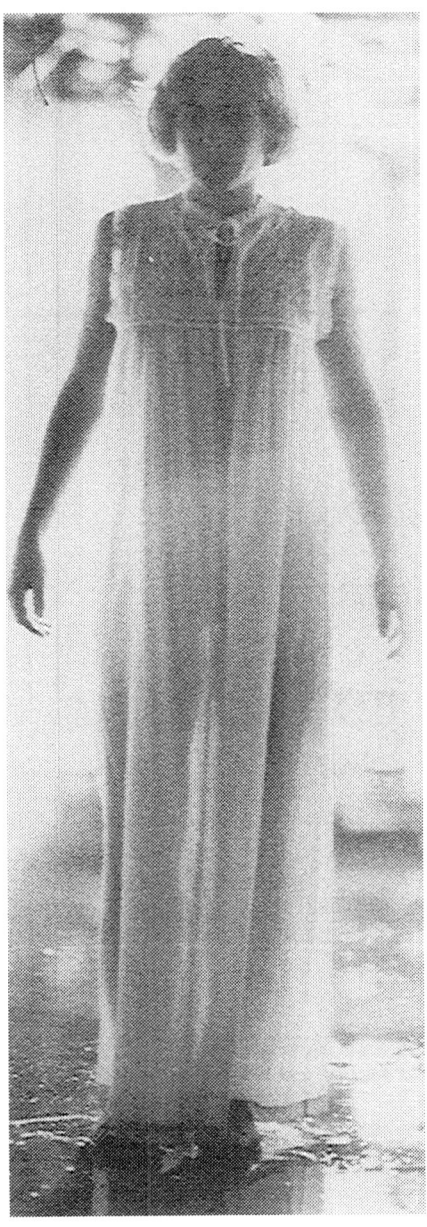

The nightmare is just beginning for Tina (Amanda Wyss) in the spellbinding opening of *A Nightmare on Elm Street.*

In a shocking sequence, from *A Nightmare on Elm Street*, Tina is trapped by an invisible Freddy and dragged across the ceiling.

and survives this attack. Realizing she cannot sleep, she downs several Stay Awake pills and goes to her room.

Nancy turns on the television and watches *The Evil Dead*. After a few minutes, she turns off the TV and listens to a noise outside her window. Glen has climbed up the trellis, and he lets himself in through the window. He is worried about Nancy, and with good reason: She has not slept in days and is becoming obsessed with the notion of a killer who stalks her in her dreams. Nancy decides to conduct an experiment. She wants Glen to stay awake and watch her while she tries to find the bogeyman...

Nancy leaves her house, walks to the police station and sees the nightmare man hovering close to Rod. She tries to warn him, and the nightmare man comes after her. Nancy is confronted with Tina again, but this time snakes roll out of Tina's dead mouth. Nancy screams in horror and runs for home with the nightmare man in hot pursuit. She runs inside and up the stairs, but her feet become caught in the stairs, which have turned to glue. She makes it to her room, the monster in pursuit.

Finally, she wakes up. Nancy is furious with Glenn because he has fallen asleep and was not watching over her while she dozed! Still, she now knows where the killer will strike next. Nancy and Glen head for the police station to save Rod's life. When they get there it is too late: He has been hanged by his bedsheet. Lt. Thompson thinks Rod committed suicide but Nancy knows better.

After Rod's funeral, Marge Thompson takes her daughter to the Katja Institute for the Study of Sleep Disorders. There, Dr. King agrees to test Nancy. She is wired up and put to sleep while King and Marge monitor her EEG from an observation room. Marge tells the doctor that Nancy thinks her dreams are real, and asks what dreams are. The doctor's response is terrifying. He says that dreams are mysteries, "hocus pocus," and that nobody really knows where they originate, or even why people dream at all. The doctor continues to monitor Nancy and all signs are normal. She slips into REM sleep and typical dream parameters. Dr. King indicates that a nightmare would register on the EEG as a five or six point spike.

Nancy convulses and the EEG spikes 15 points and higher. Dr. King rushes to awaken her and finds that Nancy's hair has gone mysteriously gray. Even more disturbing, her arm is cut ... as if by four razors. And she has brought something out of her nightmare too: the killer's beat-up hat!

Days later, Nancy still has not slept. She tells her mom that the killer is after her in her dreams, and thanks to his hat she knows his name: Fred Krueger. Her mother assures her that Fred Krueger is dead, but Nancy still will not sleep. She meets with Glen and they talk about the dream skills of the Balinese people. They have a system of dreaming where they can turn nightmares into beautiful visions. Nancy asks Glen what happens when a person sees a monster in a dream. Glen replies that the dreamer should turn her back on the monster, take away its energy, and it will disappear. If the dreamer does not do so, he or she will never wake up. This knowledge empowers Nancy, as does the book she has just purchased: *Booby Traps and Improvised Anti-Personnel Devices*. She tells Glen that she is "into survival."

Nancy returns home and discovers that her mother has installed bars on the doors and windows. Inside, Marge leads Nancy down to the cellar and the furnace where she tells Nancy the truth about Fred Krueger. He was a child murderer, a man who killed 20 kids in the neighborhood. He was finally caught but

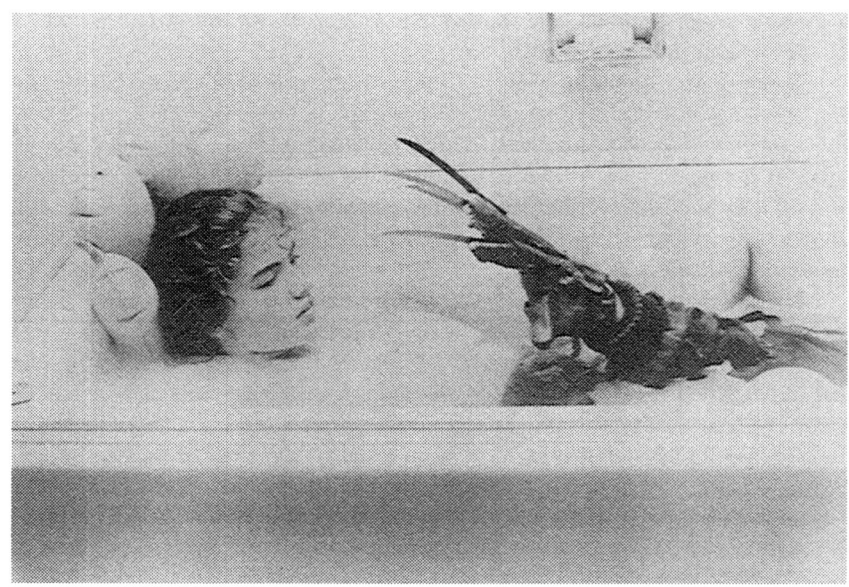

A Nightmare on Elm Street: Echoing his "snake in the bathtub" sequence from *Deadly Blessing*, Craven threatened a bathing Nancy Thompson (Heather Langenkamp) with another serpent from hell: Freddy Kruger.

he escaped justice on a technicality. The Elm Street parents were outraged and they tracked him down to the boiler room where he abused the children. They poured gasoline all over the place and burned it to the ground. Freddy was killed in the fire. Marge has kept his finger-knives stored inside her furnace. She shows the knives to Nancy, who is horrified. Realizing that Freddy is killing children for the sins of their parents, Nancy and Glen formulate a plan to bring Freddy out of the dream world and into reality, much as she brought his hat with her back to "real life." Unfortunately, Glen's parents intervene. They forbid Glen to see Nancy, who they think has gone crazy. Nancy tries to call Glen but his parents intercept her calls. Nancy tries one more time and Freddy's tongue stretches out of the telephone and licks her face. "I'm your boyfriend now," Freddy tells Nancy.

It is too late for Glen. He falls asleep and is sucked down into his bed by Freddy Krueger. His body is ripped apart and spit up at the ceiling in a torrent of blood. Nancy mourns as the authorities arrive. Nancy rings Glen's house again, this time to talk to her father Lt. Thompson. She tells him that she knows where the killer is and that she is going to get him. All he has to do is be there to capture him in 15 minutes. Thompson promises to be there, but he is just humoring Nancy.

Nancy prepares for the final conflict with Freddy Krueger. She rigs her house with booby traps, including a trip-wire to an explosive lightbulb and a rigged-up sledgehammer. Then she sets her watch alarm and forces herself to sleep. She has ten minutes to find Freddy in her dreams. At the end of that time, she must pull him into reality so her father can capture him. Once again, Nancy slips into the dream world and finds herself in Freddy's boiler room. She finds Glen's bloody headphones and realizes that Krueger not only kills people in reality, he torments their souls for eternity. Nancy meets up with Freddy and they wrestle. With only seconds left before her alarm goes off, she holds onto the beast feverishly. Nancy wakes up and ... nothing. She finds herself alone in her room. Nancy wonders if she really has gone crazy.

Freddy pops up from under the bed and pursues his prey. Nancy smashes a coffee pot on his head and leads him through the booby traps. The sledgehammer pummels him in the gut, and he falls over the trip wire and is caught in an explosion. Then, he chases Nancy into the cellar where she dumps gasoline on him and lights him on fire. She runs back upstairs and locks him in the basement. She then calls across the street to her father, begging him to help her. Thompson finally arrives and wonders what has happened. Nancy leads him to the basement, but the lock is shattered and there are fiery footprints leading upstairs. Thompson and Nancy follow the trail and find Krueger, still on fire, choking the life out of Nancy's mother. Then Marge's corpse and Freddy both vanish through the bed into another dimension. Thompson tells Nancy it is over and comforts her. He leaves her alone in the bedroom to grieve for her mother, but Nancy knows she is not alone.

Freddy cuts his way out of the mattress and Nancy knows what she must do. She turns her back on Krueger and takes away his energy. She demands the return of her mother and friends and says that Freddy will no longer benefit from her strength. Without Nancy's belief, Freddy crumbles to dust and disappears. Nancy opens the bedroom door and...

...finds herself and her mother on the front porch. It is a beautiful, sunny day. A convertible pulls up to the house. Inside are Glen, Rod and Tina, all alive and well. Nancy joins them in the car and waves goodbye to her mother. Suddenly, the car roof pops up ... it is the color of Freddy's sweater! The windows roll up and the doors lock. Out of control, the car drives on. Nancy looks back and sees a gloved hand reach through her front door and pull her mother away.

Further down the street, a group of children sing an old jump rope song about Freddy Krueger: "One, two, Freddy's coming for you..."

COMMENTARY: *A Nightmare on Elm Street* is recognized today as a classic of the horror genre, and for good reason. From the Freudian opening dream sequence in a boiler room to the battle royale between a determined teen and the monstrous Freddy Krueger, *Elm Street* is virtuoso filmmaking. The cinematic techniques utilized throughout powerfully propel the drama, but *A Nightmare on Elm Street* reaches greatness not just through technique and special effects, but through its characterizations and provocative theme.

A Nightmare on Elm Street's plot unfolds rapidly. The villain, Fred Krueger, is revealed in the opening shot as he builds his weapon, the glove with razor blades. Within five minutes, clever dialogue and pointed glances have indicated that all four of the central teens (Tina, Nancy, Glenn and Rod) are experiencing nightmares. Within ten minutes, it is established that the hunted teens are dreaming of the same monstrous man. And, in less than 20 minutes, Tina has been attacked and savagely murdered. The threat has been established quickly and the audience is hooked. Timing and pace are so important in horror films because too much exposition diffuses the terror and too little characterization prevents the audience from investing in the concerns of the protagonists. Except perhaps for *Scream*, Craven has never created a better-paced film than *A Nightmare on Elm Street*. There is not a wasted shot throughout.

Craven cunningly deploys a gaggle of cinematic techniques in *A Nightmare on Elm Street*. As is typical of a Craven movie, film cutting and editing are the artist's primary weapons. Accordingly, Tina's shocking murder is artfully spliced together from two deliberately contrasting perspectives. The audience sees first what Tina experiences as Freddy appears under the bed covers with her and attacks ferociously. Importantly, the other perspective in the scene is Rod's. Since he is awake, Rod sees no "real" bogeyman, just invisible knives slicing into his screaming girlfriend and throwing her violently across the room. The divergent perspectives of victim and eyewitness make it clear to viewers that in this film dreams *do* have a deadly impact on reality.

Unlike *Carrie* (1976), in which the final "scare" sequence is just a dream that Amy Irving survives, dreams in *A Nightmare on Elm Street* are fully incorporated into the plot. Dreams cannot simply be forgotten once a character has awakened; they are a continual source of dismay and terror that can actually result in death. In combination with the clever editing, a spinning bedroom, a stuntwoman suspended on wires and gallons of stage blood also make this death scene something of a horror film landmark. Until Craven's use here, the "spinning room" technique was a Hollywood gimmick seen mostly in musicals with Gene Kelly, Fred Astaire or the like merrily dancing their way up walls and onto the ceiling. It was adapted to horror first in Tobe Hooper's *Poltergeist*, but to a much lesser degree than in *A Nightmare on Elm Street*. Craven was the first director to place *two* people in a rotating cubicle on *different* planes, and thus the first artist to really sell the illusion that one person has defied gravity and been pulled into a supernatural vortex which breaks the laws of physics. Better than anything else, this nightmare sequence sells the terror and danger of Freddy Krueger.

"Rubber reality" is the phrase most often mentioned to describe Craven's stunning transitions from reality to dream, and a thrilling and novel aspect of *A Nightmare on Elm Street* is the ease with which characters glide from one plane of existence to the other without realizing it. There is no warning of this transition, and the audience does not "see" Tina or Nancy actually falling asleep in the early scenes. The film's structure therefore makes ample room for the unexpected. The final twist is a clever reversal/transition. The audience has not truly witnessed characters stepping in and out of their various dreamscapes, but a film which is itself a single dream of the protagonist, Nancy. The "is-this-all-a-dream-or-not?" format is a challenging one that Craven uses extremely well.

Although Don Coscarelli's *Phantasm* (1979) also attempted to walk the tightrope between dreams and reality, it was not nearly so adept in defining the rules of the game. Why did the Tall Man (Angus Scrimm) exist in Mike's dreams? What was his purpose in dwelling there? Why was Mike worthy of special attention? Although *Phantasm* is a wonderful ride and an excellent horror film, it unfolds with little rhyme or reason. Such is not the case in *A Nightmare on Elm Street*, where it is established that Krueger is a supernatural entity crossing over into dreams for the express purpose of revenge. Even more dramatically, the film suggests that the return of Krueger may be due to Marge's repressed feelings of guilt over killing him, or even a result of Nancy's repressed childhood memories. Although this notion would be abandoned in the sequels, in which it is clear that Freddy is a real entity from "the other side," the idea that a killer might be "sin" personified fits perfectly into director Craven's continuing thesis about the repression of emotions and the inherent dishonesty in American family units.

The rubber reality of *A Nightmare on Elm Street* is assembled through a variety of trick shots, and Craven leaves out nothing in his quest to unsettle an audience. The spinning room is utilized again, but for a different purpose, in the murder of Glen (Johnny Depp). Here the room is simply filmed upside down and gallons of blood are dropped through a hole in Glen's bed. On film the bed appears to be on the floor, so the blood seems to spurt upwards with incredible force. An upside-down shot is a simple technique but one which perfectly expresses the violence of Krueger's ambush. He annihilates Glen in a burst of blood so powerful that it is like a waterfall in reverse, a massive ejaculation of hatred into the real world.

Also evocative of nightmares is Craven's use of false stairs. As Nancy is pursued by Freddy in her nightmare, she ascends the staircase to her bedroom only to crash through the stairs and find her feet stuck in a milky, glue-like mush. Anyone who has ever had a nightmare of being pursued can identify with Nancy's dilemma: the very landscape of the dream prevents her escape and aids the bogeyman. Escape is impossible because Freddy manipulates this world.

The fast pace and excellent special effects would be meaningless if *A Nightmare on Elm Street* did not succeed on other fronts, particularly in characterization and theme. On the first subject, Heather Langenkamp's performance is terrific. She portrays a character who is in turns sincere, exhausted, determined, defeated and victorious. As written by Craven and performed by the talented Langenkamp, Nancy is an intelligent youth who is capable of making important connections in her life. This is an ability that other characters such as Rod, Lt. Thompson and Marge fail repeatedly to demonstrate.

Only Nancy can recognize the link between worlds and see below the

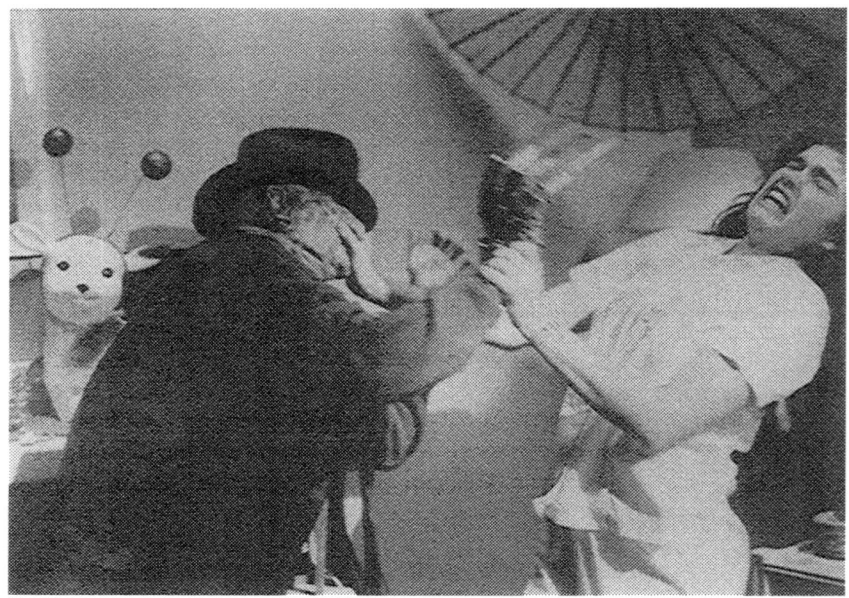

The final battle? After pulling Freddy Krueger (Robert Englund) into reality, Nancy Thompson finds her opponent ready for combat in *A Nightmare on Elm Street*.

surface of reality because she is already trained to do so ... through family experience. Nancy is prepared for her battle with Freddy because she has already seen the dark truth beneath the affluent reality of Elm Street. She has suffered through her parents' divorce, her mother's alcoholism and the lies which dominate her family, and is thus able to see the dark nature of the dreams which haunt Tina and the others. Nancy is the best-developed character up to this point in any Craven film and a totally sympathetic heroine.

With Nancy and Langenkamp, there is a perfect symbiosis between character and actress. Langenkamp catches not only the resourcefulness of this young character but the unconscious, almost unknowing humor of teenage years as well. After having stayed awake for seven days straight, Nancy comments sincerely, "God, I look 20." Langenkamp delivers the line with a perfect child-like innocence, proving that despite the divorce, the alcoholism, the denial and even the horrible death of friends, Nancy is just a kid.

In a review of *A Nightmare on Elm Street*, *People* magazine reviewer Ralph Novak referred to Craven as a "generational turncoat," a very astute observation. For Craven, the future resides not with selfish parents who look away from the truth rather than confronting it, but with the next generation. Nancy Thompson is the ultimate Craven heroine because she faces rather than denies the darkness inside, and takes responsibility for her own life. Appropriately, Freddy is vanquished when Nancy takes away "all the energy" she has afforded him. She is the core of Freddy's power, the fulcrum for all of Marge and Don's anxieties and repressed fears, so she is the character who can end the terror by taking control of her life. She does this willingly, instead of becoming just another victim.

As interesting as characterization in *A Nightmare on Elm Street* is Craven's depiction of the modern American family. The first adult seen in the film is Tina's mother. She awakens Tina from a nightmare and scolds her for having a nightmare. She is interrupted by an obviously drunk boyfriend who asks, "Are you coming back to the sack or what?" Later, Craven's dialogue also informs the audience that Tina's father abandoned the family ten years earlier. And, when Tina is murdered, her mother is hundreds of miles away in Las Vegas with the degenerate boyfriend. It is no wonder then that Tina feels vulnerable and is victimized by a child-hating male creature (Freddy). She has no positive male role models in her life, only an absentee father and her mother's selfish lover. Freddy is the ultimate extension of Craven's "bad father syndrome." He is a man who not only actively despises children, he takes pleasure in murdering them.

Nancy's family is not much better: Donald Thompson is accusatory and patronizing to his daughter. Even though she is almost an adult, he calls her "baby." When Nancy can advance his investigation, Thompson does not hesitate to use her as bait, proving also that he is opportunistic/lazy in his approach to work. Furthermore, both parents completely misunderstand Nancy's good nature. "Maybe you don't think murder is serious," they bark at her in the police station, suggesting that it is Nancy who lacks morality. On the contrary, it is Marge and Donald who are the hypocrites. They are the ones who "don't take murder" seriously: They killed Freddy Krueger without remorse.

Although Donald is an overbearing father who sees Nancy more as an object than as a person, it is Marge Thompson who comes off the worst. She is an alcoholic who keeps a vodka bottle handy in the linen closet. Like Bobby's mother in *The Hills Have Eyes*, she is also very much into denial as a way of life. She hides the truth about Fred Krueger well past the point of logic or sanity, as if keeping his identity secret will make him go away. Just as Bobby's decision to keep quiet about Beauty's disappearance in *The Hills Have Eyes* has serious repercussions, Marge's decision to withhold the truth from Nancy is incredibly damaging. If Nancy had known who or what she was up against earlier, she might have saved Rod or Glen or even Marge herself.

Marge Thompson has the protective instincts of a matriarch but no idea whatsoever how to channel them effectively. She installs bars on the doors and windows, but is unaware that such devices will not keep the horror out. Horror invades the home through nightmares, not through the front door. Perhaps this is Craven's subtle comment about the middle class response to crime in modern America. We will put bars on our houses and lock ourselves inside fortresses before we will examine why our society creates criminals in the first place.

Finally, Marge shares a quality with the Collingwoods in *The Last House on the Left*: She puts herself above the law and kills Freddy. This is bloody retribution pure and simple. Since the law failed, she and Don took matters into their own hands. The implication of *A Nightmare on Elm Street* is that it was the violent act of murder that de-stabilized the Thompson family. The murder of a man, even a bad man, and the confrontation of inner violence led the Thompsons to marital chaos and alcoholism. Their repressed feelings of guilt and sin are passed onto Nancy in the form of the demonic Krueger ... a walking, talking creation of their id.

Glen's parents are also dramatized in the most negative terms imaginable. They think they are being forceful and decisive ("You've got to be firm with these kids!") when in fact they are responsible for the death of their son. They make judgments about others, believing Nancy to be a lunatic, and have no understanding of what is happening in Glen's life. To them, it is better to live a lie than to confront an uncomfortable or unpalatable truth. Together, these "negative" families create the environment in which a demon such as Freddy Krueger thrives. What tears most families apart is not external tragedies or large-scale disasters, but the inner demons which, having been repressed for years, burst forward in a torrent of hatred. Craven believes that by repressing the truth, denying reality and taking solace in addiction, modern parents damage or actually kill their childrens' spirits. Importantly, these wounds are played out in the childrens' psychological landscape, in dreams, because their parents are not open and honest with their sons and daughters.

Because the Thompsons and the other Elm Street parents are of no help in *A Nightmare on Elm Street*, the film serves as an indictment of the American middle class. On a more basic level, parental refusal to believe Nancy's story makes the film scary. There is no help or support anywhere in *A Nightmare on Elm Street*. Like *The Last House on the Left*, the mechanisms of society have failed the young. In this case not only is law enforcement a failure, but science is as well. Nancy visits a dream clinic and Marge is airily told that dreams are "mysteries" and that "we don't know what they are or where they come from." This explanation proves that science lacks the answers required for survival and it also leaves the door open for Craven's subversive interpretation of dreams. To Craven, dreams originate deep in our subconscious, from the parent's guilt and sin, and even perhaps from repressed childhood memories.

Because no one believes Nancy, *A Nightmare on Elm Street* is similar to the feature film version of *The Twilight Zone*. As in "A Nightmare at 20,000 Feet," the protagonist's task is not just to stop a horrible monster, but to convince a skeptical world that he or she is not crazy and there really is an impending threat out there. Beyond this premise, what makes *A Nightmare on Elm Street* unnerving is that Freddy strikes people when and where they are defenseless. Everyone must sleep sometime. People are vulnerable in that state, and all of us have heard the stories that if you die in a dream, you die in reality too. *A Nightmare on Elm Street* explores that premise to its most frightening conclusion.

For this reason, *A Nightmare on Elm Street* is not like *Psycho* ("Just when you thought it was safe to take a shower") or *Jaws* ("Just when you thought it was safe to go back in the water"). Sleeping is not analogous to showering or swimming. It is not a voluntary act that can be avoided. In *A Nightmare on Elm Street*, Freddy inhabits a world that, sooner or later, *everyone* must visit.

A Nightmare on Elm Street also serves as a thematic counterpoint to another horror classic, John Carpenter's *Halloween*. Both films have strong world-views and in some senses they use the same milieu to philosophize about that view. Both films feature intelligent and likable teenagers in modern suburbia; and the high school setting plays an important role in each production.

In *Halloween*, Laurie Strode (Jamie Lee Curtis) sits in English class while the teacher drones on about "fate" and "destiny." In the midst of the class, Laurie is distracted when she spots Michael Myers' car on the street. The implication is that she has just glimpsed her fate. As the teacher explains on the soundtrack "you can't escape fate," and Laurie cannot escape her impending connection with the escaped serial killer.

By contrast, *A Nightmare on Elm Street* finds Nancy Thompson in English class while the teacher discusses the resourcefulness of the melancholy prince in *Hamlet*. The teacher notes that Hamlet stamps out the lies of his mother, something which Nancy will do in *Elm Street* as well, and that the prince probes and digs to find the truth, again as Nancy shall do. The *Elm Street* philosophy suggests that only by digging beneath the surface, by looking for the truth, can one overcome the lies of one's parents and survive.

Halloween's discussion of fate and pre-destination effectively makes Laurie a passive screen heroine. No matter what, she cannot escape her fate. *A Nightmare on Elm Street*'s literature discussion reflects Craven's view that a resourceful person *can* survive by digging for the truth. Nancy is active and positive, not a passive object victimized by a cruel destiny. Both philosophies are fascinating ones, and both are stated in high school English classes, but it is Craven's view which is the more hopeful.

A Nightmare on Elm Street also serves as a bridge between early Craven films and later epics by the director. Pointing backwards, the film regurgitates the bathtub sequence from *Deadly Blessing*, the self-defense/booby trap subplot from *The Last House on the Left*, the mother-in-denial syndrome from *The Hills Have Eyes*, the snakes as harbingers of evil (*The Hills Have Eyes, Deadly Blessing, Swamp Thing, The Hills Have Eyes Part II*) and even the boyfriend's visit to the heroine through her second-story bedroom window (*The Hills Have Eyes Part II*). Looking forward, the film is dominated by dream sequences (*Deadly Friend, The Serpent and the Rainbow, Shocker*), utilizes the telephone in important scare sequences (*Wes Craven's New Nightmare, Scream, Scream 2*) and focuses squarely on the supernatural (*The Serpent and the Rainbow, Shocker, Wes Craven's New Nightmare*) as an avenue through which a villain can gain retribution for perceived wrongs.

After *A Nightmare on Elm Street*, Freddy Krueger became a pop icon. His popularity is not difficult to understand, nor does it reflect a particularly twisted society. For generations, children have grown up idolizing King Kong, the Frankenstein Monster, Dracula, Darth Vader and Godzilla. People like to be scared, albeit in an entertaining fashion, and Freddy is just a logical extension of this development. In *A Nightmare on Elm Street*, however, Freddy is not the joke-spewing humorous creation of later films. He is a diminutive creature (almost like a troll) with the personality of an evil witch (from a production like *Snow White* or, perhaps more appropriately, *Sleeping Beauty*). He is a disfigured, almost pitiful thing who wields a distinctive weapon. Once in the real world, he loses much of his power and Nancy is able to defeat him handily. Still, Freddy is the ultimate pervert ... stalking teenagers in their pajamas, all the while licking his lips and playfully sticking out his tongue. Unlike Jason in the *Friday the 13th* series or the shark in *Jaws*, Freddy is not merely a killing machine. He offers a much more personal style of horror. He is terrifying to audiences because he *knows* his victims.

He knows where they live, what they dream of and what their vulnerabilities are. He is not just a machete-wielding maniac who kills anyone who happens upon him. He kills specific people for a specific reason (revenge), and he is therefore a bit more of a personality and a little less of a killing automaton than most stalkers. In *A Nightmare on Elm Street*, Englund plays the character to the hilt. Like the nightmare man who once stalked young Craven, Englund plays a killer who is amused by the terror he generates. Perhaps it is that quality which makes him scary.

There is some interesting cross-continuity between *A Nightmare on Elm Street* and the film *Shocker*. In *Shocker*, Langenkamp is Horace Pinker's first victim. And in *A Nightmare on Elm Street*, Lt. Donald Thompson calls for one of his deputies near the climax: "Parker! I need some help here!" he yells. A policeman named Donald Parker is a central character in *Shocker*, an in-joke referring to the character mentioned off-handedly in *Elm Street*. Also, both *Shocker* and *A Nightmare on Elm Street* open with a scene of a killer working in his grungy workshop.

Another possible connection ties *A Nightmare on Elm Street* to *Scream*: Joseph Whipp plays a police officer in both films. On the Director's Cut laserdisc of *Scream*, Craven suggests he is the same character — a man so haunted by what he saw on *Elm Street* that he moved to Southern California and became a town sheriff!

Deadly Friend (1986)

Craven ... plays up a script that's full of friendly banter. With the exception of blood spurting from dying people with the abandon of a Grade Z movie, Craven doesn't go for overkill, allowing the actors and the audience to have a good time.— Jami Bernard (*The New York Post*, October 14, 1986, page 27)

Has its familiar Craven miscues, like "nightmare" sequences that fool no one, and a "surprise" ending that makes no sense. On the whole, *Deadly Friend* is a routine horror movie poorly photographed (by old-time cinematographer Philip Lathrop) and poorly performed (with the exception of New York stage actress Anne Twomey, as Paul's mother).— Paul Attanasio (*The Washington Post*, October 11, 1986)

Deadly Friend is a disappointment for long-time Craven followers. There are plenty of shocks, and even a tinge of sadness, in this nifty little thriller, but not enough razor-edge electricity.— Patrick Goldstein (*The Los Angeles Times*, October 14, 1986)

[The film] maintains its undercurrent of suspense all along. ...It's strictly kid stuff, but, at times, suspenseful kid stuff."— Bill Kaufman (*Newsday*, October 11, 1986)

More silly than frightening."— Howard Maxford, *The A-Z of Horror Films* (Indiana University Press, 1997, page 74)

Writer Bruce Joel Rubin ... wants to tell a bittersweet love story... Director Wes Craven wants to retell *A Nightmare on Elm Street*, loading up on nightmares, tacked-on shock scenes and effects for their own sake...— John Stanley, *Creature Features Strikes Again* (Creatures At Large Press, 1994, page 98)

CAST: Matthew Laborteaux (Paul Conway); Kristy Swanson (Samantha); Michael Sharrett (Tom); Anne Twomey (Jeannie Conway); Ann Ramsey (Elvira Parker); Richard Marcus (Harry); Russ Marin (Dr. Johanson); Lee Paul (Police Sgt. Volcheck); Andrew Roperto (Carl Denton); Charles Fleischer (Voice of "BB"); Robin Nuyen (Thief); Frank Carestant (Angry Resident); Merritt Olsen (CAT Scan Technician); William H. Faeth (Doctor in Sam's Room); Joel Hile (Deputy); Tom Spratley (Neighbor); Jim Ishida (Coroner)

CREDITS: A Warner Brothers Release of a Pan Arts/Layton film. A Wes Craven Film. *Music:* Charles Bernstein. *Film Editor:* Michael Eliot, A.C.E. *Production Designer:* Daniel Lomino. *Director of Photography:* Philip Lathrop. *Based on the novel "Friend" by* Diana Henstell. *Co-Producer:* Robert L. Crawford. *Executive Producer:* Patrick Kelley. *Producer:* Robert M. Sherman. *Screenplay:* Bruce Joel Rubin. *Director:* Wes Craven. *Unit Production Manager:* Phil Rawlins. *First Assistant Director:* Nicholas Batchelor. *Second Assistant Director:* Peter Graupner. *Set Decorator:* Edward J. McDonald. *Set Designer:* Roy Barns. *"BB" Robot:* Robotics 21, Ray Raymond. *"BB" Shell Design:* Keith Huber. *Mime Coach for Kristy Swanson:* Richard Shepherd. *Medical Advisor:* William H. Faeth, M.D. *Associate Film Editor:* John P. Morrisey. *Supervising Sound Editor:* Dale Johnson. *Sound Editing:* SoundFX, Inc. *Music Editor:* John LaSalandra, S.M.E. *Production Mixer:* Richard Church. *Boom Man:* Eugene Ashbrook. *Re-Recording Mixers:* Dan Cohn, Allan Stone, Jim Williams. *Camera Operator:* Bill Johnson. *First Assistant Camera* Ken Zunden: Horace Jordan. *Second Assistant Camera:* Paul Mindrap. *Still*

Photographer: Carol McCullough. *Script Supervisor:* Marion Tumen. *Men's Costumer:* Barton "Kent" James. *Women's Costumer:* Carole Brown James. *Makeup Artist:* Mike Hancock. *Hairstylist:* Better Iverson. *Gaffer:* Buddy Bowles. *Electrical Best Boy:* William Peets. *Key Grip:* Howard Anderson. *Grip Best Boy:* Jon Robinson. *Property Master:* Victor Petrotta, Jr. *Assistant Property Master:* John Sweeney. *Special Effects Foreman:* Peter Albiez. *Location Manager:* Bruce Lawhead. *Transportation Coordinator:* Bob Neilson. *Transportation Captain:* Dave Robling. *Construction Coordinator:* Larry Verne. *Leadman:* Fred Morrison. *Stand-by Painter:* Mel Holman. *Production Accountant:* Susan Montgomery. *Production Secretary:* Kara Shaw. *Unit Publicist:* Patti Birznieks. *Assistant to Mr. Craven:* Marianne Maddalena. *Assistant to Mr. Sherman:* Ruth Ellen Daniels. *Additional Special Makeup Effects:* Lance Anderson. *Opticals and Title Design:* Pacific Title. *Title Design:* Dan Perri. *Lenses and Panaflex Cameras:* Panavision. *Color:* Technicolor. *Stunt Coordinators:* Terry Leonard, Tony Cecere. *Stunts:* Linda Arvidson, Pam Benson, Doc Charbonneau, Mark Donaldson, Leslie Hoffman, Tracy Lynn Keehn, Lane Leavitt, Mike McGaghy, Tom Oldberg, Patricia Romano, Debby Lynn-Ross. From Warner Brothers. *Running Time:* 91 minutes. *MPAA Rating:* R

SYNOPSIS: In a small parking lot, a thief breaks into a Volkswagen van but is prevented from stealing by a robotic hand gripping his neck. The robot releases him and the thug runs off, dazed. The Conways, the owners of the robot and the van, return from their shopping excursion and drive off. They are headed for their new home in the town of Wellington.

The next morning, they arrive at their new home, a beautiful Victorian house. Teenager Paul Conway lowers a ramp and out of the van strolls the yellow robot BB, replete with big red eyes. As BB surveys his new home, he makes gleeful chirping noises. He also inadvertently frightens the local paperboy, Tom.

Paul, Tom and BB quickly become friends. Tom is fascinated by BB and Paul tells him that the robot represents the latest advances in artificial intelligence. BB is constantly learning and developing. Paul also tells Tom that he has a scholarship at Polytech University, studying the human brain with Dr. Johanson.

Paul and his mother move into their new home. BB's batteries run low, so he shoves the piano away from the wall and plugs himself into a socket to facilitate recharging. Later, Paul, BB and his mother meet Dr. Johanson at Polytech and are given a tour of Paul's amazing new laboratory. As the days pass, BB and Paul clean the front yard. Paul heads into the backyard to the shed and meets his neighbor, Samantha. Paul notices immediately that the blond beauty has bruises on her arm, but Sam tries to hide the wounds. Still, the two young people quickly develop a rapport. Their friendship is aborted when Sam's father bursts out of his house and glares at her with menace. Sam seems frightened and returns inside.

That night, Sam comes over with some doughnuts as a housewarming gift.

2. The Feature Films

Samantha (Kristy Swanson), BB and Paul (Matthew Laborateaux) share good times in *Deadly Friend*.

After Paul gives the girl a tour of his bedroom and the attic, her father soon arrives, angry. He demands that Sam come home immediately and then physically drags his daughter away. That night, Sam is terrified. Her father enters the bedroom and makes physical advances, calling her a slut "like her mother!" Then, as he gets too close, Sam breaks a vase on her nightstand and stabs her father in the stomach with it. The vase ejaculates blood all over Sam and the bed. Sam wakes up screaming: It was just a bad dream. She goes to her bedroom door and hears her drunken dad stumbling around the house. She locks her door and props a chair against it.

Paul and Tom teach BB to deliver papers. One day as they are walking the route, Tom stops at Elvira Parker's house. She lives behind a locked fence and Tom tells Paul that she is a paranoid old loon. Sure enough, a mean old lady comes out on the front porch and threatens the boys with a shotgun. She also expresses immediate dislike for BB. The boys move on with their robot and Tom reveals that his dad is a security guard for the University Hospital. While walking further, the boys are confronted by a gang of motorcycle punks who insult Tom and push Paul into a garbage bag. BB responds with force and grabs the leader of the gang by the crotch. The gang rides away, frightened. Only when BB is satisfied that the danger to Paul is passed does it finally release the punk leader. He rides away screaming that he will "get" Paul for this!

Paul instructs undergraduates at the University about recent advances in artificial intelligence. During his free time, he, BB Tom and Sam develop a strong friendship. One day, they play basketball together until BB accidentally tosses the basketball onto Elvira Parker's front porch. She stomps out angrily and takes the ball inside, refusing to give it back. As she slams the door, BB's eyes seem to freeze on Elvira and the house, as if he will not forget this insult. Back at school, Paul's experiments continue and he dissects the brain of a corpse. He is making incredible advances and thinks one day he may be able to power the human mind with robotic control chips.

On Halloween, Paul and his mother carve a pumpkin together. Sam comes over with a bloody nose and asks for ice. She claims that she gets nosebleeds, but Paul and her mother suspect that her father is abusing her. She is angered by this suggestion.

Paul, Tom, Sam and BB go out for Halloween night. They decide to play a little prank on Elvira Parker. The robot unlocks her gate in seconds and Sam goes up to ring her doorbell — the first time anyone has gotten to her doorbell in years. As Sam steps on the porch, alarms go off and Sam screams. She runs for the gate but falls down. Tom sees Elvira coming and he, Paul and Sam hide in the shrubbery. When Elvira steps out onto the porch she is armed with a shotgun. Elvira shoots BB. She blows him apart, striking him first in the arm, then in the head and finally in the chest. Paul is shattered by the loss of his beloved friend, and Tom blames himself for suggesting the stunt.

On Thanksgiving Day, Sam, Paul and his mom share turkey dinner. Afterwards, Paul and Sam have their first kiss. Sam returns home late that night, and her father is outraged. He slaps Sam, punches her in the face and then pushes the teenager down the stairs. The fall breaks Sam's neck and she is rushed to the hospital. The doctors can do nothing for her, and Sam is left brain-dead. Dr. Johanson tells Paul that Sam will be kept on life support for 24 hours, and then the plug will be pulled. Enraged, Paul runs away.

At home, he mourns the loss of Sam and BB and then remembers BB's special computer chip. It links artificial intelligence and the human brain — and maybe it can help Sam. Paul runs to Tom's house and asks for a favor. He needs Tom's father's University Hospital keys so he can break into the hospital and save Sam before the plug is pulled. That night, Tom comes over for dinner and he and Paul mix a sedative into Mrs. Conway's coffee. Once she is unconscious, they rush to the hospital and execute Paul's plan. Tom deactivates hospital power from the basement.

Upstairs, Dr. Johanson pulls the plug on Sam while her father watches heartlessly. Then the hospital goes dark and Paul slips into Sam's room and drags her out in a laundry sack. As the boys leave the hospital, Tom is horrified, afraid they will be caught.

At Paul's lab, young Conway inserts BB's control chip into Sam's brain. The tiny computer will act as a sort of pacemaker for the damaged gray matter. Paul then brandishes his remote control and activates Sam. Her foot moves, and Tom faints. Realizing they have saved her life, Paul and Tom take Sam to his house and let her sleep in the shed behind the house. When they return home, Paul's mother is still out cold. Paul thanks Tom for all his help, but Tom is finished with this ghoulish business now. Paul returns to Sam in the shed and activates her. Her eyes open mechanically and she starts to breathe. Paul teaches her to sit up and she responds slowly, her hands stuck in the position of BB's robot pincers.

The police arrive at Sam's house and inform her father that her body has disappeared from the hospital. In the middle of the night, Paul awakens to find Sam watching her father through the shed window. Paul deactivates her.

The next morning, Sam is missing. Paul runs up and down the street searching, but there is now sign of her. She has returned to her house to wreak vengeance upon the abusive father who killed her. Her father finds a door to the cellar open and walks down the stairs. Sam yanks him off his feet and drags him to the furnace. First she breaks his wrist and then she snaps his neck. When Paul finds Sam in the cellar, her father's head is burning inside the furnace. Paul is horrified and hides the corpse in a pile of coal. He returns home with Sam and locks her in his room.

That night, Sam breaks free again, this time paying a visit to Elvira Parker. Elvira calls the police when she sees Sam, but they think Elvira is crazy. Sam breaks into her house and a basketball bounces ominously into Elvira's living room. The old lady picks up her shotgun when Sam jumps out and throws her against the wall. The reanimated girl tosses the basketball at Elvira so hard that it splits her skull into bloody fragments. Elvira ends up a decapitated hulk spurting blood and rolling on the floor.

In his bed, Paul dreams of a bouncing basketball that rolls slowly into his room and up into his bed. He pulls up the covers and it is not a basketball at all but the burned head of Sam's father.

At Elvira's house, the police find Elvira's body, and the corpse of Sam's father. Tom learns that Sam has been killing people, and threatens to go to the police. Paul promises Tom that things will change, but Tom refuses to budge and the two get into a knock-down, drag-out fight. During the battle, Sam attacks Tom, believing he has injured Paul. Paul and his mother save Tom, but now Sam is out in the open. Scared, she runs down a dark alley. Paul runs after her but is stopped by the motorcycle punk who once attacked him. Sam saves Paul from the punk as a police car arrives on the scene. Sam throws the punk into the car, smashing the windshield, and runs off.

Sam is soon confronted by police on all sides. She makes her way back to the shed behind the Conway house. Paul meets her there and comforts her as she cowers in a corner. Amazingly, Sam is becoming human. She starts to develop normal human vision and for the first time since her death she speaks in her own voice, saying Paul's name tenderly. The police arrive and BB's survival instinct

A portrait of innocence — but beautiful Samantha (Kristy Swanson) has a grim fate in store for her in *Deadly Friend*.

kicks in again. Sam rushes the police and they shoot her down. She dies uttering Paul's name.

Later, Paul breaks into the hospital and pulls Samantha's body out of the freezer. He thinks he can still save her. Strangely, she begins to change. Her skin ripples and BB's evil, smiling face protrudes. The robot/girl grabs Paul by the throat and he screams as he is pulled to his death.

COMMENTARY: *Deadly Friend* is an inoffensive collection of clichés which bears the tell-tale marks of heavy studio interference. Although Craven strikes some different notes than are customary in his films, *Deadly Friend* "finds its voice" in scenes which concern his favorite theme: dysfunctional families and society's failed institutions. Severely lessening its potential impact on audiences, *Deadly Friend* is packed with stock situations and "rerun" characters. Typical of the time period when it was produced, the central character is a brilliant adolescent (*Real Genius* [1985], *War Games* [1983] and *Whiz Kids* [1984] on TV) who owns a cute robot capable of more "humanity" than expected (*Short Circuit* [1986], *SpaceCamp* [1986]). The teenager is frequently harassed by bullies (*Back to the Future* [1985], *Weird Science* [1985]), but the nasty teens eventually receive their comeuppance.

In *Deadly Friend*, there is also the "evil" neighbor (Anne Ramsey's Elvira Parker) living in a fortress-like home (Polly Holliday in *Gremlins* [1984]). Importantly, the "evil" neighbor, an older female in both movies, is punished for her misdeeds by the "monster" of each production. Typically, the teenage genius discovers love with a beautiful girl (Phoebe Cates in *Gremlins*, Ally Sheedy in *War Games*, Michelle Meyrink in *Real Genius*, Elisabeth Shue in the various *Back to the Future* films, Danielle von Zerneck in *My Science Project*, Mary Kay Place in *Explorers* and Kristy Swanson in *Deadly Friend*) and a first kiss has paramount importance in the proceedings (*Explorers* [1985]).

Even the *Frankenstein* aspect of *Deadly Friend* is reminiscent of earlier teen dramas. Like the mechanical central character in *D.A.R.Y.L.* (1985), *Deadly Friend*'s BB develops human feelings and a personality. With so many similarities to other hit films of the time period, *Deadly Friend* is not only derivative, but typical of the standard Hollywood approach: If one teenage film is a hit, crank out as many clones as possible to bring back the same audience.

Unfortunately, Craven's very name hinders *Deadly Friend* from being just another pleasing variation on the teenage genius/cute robot films of the mid-80s. Preview audiences expected the film to be a hardcore horror picture like *A Nightmare on Elm Street* and were disappointed by *Deadly Friend*'s innocuous nature. Demanding that Craven deliver the goods, Warner Brothers ordered the inclusion of several "gore" scenes and the result is that *Deadly Friend* appears distinctly schizophrenic.

Craven initially shot a perfectly acceptable, if not terribly original, teen picture. The inappropriate gore scenes seem cut in from another production in this gentle, fun environment. Though interesting, the dream sequences do not fit into the plot as expertly as they did in *A Nightmare on Elm Street*, and the final "jolt," BB pushing his way out of Samantha's corpse, is absurd and illogical. Had the powers-that-be left well enough alone, it is possible that *Deadly Friend* would have found success as a modest and slightly macabre teen picture along the lines of all the other pictures mentioned. By tacking on several bloody "kill scenes," the picture became neither fish nor fowl. It was too gross to satisfy the teen market that fell in love with *Short Circuit* or *Weird Science* and still too soft to appeal to *A Nightmare on Elm Street* aficionados. Above all, *Deadly Friend* is evidence that studio tampering in post-production is counterproductive.

Despite *Deadly Friend*'s derivative and confused personality, the film is not without merit. Bruce Joel Rubin's screenplay hits some nice notes and his droll dialogue is well delivered by the three primary youngsters, Matthew Laborteaux, Kristy Swanson and Michael Sharrett. Craven also shows a knack for comedy by employing fast-motion photography early in the proceedings to dramatize the superior abilities of BB.

The sequence in which Paul must incapacitate his mother (Anne Twomey) at the kitchen table also comes off without a hitch, and is one of the film's funnier moments. Voiced by Roger Rabbit himself, Charles Fleischer, BB is a unique creation. Craven builds tension by dramatizing in the very first scene that the robot is capable of violence, thus laying the groundwork for BB's final transformation into vengeful killer (in Sam's body). Craven is also a big *Frankenstein* fan, and that subplot comes through with clarity in *Deadly Friend*. Like Victor Frankenstein, Paul cannot stomach death and so he attempts to beat it. In the end, as in Mary Shelley's story, Paul's entire life is consumed by death.

The film, though nowhere near as cohesive as Craven's *The Last House on the Left*, *The Hills Have Eyes* and *A Nightmare on Elm Street*, is propelled forward effectively by two tragedies. It is these twin losses (BB and Sam) that send young Conway over the edge and into desperation. If *Deadly Friend*'s screenplay had more fully incorporated horror at an early stage instead of retroactively, the film really might have been something special.

Akin to most of Craven's film work, *Deadly Friend* concerns a middle-class American community that has failed its teens. Sam's father is not only overbearing, but abusive. He punches her in the face and throws her down the stairs. He is a murderer and by far the worst of Craven's bad fathers. He is an alcoholic, like Marge in *A Nightmare on Elm Street,* but this addiction is more forcefully handled in *Deadly Friend.* The revived Sam lures her dad to his death with a bottle of booze, proof positive from Craven that alcoholism will kill you!

Interestingly, the rest of the community also bears a measure of responsibility for Sam's death. No one does *anything* to protect this girl from a threat inside her own household. At one point, Mrs. Conway suggests action to prevent the abuse, and Sam is offended, but the fact of the matter is that Sam dies because no one in the community comes to her aid. At one point, Mrs. Conway prays for Sam ("May God keep Sam's father dead to the world for the rest of the night"), but this strategy is hardly an effective one. Like Ethel Carter's prayer for the Lord to watch over her family in *The Hills Have Eyes,* Conway's prayer in *Deadly Friend* actually has the opposite effect. That very night, Sam is killed after enjoying Thanksgiving dinner at Paul's house. Craven is not only suspicious of religion, he is scornful of it. It is not only ineffective, it is a precursor to death. In *Last House on the Left, The Hills Have Eyes* and *Deadly Friend,* protagonists die *immediately* after scenes of prayer and in *Deadly Blessing,* Isaiah's id is an avenging incubus who kills all those who are not "God's kindred."

Sam's neighbors are not the only ones who fail her in *Deadly Friend.* The police are also to blame. As in *The Last House on the Left,* the police force in *Deadly Friend* is depicted as a squad of buffoons. The sheriff sits on his ass and wolfs down a hoagie, assuring a deputy that he will investigate a possible crime "as soon as is humanly possible." Meanwhile, he continues eating.

The police are notable for their absence. Where are they when motorcycle punks attack Paul on the street? When Elvira Parker threatens harmless teenagers with a shotgun and blasts BB to pieces? When Sam is being beaten? Just as the cops failed to protect Mari Collingwood in *The Last House on the Left,* the policemen fail to protect Sam in *Deadly Friend* even though everyone in the neighborhood is aware of her father's abusiveness.

Another modern institution fails in *Deadly Friend* as well: science. The hospital doctors who operate on Sam are unable to save her and are finally reduced to saying wistfully, "Gee, she was a beautiful kid." Dr. Johanson, Paul's mentor, is an expert in the field of brain trauma and yet he too is unable to apply his research to a real-life scenario. Overall, Johanson is a rather pitiful character. Virtually every scene reveals him to be less-intelligent, less-resourceful and less-motivated to discover new methods than his young friend. This depiction shows not only that the scientific community has failed today's youth, but reveals further evidence that Craven is, in the words of Ralph Novak, "a generational turncoat." As in *A Nightmare on Elm Street,* Craven finds promise not in the baby boomers or the World War II generation, but in America's pliable youth. Of course, that great promise is twisted by obsession in *Deadly Friend*, but it is still visible.

Though awkwardly placed within the narrative, the nightmare sequences in *Deadly Friend* are interesting, well-executed horror vignettes. The first dream sequence is successful because it develops a character in a way the dialogue does not. Sam is asleep in her bed when her father breaks in and begins to touch her. This scenario suggests that his abuse of Sam goes beyond the realm of physical beatings and into the sexual arena, something heretofore unmentioned in the screenplay ... but not difficult to believe. The sexual metaphor is completed by the punchline of the dream sequence: Sam jabs her father in the mid-section with a broken vase and he ejaculates blood through what is a fairly obvious phallus-symbol. He sprays not only his daughter with the liquid, but also her bed sheets.

This single "nightmare" hints that there is a deeper subtext to *Deadly Friend*, a sexual one, but unfortunately it is not pursued in a substantive way. The lack of narrative depth is hardly surprising since this dream, like the others, was tacked on once the rest of the film had already been lensed.

The second dream vignette is also frightening, if not as illuminating. Paul pulls up his bed sheets to grab what he thinks is a basketball, but the orb is actually a human head. This is a "jolt" moment pure and simple. Still, it is an effective scare in a movie without many nail-biting moments.

In the final analysis, *Deadly Friend* fails as a horror film because it is not terrifying. Once Kristy Swanson has been revived as a killer-robot, she stumbles around town with her arms outstretched and her hands locked in BB's "pincer" pose. Unlike traditional zombies, Sam's corpse remains pristine throughout the picture except for heavy blue eye-liner. Because she is essentially a teenage girl walking around with a "blank" stare and rigid limbs, an element of unintentional comedy enters the picture. She is not a figure of fright but a childish variation on the Frankenstein Monster. Since there is no effort to shroud Sam in shadows or cloak her in darkness, she remains a familiar person rather than the specter of death seeking retribution that the script seemingly requires.

In his analysis of horror, *Danse Macabre*, Stephen King wrote that terror was the finest emotion he could generate in readers. If he failed to terrify, he would attempt to horrify. Failing that, he would go for the gross-out. Sadly, *Deadly Friend*, conceived as a teenage adventure rather than a horror picture, could not terrify an audience (even with punched-up dream sequences), and so Craven did what he could: He went for the gross-out. Accordingly, the murder of Elvira Parker is a disgusting bit of business wherein her head is smashed by a basketball and her headless body staggers around the room spewing blood through the neck for a few seconds. It is a disgusting moment but it lacks the visceral impact of Tina's terrifying death in *A Nightmare on Elm Street* because the overall mood of *Deadly Friend* does not support such a grim death. In fact, the basketball murder sequence actually comes across as fairly humorous since a basketball hardly seems an appropriate weapon of destruction.

A revived Samantha stalks those who harmed her, including her alcoholic father, in a grisly scene from *Deadly Friend*.

Another gross-out scene is the death of Sam's dad in the furnace. Like the basketball scenario, this scene is competently shot but, again, the mood seems appropriate to a different film. And, unlike *The Last House on the Left*, this is a sequence that seems to be in favor of violent retribution. The audience hates Sam's dad and enjoys when he gets what's coming to him.

The weakest element of *Deadly Friend* is the ludicrous special effects ending in which a diabolical BB bursts out of Sam's corpse. This ending intimates that the presence of BB's microchip in Sam's skull has "rewritten" her DNA to make her a Borg-like entity of evil. It is a ridiculous suggestion since, just moments before her death, P.O.V. shots from Sam's perspective established that the human within her was once again re-asserting itself. The "shock" ending of *Deadly Friend* is only startling in its lack of continuity with the rest of the film.

Deadly Friend is not a satisfying film because of its conflicted dual nature, yet it is not a terrible film. The performers are all very good, and Craven shows an admirable light touch with material that should not have been contaminated with hardcore horror. *Deadly Friend* is one of Craven's most hated ventures because it is so "soft" in some scenes yet so over-the-top in its outrageous effects. Since it does not have a consistent atmosphere, people just did not know how to feel about the film. Fortunately, Craven would find himself back at the top of his form in his next venture, *The Serpent and the Rainbow*.

There is one final footnote of interest regarding *Deadly Friend*. At the time of its release in 1986, many critics were openly disdainful of the film's premise that a computer chip could be successfully mated to a human brain. It was neither possible nor believable, they insisted. Ironically, *The Washington Post* reported on October 27, 1997, in a story entitled "Need Computer in Head? Chip Links with Brain" that computer chips which interface directly with human brain cells are now a technological possibility. These chips were discussed in New Orleans on October 26 at the annual meeting of the Society for Neuroscience. What seemed impossible only a decade ago in *Deadly Friend* may someday be a reality. *Deadly Friend* still has many problems, but at least in this arena it proved prophetic.

The Serpent and the Rainbow (1988)

> It's a campy romp through the occult from that master of the gore genre, Wes Craven ... Most of the gore — and there's gore aplenty — comes from those is-this-reality-or-is-it-a-nightmare sequences which Craven overdoes. But if you're a fan of such foolishness, this movie should be right up your dark alley.— Tom Cunneff (*People Weekly*, February 15, 1988)

> The visual look of the movie is stunning; there's never the sense of sets, of costumes, of hired extras, but more a feeling of a camera moving past real people in real places. Even the obviously contrived scenes, including some of the hallucinations and voodoo fantasies, have an air of solid plausibility to them... He [Craven] has a sure touch for horror and the macabre, and *The Serpent and the Rainbow* ... takes the most lurid images and makes them plausible.— Roger Ebert (*The New York Post*, February 2, 1988)

> As you would expect from Craven, there are some good set pieces but, given the material, they seem highly inappropriate. ...[O]ne of the most chilling scenes is when the screen is completely black and we hear nothing but the sound of being buried alive. The horror of nothingness is far more disturbing than the villain, who ... has deteriorated into Freddy Krueger's poor relation.— Suzanne Moore (*New Statesman & Society*, March 28, 1989)

> Craven's films have always been distinguished by their striking visual imagery and *The Serpent and the Rainbow* is no exception. From the film's opening moments, Craven begins to blur the line between hallucination and the perceived real world, weaving lush Haitian landscapes, shadowy darkness and dazzling special effects into a tapestry of alternate realities.— Bob Morrish (*Cinefantastique*, July 1988, page 48)

CAST: Bill Pullman (Dr. Dennis Alan); Cathy Tyson (Marielle DuChamps); Zakes Mokae (Police Capt. Peytraud); Paul Winfield (Lucien Celine); Brent Jennings (Louis Mozart); Conrad Roberts (Christophe); Badja Djola (Gaston);

Theresa Merritt (Simone); Michael Gough (Schoonbacher); Paul Guilfoyle (Andrew Cassidy); Dey Young (Mrs. Cassidy); Aleta Mitchell (Celestine); William Newman (French Missionary Doctor); Jaime Pina Gautier (Julio); Evencio Mosquera Slaco (Old Shaman); Kimberleigh Burroughs (Margrite); Philogen Thomas (Priest); Ana Rosa Smith Avila (Mulatto Nurse); Francis Guinan (American Doctor); Sally-Ann Munn (Nurse); Jean-Baptiste Rosvelt (Black Waiter); Robert De James (Old Lame Peasant); Jackson Delgado (Possessed Dancer); Barbara Guillaume (Mozart's Whore); Betty Garcia Rodriguez (Pretty Whore); Luis Tavare Pesqiera (Kyle Cassidy); Claudia Pimentel (Old Crone); Michael Jackson (Newscaster)

CREDITS: A Universal Pictures Release. Keith Barish Presents A Rob Cohen/David Ladd Production. A Film by Wes Craven. *Casting:* Dianne Crittendon. *Costume Designer:* Peter Mitchell. *Music:* Brad Fiedel. *Film Editor:* Glen Farr. *Production Designer:* David Nichols. *Director of Photography:* John Lindley. *Executive Producers:* Rob Cohen, Keith Barish. *Inspired by the Book by:* Wade Davis. *Screenplay:* Richard Maxwell, A.R. Simoun. *Producers:* David Ladd, Doug Claybourne. *Director:* Wes Craven. *Stunt Coordinator:* Tony Cecere. *Stuntpeople:* Ray Woodfork, Marvin Walters, Eric Chambers, Al Lee, Dane Farwell, Irving Lewis, Eric Mansker, Perry Nicholls, Mark Orrison, Debbie Lynn Ross. *Associate Producer:* David B. Pauker. *Unit Production Manager:* Michael Bennett. *First Assistant Director:* Bob Engelman. *Second Assistant Director:* George B. Gregg. *Production Executive:* Curtis Burch. *Sound Design:* Joy Boekelheide. *Additional Editing:* Peter Amundson. *Special Makeup Effects:* Lance Anderson, David Anderson. *Special Mechanical Effects:* Image Engineering. *Supervisor of Special Effects:* Gary Gutierrez. *Dialogue and Dialect Consultant:* Nora Dunfee. *Special Choreography:* Carmen de Lavallode. *Choreographer:* Juan Rodriguez. *Research Anthropologist:* Julia Tavares. *Production Consultant:* Ramiro Joloma. *Production Manager:* Jaime Pina Gautier. *Additional Second Assistant Directors:* Jose Louise Ortega, Miguel Heded, Felipe Vicini. *Assistant to Mr. Ladd and Mr. Claybourne:* Jill Simpson. *Assistant to Mr. Craven:* Marianne Maddalena. *Script Supervisor:* Carmen Soriano. *Production Coordinator:* Loolee Deleon. *Production Auditor:* Dianne Cheek. *Assistant Auditors:* Denise Morgan, Eugenia Orlowski, Abdelilah Marrackchi. *Production Secretaries:* Stel Deleon, Nancy Hynes. *Production Associates:* Victoria Kluge, Robbie Tucker. *Key Production Assistant:* Janice Convery. *Production Assistants:* Adam Smith, Mariella Garcia, Alexandria Lutard, Francia DeCamps. *Post Production Assistants:* Joe Heffenan, Clayton Corrie. *Location Casting:* Sue Parker. *Extra Casting Assistant:* Heig Beck. *New York Casting Assistant:* Sarah C. Koeppe. *Creole Dialogue Coach:* Nicole Alvarez. *Assistant Editors:* Bill Ohanesian, Michael Murphy. *Apprentice Editors:* James Brewer, Julie Offer. *Art Director:* David Brisbin. *Assistant Art Director:* Andy Keesee. *Set Designer:* Dawn Snyder. *Draftsman:* Joan Diego Vasquez. *Sketch Artists:* James Hegedus, Bruce Pierce. *Art Department Assistant:* Emma Sanchez. *Art Department Manager:* Juan Santana. *Set*

Decorator: Rosemarie Brandenburg. *Leadman:* Barry Frankenburg. *On Set Decorator:* Jonathan Craven. *Swing Gang:* Jess Moreno, Victor Nunez, Ricardo Masy-Dulve, Jose Hernandez. *Dresser:* Daniel Prati. *Property Master:* Charles Stewart. *Assistant Props:* Linda Kiffe. *Props Person:* Jeanette Rodriguez. *Camera Operator:* Ken Ferris. *First Assistant Camera:* Larry Karman. *Second Assistant Camera:* Findlay Bunting, Gordon Miller. *Additional Camera Operator:* Henry Lynk. *Steadicam Coperator:* Alan Caso. *Assistant Steadicam Operator:* Rick Fee. *Still Photographer:* Gary Farr. *Second Unit Director:* Rob Cohen. *Additional Photography:* George Koblasa, Len Gitleman. *Sound Mixer:* Donald Summer. *Boom Operator:* Steve Soillars. *Utility:* Chrstine Lemoine. *Gaffer:* Patrick Reddish. *Best Boy:* Bruce McCleery. *Electricians:* George Hock, Michael McFadden, Freddy Aquino, John Carney, Rafeal Ariuss. *Generator Operator/Technician:* Sean Grey. *Grips:* Timothy Pershing. *Best Boy Grip:* Daniel Pershing. *Dolly Grip:* Dwight Lavers. *Grips:* Ario Cruz, Gustavo J. Reynoso, Larry McCarron, Luis Llinas. *Key Makeup Artist:* Michelle Buhler. *Hairstylist:* Robert Hallowell. *Makeup Technicians:* Jeff Farley, James McPherson, Leonard McDonald, James Kagel. *Costume Supervisor:* Shawn Barrie. *Wardrobe Assistant:* Lynda Foote. *Special Effects Coordinator:* Peter Chesney. *Key Technician:* Bruce Hays. *Special Effects Technicians:* Emmet Kane, Bob Ahmanson. *Special Effects Assistant:* Sandra Steward. *Image Engineering Coordinator:* Robin D'Arcy. *Location Manager:* Rien Navez. *Running Time:* 105 minutes. *MPAA Rating:* R

SYNOPSIS: In Port-au-Prince, Haiti, in the year 1978, Baron Samedi rules the streets and the secret police of "Baby Doc" Duvalier (the Ton-Ton Macoute) abuse their authority and knowledge of voodoo to silence the enemies of the state. An outspoken proponent of liberty and freedom, a schoolteacher named Christophe is found dead and transported to the local hospital. He is pronounced dead by the white doctor on the scene, but the poor man is not truly dead, just paralyzed by the deadly zombie powder wielded by Peytraud, head of the Ton-Ton Macoute. As the paralyzed Christophe is lowered into the ground in a casket and buried, a single tear rolls down his cheek.

Several years later, on August 15, 1985, Dr. Dennis Alan travels to the Rio Negro area of the Amazon basin. Flown there by helicopter, Alan meets with the local shaman, a powerful man in the Amazon. The Shaman senses an evil force closing in on Dennis and wants to show the scientist what it is. To facilitate such a view, he gives Dennis a potion. After sipping the strange concoction, Alan falls asleep and encounters his spirit guide, a playful jaguar. Then the vision turns grotesque. A cold wind blows in the jungle and in the dream world the Shaman turns into a grinning, devilish black man: Peytraud of Haiti! Groping hands pull Alan beneath the ground, deeper and deeper into the rotting core of the Earth.

Alan awakens to discover the vision was all a dream, yet in reality his helicopter pilot has been killed ... his face consumed by maggots. Terrified, Alan runs across a river to escape. He senses an evil presence pursuing him but a jaguar, his spirit guide, leads him safely to a road nearly 200 miles away. Alan survives this strange incident and returns to the United States.

After less than a week in Boston, Alan is summoned to meet his old friend Earl Schoonbacher, a consultant to the large corporation BioCorp. Earl insists that he has a job offer for the versatile Alan. Dennis listens politely as he is introduced to the head of Boston BioCorp, Dr. Cassidy. Cassidy asks the anthropologist what he knows about zombification. Alan thinks this line of questioning is a joke but he is soon presented with a death certificate and doctor's report on Christophe Juran, who was pronounced dead and buried in 1978.

Accompanying the medical records is a photograph of Christophe, alive and well, in the People's Clinic in Port au Prince. Amazingly, the picture was taken only a week ago. Dr. Cassidy wants to know who brought Christophe back from the grave and how it was done. Alan suggests that a new drug might be responsible, a Haitian anesthetic that could revolutionize modern medicine. Schoonbacher believes this powder may offer proof about the soul, but Alan dismisses the notion. He then agrees to fly to Haiti to acquire the new drug.

In Haiti, revolution is in the air, a ruthless dictator is in the palace and poverty dominates the streets. Alan senses the same dark presence he encountered in the Amazon. He soon meets Dr. Marielle DuChamps, the beautiful psychologist who sent BioCorp the picture of Christophe. She leads Alan into the clinic and stresses the terrible conditions in the establishment. She introduces the American to Marguerite, a woman who died and was buried 15 years ago, but who was found a year ago wandering in the marketplace of her village. Alan interviews Marguerite and notes that her hands are scarred — ripped apart from clawing her way out of the grave. There is also an unending horror in her eyes, and she cannot speak. Alan is shaken by his encounter with Marguerite, but is most interested in meeting Christophe, a "zombie" who supposedly has his memory and speech still intact.

That night, Marielle takes Dennis to meet Lucien Celine, a local magician powerful both in politics and voodoo. He is the owner of a nightclub for tourists and an information broker with knowledge of Christophe. Alan converses with Lucien, but the man warns Alan that there are some secrets in Haiti that people there hide even from themselves. Then Lucien asks Marielle to dance for the crowd in celebration of Erzulie, the Goddess of Love. Marielle is angered by the request and leaves the club. On the way out, a man spits a substance at her and she freezes in her tracks. At the same time, Peytraud, head of the Ton-Ton Macoute, enters the club. Lucien warns Alan that Peytraud is a black magician and a very dangerous man.

Soon, Marielle has changed into a beautiful dress and begins to dance for the crowd. Lucien claims she is possessed by the spirit of the Love goddess and that possession is as natural to Marielle "as breathing." During Marielle's performance, Peytraud taps on his glass and uses black magic to bollix the dance. The dancers go crazy and one tries to kill Marielle. Alan intervenes, breaking a

Dr. Alan (Bill Pullman) and Dr. DuChamps (Cathy Tyson) are fingered by a minion of Peytraud in *The Serpent and the Rainbow*.

bottle over the dancer's head. Peytraud leaves the club, his eyes never wandering far from Alan. The next morning, Marielle remembers nothing of her dance or the experience at the club.

DuChamps and Alan travel to Christophe's village, but no one there will help them find him. Finally, Christophe's sister locates them and suggests that they begin searching nearby graveyards. Dennis and Marielle spend most of the night doing just that; at the third graveyard they encounter grave robbers, but no sign of Christophe. Then, suddenly, Christophe steps out of the shadows. Marielle and Alan interview him and he recalls everything that happened to him during his burial. He claims that his soul has been stolen and that he is forced to do evil things at the bidding of a powerful man. He also warns that he is often sent to haunt the dreams of other people. Alan probes further and Christophe reveals the existence of a poison powder. Alan realizes this powder might be the anesthetic he seeks.

The next morning, Alan returns to his hotel room to find it covered in blood. Strange voodoo symbols have been scribbled all over the walls. Alan turns a corner and sees the shadow of an assailant, armed with machete, approaching him. He ducks out a window and goes to speak with Lucien again, but Lucien steadfastly refuses to talk about the powder. After much prodding, he gives up the name of the man who produces the powder: Mozart.

Alan and Marielle go to a cockfight and meet with Louis Mozart. He informs them that he will make the powder for them. Alan replies that he will need proof that the formula works. Mozart agrees and tests the poison on a goat. After drinking just a little bit of the substance, the goat collapses. Alan carves a small symbol in its hoof and says he will return the following day to see if the goat is raised from the dead. After Alan leaves Mozart, Marielle talks to him about voodoo and the culture of Haiti. She tells him that the God of Voodoo dwells not just in Heaven but in the bodies and the flesh of the people of Haiti. The psychologist sees no conflict between her religion and science.

To further expose Alan to the mysteries of the land, Marielle leads him on a religious pilgrimage. Thousands of people holding candles walk through a beautiful countryside singing. That night, Alan sees Christophe standing close by with a strange, veiled bride beside him. The bride approaches seductively and Alan lifts her veil. The bride is a desiccated corpse. Alan jumps back in fright when the bride opens her mouth and a giant snake leaps out at him. Dennis awakens from the nightmare, shaken. The next morning, following the end of the religious processional, Alan and Dr. DuChamps become lovers inside a concealed mountain cave.

Returning to Port-au-Prince, Alan is apprehended by the secret police and taken to the headquarters of the organization. Peytraud confronts him and demands to know why he is in Haiti. He also tells Alan that DuChamps and Christophe are dangerous radicals. Alan maintains his innocence and claims he is a tourist enjoying the beauties of Peytraud's country. Peytraud warns Dennis that Haiti is not Grenada, and that there will be no anarchy here. After Alan is released, he returns to Mozart to check on the "zombie" goat. He cons Mozart into including him in the mixing process of the powder. For $1,000, Mozart agrees to show Alan how to make the dangerous poison.

They travel to a cemetery by moonlight because they need fresh bones. They open up a small casket and Alan is horrified to see the body within it: It is the bride he saw in his nightmare! Mozart reveals that this woman once had powerful voodoo powers and that her bones will make the potion strong. The next morning, DuChamps and Alan return to the clinic to get some sleep but the Secret Police attack. Alan is brought before Peytraud again, this time to be tortured. Alan offers to leave the country but his nemesis warns that it is too late for that. This time, Peytraud does not want lies; he wants to hear Alan scream. With vicious speed, Peytraud hammers a spike into Alan's scrotum. Later, the police release the injured Alan and Marielle tends to his wound. Fortunately, the blow was struck to create fear, not injury, and Alan is not badly hurt.

Alan continues to work with Mozart in collecting and mixing the powder. Further ingredients include poison sea toad, puffer fish, herbs and minerals, all charred and then mixed together with crushed human bones. The mixing process takes three days and three nights.

While Alan waits for the formula to be completed, he and Marielle stay at a small cottage on the beach. One night, Alan awakes to discover a boat sailing to his door. It is on fire, and standing at the ship's fore is the dead bride! Alan panics when his room shifts and transforms into a coffin. As he pummels the top of the coffin, blood surrounds him. He wakes up screaming and discovers the decapitated body of Christophe's sister in bed next to him. Before Alan can make sense of this scene, the Secret Police break in and take photographs of him with the dead bodies. Alan is again brought before Peytraud, who warns him to leave Haiti before those photographs are made public. Peytraud also shows Alan his collection of souls. He has hundreds of small jars, each holding a soul of an enemy. Peytraud claims that these souls now serve him and that he can reach Alan anywhere, inside his mind. Then Peytraud promises Alan he will not harm Marielle, and he orders his men to escort Alan to the airport. Alan is forced aboard a plane. As he awaits take-off, Mozart sneaks aboard and gives Alan the powder they mixed together. Alan will not go home empty-handed after all.

In Boston, Alan tests the powder at BioCorp using a baboon as a guinea pig. Dennis learns that the zombie anesthetic affects only certain parts of the brain. Although the animal is paralyzed, it is still conscious. It sees and feels everything happening to it but is unable to move. Essentially, the powder makes an animal or person a prisoner in their own body. Fortunately, Alan also learns that the powder wears off in 12 hours. Still, people might be buried in 12 hours, only to awake deep beneath the earth in a cramped, airless coffin.

One night, Alan attends a dinner party at the home of Dr. Cassidy. He tells Schoonbacher that he feels bad about leaving Marielle in Haiti. He has attempted to contact her but has been unsuccessful. Schoonbacher warns him not to return to Haiti, but Alan decides that he must. In Haiti, Peytraud casts a spell that travels all the way to Boston and affects Mrs. Cassidy. The hostess becomes possessed with Peytraud's spirit and, after chewing her own wine glass, she tries to kill Alan with a table knife. Alan leaves the house after realizing that Peytraud can reach him anywhere in the world.

Upon his return to Haiti, Alan is apprehended immediately — not by the police, but by Lucien's men. Lucien informs Alan that Marielle is safe at the clinic. He also takes steps to give Alan some psychic protection from Peytraud's evil powers. At the same time, Mozart is captured and taken to Peytraud's dank headquarters. His head is chopped off with a machete and Peytraud drinks his blood and traps his soul. Now the villain is even more powerful. In the courtyard outside his nightclub, Lucien and Alan experience further horror. Lucien seizes up and dies. Out of his dead mouth crawls a scorpion. Alan backs up in horror, only to be met by a man who blows the paralyzing powder in Alan's face. Alan begs the locals for help, informing them that he has been poisoned. Of course, they think he is crazy. As the poison begins to paralyze his body, Alan falls to the ground. Curious onlookers gather around and he begs them not to bury him. Alan is taken to the hospital and pronounced dead. Peytraud visits him there and tells him that he will experience "no rest" and that he will see everything. He also promises to decapitate Marielle that very night.

Alan is unable to move or protest as he is dumped inside a coffin and lowered into a hole six feet deep. To make sure that Alan does not grow lonely in the grave, Peytraud throws a spider in with him. Then Alan is sealed into the casket and left for dead. Twelve hours later, Alan awakens, gasping for air. He screams for help and tries to maneuver in the tightness of his coffin. Then he feels the spider crawling along his trapped body and pounds furiously to be released. He is saved by Christophe, who still wanders these cemeteries at night.

Christophe informs Alan that he has been to "the other side" and so now has the powers of that realm as well. He also warns the American that the final battle with Peytraud will be fought not in reality but inside Alan's mind. Regaining his strength, Alan heads for the Secret Police headquarters hoping that he is not too late to save Marielle. At the same time, newscasters report that Baby Doc Duvalier and his family have fled Haiti. The fires of revolution boil and riots break out across the country.

Peytraud realizes that time is running out for his evil regime and he prepares to separate Marielle's head from her body so that her soul will also serve his dark purposes. Haitians attack the police headquarters and rip it to pieces. At the same time, Alan breaks in and tries to find his opponent. He is tormented by a torture chair which comes to life and pursues him. Then he is attacked by a revivified Lucien, who pulls his own head off in a fit of rage. The torments do not end and Alan must traverse a corridor of pain where decaying hands grope blindly for him from prison cells. Alan falls down a staircase and finally enters the lair of his enemy.

The two men fight to the death and Marielle shatters the soul containers. The captive souls are released and they surround Peytraud. Attacked by the spirit of his former victims, Peytraud catches fire and collapses on a mountain of skulls. His body vanishes. Thinking the battle over, Alan and DuChamps attempt to escape the headquarters but are confronted by Alan's nightmare bride. Peytraud returns from the other side horribly burned, and warns there will be no rest for Alan. The two men grapple and with the help of the jaguar, Alan's spirit guide, the American defeats Peytraud. Realizing that the nightmare is occurring inside his mind and soul, Alan uses his spiritual powers to strap Peytraud to the torture chair. Then, Alan telekinetically causes a spike to impale Peytraud's scrotum. Peytraud screams as he is pulled downwards into hell.

Marielle assures Alan that the nightmare is finally over. The trapped souls are free and Haiti will awake to freedom for the first time in many years. Beyond these triumphs, Alan finally has concrete evidence of man's "soul."

COMMENTARY: The book *The Serpent and the Rainbow*, a fascinating

Wes Craven on location in Haiti during principal photography on *The Serpent and the Rainbow*.

non-fiction journey into the world of voodoo, was written by Wade Davis and published in 1985 by Simon and Schuster. At 297 pages, the book served not only as a travelogue and history of Haiti, but also as startling exploration of "the boundaries of death." As such, it was perfect material for Hollywood and little time was wasted in adapting the book to film. Craven and writers Richard Maxwell and A.R. Simoun have remained substantively true to the spirit of Davis's work.

In print, *The Serpent and the Rainbow* begins with a note on orthography. The history of the word "voodoo" is discussed, including its roots in the Fon language of Dahomey and Togo. Most importantly, the note comments on how voodoo (or "vodoun,") as Davis chooses to call it refers not to the typical Hollywood vision of fantasy, sorcery and black magic but to a specific event: a dance in which spirits arrive to mount and possess the living.

The opening note also discusses the spelling of the word "zombie" and what it means (to Haitians: the spirit of a dead man). The tenor of the book is immediately established as one of respect and understanding for customs quite different from Western tradition. Though different in some graphic details, Craven's adaptation of the film is faithful to the spirit of the book because it also attempts to understand voodoo rather than merely exploit it as a Hollywood construct representing mysticism and the occult. On the contrary, Craven's picture carries over the travelogue aspects of the book and the respect for a fascinating culture.

Even the structure of the film is faithful to the book. In the first chapter of *The Serpent and the Rainbow*, ("The Jaguar"), Davis recounts a 1974 visit to the Amazon jungle. Once there, he journeys with an English journalist across 250 roadless miles of rain forest which separate Colombia from Panama. During the journey, a black jaguar appeared before Davis and pointed the way to safety. In the film, protagonist Dennis Alan also finds himself in the Amazon rain forest. Although this scene in the film is utilized to establish the threat of the dangerous magic man Peytraud (a character not in the book), Alan escapes from the jungle when his spirit guide, a jaguar, leads him to the road. There are slight changes but for the most part unimportant ones. The jaguar serves the same purpose in the book and in the film.

In Chapter 2, "The Frontier of Death," Wade Davis meets with his old professor Dr. Schultes (Dr. Schoonbacher in the movie) and a psychiatrist and pioneer in psychopharmacology named Dr. Nathan S. Kline (Dr. Andrew Cassidy in the movie). They present Davis with a tempting offer. They show him the death certificate of Clarvius Narcissus (Christophe in the film), a man who died in 1962, but who has recently been seen alive and well in Central Haiti. He is the victim of a voodoo cult — a zombie risen from the grave. Craven's movie is especially faithful in this section, capturing the mood and even much of the dialogue from this chapter. Interestingly, the film leaves out one detail. In Davis' book, the zombie powder is important not just as a new anesthesic, but in an entirely different context. It is to be used to keep NASA astronauts sedated, a kind of suspended animation for interplanetary trips. Perhaps this is one case where truth really is stranger than fiction, and the filmmakers opted to leave out this detail ... perhaps considering it too far-fetched for audiences to accept.

From there, Craven's film continues to mirror its source material. Although details such as those found in Chapter 3 ("The Calabar Hypothesis") are left out, most of the characters in the book show up in the film. Maximillian Beauvoir, Lucien in Craven's picture, is club owner and vodoun expert. Rachel Beauvoir is his daughter, but in the film this relationship has been removed and Marielle Duchamps (Cathy Tyson) is the re-named character (who also serves as the director of the Centre de Psychiatric et Neurologie in Port-au-Prince). The Haitian chemist who produces the zombi powder (tetrodotoxin) is Marcel Pierre in the book and Mozart in the film. Although the sequences in which the American ethnobiologist negotiates for the powder are translated successfully from book to film, the history of the character is quite different. In the book, Marcel is a member of the villainous Ton Ton Macoute, the film's antagonists, not a victim of the police force as Mozart is in the picture.

Where the two versions of *The Serpent and the Rainbow* really differ is in the character called Peytraud (Zakes Mokae). There is no such powerful "voudon" villain in Davis' book. Instead, Davis encounters strange secret societies which use the zombie powder as a kind of punishment for those who have broken unspoken laws. Clairvius Narcisse, for instance, is depicted in the book as a man who did not share his wealth and who had many mistresses he did not support. He hoarded his money and was the first man in his village to have a tin roof atop his house. One of his enemies, possibly in his own family, sold him out to a secret society and they made him a "zombi." In the film, Christophe is made a zombie by Peytraud as punishment for speaking against Haitian authority. Thus the character changes from "bad" to "good" in adaptation.

The tetrodoxotin remains a tool in both media, a tool by which Haitians (secret societies in the book, Police Chief Peytraud in the film) control people. Otherwise, what the film misses is something that would have been impossible to convey in two hours: the long history of slavery in Haiti. Much of the book is concerned with the "maroons," escaped slaves who fled the French plantations and formed their own society based on African tradition in the mountains of Haiti.

Fortunately, the film does capture many fascinating specifics of the book. In both cases, the Haitian night club owner warns the American interloper that Haiti is a land "where things are not the way they seem." In both media, the American witnesses a voodoo dance wherein a woman is possessed by a God (Erzulie in the motion picture, the divine horseman in the book). The book and the film also share a fantastic religious pilgrimage, scenes of possessed people eating glass and dramatic examples of the zombie powder's power, although in the book Davis is not made a zombie himself.

What Craven's *The Serpent and the Rainbow* lacks in the "history" department is easily compensated by the amazing visuals the movie provides. Much of the film plays out as a sort of documentary as Craven leads his camera and crew all over Haiti and the Dominican Republic. The result is a film that feels authentic and is all the more frightening because of that "realism." The documentary approach, authentic locations and "real" extras lend a plausibility to the plot which on film is essentially a battle between two men: Alan and Peytraud.

Like *A Nightmare on Elm Street*, this battle unfolds not only in reality, but in the dream landscape of the mind. Because Peytraud is a magician extraordinaire, he is able to haunt Alan's dreams with terrifying regularity. From the scene in the Amazon to the final battle, Peytraud is always a presence and he thus provides a sense of cohesion that only a supernatural villain (which the book lacked) could provide. Though Davis may not have been happy with the addition of an "evil" character to challenge his hero, it makes sense from a movie perspective. In the book, Davis fights against prejudice, secret societies and a world where rational causality is meaningless, but those threats are separate and unfocused ones. By making Peytraud a figure outside rational causality who threatens Alan's very soul, Craven's film hones the terror in the situation while also maintaining the "stranger-in-a-strange land" atmosphere of the book.

Having established the world of Haiti through scenes in the night club (where voodoo ceremonies are practiced for tourists) as well as the incredible pilgrimage up the mountain, Craven then sets out to terrify his audience with the most frightening images imaginable. As in *A Nightmare on Elm Street*, "rubber reality" is the order of the day as Peytraud infiltrates Alan's mind and wages war there. In one harrowing scene, Alan runs to a door and pounds on it. The camera turns on its side and the walls close in on him, revealing that he is no longer in a room but a coffin instead. Just when the feeling of claustrophobia is unbearable, the coffin fills with blood and Alan drowns in the thick scarlet substance. It is a frightening image that foreshadows Alan's later experience inside a real coffin.

In other instances, Craven is more subtle with his imagery. Following a night in the cemetery, Alan returns to his hotel to find strange markings all over his walls. As his attention turns to a nearby hallway, a shadow on the wall is glimpsed. It is approaching and wielding a machete. Alan jumps from the window and darts away before the assailant is more than a shadow, but the effect is adrenaline-inducing. By instinct, the audience fears the unseen and this approaching shadow is an unseen specter of incredible menace.

Craven is also at his macabre best in depicting Alan's paralysis and brief time spent in the grave. The scene begins powerfully when a figure from a crowd unexpectedly steps forwards and blows the poison into Alan's face. In a previous scene, Boston scientists established the effects of the poison, so the audience is aware that it perfectly mimics death, but that the victim of the powder is conscious. Thus they share Alan's panic as he begs for help from locals who do not understand what he is saying. As Alan collapses, Craven switches to Alan's point of view, thus putting the viewer into his head. Now the audience is paralyzed too. The director sticks with the point-of-view perspective as doctors pronounce Alan dead. Then they see Alan being lowered into a coffin and the lid being hammered on ... again from the first-person point of view.

After the audience sees dirt being thrown onto the coffin (and spraying Alan's face) there is only darkness, (the screen goes totally black). When the poison wears off, Alan awakens in darkness and pounds at the coffin to escape. Still, the audience sees nothing but black. Alan's breathing becomes labored and then he feels the spider crawling across his body. It is a spine-tingling sequence so terrifying that one review accused Craven of "directorial sadism" for his decision to bury his viewers alive with their protagonist. Sadistic or not, it is a terribly effective technique and one of the scariest sequences in horror film history. Anyone who fears suffocating, spiders or being buried alive will find it almost intolerable in its intensity.

The final battle between Peytraud and Alan is a descent into a twisted reality. Alan must pass through a prison where grotesque bony arms grope blindly for him. To enter Peytraud's den of evil, he must also descend a strange staircase resembling one of M. Escher's paintings. Many critics have complained about this finale, because the documentary-like style which dominated the early part of the film is jettisoned in favor of a dark fantasy world where the laws of physics seem no longer to apply. These naysayers have missed the point, because Craven has already established the validity of this strange fantasy realm not only through the dream sequences which punctuate the film but through dialogue. Once rescued from the grave, Alan *is* a zombie and Christophe tells him that he can now see and do things that others cannot. Likewise, Lucien informs Alan that the final battle with Peytraud will take place in *Alan's mind*. If one considers these clues, the landscape of the battle royale is perfectly acceptable and logical from a dramatic standpoint. It takes place in a world outside "causal reality," like Davis' book, and inside the world of superstition and magic.

If the climax of *The Serpent and the Rainbow* is disappointing in any regard, it is only that Peytraud (wearing a red shirt), becomes a horribly burned specter from the "other side" who resembles the red-and-green garbed Freddy Krueger. Since both villains operate in a fantasy landscape instead of what we consider reality, and since both capture the souls of their victims, the similarity is further highlighted. The connection between Peytraud and Krueger is disturbing to some critics because *The Serpent and the Rainbow* begins as an astonishingly complex film with grand locations, interesting characters and a compelling premise. The final supernatural battle is thus seen as a reduction to easy "horror movie" clichés.

On the contrary, the final battle is surely the apex of the film, the sequence in which a cynical Westerner finally "understands" the Haitians and even gains knowledge about man's soul. Any conclusion that did not occur on a psychic landscape involving captive souls and the man who exploited them for his own strength would not have satisfied the themes at the heart of the picture.

The Serpent and the Rainbow is also commendable for its efforts to develop an interesting sort of political tyranny. Peytraud, an officer of the Ton-Ton Macoute and loyal servant to "Baby Doc" Duvalier, is a ruthless despot like his master. He controls people not only through a brutal police force but also by enslaving their very souls. People in Haiti who espouse the principles of liberty, such as Christophe, are censured not by captivity but through zombification! The tyrannies of Haiti's government in general and of Peytraud's in particular are also mirrored in the conclusion: Both forces collapse at the same time and the forces of freedom recapture not only the halls of government, but also the souls that have been enslaved by a despotic state. Craven has often referred to *The Serpent and the Rainbow* as a "political thriller" and with good reason. The personal story of Alan and Peytraud echoes the grander story unfolding in the country at the same time. As Alan deposes Peytraud, so do the Haitian people finally free themselves from "Baby Doc" Duvalier.

Like virtually every Craven flick, *The Serpent and the Rainbow* is packed with unforgettable imagery. An evil old crone in a wedding dress appears to Alan again and again. In one shocking scene, a snake leaps from her mouth and locks onto Alan's face. Of course, the snake is an image familiar from *The Hills Have Eyes, Swamp Thing, Deadly Blessing* and *A Nightmare on Elm Street*, but this strange skeletal figure is the symbol that lingers in the memory after the film has ended. With a wedding veil draped over her decaying face, this creature shuffles through Alan's dreams and squeaks and groans in the most disturbing manner imaginable. Since she is always seen in a wedding gown, an unstated, almost subconscious connection is forged between this creature and the protagonist: The old crone (representing death) is Alan's bride. Yikes!

Other images are equally terrifying. In one harrowing passage, Alan is strapped naked to a chair and Peytraud drives a metal stake through his scrotum. Like the "buried alive" sequence, this genital torture is guaranteed to generate some pretty severe squirming, especially among male viewers. Even more disgusting is the aftermath of that scene: The minions of the Ton-Ton Macoute throw the mutilated Alan from a speeding truck. As he lands in the street, his white underwear is soiled with a dark patch of blood. Grisly stuff.

When viewed in the context of Craven's film career, *The Serpent and the Rainbow* is a bit of an anomaly as it does not focus either on the American middle class or the destruction of the family. Instead it is a horrific adaptation of a good book that allows him to further indulge in his penchant for adeptly creating nightmarish fantasy worlds. It is a logical extension of the dream-motif begun in earnest in *A Nightmare on Elm Street* (after a brief flirtation in *Deadly Blessing*) and continued in *Deadly Friend*. In many ways, *The Serpent and the Rainbow* is Wes Craven's most technically adroit film until *Wes Craven's New Nightmare* in 1994. It carries no jokey satire (like *Shocker*), no teenagers (like *Deadly Friend*), and the characters and locations are captured with remarkable flair. It is a literate film thanks, no doubt, to its beginnings in Wade Davis' excellent source material, and a terrifying adventure which successfully navigates the "boundaries of death."

Shocker (1989)

Craven has constructed the escalating mayhem with such craft that disbelief is ... at least given pause. The narrative is furiously driven along by bursts of heavy metal on the soundtrack and punctuated by scenes of wicked black humor... Effects are often spectacular... Its highs are freaky and unpredictable enough to endow it with some real potential as a rollicksome midnight cult movie.— Elliott Stein (*Village Voice*, November 7, 1989)

This time around, [Craven] lacks a consistent vision, though there are some nice touches ... Craven relies too much on dreams to advance and justify his plot.— Richard Harrington (*The Washington Post*, November 2, 1989)

One of the most entertaining bad movies of the year... It's a campy comic book thriller: junk food filmmaking with some style and a sense of humor... The film's climax is a brilliantly edited montage sequence...— Kevin Sweeney (*Films in Review*, January 1990)

Craven, like David Cronenberg or George Romero, is a real virtuoso of lowercase horror and *Shocker* is crammed with dazzling bursts of macabre technique.— Michael Wilmington (*The Los Angeles Times*, October 27, 1989)

So how scummy is Wes Craven? Scummy enough ... to put a vile obscenity in the mouth of a little girl ... for no other reason than minor shock value... Craven is as tasteful as a septic system, as witty as a potato and as possessed of a sense of pace as a sidewalk. This tiresome horror film borrows liberally from *Frankenstein*, *The Thing* and ... the old TV series *The Outer Limits* yet still ends up as almost two hours worth of violent hemming and hawing.— Ralph Novak (*People Weekly*, November 13, 1988)

Shocker has a bright moment now and then. The best is a little girl, her body commandeered by Pinker, dragging her leg as she scampers through a park. Pretty funny. ...On the whole, though, *Shocker* is second-rate, ugly, predictable exploitation sadly lacking in logic or even in zippy special effects.— V.A. Musetto (*The New York Post*, October 27, 1989)

CAST: Mitch Pileggi (Horace Pinker); John Tesh (TV Newscaster); Heather Langenkamp (Victim); Peter Berg (Jonathan Parker); Jessica Craven (Counterperson); Cami Cooper (Allison); Richard Brooks (Rhino); Sam Scarber (Cooper); Theodore Raimi (Pac Man); Keith Anthony Lubow-Bellamy (Football Player); Virginia Morris (Diane); Emily Samuel (Sally); Michael Murphy (Lt. Donald Parker); Peter Tilden (Reporter); Bingham Ray (Bartender); Sue Ann Harris (Waitress); Eugene Chadbourne (Man in Bar); Jack Hoar (Sergeant); Stephen

Held (Rookie); Richard J. Gasparian (Cop #1); Joyce Guy (Cop # 2); Bobby Lee Swain (Priest #1); Joseph Roy O'Flynn (Priest #2); Linda Kaye (Woman at Stairs); Vincent Gastuaferro (Pastori); Janne K. Peters (Doctor); Bruce Wagner (Executioner); Marvin Elkins (Guard #1); Christopher Kriesa (Guard #2); Michael Matthews (Evil Mouth); Ricardo Gutierrez (Guard Sergeant); Ernie Lively (Warden); John Mueller (Fireman); Jonathan Christian Craven (Jogger); Lindsay Parker (Little Girl); Deirdre Allyn Taylor (Young Mother); Kane Roberts (Bruno); Dr. Timothy Leary (TV Evangelist); Marji Martin (Woman Couch Potato); Ray Bickel (Man Couch Potato); Mark Slama (Kid With Crow Bar); Karl Vincent (Kid With Mask); Wes Craven (Man Neighbor); Holly Kaplan (Woman Neighbor)

CREDITS: A Universal Pictures Release of an Alive Films Presentation. *Executive Producers:* Shep Gordon, Wes Craven. *Casting:* Gary M. Zuckerbrod. *Co-Producers:* Peter Foster, Bob Engelman. *Costume Designer:* Isis Mussenden. *Musical Supervisor:* Desmond Child. *Music:* William Goldstein. *Production Designer:* Cynthia Kay Charette. *Editor:* Andy Blumenthal. *Director of Photography:* Jacques Haitkin. *Producers:* Marianne Maddalena, Barin Kumar. *Writer and Director:* Wes Craven. *Stunts:* Charlie Brewer, Tony Cecere, Laura Dash, Oscar Dillon, Dane Farwell, Greg Gault, Jeff Hasserstad, Ed Hamilton, Gary Jensen, Karen E. Laine, Al Lee, Dennis Madalone, Dennis R. Scott, Charlie Sween, Pat J. Tallman, Timothy P. Trella, Steve P. Vandeman, Lee Waddell. *Unit Production Manager:* Barin Kumar. *First Assistant Director:* Robert Engelman. *Second Assistant Director:* Jeffrey Wetzel. *Assistant Producer:* Warren Chadwick. *Unit Manager:* Rick Reynolds. *Second Assistant Directors:* Mark S. Glick, W. Thomas Snyder. *Production Auditor:* Catherine Webb. *Script Supervisor:* Susan Bierbaum. *First Assistant Camera:* Robert N. Gesicoff. *Second Assistant Camera:* Lee Dublin. *Apprentice Camera Technician:* Tami Maimon. *"B" Unit Camera Operator:* Allen Blaisdell. *"B" Unit First Assistant Camera:* Doug Sheldon, Beth-Jana Friedberg, Richard Mosier. *"B" Unit Second Assistant Camera:* Sean Hise, Tom Jenson, Susan Beth Horton, John C. Bailey. *Sound Mixer:* Robert Janiger. *Boom Operator:* George M. Scott. *Gaffer:* Alan B. Brownstein. *Electrical Best Boy:* Steve Reinhardt. *Electricians:* Michael Winterburn, Randall Ott, Fred Beese, Edward Alan Frazier. *Key Grip:* Thomas J. Keffer. *Grip Best Boy:* Michael A. Perez. *Dolly Grip:* Thomas Craig Mitchell. *Grips:* Jerry F. Day, Michael J. Fahey. *Swing:* Michael Sapp Chun. *Art Director:* Randy Moore. *Set Decorator:* Naomi Shohan. *Set Designer:* Keith M. Burns. *Set Dresser:* Mark C. Haskins. *Lead Mixer:* Gene Bishop. *Property Master:* Gerry L. Franenberg. *Key Assistant Props:* Richard L. Bioni. *Assistant Props:* Jack Alex. *Wardrobe Supervisor:* Priscilla Poore. *Wardrobe Assistant:* Kimberly Adams. *Key Makeup and Hairstylist:* Suzanne Parker Sanders. *Makeup and Hair:* Laura Gorman. *Rigging Gaffer:* Paul W. McIlvaine. *Rigging Electrician:* Craig Allen Brink. *Rigging Key Grip:* Charles Belisl. *Stunt Coordinator:* Tony Cecere. *Special Effects:* Special Effects Services and Larry Fioritta. *Special Effects Lead:* Bob Phillips. *Special Effects Technicians:* Ted Coplen, Joe Hefferman. *Special Makeup Design:* Lance Anderson. *Key Special Makeup:*

David L. Anderson. *Special Makeup Lab Technicians:* Scott Coulter, Jeff Farley, David Artherton, Roger McCoin. *Production Coordinator:* Nancy King. *Assistant Production Accountant:* Lydia Sarmiento. *Location Manager:* David Halloman. *Assistant Location Manager:* Dan Gorman. *Additional Location Scout:* Geoff Harding. *Construction Coordinator:* Robert A. Maisto. *Construction Foreman:* Alan Macrae. *Lead Carpenter:* Gary Sagliardo. *Carpenters:* John C. Cales, Glenn Consbruck, Keith Cox, Dave Florence, Hal. B. Forsen, John M. Holliday, William Jones, John S. Reynolds, Ray Turnberg, Lance C. Amflick. *Stand-by Carpenters:* Frank Lews, Dan Whiffier, Victor Price. *Lead Scenic Artist:* Donna F. Slager. *Scenic Painters:* Catherine Burns, Dennis Stephens. *Set Dressing Swing:* Jonathan Bobbitt, Philip Chapwick, Kristin Jones. *Steadicam Operators:* Randy Nolan, Mark O'Kane. *Still Photographer:* Peter Iovino. *Storyboard Artist:* Mark Baird. *Transportation Coordinator:* Stephen Hudis. *Transportation Captain:* Kevin Hudis. *Drivers:* John P. Menese, John Moore, Michael Long, Marc Christopher, Charles Hindman. *Production Van Driver:* Tony Gene Sackman. *Assistant Production Coordinator:* Martha J. Liermann. *Assistant to Mr. Craven and Ms. Maddalena:* Jeffrey Fenner. *Assistant to Director:* Toby Forlenza. *Production Assistants:* James D. Deck, David Topor, David Grace, Hugh R. Moss, Tony Sina-Schwartz, Rex Cook, Donna Leonard, Dan Spaulding, Richard A. Saustegun. *Set Medic:* Arnold Peterson, Rescue Ambulance. *Catering:* Cast Supper. *Unit Publicist:* Stacy Ivers. *Extra Casting:* Nancy Mott. *Casting Assistant:* Jodi Rothfield. *Stand-ins:* Mark Slama, Dennis Tracy, Karl Vincent. *Production Legal:* Wyman, Isaacs and Green. *Completion Bond:* Film Finances, Inc. *Additional Photography:* Mac Ahlberg. **Second Unit:** *First Assistant Directors:* Stuart Lyons, Stephen Lofaro. *First Assistant Camera:* Stephan Collins, Chris Moseley. *Second Assistant Camera:* Debbie O'Brien, Chris Hood. *Script Supervisor:* Lori Gerson. *Art Director:* Randy Moore. *Costumer:* Janice Kopelon. *Makeup:* Rosalia Altamura. *Gaffer:* John Bertram. *Key Grips:* Rhen Alderman, Thomas V. Browne. *Grip Best Boys:* Steph Blakemore, Pascal Frenchot. *Electrical Best Boys:* Anthony Varuola, Brian Devin. *Dolly Grip:* Larry Roth. *Grip:* Randle P. Little. *Electrician:* Richard Kelly. *Boom Operators:* Arthur Jackson, Eric Goldstein. *Set Dresser:* Alyson Starbird. *Scenic Artist:* Matt Flynn. *Assistant Scenic Artist:* Mona May. *Carpenters:* Buzzy James Dudley, Kirk M. Petruccelli, Johannes Spalt. *Art Department Swing:* Renee Landry. **Post Production:** *Post Production Supervisor:* Warren Chadwick. *Post Production Coordinator:* Mark G. Coleman. *Assistant Editor:* Karen Joseph. *Apprentice Editor:* Jonathan Christian Craven. *Post Production Accounting:* Production Accountant Services. *Visual Effects Wrangler:* Jeff Okun. *Visual Effects Editor:* Robert Yamomoto. *Visual Effects Coordinator:* Jonathan Craven. *Digital Visual Effects:* The Polycom Group, Inc., Alan Barnett. *Visual Effects Assistant:* Mark Phillips. *Technical Animation Supervisor:* Samuel E. Recros. *Motion Control:* The Chandler Group. *Motion Control Operator:* Joshua Cushner. *Visual Effects Assistant:* Charles May. *Video Services and Assembly:* John Bryant. *Video Playback:* Fred Donelson. *Photo Roto:* Nick Vasu, C & D Inking. *Visual Effects:* Apogee Inc.— Roger Dorney, Perpetual

Motion Pictures, David J. Williams, Hollywood Optical Systems, Inc., Cinema Research Group, Pacific Title and Art Studio, Planet Blue. *24 Frame Video Displays:* Video Image. *Supervising Sound Editors:* Michael Redbourn, Richard Shorr. *Sound Effects:* Richard Shorr. *Re-Recorded at:* Lorimar Studios. *Re-recording Mixers:* Wayne B. Heitman, John Boyd, Tennyson Sebastian II. *ADR Mixer:* Martin Church. *Foley Mixer:* Robert Perissi. *Foley Artists:* Robert Friedman, Keith Olson, George Borghi. *Sound Editing:* Top Sound, Inc. *ADR Editor:* Robert Hefferman. *Music Editors:* Richard Shorr, Laura Pearlman. *Sound Track Music Coordinators:* Pat Lucas (SBK Records), Ed Gerrard (Alive Records). *Sound Editors:* Dan Yale, Val Kukloski, John Kwitkowski. *Assistant Sound Editors:* Daryl Hall, Ken Troise. *ADR Group Coordinator:* Leigh French. *Color Timing:* Mateo Deravenessian. *Negative Cutter:* Dode Weyant. *Special Visual Effects:* Available Light, Ltd. *Titles:* Mercer Titles and Optical Effects, Ltd. *Lenses and Cameras:* Clairmont Camera. *Production Services and Equipment:* Keylite Product Services, Inc. *Color:* Foto Kem. A Universal Release. In Memory of Barin Kumar. *Running Time:* 111 minutes. *MPAA Rating:* R

SYNOPSIS: A man works obsessively in his filthy workshop. Impaired by a limp, the psychopath works with TV sets, electronic boards and a bloody hunting knife. On his arm is the tattoo of a spider, its legs in the shape of lightning bolts. After a few moments, TV sets come to violent life with terrible images. Riots, Nazi war footage, nuclear blasts and news footage of a recently massacred family appear and disappear, one after the other. The news footage is punctuated by a frightening report that the killer of a family is still loose. He has been killing for nine months and the police have no leads. All they know is that an unidentified man breaks into homes and butchers whole families without mercy.

In Meriville, young Jonathan Parker is the toast of the town. He is attending college on a football scholarship and everything seems to be going his way. During football practice one afternoon, Jonathan is distracted by the presence of his girlfriend Allison Clemen, and is tackled by his buddy, Rhino. Coach Cooper harasses Jonathan for his lack of concentration. On the next run, Jonathan is distracted again and runs smack into the goal post. Afraid he has a concussion, Jonathan leaves practice and heads for his rented home off-campus. He is accompanied by Allison, who is worried about the injury. While walking home, Jonathan and Allison end up in a neighborhood that is familiar to Parker. It is the block where he grew up and where his foster family still lives. Outside his house, a repair van with "Pinker's TV Repair" emblazoned on the side is parked. Since it is now late at night, Jonathan thinks this is odd. He goes into the house alone and finds his mother and sibling under attack by the vicious Horace Pinker. Jonathan tries to save his family but when he tackles Pinker, he goes right through him. Jonathan wakes up suddenly in his home and realizes that he has had a vision of his family's massacre. The truth of his vision is confirmed when he receives a telephone call from his foster father, Lt. Donald Parker, who tells him that his family has been murdered.

After attending the funeral, Jonathan tells his father in a local bar that he dreamed of the murderer. Donald thinks this is crazy, but Jonathan reveals the exact details of the crime scene, things that he could not possibly have seen. Furthermore, he remembers the name he saw on the van: Horace Pinker. Although Donald does not believe Jonathan's story about a prescient dream, he agrees to check out Pinker.

That night, Jonathan, Donald and a squad of policeman surround the Pinker repair shop. They enter the store and find it filled with TV sets, all playing scenes of carnage like fire bombings in Vietnam. From his hiding place, Pinker watches the intruders. When one officer strays too close, Pinker springs and drags the policeman into the alcove. Jonathan spots blood pouring out on the floor and he and his father find the dead cop in Pinker's secret room. Also clearly visible are several dead animals hanging from hooks. Most disturbingly, the dead cop's uniform is missing. Outside, Pinker murders two more cops thanks to his disguise. Before the night is over, four policemen are dead and Pinker has escaped.

The next morning, Pinker's face is all over the news. Reports about the cop massacre and Jonathan's unconventional means of fingering the killer proliferate. Jonathan goes to class, leaving Allison at his house. Before he leaves, Jonathan presents Allison with a birthday present: a necklace with a heart around the chain. After Jonathan has left, Horace breaks into his house and brutally murders Allison. At football practice, Coach Cooper tells Jonathan he needs to go home at once. Parker passes the police in his house and sees that blood has been sprayed all over the bathroom. Allison lies dead in the bath tub, floating in her own blood. Jonathan mourns another loss and decides that it is up to him to stop Pinker. With his football buddy Rhino beside him, Jonathan goes to sleep and dreams of Pinker again. When he awakens, he knows where Pinker will strike next, and he and Rhino rush to the scene. Donald Parker, afraid that his foster son has really gone around the bend, follows him with several police officers.

The police, Jonathan, Rhino and Donald Parker corner Pinker on Maddalena Avenue. Pinker flees to the roof of an apartment building and Jonathan pursues him. The two men fight and the police arrive and apprehend the serial killer. As he is being dragged away, Pinker tells Jonathan that killing is in their blood. Jonathan is shaken, but Donald assures him that the nightmare is over. Jonathan says he wants to be present when Pinker gets the chair. He feels he has earned the right to see Pinker die.

As Pinker awaits execution, he conducts a black magic ritual in his death row cell. A spirit springs out of a television set and grants Pinker a special gift. As it does so, Pinker is seemingly electrocuted. Security guards arrive just in time to see Pinker collapse and they think he has committed suicide. One officer attempts mouth-to-mouth, but Pinker rips his lips off! Pinker is then dragged to the execution chamber and strapped to the electric chair. He sits there laughing, looking into Jonathan's face, and reveals that he is actually Jonathan's natural father. He tells him to remember how Pinker murdered his mother. Jonathan does remember: He shot Pinker in the leg when he was just a kid! The execution switch is pulled and Pinker shakes. The lights go out, and when they come back on, Pinker is still holding onto life. A female doctor runs to assess his situation but when she touches him, she receives a stunning electric shock. The lights go out again and when they return, Pinker is gone. Donald Parker, Jonathan and the police search the execution chamber as the injured doctor is carried away, and Pinker's dead body is found in a corner. But Jonathan suspects that somehow the reign of terror is just beginning.

Pinker's consciousness has hopped bodies: His soul is now hiding inside the female doctor! She awakens in a squad car and attacks her police drivers. The car crashes and there is an explosion. The doctor and one officer die in the blaze, and the other officer, Pastori, is rushed to the hospital.

Jonathan goes home and sleeps. In his dreams, he encounters a bloodied Allison in the shower. She warns him that Pinker is still loose and "learning to move." She gives him back the heart necklace, the symbol of their undying love, and tells him that it will ward off the serial killer. When Jonathan wakes, the necklace is in his bed. Fearing that he has gone crazy, Jonathan decides to move because there are too many bad memories in the house. Suddenly there is a knock on the door: It is Sgt. Pastori. Jonathan is taken by surprise when Pastori reveals the same limp that afflicted Pinker and starts shooting at him. Jonathan runs to a nearby park but Pastori/Pinker, still shooting, follows. Finally, Pastori has a heart attack, immobilizing Pinker momentarily. Realizing he needs a new body, Pinker shoots a passing jogger and jumps into his body. Then he switches bodies again, this time inhabiting a little girl, Amanda, who boards a bulldozer and tries to run over Jonathan. When she crashes, Amanda runs away. Jonathan runs after her and starts beating her, but Amanda's mother sees the battle and thinks that Jonathan is attacking her child. When Jonathan drops the heart necklace on Amanda the talisman forces Pinker to abandon her body. He jumps into her mother's body and then rapidly into a muscular construction worker. With a pick-axe in hand, the construction worker hooks Jonathan's necklace and tosses it into the middle of the lake. With no means of defense, Jonathan retreats.

Later, Jonathan reveals to Rhino, Coach Cooper and his friend Pac Man that Pinker is still alive and trying to kill him. He explains that what he needs to defend himself is the necklace. He asks Coach Cooper if he will return to his (Jonathan's) home and get a diving mask so Jonathan can dive into the lake to retrieve the talisman. Cooper agrees and he and Pac Man head for Jonathan's place. Time goes by and the coach and Pac Man fail to show up. Jonathan realizes something has gone wrong and returns home to find that Pinker has jumped into Coach Cooper's body and murdered Pac Man. The coach tries to murder Jonathan but Allison arrives from the other side and tries to will Pinker out of

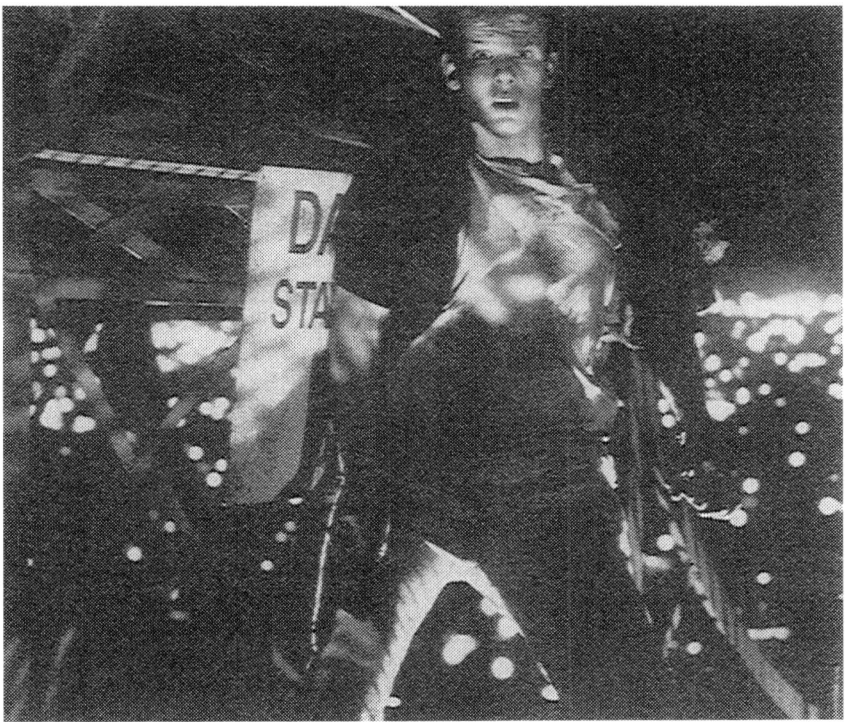

"I'm nationwide now!" A stunned Jonathan Parker (Peter Berg) watches as Horace Pinker enters the world of television via a satellite dish in *Shocker*.

the coach's body. The coach cannot beat Pinker but he has the willpower to kill himself. He stabs himself in the heart and Pinker is forced into the open. Allison fires a beam of pure light through the serial killer, but Pinker escapes death by jumping into an electrical outlet. Drained, Allison disappears.

Donald Parker arrives at Jonathan's house and sees the carnage. He now believes that Jonathan is a copycat killer and he reads the boy his rights. Parker touches a lamp and it sparks. Now, Pinker is inside Parker! Jonathan realizes this and runs away, his father/Pinker in hot pursuit. Jonathan runs down an alleyway and climbs up a TV broadcasting tower. Still in Parker's body, Pinker pursues. High above the city, the two men fight. Pinker finally ceases when Parker has a heart attack. With no other body to escape to, Pinker slips into a satellite dish and as a consequence becomes infinitely more powerful. "I'm nationwide now!" he tells Jon as he flies merrily away on the TV airwaves. Jonathan rescues his father, who reveals that he faked a heart attack to fool Pinker.

Now that Pinker can enter any American home with a TV set, the murders continue. Jon pulls Rhino and his football team together for a plan: He convinces them to break into a power station close to midnight and turn off the power. Then Jonathan asks a TV reporter to set up a live feed in his mother's home, promising that he will bring the killer right to him (and consequently make him a TV anchorman). The camera has to be operating at 11:55 p.m. so Jonathan returns to the lake, dives in and recovers the necklace with Allison's assistance. Once on shore, they kiss and make love. All of Pinker's victims then appear to Jonathan and beg him to awaken now and stop Pinker forever. When Jonathan awakens from his dream (with the necklace), Pinker has already entered his apartment. The two duke it out until Horace jumps back into the television. Hoping the necklace will allow him to follow, Jonathan dives into the set after him.

Jonathan and Pinker traverse various TV channels. Jon chases the killer through World War II aerial bomb footage, through a *Leave It to Beaver* episode, an Alice Cooper concert and a newscast starring John Tesh. The channels continue to switch and Pinker and Parker find themselves inside the film *Frankenstein* and then nuclear test footage. Finally, they jump out of the TV and land in the living room of a family of couch potatoes. Pinker destroys the living room, beats up the father of the family and returns to the television set, this time ending up in an evangelistic program. Jonathan leaves the couch potatoes too, but not before stealing their remote control. He follows Pinker back into the dangerous world of television, but this time he has a weapon. With the remote control, Jonathan switches channels and he and Pinker find themselves in the Parker household where the news reporter is broadcasting "live."

Jonathan reveals to Pinker that the killer is now bound by "TV rules." He uses the remote control like a weapon and throws Pinker into various modes such as fast forward, rewind and freeze frame! As Jonathan is finishing with Pinker, Rhino and the football team turn off the power. Jonathan and Pinker realize that they are still inside a TV channel (one broadcasting from the Parker home) and that they must escape before the power goes off and that electric domain no longer exists. Pinker tries to jump through the TV set, but he does not make it in time: His head crashes into the TV set and he is electrocuted. Jonathan puts the necklace talisman around the camera and he jumps through the camera lens back into reality. Pinker is caught in a dying broadcast and disintegrates to static.

With Pinker gone, Jonathan leaves his home and looks up at a beautiful starry sky. A neighbor asks if that was him on the tube, but Parker has eyes only for the heavens.

COMMENTARY: *Shocker* is a rollicking horror satire filled with thrills, chills and laughs. Although it lacks the thematic complexity of *The Last House on the Left* and *The Hills Have Eyes* as well as the serious tone of *A Nightmare on Elm Street* and *The Serpent and the Rainbow*, *Shocker* is nonetheless an enjoyable picture designed solely to introduce the world to yet another horror franchise, *à la* the Freddy Krueger films.

Since *Shocker*'s purpose is to create another super-villain to charm and alarm audiences weaned on Freddy's wisecracks, much of the film's storyline is a blow-by-blow repetition of Craven's own now-seminal *A Nightmare on Elm Street*. Both films open in the filthy workshop of a mass murderer and involve the creation of a distinctive weapon. In Freddy's case, that weapon is a glove with razor blades; in Horace Pinker's case, the weapon is an array of TV sets which ostensibly receive transmission straight from Hell! Like Freddy, Horace is also physically distinctive, and therefore set apart from the rest of humanity. Instead of being a burn victim, *Shocker*'s villain sports a terrible limp (the result of an old gunshot wound) and a chrome-dome top that makes him look like Mr. Clean's doppelganger.

The similarities between *Shocker* and *A Nightmare on Elm Street* do not end with the characteristics of the villain. The protagonist in both films is the child of a local police lieutenant, both of whom are named Donald (Don Parker in *Shocker*, Don Thompson in *Elm Street*). The protagonists are also the only people aware of the killer's identity in both scenarios, and they share a strange bond with their nemesis in the landscape of dreams. Protagonists Nancy Thompson and Jonathan Parker are connected to the murderers not only through dreams but through a special relationship. Nancy is the daughter of the people who torched Freddy, and Jonathan is actually Pinker's biological son who wounded him. Even more interestingly, *Shocker* reveals specifics about Pinker's life that *Elm Street* only confronted in Marge Thompson's dialogue in the basement with daughter Nancy listening in rapt attention. Since *Shocker* tells of the serial killer's murder spree, his apprehension by the law, punishment *and* his ascension to the position of supernatural avenger, the point of attack is an early one. By contrast, *A Nightmare on Elm Street*'s late point of attack begins with the supernatural creature avenging his own death and works backwards to his origin in the guilt-ridden folks of Springwood. In this regard, *A Nightmare on Elm Street* is far more satisfying than *Shocker* because of its focus on several mysteries. The audience wonders who the killer is, why he attacks the kids on Elm Street and how he came to be burned. These questions make the story compelling and the late point of attack gives the film's structure an artistic veneer. By starting so resolutely at "the beginning" and leaving so little to the imagination, *Shocker* feels a bit more mundane and much less involving than its illustrious predecessor.

Shocker's thorough recycling of elements from *A Nightmare on Elm Street*, including identical protagonists, identical police "fathers," identical supernatural avengers and even a similar focus on dreams comes at a heavy price. For much of its overly long running time, almost a full two hours, the picture seems derivative, like ground Craven has already covered. Even Michael Murphy's character, a father and authority figure in denial, and Horace's role as another ultimate "bad father," are thematic leftovers from *A Nightmare on Elm Street* and other, better Craven productions. What finally rescues *Shocker* from the label of "rip-off," and makes it quite an individual picture, is Craven's all-out efforts to go for laughs. This humor is best displayed in two pivotal scenes

The humorous elements of the picture first come into focus during an extended set-piece in an idyllic park. Jonathan is chased by the deceased Pinker, who now inhabits the body of a cop. Pinker is so determined to catch his prey that he draws innocent bystanders into the chase and possesses their bodies with increasingly funny results. The punchline of the scene finds the desperate Pinker inhabiting the body of a cute six-year-old girl. Displaying Pinker's tell-tale limp as well as his predilection for cussing, this little darling attacks Jonathan with a vengeance, even spitting a disgusting wad of saliva in his face. It is an over-the-top, wicked moment which reminds one briefly of *The Bad Seed* (a film referenced by Craven in *Deadly Friend*).

Furious at Pinker's resilience, Jonathan tackles the child/killer just as her concerned mother wanders into sight. Of course, poor Mom thinks this crazy guy is hurting her child and she rushes in to defend her offspring from a man she assumes is a maniac! The ironic result of this scene is that Jonathan is prevented from defeating Pinker and treated as if he himself is the monster.

People's reviewer found this silly scene (and Craven himself) "scummy" for putting a child through such harassment. Movie critics are often downright silly themselves about horror films and Ralph Novak's morally indignant response to *Shocker* is certainly an example. On another memorable occasion, Gene Siskel gave thumbs-down to James Cameron's *Aliens* (an acknowledged genre landmark) because the film put a little girl (Carrie Henn) in mortal danger. Siskel apparently could not stomach the thought of a child being menaced, but his argument does not stand up under scrutiny. Does anyone (even a sheltered movie critic) seriously expect a saliva-dripping, gut-busting, face-hugging alien or a re-animated psychotic killer (as in *Shocker*) to spare a child should he or she run across one? If an evil alien or the despicable Pinker did so, it would surely be a violation of situational and dramatic logic. Ironically, such a violation would no doubt have the very same critics screaming that the director "copped out." Both *Aliens* and *Shocker* are honest in that, like their villains, they show no respect for the sanctity of childhood.

Novak's unfortunate remark about Craven's "scumminess" proves two things. The first is that horror films frequently find themselves in a no-win scenario. If they are true to their premise and put children in danger, they are reviled. Contrarily, if they fail to respect the logic of their nightmare world, they are dismissed as unbelievable and similarly disdained. Secondly, the comment reinforces what Tim Bywater and Thomas Sobchack asserted in their handbook for first-year film students, *Introduction to Film Criticism*:

> [T]he journalist approach ... seems as shallow as the average review in a daily newspaper: simply the unsupported opinions of the reviewers about a recent film.[6]

That a reviewer would label a director "scummy" because of a movie's content is absurd. Is *Boogie Nights* scummy because it unfolds within the porn industry? Is *Deliverance* scummy because it deals with rape? Are *The Exorcist* and William Friedkin also scummy because that film forces a youngster to do perverse things with a crucifix? Is *The Last Boy Scout* and its director also to be labeled "scummy" since young Danielle Harris spouts four-letter words (she is not even possessed by a serial killer or Satan?) Or, more directly, is "scumminess" merely an unsupported opinion by a man who does not like the maligned horror genre in general and Craven specifically?

Movie reviewers have no right to judge that another human being is "scummy" simply because *the reviewer* does not approve of the director's subject material. That kind of attitude is perilously close to censorship. If any critic legitimately dislikes *Shocker*, he or she should share with his readership why the film fails for him, not offer an unsupported personal opinion of the director as a substitute for credible and intelligent analysis. Fortunately, all movie reviewers are not dunderheads when it comes to horror. V.A. Musetto of *The New York Post* and others acknowledged that *Shocker*'s park set-piece is a funny and clever bit of business.

For the record, the swearing child in *Shocker does* serve a purpose far grander than either "minor shock value" or comic relief. She is a critical link in a chain. The evil Pinker becomes "respectable" by jumping into the bodies of middle-class citizens throughout the film. He is able to use these bodies like suits and therefore manipulate the rest of society into believing his deception. First, he becomes a cop and chases Parker through the park. Nobody interferes because what they see is a police officer chasing a fugitive. They are unable to see that beneath the surface there is a darker truth: The police officer is a monster and the man being chased is society's defender. At another point, Pinker changes into Jonathan's coach, another authority figure to whom people have automatic, unthinking loyalty. Pinker uses this loyalty to kill Pac Man and further hurt Jonathan.

The little girl is a perfect disguise for Pinker because, like the policeman and the coach, the young and innocent are protected by society. On the surface, all a mother can see is that a man is attacking her child. She is unaware that underneath the skin, her child is actually a monster. Craven's theme, that one should not judge a book by its cover, is expertly forwarded by Pinker's forays into other bodies, including a child's. In addition to serving this purpose in the narrative, the scene is also funny and it is also good for shock value. This is *Shocker*, after all, not *The English Patient*.

The second bit of humor in *Shocker*, one a lot less controversial than a swearing child inhabited by a serial killer, is the over-the-top conclusion. In a spellbinding montage that features rapid-fire editing, amazing *Forrest Gump*–style special effects (before there *was* a *Forrest Gump*) and footage from *Leave It to Beaver*, *Frankenstein* and other sources, Jonathan chases Pinker through the perilous land of TV. What the hero and Pinker find there is an overwhelming universe of hundreds of channels that neither one is ready to cope with. At one

Possessed by Horace Pinker, Lt. Parker (Michael Murphy) attacks his son (Peter Berg) in *Shocker*.

point, Parker begs "the Beaver" to help him, but the Cleavers forge blissfully onward in the family car. The implication is that nothing stands in the way of a perfect, blissfully ignorant American middle class. Like the people who saw Pinker assault Jonathan in the park, the characters on *Leave It to Beaver* are unable to conceive of a dark side beneath their perfect surface existence.

The humor of the final sequence is not derived just by the seamless blending of *Shocker* characters with TV icons and filmclips, but through other staged vignettes. At one critical juncture; Pinker and Jonathan jump out of the TV world and into the living room of some overweight couch potatoes. The family is hardly alarmed by the presence of strangers in the household and its members continue to eat junk food. Craven's thrust is that TV makes zombies of Americans. Even people jumping out of the screen and fighting is just more "bread and circuses" for the masses.

Another vignette finds Pinker and Jonathan battling within inches of news reporter John Tesh, who is nearly drawn into combat himself as his perfectly stacked notes are scattered across his desk. Tesh is a likable personality and this scene demonstrates his willingness to be a target of fun. After the combatants have finished with him, Tesh looks to the cameraman (off-screen) and asks if he "got that," perfectly capturing America's bottom-line approach to journalism. There is no time to wonder if the newsman is okay or how this strange event has occurred. All that matters is that the cameras keep rolling and that the people at home are continually fed a stream of images.

When Pinker and Jonathan, who are quite literally "channel surfing," arrive at Timothy Leary's evangelical program, Craven's satire reaches full strength. While Leary begs his audience to send more money for God, the *Shocker* enemies duke it out. These events ask the pointed question, where is God while this is going on? The evangelicals believe that God wants their money, but their hypocrisy is exposed by evil's presence in their very midst. They wanted to ring up the Lord, but Satan answered the call instead.

In toto, *Shocker*'s go-for-broke final montage suggests that TV is a portal of evil. Carried on the airwaves, Pinker has instant access to all of America. Craven's theme about the insidious nature of television is an echo of *Poltergeist*, another horror picture wherein the TV served as a gateway for evil spirits. Attacking television as evil's portal is an easy solution, but, Craven's picture builds beyond that simple lesson. His final comment is not that TV is just evil, it is actually all-consuming. American television is so cutthroat that it devours even those people who exploit it! Sure, television is Pinker's strength and introduction to America, but it is also his weakness. Once he jumps into the world of TV, he is bound by its rules and therefore able to be manipulated by others (including Jonathan). Thus the director was reminding a nation which had witnessed the televised downfalls of Oliver North, Jim and Tammy Faye Bakker and Jimmy Swaggart of the medium's dual nature.

In *Shocker*, Pinker is finally done in by the boob tube. He tries to re-enter television but finds it unwilling to accept him again. His head smashes through the screen and he is electrocuted. It is a death that pointedly suggests the fickle nature of TV audiences. Pinker's "death by TV" was later repeated in *Scream* (1996) when Stu (another TV junkie) also found himself electrocuted by the boob tube. At an even more basic level, Pinker's national reign of terror ends only when television sets are finally turned off, something that as a nation we are unwilling to do.

Beyond the humorous and satirical moments which give *Shocker* a unique personality, the film is strong in one other notable area: lighting. The movie is suffused with a muted blue light. Jonathan's bedroom, the shore by the lake and even the dream sequence near Maddalena Avenue (named after producer Marianne Maddalena) are all lensed in a weird blue light that perfectly mirrors the eerie luminescent light generated by television sets left on in darkness. This approach to lighting ties in nicely with the film's TV obsession and subconsciously makes viewers aware of the television motif even before the final sequence.

On the negative side, *Shocker* is tiresome in its over-reliance on dreams. Rubber reality was completely mined by the late '80s in a variety of productions, including the *Nightmare on Elm Street* franchise, *Waxworks* (in which characters stepped through wax exhibits into the fantasy world of Dracula, Wolfman, the Mummy and the Marquis De Sade[!]), *Hellbound: Hellraiser 2* (wherein protagonists visited the personal Hell of various souls, including one where invisible babes always promised but never delivered) and *Phantasm 2* (which played with a dream versus reality structure). Even *Poltergeist III* went the route of "rubber reality" by revealing a world of evil inside mirror reflections. Though Craven is arguably the initiator of this rubber reality horror trend, his return to his own subject matter seems rather lackluster after so many variations on a theme.

Secondly, *Shocker*'s plot is driven by a humor-spouting anti-hero. Although Mitch Pileggi is charismatic as Horace Pinker, the character is another Freddy wannabe. Audiences stayed away, already having seen the wise-cracking Chucky of *Child's Play*, the irony-dripping Pinhead of the *Hellraiser* franchise and Richard Lynch's supernatural cult-leader in *Bad Dreams* (1987). *Shocker*'s original concept was always to knock Freddy from his throne as the king of horror, but by mimicking the wisecracks of his better-known nemesis, Pinker fails to emerge as a real individual rather than a clone.

There is also an element of self-mockery permeating *Shocker*. With a football team and coach playing prominent roles, sports clichés are in evidence. At one point, Jonathan energizes his possessed coach with a speech about willpower. It is a campy moment rather than a genuinely moving one. Jonathan's spectral girlfriend/other-worldly protector is also rather hokey. She returns to Earth in an immaculate white dress and shoots laser beams of purity from her chest. This camp approach to the characters (a far cry from *A Nightmare on Elm Street*) proves distancing in *Shocker*. The humor which exposes society's "appearance is reality" prejudice in the park and derides TV as an all-consuming entity in the finale works really well, but the campy approach to characters is not effective.

It is hard to reconcile the self-mocking tone of *Shocker* with the extreme violence and gore that surfaces, but Craven was again ahead of the curve. His approach on *Shocker*, mixing satire and laughs with graphic violence, was followed explicitly by popular Quentin Tarantino-penned films such as *Jackie Brown* (1997), *From Dusk Till Dawn* (1995), *Natural Born Killers* (1994) and *Pulp Fiction* (1994). If one considers that *Shocker* also pioneered the effects techniques made popular in *Forrest Gump* (1994), Craven's status as the most progressive voice in modern horror cinema is virtually unimpeachable. He predicted the path of two '90s Academy Award winners before the '90s even began! And, *Shocker* was re-made, unofficially, in 1998 as the similarly plotted *Fallen*.

In the final analysis, *Shocker* is rather scattershot. The family politics are another Craven rerun (another comment on our TV culture?) and the satirical edge is less effective than in the remarkable *The People Under the Stairs*. In the Craven roster, *Shocker* is surely better than *Deadly Friend*, *The Hills Have Eyes Part II* or *Swamp Thing*, but it lacks the scope of *The Serpent and the Rainbow*, the intensity of *The Hills Have Eyes* and *A Nightmare on Elm Street*, and the purity of *The Last House on the Left*. *Shocker* also failed in the very realm it had been conceived: It did not generate a franchise.

The People Under the Stairs (1991)

...a terrifically effective scare show, a virtuoso work of cinematic terror incorporating superior cinematography and production design and, most important of all, comic relief... Craven displays a genuine and all-crucial mastery of shifts in tone...— Kevin Thomas (*The Los Angeles Times*, November 4, 1991)

This revival of the plot-driven, exhausting, funny-pointed suspense-horror picture is a welcome change from the flip, sequel-generating product that has characterized the horror film in the late '80s and early '90s.— Kim Newman (*Sight and Sound*, November 2, 1991)

Craven's politically charged plot takes dead aim at the racial divisiveness and class warfare of the Reagan '80s. It is also a fairly cynical attempt to pander to the inner city black audience, always core devotees of exploitation horror films.— Thomas Doherty (*Cinefantastique*, April 1992, page 59)

Wes Craven has been directing downhill since his terror triptych of *Last House on the Left*, *The Hills Have Eyes* and the original *Nightmare on Elm Street* so it's hardly surprising that he hits rock bottom with *The People Under the Stairs*. ...[S]cary how far Craven has fallen.— Richard Harrington (*The Washington Post*, November 6, 1991)

CAST: Brandon Adams (Fool); Everett McGill (Man); Wendy Robie (Woman); A.J. Langer (Alice); Ving Rhames (LeRoy); Sean Whalen (Roach); Bill Cobbs (Grandpa Booker); Kelly Jo Minter (Ruby); Jeremy Roberts (Spenser); Conni Marie Brazelton (Mary); Joshua Cox (Young Cop); John Hostetter (Veteran Cop); John Mahon (Police Sergeant); Theresa Velarde (Social Worker); George R. Parker (Attic Cop); Yan Birch (Stairmaster); Wayne Daniels (Stairperson 1); Michael Koeplow (Stairperson 2); Brutus/Bubb/Schultz and Zeke (Prince)

CREDITS: A Universal Pictures Release of an Alive Films production. A Wes Craven Film. *Casting:* Eileen Knight, C.S.A. *Executive Producers:* Shep Gordon, Wes Craven. *Costume Designer:* Ileane Meltzer. *Co-Producer:* Dixie Capp. *Music:* Don Peake. *Production Designer:* Bryan Jones. *Editor:* James Coblentz. *Stunts:* Brigit K. Schier, Lori Lynn Ross, Dane Farwell, Dan Rycerz, Lynn Salvatori, Marian E. Green, Beth Nafer, Paula Moody, Melvin Jones, Eric Mansker, Rex Lee Waddell, John Branagan, William R. Perry, Linda Arvidson, Kelsee Devereaux, Sandy Gimpel. *Director of Photography:* Sandi Sissel. *Producers:* Marianne Maddalena, Stuart M. Besser. *Writer/Director:* Wes Craven. *Stunt Coordinator:*

Tony Cecere. *Associate Producer:* Peter Foster. *Unit Production Manager:* Stuart M. Besser. *First Assistant Director:* Nick Mastandrea. *Second Assistant Director:* Rosemary C. Cremona. *Additional Editing:* Tom Walls. *Second Unit Director:* Peter Chesney. *Camera Operator:* George Billinger. *First Assistant Camera:* Terry J. Pfang. *Second Assistant Camera:* Craig Cockerill. *Additional Operator:* Chris Hayes. *"B" Camera First Assistant:* Dana Altomore. *Steadicam Operators:* Dan Kneece, Jeff Mart. *Steadicam Assistant:* Lex Dupon, Ted Chu. *Leader:* Brenda Ryan. *Still Photography:* Carol Westwood. *Video Playback:* Intervideo. *Sound Mixer:* Donald Summer. *Boom Operator:* Walter Charles Gorey. *Production Coordinator:* Sarah James Arbeid. *Post Production Coordinator:* Yvonne Valdez. *Assistant Production Coordinator:* Jill Simpson. *Script Supervisor:* Joi Andreoli. *Production Accountant:* Albert Belmont, Jr. *Assistant Production Accountant:* Paul Seitzinger. *Extras Casting:* The Casting Group, Rick Montgomery. *Assistants to Mr. Craven and Marianne Maddalena:* Jeffrey Fenner, Chris Parker. *Location Manager:* Judson Neil Schwartz. *Location Assistant:* Christopher W. Trott, Henry Castillo. *Casting Assistant:* Andrea Mack. *Second Second Assistant Director:* Melanie Knox. *Art Director:* Steven Lloyd, S. Kroyer. *Set Decorator:* Molly Flanegin. *Assistant Set Director:* Lisa Thompson. *Leadperson:* John Fortino. *On-Set Dresser:* Daniel M. Butts. *Property Master:* Will Blount. *Assistant Props:* Monica Ragan. *Second Assistant Props:* Bruton E. Jones, J.P. Jones. *Stand-by Special Effects Carpenter:* Chester E. Hewett III. *Standby Carpenter:* Daniel Kopeli. *Standby Painter:* Douglas G. Bruce. *Set Construction:* Design Setters. *Construction Foreman:* Fernando Lau. *Storyboard Artist:* Philip Mayor. *Swing Gang:* Steve M. Alacantra, Ronald M. Price, Jr., Ken Luttrell, Robert Roule, Tony Ramos, Hal Olofsson, Ronald Davis. *Wardrobe Supervisor:* Tim Wegnan. *Set Costumer:* Yvette M. Walsh. *Makeup Artist:* Michelle Buhler. *Hairstylist:* Barbara Olvera. *Assistant Makeup:* Denise Dallvalle. *Second Assistant Editor:* Angela T. Robinson, Tim O'Neil. *First Assistant Editor:* Sandra Davis. *Gaffer:* Bruce McCleery. *Best Boy Electric:* Dave Robey. *Electricians:* Jeff D. La Rosa, Jerry Mandley, Samuel "Skip" Smith. *Rigging Gaffer:* Huston Beaumont. *Key Grip:* Joe Celeste. *Dolly Grip:* Jamie Young. *Best Boy Grip:* Brian Robertson. *Grips:* Gary Williams, Spin Tencer. *Rigging Grip:* Ned Nedrow. *Special Effects:* Image Engineering, Inc. *Special Effects Supervisor:* Peter Chesney. *Key Effects Coordinator:* Dean Miller. *Special Effects Projects Coordinator:* Kate Steinberg. *Effects Technicians:* J.D. Streett, Sandy Stewart. *Mechanical Dog Effects:* Robert Clark and Roark Productions. *Dog Effects Crew:* Camilla Henneman, Rikelle Kerr, Mark Goldberg, Jim McLaughlin, Mark Goodell, Kent Jones. *Special Makeup Effects:* KNB. *Effects Supervisors:* Gregory Nicoreto, Robert Kurtzman, Howard Berger. *Key Effects Technicians:* Rick Matire, Earl Ellis. *Effects Assistants:* Rick Lalonde, Jerry Baker. *Fiberglass Molds:* Make Believe Productions. *Animals Supplied By:* Birds and Animals Unlimited. *Head Trainer:* Roger Schumacher. *Trainers:* Jim Dew, Angelo Rivers. *Supervising Sound Editor:* Paul Clay. *Sound Editors:* Carin Rogers, Susan Kurtz, Jeff Sandler, Mike Szackmeister, Rick Bozeat. *ADR Editors:* Pat Somerset, Ernesto Mas. *Assistant Sound Editors:* Dave

Jonsen, Drake Jenevin, Karyn Foster. *Music Editor:* Dick Bernstein. *Scoring Synchronization:* Offbeat Systems. *Foley Artists:* Diane Marshall, Jerry Trent. *Loop Group:* L.A. Loopsters. *ADR Mixer:* Tanya Sharpe David. *ADR Recordist:* Greg W. Lowe. *Foley Mixer:* Karin Roulo. *Supervising Re-Recording Mixer:* Peter Reale. *Re-Recording Mixers* Howard Wilmarth, Roberta Doheny. *Recordist:* Rich Coleman. *Re-recorded at:* Universal Studios Sound Department. *Production Assistants:* Jim Goldthwait, Crystal Weaver, Catherine Anderson, Jon Davis, Fabio Golombeck, Richard Edgar Rollins IV. *Post Production Assistant:* Anne Trumbore. *Negative Cutting:* In Frame, Inc. *Transportation Coordinator:* Jimmy Jones. *Transportation Captain:* James Oberman. *Drivers:* Mark Jones, Thomas G. Barlow, William Condit, Betty Ann Konz, Steven Lloyd, James Jones, Sr. *Unit Publicist:* Henri Bollinger. *Studio Teacher:* Richard Wicklud. *First Aid:* John Blue. *Catering:* Mobile Star Catering. **Second Unit:** *Second Unit Director of Photography:* Tony Cutrono. *First Assistant Camera:* Jerry Gorman. *Second Assistant Camera:* Wendy Van Dyke. *Gaffers:* Jules La Barthe, Felix Rivera. *Stand-Ins:* Wanda Welch, David Riggon, Julie Mondin, Sean Lemar, Roxanne Meyers, Van johnson. *Stage Hand:* James Needham. *Special Thanks to:* Madison Ruth, The American Humane Society, Bea Wallace. *The People Under the Stairs:* Nick Cramer, Earl Dax, Gregory Kauter, Burton Pierce, Robert Michael, David Robinson, Daniel Windtree. "Do the Right Thing" written by David "Readhead" guppy and Markell Riley and performed by Readhead Kingpin and the F.B.I., courtesy of Virgin Records. "Threnody to the Victims of Hiroshima for 52 String instruments" written by K. Pendrecki, performed by the National Philharmonic Orchestra in Warsaw, conducted by Witold Rowicki, courtesy of Polskie Negrania. *Additional Orchestral Score:* Graeme Revell. *Bonding Company:* Film Finances. *Insurance:* Transamerica Insurance Inc., Co. *Financing Company:* Yasuda Trust and Banking company, Mr. Brian Maki. *Studio Facilities:* Renmar Studios. *Color Timing:* David Orr, Bill Pine. *Title Design:* Kathy Broyles, Jeff Okun. *Opticals:* Howard Anderson. *Man's Leather Outfit:* Peter Camonier of Wayne's Leatherack. *Dolby Stereo Consultant:* Steve F.B. Smith. *Cameras and Lenses:* Clairmont Camera. From Universal City Studios, Inc. *Running Time*: 101 minutes. *MPAA Rating:* R

SYNOPSIS: On the eve of his thirteenth birthday, Poindexter, an African American boy, is given a tarot card reading by his older sister, Ruby. Poindexter, who has been nicknamed "Fool," listens intently as Ruby predicts a dangerous year for him. It is a year on a cliff or a precipice, a year that will require the boy to walk through fire and either burn or come out the other side a man. Although Fool does not know the particulars of the challenges he will face, his life is already filled with problems. His mother is growing sick because of cancer and the family does not have the money to pay for an operation even though any doctor could easily excise the growth. Furthermore, the family is three days late paying the rent. Their lease stipulates that the family will have to pay triple or get out. Of course, the family does not have the money to pay triple and therefore the landlords have delivered an eviction notice. Fool's family has one day before it must vacate the tenement.

Fool meets Leroy, Ruby's boyfriend. Leroy offers the young man a way to make money and save the family but Fool is reluctant to assist Leroy. He wants to be a doctor, not a crook, but Leroy proposes a robbery of the landlord's house! During a recent liquor store robbery, Leroy found two items: a schematic of the landlord's fortress-like home and a letter from a man asking to buy the collection of gold coins that the landlord has acquired. Fool is reluctant to rob anyone, even the cruel landlords who charge outrageous rent and have evicted his family, but Leroy reminds him that the landlords do not care about people or family, only money.

Across town, in the luxurious mansion of the landlords, a family lives a twisted existence. The husband and wife who live inside the gigantic house have a daughter named Alice whom they discipline cruelly and often abuse. The man and the woman are determined to evict Fool's family because his is the last one in the slum. Once Fool's family is gone, the landlords will build a condo and bring "clean people" there so they can become even richer. When Alice asks what happens to the people who are thrown out of their homes, her mother responds that children should be seen and not heard. Later, Alice is punished for losing a piece of silverware. She has given it to one of the boys who dwells under the stairs, which is a violation of house rules. Accused of feeding "one of those things" between the walls, Alice's father takes off his belt and whips her with it.

The next day, Fool disguises himself as a boy scout and approaches the home of his landlords. He knocks on the door and meets the mother. He informs her that he is selling cookies, but the Woman will not let him inside. Fool insists that he has to go to the bathroom but she still refuses him access to her house. Fool leaves the premises, but not before getting a good look at the house. There are padlocks on the windows outside, as if designed to keep something inside. Leroy's accomplice Spenser also wants to take a look at the house before they break in on Sunday. He dresses up as a gas company worker and knocks on the door. He informs the Woman that there is an emergency gas leak nearby and that he needs to come inside and read her meter. The mother sees through his guise because Spenser is wearing a skull ring on one hand, but she lets him in anyway.

Leroy and Fool await Spenser in a van parked across the street. They are amazed when they see the mother drive away from the house. Spenser is alone inside and this is the perfect opportunity to conduct the robbery! Leroy and Fool break into the house and find a steel door blocking their way to the kitchen. Leroy forces open the door with a crowbar and is attacked by the vicious family dog, Prince. Fool thinks quickly and manages to lock the dog in the anteroom as he and Leroy enter the kitchen. A small plaque catches Fool's eye: "See No Evil, Hear No Evil, Speak No Evil." The window sills are lined with dead flies and the whole kitchen reeks of death and human waste.

Fool wants to leave but Leroy keeps him in line by suggesting that he is "too chicken" for this kind of work. Leroy heads up the grand staircase into the house while Fool descends into the basement to find Spenser. On the staircase, the young boy finds Spenser's clipboard and pen abandoned. He hears a noise and heads further downstairs. Deep in the giant basement, a TV set is on and playing footage of the Gulf War. Fool hears people moving behind a wood partition and goes to investigate when he trips over Spenser's body. Spenser is dead and his hair has turned stark white. He died clutching a gold coin. As Fool soon discovers, the basement is inhabited by hordes of savage people. They stretch from behind a wood fence and try to grab Fool. He runs from the basement but the stairs collapse into a ramp and he tumbles back to the cellar. Fool is saved when Alice opens the door for him. She disappears as mysteriously as she appeared and Fool wastes no time in locating Leroy.

The owners of the house return and Fool realizes it is time to leave. Unfortunately, the house has unbreakable windows with bars on them and the front door has been rigged to deliver an electric charge if touched. Leroy and Fool are trapped, and after contending again with the family dog, run upstairs and hide. Before long, the Man and Woman activate their internal security system and put the house on "lockdown" mode. Daddy readies his automatic pistol with laser sighting. Leroy is caught and the Man shoots him to death, leaving Fool all alone in the house while the man and woman dance over Leroy's perforated corpse.

Hoping to escape the same fate as Spenser and Leroy, Fool crawls into a vent and finds human skeletal remains. At the end of the long tunnel he spots Alice again, and she leads him to safety. Together they hide in the bathroom and Alice reveals that she has never been allowed outside. Furthermore, no one has ever gotten out of the house. The people in the cellar are young boys kidnapped by the demented family. For one reason or another, each boy was "bad" and so the father cut out the bad parts and trapped each one under the stairs. Alice lives in mortal fear of the same fate and survives by seeing, hearing and speaking no evil. Alice also tells Fool about Roach, a boy who has escaped the cellar and who now dwells inside the walls of the house. Alice opens a cabinet that leads into a dark labyrinth and says that it will lead to Roach. Fool is reluctant to step inside because he wants out of the house, not into it. Fool looks out the window and sees the cops arrive. He bangs on the window but they do not hear him. In the back of Spenser's van, the man and the woman discover Fool's boy scout outfit and realize they still have an intruder in their home — one who even now might be with their Alice!

After dressing up in a black leather hunting outfit, the Man searches for Fool. Alice has returned to her room but Fool is trapped in the bathroom. The Man finds him there and Fool smashes the toilet lid over his head. Then Roach appears and pulls Fool to safety inside the bowels of the crazy house. Angry, the Man sends his killer dog into the maze after them. With Prince in hot pursuit, the boys find their way through the darkness and spring a trap on the dog. Prince

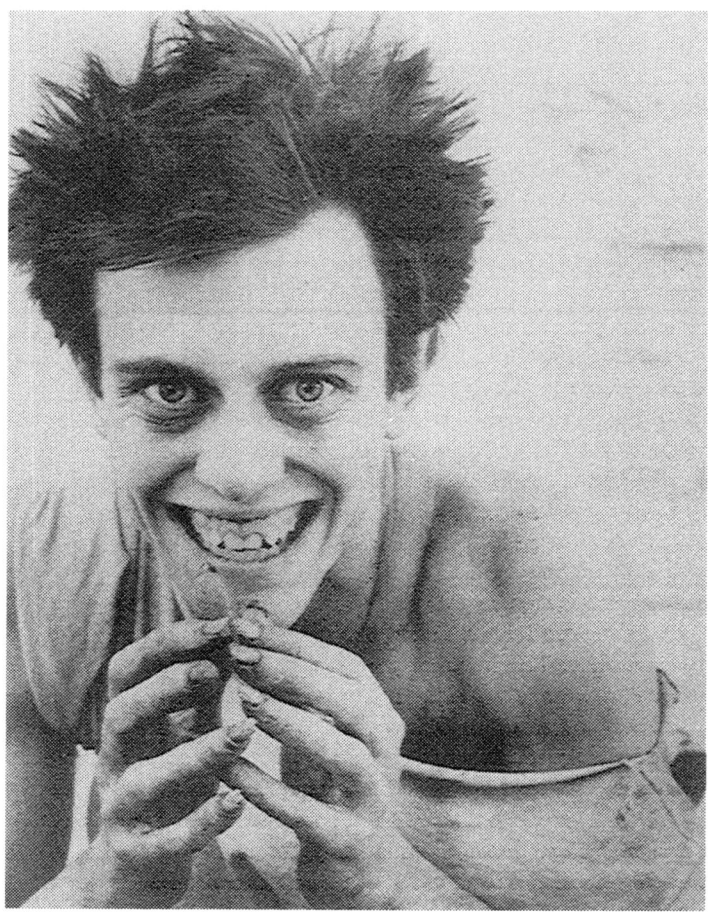

Roach (Sean Whalen) hides behind the walls in *The People Under the Stairs*.

trips a booby trap and falls down the dumbwaiter into the kitchen. After a few more moments, Roach and Fool reach safety in Alice's room. Fool thanks his rescuer and learns that Roach's parents cut his tongue out so he would never speak evil to them. He also discovers that Alice is a seamstress. She makes tiny cloth dolls, memorials to all the burglars, visitors and lost souls who have ended up dead inside this house. Among the dolls are ones commemorating Spenser and Leroy. Unexpectedly, the Man and Woman burst into the room. Roach is fast and manages to escape into a vent. As he crawls through the walls, the Man shoots at him and manages a hit. Then Fool is apprehended and thrown into the basement with Leroy's corpse. While the Man tends to Fool, the Woman disciplines Alice by forcing her to clean up Leroy's bloody remains in the living room. When Alice slips in the blood and soils her dress, the Woman becomes furious. She runs a bath of boiling water and viciously forces Alice into it, shouting that the "flames of Hell are hotter!"

Fool is forced to watch as his captor guts Leroy, eats his liver and throws his remaining organs to the boys starving under the stairs. The Man disposes of Leroy by hurling his body into a pit of human filth and then he throws Fool to the people under the stairs. Fool is soon surrounded by long-haired, pasty-faced adolescents who have been reduced to savagery. Roach once again appears and leads Fool to safety through a pipe in the furnace that leads up into the kitchen. Fool thanks his friend, who has been mortally wounded. As Roach expires, he presents Fool with a bag of gold coins and scrawls the name "Alice" on the wall of the ash-covered furnace. Fool promises he will save Alice before escaping. With his guide in this nightmare house gone, Fool climbs straight up, floor after floor, towards Alice. He enters Alice's room and saves her from another incident of vicious abuse by punching the Man in the crotch. Fool pulls Alice back into the vent and they escape into the walls. Furious, the Man sends his dog into the corridor after them. Fed up, Fool wrestles the dog to the wall. The Man has heard noises of the fight and plunges his bayonet through the wall, but he kills his dog, not Fool. Alice and Fool escape to the attic while the insane couple mourns the death of their dog.

The attic offers Alice and Fool an escape route, but Alice has never been outside and is scared. Fool opens a window and spies a pond in the garden far below. He knows they can jump and survive but Alice refuses to leave. As the Man bursts into the attic, Fool promises to return and then makes his escape. He slides to the edge of the roof and jumps into the pond.

Fool returns to the ghetto and meets with his Grandfather Booker. He shows him the gold coins, and Booker assures the boy that they are more than enough to pay the rent and for his mom's operation. He also warns Fool to be careful because he has messed with an evil family. The twisted couple is not just husband and wife, but brother and sister! While Fool listens, Booker recounts the family history of the lunatics. They used to sell cheap coffins for extravagant prices, but the more money they got the greedier and crazier they grew. They turned their giant funeral parlor into a house of horrors. Fool is shaken by this news but he knows he must fulfill his promise to Alice and save her from the evil landlords. Before he plots his return to the house, he visits with his sick mother and tells her that he feels bad for stealing. He promises to make it up to her by doing something good.

Fool calls the police department and reports child abuse at Alice's home. Several squad cars and representatives from the Department of Child Welfare soon arrive and search the house. The demented couple put up a good front and serve their visitors coffee and cookies. They claim that they have no children, but the cops find Alice's room. The mother lies that Alice died several years ago and that they have not been able to touch the room since. The police believe the story and leave. While the doors were open and unguarded, however, Fool has returned. He creeps upstairs and listens to the couple praying. But the prayers are being played on a tape recorder: Fool has walked into a trap. He breaks free after beating the mother with a fireplace poker and then escapes into the fireplace. Fool climbs to the attic and releases Alice from captivity. This time the duo cannot escape by jumping into the pond below because the Man has emptied it and filled the bottom of the pool with glass fragments. While Fool tries to think of another method of escape, he tells Alice that she was stolen as a baby. The crazies are not her real parents at all. This fact is liberating to Alice and she realizes she owes her "parents" no further loyalty.

Fool and Alice climb onto the roof and re-enter the house through the chimney. He bypasses the evil parents by dropping a brick on the Man's head. The two children slip down the chimney and split up. Fool manages to find the Man's shotgun and he faces him down with it on the stairs to the basement. The Man trips the booby trap and the stairs become a ramp again. Fool falls to the bottom of the cellar and the Man recovers his gun. He is about to shoot Fool when there is a knock on the door. The Woman instructs the Man to be quiet while she investigates. She opens the door and discovers Ruby there. Ruby claims she represents evicted people but the Woman slams the door on her. Ruby rings the doorbell again and this time she has hundreds of supporters behind her. Furious, the Woman levels a pistol at Ruby but is knocked unconscious by Alice.

Back in the basement, the people under the stairs save Fool's life. Shooting wildly, the Man blows up the lock holding the boys back and soon the people under the stairs are free. In exchange for showing them the way out, the savage boys show Fool to the embalming room. Inside is a stash of money: millions of dollars in cash and gold coins. Fool also discovers crates of dynamite.

Upstairs, the Woman has awakened and locked Ruby out of the house again. Eager to discipline her Alice, she stalks her with a butcher's knife. Before she can strike, the people under the stairs break out of the cellar and through the walls to attack their captor. Alice wrests the knife away from her "mother" and stabs her in the gut with it. The Woman is then set upon by dozens of savage boys and thrown down into the cellar, dead.

In the embalming room, Fool confronts his nemesis. He has rigged dynamite all over the room and threatens to blow it up unless the Man drops his gun. The Man refuses and Fool keeps his promise. The house goes up in flames and money rains down from broken windows and the chimney, flooding the gathered community with cash. Fool escapes with Alice after the Man is blown into his pit of human refuse. As they exit the house with the people under the stairs, Fool knows he will never be called Fool again but "King" instead. For the first time in a long time, the people under the stairs are free and there is money in the neighborhood again.

COMMENTARY: Eschewing the dream landscape and supernatural special effects of *Shocker*, Craven finds himself back on solid ground in *The People Under the Stairs*. The film is exciting not only its production design and directorial technique, but in Craven's ultimate exploration of the American middle-class family.

On the surface, *The People Under the Stairs* is another frightfully well-conceived horror flick. The production designers have built a house that is a memorable chamber of horrors. Filled with booby traps, dead-ends and deadfalls, the house is as much Fool's nemesis as its owners are. With secrets in the basement, behind the walls and inside a rotting interior, the house perfectly reflects the insanity of the villainous couple. With its labyrinthine twists and turns, it is the living embodiment of their

A Lost Boy — one of Wes Craven's *People Under the Stairs.*

twisted psyches. The house is captured expertly by the talented Craven, who often positions the camera above eye level and points it "down" towards the corners of long hallways or staircases. This high angle not only captures all the action, it successfully makes star Brandon Adams appear small amidst the detritus of the interior. Furthermore, many shots inside the house are slightly cock-eyed. It is not an extreme angle, but enough to be unsettling and to suggest that there is something off-kilter inside the mansion.

For his chases inside the walls, Craven utilizes tracking shots, P.O.V. sequences and tight framing to heighten the mood and pace of the action. The audience thus feels Fool's entrapment and breathes a sigh of relief when finally, after an hour, Fool makes it outside again. Of all Craven's films, *The People Under the Stairs* is among the most cohesive. It takes place in one claustrophobic locale and explores the terrain of that "inner space" relentlessly.

Perhaps of more interest than the feel of the house or the techniques which Craven employs to build tension is the film's relevant screenplay, which comments ironically about religion, the yuppie era and the degradation of the American family. Like *The Hills Have Eyes*, *The People Under the Stairs* is foremost a battle between the "haves" and the "have nots." It is also a reversal of *The Hills Have Eyes* because the protagonists in the later film are the "have nots." The "haves" in *The People Under the Stairs* are twisted by wealth and religion, and have become crazy. Like an exaggerated version of the "whitebread" Carters, the white antagonists in *The People Under the Stairs* are racists who call black people "niggers" and who want to evict the black people from the ghetto so they can bring in "clean" people. Also, they have great affection for their ferocious family dog. Unlike the Carters, however, the couple in *The People Under the Stairs* is not just dysfunctional, but stark raving insane. Thus Craven chronicles an important shift from the '70s to the '90s. In his eyes, middle-class families have gone from bad to worse.

What Craven apparently blames for this downward shift to insanity is the Reagan '80s, the era between *The Hills Have Eyes* and *The People Under the Stairs*. Therefore, as Thomas Doherty wrote in *Cinefantastique*, Craven takes "dead aim" at the hallmarks of the Reagan revolution: racial divisiveness, the yuppie mentality and religious conservatism.

Racism is an issue at the heart of this picture. Not only does the evil family hurl racial epithets at black people with alarming regularity, it actively oppresses the African-American community. The evil landlords own not only the ghetto apartment buildings which have become crackhouses where rabid dogs fight over scraps of meat, but also the local liquor store. They feed the community's addictions and make a fortune doing it. Furthermore, they take all the money out of the ghetto by charging extravagant rents and by selling alcohol.

In the first portion of the film, Craven powerfully documents the desperation of Fool's "have not" family. It cannot afford the rent, the apartment is a hellhole, and there is no money coming in. Fool's only chance to save his mother's life is to join Leroy in a robbery. Ironically, Fool's brother Washington is in prison because he also tried Fool's route, to "put food on the table" through robbery. From these examples, Craven sees the plight of America's inner cities as a consequence of white wealth rather than as a result of the behavior of the black community. Unfortunately for the people in the ghetto, the money of the "successful" 1980s never "trickled down" to them. Instead, the money stopped in the hands of the wealthy who were too selfish to share. Instead of passing money through their hands to the community, they bought liquor stores and apartment buildings and further lined their own pockets. As *The People Under the Stairs* points out, the gap between rich and poor has widened because of 1980s economics and the greed of an upper-middle class who sees, as Wendy Robie remarks in the film, "no community here."

The yuppie mentality and middle-class "concerns" are also lampooned in *The People Under the Stairs*. The landlords have only one concern in life: making more money. They murder, evict, steal and collect to gain more money. The accumulation of wealth does them no service, however, because they literally just throw sacks of cash and gold into their basement. The money they have taken from the community does not go back to it because the evil Robsons, representing the middle class, intercepted it and have taken it out of circulation. Craven equates moneylust with insanity. The more the Robsons get, the more they want.

The couple in *The People Under the Stairs* share other concerns of every "respectable" middle-class American family. The man and woman comment to the police that crime is "out of control" in their neighborhood ... when their own materialism is a root source of urban crime! Rather than address the behaviors that cause criminal activity, the demented family in *The People Under the Stairs* puts bars and padlocks on their doors and windows, just like the Thompsons in *A Nightmare on Elm Street*. They hide behind security systems and electrified doors, but the truth of the matter is that what lurks inside the house is far worse than an intruder from the outside world.

As is typical for Wes Craven, he is absolutely scathing in his portrayal of contemporary America. Not only are the antagonists selfish yuppies, they are also child abusers who are twisted by a repressive religious upbringing. The "bad" parents of *The People Under the Stairs* constantly use religion as a justification of their behavior. When they punish their children for expressing themselves, they cut out the body parts that offend them ("If thine eye offends thee, pluck it out"). The mother refers to Alice as a "little Judas" when the girl betrays her, thus comparing herself to Christ! The couple is also heard praying near the climax of the film, but with a strange variation on an old refrain. With all reverence, the duo solemnly declares, "If I should *kill* before I wake"!

This religious imagery infiltrates every aspect of the couple's life. When the mother tortures Alice and throws her into the boiling water of a bathtub, she notes that "the fires of Hell are hotter!" When the antagonists dislike anyone, whether it be black people, the police or social workers, they align themselves with the Lord and morality by remarking, "May they burn in Hell!" They believe they are morally superior to others because they are Christians and therefore God's chosen, when in fact they are the most immoral, selfish people in the community.

Craven peppers the film with many such examples of middle-class Christian hypocrisy. Woman (Wendy Robie) and Man (Everett McGill) play their roles to the hilt, and show more affection to their dog than to their children. It is clear that these people would never hurt their beloved pet ... but that they have no compunction about mutilating their own children. Furthermore, this couple blames their children for expressing their opinions freely and not sharing their twisted sense of morality. As punishment, they censor their children, chopping off tongues, gouging out eyes or slicing off ears so that the children cannot repeat these "mistakes."

Importantly, the parents offer no instruction in morality to their kids, they just punish them when they prove disappointing. Continuing his criticism of TV, Craven has the crazy couple put a TV in their basement "day care." In essence, they leave the punished children alone for days on end with only the TV as company! Like many parents, they complain about the loose morality of American society and then dump their children in front of the TV set for hours while they concentrate on accumulating more wealth.

As in *A Nightmare on Elm Street* and *The Last House on the Left* Craven also expresses the notion in *The People Under the Stairs* that society has failed the next generation. The police are again incompetent, and they fail to save Alice or Fool because, as Grandpa Booker says, they don't take the stories of wrongdoing seriously. After all, the evil couple are business people with *assets*. They live in a nice house in a nice part of town and on the surface they appear respectable. The police and even social services are not interested in looking below that surface and discovering the truth.

At one point in *The People Under the Stairs*, Craven shows the abandoned children watching a small television set. On the TV, Gulf War footage plays endlessly. By affording a view of Baghdad's bombing, Craven makes a connection between our middle class and this 1991 war. America wages war outside our borders, but the real horror is what is occurring inside the country. *That* is what needs to be addressed. In Baghdad we fight so we can save a dollar every time we go to the gas pumps, and our expensive technology levels an enemy city. By showcasing this footage, Craven reminds audiences that our money is *not* in the ghetto or our educational system but in the planes, ships and missiles we use to so violently protect our pocketbooks. Considering all of this social commentary, *The People Under the Stairs* is Craven's most searing indictment of American values yet.

Like *The Hills Have Eyes* and *The Last House on the Left*, *The People Under the Stairs* is a distinctly Freudian vision. Craven believes that repressed feelings do not disappear, but return as symptoms. The house, filled with cast-off children and dark secrets, is a realm of repression. Call it "Alice in Denial-Land." The incestuous yuppies deny their sins, but in the end the very things they repress return to haunt them. The children (a dark secret, a repressed "failure") literally burst out of the house, out of the walls, and out from the stairs to kill those who have forgotten them. The Robsons learn the hard way that their repressive behavior will return as the "symptoms" that lead to their deaths. In a split-second of self-awareness, the mother is conscious of this fact. She pauses briefly and repeats that the children will be "the death" of her. Not surprisingly, she is correct.

Even though *The People Under the Stairs* is packed with social commentary, it is not "heavy-handed." Quite the opposite is true and this film emerges as one of Craven's most consistently entertaining productions. The script is literate and filled with appropriate humor, and McGill and Robie create real individuals rather than Freddy Krueger clones. The film can even be read as an urban fairy tale to a degree since so many of its details are timeless and archetypical. Consider: Fool lives in a poor kingdom ruled by an evil King and Queen. He does not have the gold coins to pay for his mother's operation, so he must brave the dangers of a great castle and defeat the enemy. Inside, he escapes from a dungeon of monsters and finds a beautiful damsel to rescue. At the end, all is well when the evil family is vanquished and the gold it has hoarded is returned to the community. Everyone lives happily ever after.

The People Under the Stairs also espouses marvelous values to a significant degree. Alice (a Caucasian) and Fool (an African-American) work together and build a friendship beyond the racist society in which they were both raised. Indeed, Roach is a smelly, filthy creature lacking a tongue, but he is also resourceful, brave and loving. *The People Under the Stairs* recognizes this truth and eloquently states that appearance is not what is important: a person's heart is. Even the "people under the stairs," grisly albino creatures with greasy hair and body odor from Hell, are revealed to be abandoned children who can work together and offer something valuable to the community. Has there ever been a stronger (or more powerful) plea for diversity?

At the conclusion of *The People Under the Stairs*, the community bands together to stop the greedy landlords once and for all. Working together for a common cause, instead of lining one's own wallet, is lauded. Although some of *The People Under the Stairs'* moral explorations are simplistic, the film is a courageous one that exposes the dark consequences of the Reagan revolution and revels in the joys of diversity and community.

Wes Craven's New Nightmare (1994)

With equal debts to Pirandello and P.T. Barnum, Mr. Craven brings back his prize creation ... an ingenious, cathartic exercise in illusion and fear. — Janet Maslin (*The New York Times*: "Freddy Krueger Enters the Real World. Yikes!", October 14, 1994)

It's a complicated, tricky attempt to bring out the elements of horror moviemaking ... that's deliberately self-conscious... It's post-modernism for the mall crowd... It's compelling ... it challenges you to keep up with it. — Peter Rainer (*The Los Angeles Times*, October 14, 1994)

This rippingly good movie-within-a-movie, a pop *Day for Nightmare*, revives the razor-fingered, dream-haunting Freddy Krueger... In addition to Craven's technical virtuousity, what places him in the pantheon of great contemporary horrormeisters — David Cronenberg, John Carpenter and George Romero — is his ability to hook into our fears. — Thelma Adams (*The New York Post*, October 14, 1994)

[T]he idea of a movie monster crashing through the "fourth wall" of the filmmaking process to move among the people who invented him is irresistible, particularly in a series about the blending of reality and fantasy, and Craven plays it with such deadpan earnestness, you hang on every page. — Jack Matthews (*Newsday*, October 14, 1994)

Craven is still one of the horror cinema's most imaginative creators of purely frightening moments. Dispensing with the adolescent concern of the sequels, and ditching embarrassing frills like heavy metal music, feeble teen performances and bad one-liners, this is a worthy follow-up to the first film and a sly critique of all the watering-down that has happened since.— Kim Newman (*Sight and Sound*, January 1995)

A pop Pirandellian fantasy, full of beautifully crafted visual and psychological jolts, an amusingly "inside" look at Hollywood moviemaking, and, on its most intense level, a film that tries to wreak havoc with our whole sense of reality.— Michael Wilmington (*Chicago Tribune*, October 14, 1994)

Wes Craven's New Nightmare lacks the trancelike dread of the original *Nightmare*, and it features almost none of the ingeniously demented special effects that made the series' third installment, *Dream Warriors*, a hallucinatory exercise in MTV horror. This one is just an empty hall of mirrors.— Owen Gleiberman (*Entertainment Weekly*, October 28, 1994, page 72)

A clever idea wonderfully executed with an apocalyptic climax... After this, Craven has to be considered one of the best directors in the horror genre.— John Stanley, *Creature Features: The Science Fiction, Fantasy and Horror Movie Guide* (Boulevard Books, 1997, page 557)

CAST: Jeffrey John Davis (Freddy's Hand Double); Heather Langenkamp (Herself); Miko Hughes (Dylan); Matt Winston (Chuck); Rob LaBelle (Terry); David Newsom (Chase Porter); Wes Craven (Himself); Marianne Maddalena (Herself); Gretchen Oehler (Script Supervisor); Tracy Middendorf (Julie); Cully Fredrickson (Limo Driver); Bodhi Elfman (TV Studio P.A.); Sam Rubin (Himself); Robert Englund (Himself); Claudia Haro (New Line Receptionist); Sara Risher (Herself); Robert Shaye (Himself); Cindy Guidry (Kim at New Line); Ray Glanzmann (Highway Patrol); Yonda Davis (Highway Patrolman); Michael Hagiwara (Coroner); W. Earl Brown (Morgue Attendant); Kenneth Zanchi (Minister); Nick Corri (Himself); Tuesday Knight (Herself); Beans Morocco (Graveyard Worker); John Saxon (Himself); Freddy Krueger (Himself); Tamara Mark (Patrice Englund); Fran Bennett (Dr. Heffner); Lin Shaye (Nurse With Pills); Deborah Zara Koblyt (Newscaster); Diane Nadeau (Counter Nurse); Star-Shemah (ICU Nurse #1); Lou Thornton (ICU Nurse #2); Cynthia Savage (ICU Nurse #3); Jessica Craven (Junior Nurse With Needle); Sandra Ellis Lafferty (Senior Nurse With Needle); Thomas G. Burt (Security Officer); Tina Vail (Nurse Abbott).

CREDITS: A New Line Cinema release. A Wes Craven Film. *Writer/Director:* Wes Craven. *Based on Characters Created by:* Wes Craven. *Producer:* Marianne Maddalena. *Co-Producer:* Jay Roewe. *Executive Producers:* Robert Shaye, Wes Craven. *Casting:* Gary Zuckerbrod. *Director of Photography:* Mark Irwin, C.S.C./A.S.C. *Editor:* Patrick Lussier. *Music:* J. Peter Robinson. *Production Designer:* Cytnthia Charette. *Costume Designer:* Mary Jane Fort. *Co-Executive Producer:* Sara Risher. *Unit Production Manager:* Barry Waldman. *First Assistant Director:* Nick Mastandrea. *Second Assistant Director:* Rosemary C. Cremona. *Production Executive:* Timothy Gray. *Associate Producer:* Jeffrey Fenner. *Executive in Charge of Production:* Joe Fineman. *Production Coordinator:* Pearl Lucero.

Assistant Production Coordinator: Diane Sabatina. *Assistant to Wes Craven and Marianne Maddalena:* Angela Lussier. *Production Secretary:* Lisa Harrison. *Assistant to Sara Risher:* Lynn McQuaker Kavner. *Script Supervisor:* Gretchen Oehler. *Production Accountant:* Diana Johnson. *Assistant Production Accountant:* Cynthia Walker. *Accounting Assistant:* Sonia Marie Samuel. *Post Production Assistant:* Fred Grossman. *Production Controller:* Paul Prokop. *Production Attorney:* Phillip L. Rosen. *Contract Administrator:* Liz Amsden. *Art Directors:* Troy Sizemore, Diane McKinnon. *Set Designer:* Stephen Alesch. *Draftsman:* Charles J.H. Wood. *Storyboard Artist:* Matt Golden. *Set Decorator:* Ruby Guidara. *Leadsman:* Tom Kerns. *On-Set Dresser:* Grant Scharbo. *Swing Gang:* Daniel Spaulding, Loren Patrick Lyons, Andrew V. Ciconia. *Set Dresser:* Catherine Ernst. *Prop Master:* Cheri Candido. *Assistant Propmaster:* Nino Candido. *Prop Assistant:* Chuck Askerneese. *Additional Camera Operators:* Eric Goldstein, Robert D. Tomer. *First Assistant Camera:* Gary K. Ushino. *Second Assistant Camera:* Jeffrey Civa. *Second Assistant "B" Camera:* Egor Davidoff. *Steadicam Operators:* David L. Peck, Kirk Gardner. *Loader:* Brian Heffron. *Gaffer:* Jay W. Yowler. *Best Boy Electric:* Troy White. *Electricians:* John D. Tomaso, Yariv Michaelovich, Michael Foster. *Rigging Gaffers:* Chris Culliton, David W. Strong. *Key Grip:* Charles M. Smallwood. *Best Boy Grip:* Larry Roth. *Dolly Grip:* Loren Hillebrand. *Grips:* Sandy Bloom, Don Telles, Em Marie Ishikawa, Juan Morse, Marc Polanski. *Rigging Key-Grip:* Charles A. Horns. *Sound Mixer:* Jim Steube. *Boom Operator:* Moe Chamberlain. *Wardrobe Supervisor:* Jane Lanzner. *Set Costumers:* Ann Foley, Gina Wingate. *Wardrobe Shopper:* Carolyn Greco. *Key Makeup:* Ashlee Peterson. *Key Hair:* Camille Henderson. *Assistant Makeup:* Heide Seeholzer. *Second Assistant Director:* Susan Pickett. *DGA Trainee:* Jules Kovisars. *Supervisor Visual Effects:* William Mesa. *Visual Effects:* Flash Film Works. *Visual Effects Producer:* Nick Davis. *Visual Effects Co-Producer:* Linda Landry-Nelson. *Visual Effects Technical Supervisor:* John Coats. *Visual Effects Cameraman:* Dave Stump. *Visual Effects Art Director:* Charles Wood. *Visual Effects Production Manager:* Tina Mesa. *Visual Effects Camera Assistant:* Mike Ball. *Visual Effects Digital Technician:* Dave Lockwood. *Visual Effects Assistant Editor:* Bonnie Dombrowski. *Matte Painting:* Tim Donahue. *Conceptual Artist:* Matsune Suzuki. *Film Scanning:* C.I.S. *Digital Film Recording:* Digital Filmworks. *Digital Visual Effects:* Digital Filmworks. *Mechanical Special Effects Created by* Lou Carlucci. *Special Effects Crew:* Charles Schmitz, Michael W. Menzel, John C. Carlucci, Morgan Guynes, James Ochoa, Jim Hannah, Albert Maranconi, Steven Carlton Ficke, Adam Campbell, Dwight Roberts, Martin Simon, Andre Ellington. *Special Makeup Effects:* Kurtzman, Nicoreto and Berger EFX Group, Inc., Robert Kurtzman, Gregory Nicoreto and Howard Berger. *Coordinator:* Erin Haggerty. *Makeup Effects Crew:* Wayne Toth, George Bernota, Evan Campbell, Douglas Noe, Kan Hiroshi Ikeuchi, Bill Hunt. *Freddy Krueger Makeup:* David Miller Creations. *Makeup Crew:* David Miller, Michael J. Regan, Mark Maitre, V. Jude Ruta, Mark Boley, Gino Avecedo. *Construction Coordinator:* Raymond Camaioni. *Construction Estimator:* Karri Mayo. *Construction*

Foreman: Ken Brooks. *Stage Foreman:* Richard C. Welch. *Carpenters:* Jose J. Jimenez, Anthony McNerny, Robert McNerney, Garner E. Ryan, Ralph R. Coutler, Pedro Fernandez, Larce Crawford, Marc Alan Stevens, Joseph T. Delmont, Humberto Jimenez, Rutilo L. Jimenez. *Labor Foreman:* Carlos Chavez. *Laborers:* Salvador Sahagun, Joseph Camaioni. *Lead Scenic and Krueger Paintings:* Linda Newman. *Scenic Artists:* Martha Higgins, Kiren Meyer, Leeza Ingills, Star Fritz, Jon Higgins, Craig G. Shepherd, Richard Brandt, Twyla Reppen, James R. York, Linda Castren, Daniel Beralos. *Sculptors:* Patrick Magin, Katie Karloff. *Foam-Tec:* John Bloom, Simon Loftas. *Plaster Foreman:* Jim Clements. *Metal Workers:* Michael Sean O'Harra, Wayne Erickson. *Location Manager:* Marshall Moore. *Assistant Location Managers:* Gerard Averill, Eva Schroeder, Ari Jampuisky. *Production Assistants:* Daniel K. Arrendondo, Gretchen Hyman, Rudy Scalese, Maria D. Saltzer. *Production Interns:* Chuck Mullaney, Joshua David Scott. *Nurse:* Sandra Ohifest. *Med Tech Advisors:* Lanee Gentile, Lori Robertson. *Transportation Coordinator:* Griff Ruggles. *Transportation Captain:* Danny Westerberg. *Drivers:* Richard Rizzo, Gordie Merrick, John Nardone, Ronald R. Stinton, Don Martin, Mark Brown, Tony "Bear" Mihalopoulos, Hollywood Dave Flanigan, John R. Videgain, Charles Clevering, Gregg R. Videgain, Raymond R. George, Morgan McGuinness, Glenn Mathias. *Casting Associate:* Jean Scoccimarro. *Extras Casting:* Webster-Kolich and Company, Casting. *Casting Intern:* Eric Small. *Post Production Supervisor:* Sara King. *Assistant Editor:* Edwards Abroms. *First Assistant Editor:* Peter Devaney Flanagan. *Second Assistant Editor:* Lynn Abroms. *Music Editor:* Lise Richardson. *Sound Editorial:* Clay Digital Sound. *Sound Supervisor:* Paul Clay. *Dialogue Editors:* Jerry Jacobson, Chris Rabideau, Marty Stein. *Effects Editors:* Patrick O'Sullivan, Susan Kurtz, Cindy Rabideau. *Sound Assistants:* Ken Miller, Chris Nava, Patricia Conaway, Nick Clay. *Foley Artists:* Ellen Hueur, Chris Moriana. *ADR/Foley Mixer:* Karin Roulo. *ADR Recordist:* Darrin Mann. *ADR Foley Re-recorded at:* Ivy Sound Studios. *Walla Group:* Studio City Players. *Sound Designer:* Paul B. Clay. *Re-Recording Mixers:* Peter Reale, Roberta Doheny, Tim Philben. *Re-Recorded at:* Universal City Studios. *Music Supervisor:* Paul DiFranco, Ed Gerrard. *Orchestration:* Michael McCuistion. *Additional Orchestrations:* Larry Rench, Peter Tomashek, Lolita Ritmanis, Harvey Cohen, Edgardo Simone, Scott Rogers. *Supervising Music Copyists:* Greg Buttars, Leslie Buttars. *Orchestral Music Recorded at:* L.A. Studios East. *Scoring and Mix Engineer:* Robert Fernandez. *Assistant Engineer:* Glenn Neibaur. *Studio Manager:* Robin Leishman. *Orchestra Conductor:* Michael McCuistion. *Preview Technical Supervisor:* Lee Tucker. *DTS Engineer:* Jeff Levison. *Stunt Coordinator:* Tony Cecere. *Stunts:* Christopher Doyle, Debbie Lee Garrington, Alex Gaona, Lynn Salvatori, Trisha Lane, Lisa McCullough, Deep Roy, Ed Gale, David Edward Carben, Lou Carlucci, Christine Brady, Sandy Free, Annie Ellis, Chere Rae, Maria R. Kelly, Richie Gaona, Mickey Gilbert. *Stand-ins:* Diana Nadeau, Jeffrey John Davis, Troy Larkin. *Set Teacher:* Phil Eisnhower. *Catering:* Deluxe Catering. *Craft Services:* Patrick Hibler. *Unit Publicist:* Yorke and Hill Public Relations. *Unit Photographer:* Joseph Vices. *Product Placement:* Tony Hoffman. **Freeway Unit Crew:** *Gaffer:* Rick Sands.

Best Boy Electric: Steve Bishart. *Electricians:* Mike Carter, Tim Moore. *Key Grip:* David H. Winner. *Best Boy Grip:* Jeff Ahrens. *Grip:* Frank Scibella. *Construction Foreman:* Douglas Womack. *Hair and Makeup:* Kelvin R. Trahan. *Craft Services:* Randall E. Tedesco. **Second Unit Crew:** *Director:* Mickey Gilbert. *First Assistant Director:* Jim Behnke. *Script Supervisor:* Karolyn Justin. *Director of Photography:* Eric Goldstein. *Camera Operator:* Michael Endler. *First Assistant Camera:* Brian Keith Banks, Andrew Parke. *Loader:* Taj Gombart. *Gaffer:* Donald J. Sutherland. *Best Boy Electric:* Michael Davis. *Electricians:* Katrin Schenk, Steve Kagan, Jonathan Norton, Larry Wallace. *Musco:* Brad Chelefvig. *Key Grip:* Billy Bosson. *Best Boy Grip:* Michael Flaningham. *Grips:* Brian Crane, David J. Whitham, Miles Thomas, Cesar A. Gonzales. *Precision Drivers:* The Bill Young Driving Team. *Stunt Drivers:* Lance Gilbert, Joe Finnegan, Tim Gilbert, Gene Hartune, Chuck Hosack, Jim Wilkey, Jim Lewis, George E. Sack Jr., George A. Sack. *Second Unit Special Effects Crew:* Marty Bresin, Don Hastings, Mike Brown, Scott Sand, Jeff Bresin, Steve King. *Second Unit Transport Captain:* Gordie Merrick. *Second Unit Drivers:* Gordon E. Merrick III, Chad Merrick, Michael Anderson, Guy A. Duquette, Buck Holland, Chrales D. Hindman. *Second Unit Location:* Lee Steadman. **Additional Shooting:** *Production Supervisor:* Eric McLeod. *Unit Production Manager:* Leon Dudevoir. *First Assistant Director:* Gary Marcus. *Second Assistant Director:* Robert Leveen. *Production Coordinator:* Holly Hagy. *Assistant Producer:* Marlene Hart. *Production Secretary:* Brian Odo. *Lead Scenic:* Lind Castren. *Assistant to Props:* Jonathan Craven. *Eel Wrangler:* Aquarium Center/Sean Lally. *Heather Eel Double:* Kim Litte. *Cameras:* Clairmont. *Equipment:* Filmtrucks, Inc. *Completion Bond:* Percenterprises/Motion Picture Gurantors. *Production Insurance:* Albert Reuben Insurance. *Payroll:* Media Services. *Prints:* Film House. *Color:* Foto-Kem. *Opticals:* Howard Anderson Co. *Additional Digital Opticals:* The Post Group. *Timer:* Mato. *Titles:* Howard Anderson Company. *Negative Cutter and Positive Assembly:* Magic Film and Video, Marie Helen Desbiens, Syd Cole. "Losing My Religion" written by Bill Berry, Peter Buck, Mike Mills and Michael Stipe, courtesy of Night Garden Music. *A Nightmare on Elm Street* footage courtesy of New Line Cinema, 1984. *A Nightmare on Elm Street* score written by Charles Bernstein. *Special Thanks to:* Jerry Bingham, Stuart Besser, John and Mary Hughes, Sam Focher, Dr. Judith Swerling. In Memory of Gregg Fonseca. From New Line Cinema. *Running Time:* 112 minutes. *MPAA Rating:* R

SYNOPSIS: A man works in his filthy workshop, a furnace aflame in the background. He builds himself a deadly mechanical arm complete with robotic fingers and long finger-razors. When he is finished assembling the monstrous claw, he cuts off his own hand with a meat cleaver and attaches the prosthetic monstrosity to his bloody stump. Suddenly, director Wes Craven calls "cut" and the shot is stopped because not enough blood is pouring out of Freddy's bloody wrist. Dozens of technicians are revealed to be on the set and behind the scenes sits actress Heather Langenkamp with her five-year-old child, Dylan. The duo watches as Chase, Dylan's father, adjusts the mechanical hand with two special effects technicians. Something goes horribly wrong with the mechanical hand and it springs to life. A razor-sharp knife scratches Chase's hand and he falls down, wounded. The hand goes on a rampage and kills Chuck and Terry, Chase's assistants. During the pandemonium, Heather screams as she realizes she has lost sight of Dylan. Freddy's hand strikes again, leaping up Chase's torso and readying itself for the kill when...

...Heather awakens from the nightmare, the entire house shaking around her. An earthquake is tearing everything apart! Heather and Chase run to Dylan's room to protect him and finally the tremors subside. Dylan notices that Chase's finger is badly cut, and Heather remembers that he had the same injury in her nightmare! At breakfast, Dylan sculpts Freddy's face in his oatmeal and Heather is anxious. There have been five earthquakes in three weeks and an obscene phone caller has been harassing her for six weeks. Heather tells Chase about the nightmare and he is understanding. He has a special effects job in Palm Springs and will have to leave for the day. Heather too has a busy schedule: She is to be interviewed on a local talk show that morning. As Chase drives away, a wall in his bedroom cracks open as if torn by Freddy's glove. As Heather busies herself, she notices Dylan downstairs in the living room watching the original *A Nightmare on Elm Street*. She turns the TV off and the phone rings. On the other end is a person who sounds like Freddy. After another slight tremor, Dylan's babysitter Julie arrives and Heather is whisked away by limo to the studio.

Heather is interviewed by Sam Rubin. It is the tenth anniversary of the original *A Nightmare on Elm Street*, the phenomenon is still going strong and (like most people) Rubin wants to know if Freddy is really dead. Heather is a little shaken by this question but affirms that Krueger is really gone. She is also asked about horror movies and whether having a small child changes her perspective about them. Heather comments that she would not let her young son see the original *Elm Street* flick. When Rubin asks about Robert Englund, Heather's co-star, the crowd goes wild. Englund bursts out onto the stage in full Freddy makeup and costume. The fans in the audience give him a standing ovation. There are fans wearing costumes and masks, brandishing "fake" Freddy gloves and even holding signs that read "Freddy I love you!" Heather watches all of this apprehensively, a little frightened by the specter of death dancing across the stage.

After the show, Heather watches as Robert is mobbed by crazed fans. The two actors talk briefly and Robert says he would like to work with Heather again. Heather is not so high on the notion, but she soon gets a call from Sara Risher at New Line Cinema, the co-producer of the first *Elm Street* film. Heather is chauffeured to New Line and taken to a meeting with Robert Shaye, New Line's president. Heather notices that the office is decorated with Freddy memorabilia such as paintings, books and action figures.

Shaye asks Heather to join him in "the definitive" nightmare movie. Wes

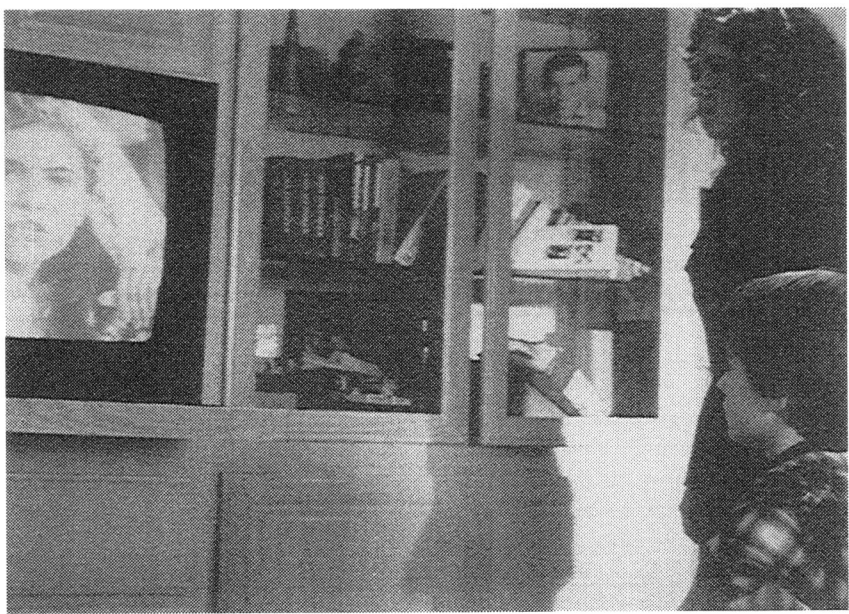

In *Wes Craven's New Nightmare*, Heather Langenkamp and son Dylan (Miko Hughes) watch *A Nightmare on Elm Street* on TV.

Craven has pitched an idea that the studio is excited about and Heather is written into the script as the star. Heather is not convinced that she needs to do another nightmare film, especially because she is now a parent, but Shaye replies that "kids love horror." He also tells Heather that Craven has not proposed a new horror movie for so long because he has not had any really scary nightmares. To Heather, this fact is ominous: If Wes is writing a new script, he must be having nightmares again. As it turns out, Wes is not the only one having trouble. Heather learns that Shaye is also being dogged by "Freddy" phone calls. The last piece of news from Shaye is the worst: Chase has been working on a brand new Freddy glove for the new film, just as Heather dreamed the night before. Heather turns down the mouse offer and leaves the office.

When Heather returns home, she discovers Julie trying to tend Dylan, who is in the midst of a convulsion. "Never sleep again!" the poor boy croaks, echoing the famous Freddy jump-rope song. Dylan finally calms down and tells his mother that Rex, his stuffed dinosaur, saved him from the "bad" man. Heather notes with fear that Rex is now slashed in four spots ... as if by Freddy's razors. Heather calls Chase with worry and demands that he come home. Chase is having a bad day because Chuck and Terry did not show up for work and no one has heard from them. He agrees to come home when Heather tells him about Dylan's convulsion. Chase leaves the set, unaware that the malevolent Freddy glove has left with him.

That night, Heather reads *Hansel and Gretel* to Dylan in bed. She nears the climax of the fairy tale and does not want to finish it. It is so violent and so scary that it cannot be good for Dylan. Dylan begs his mother to finish the story. It is important to him for the tale to close so he knows that evil is defeated. Heather acquiesces and Dylan is happy. As he prepares for sleep, he stands Rex at the edge of his bed. He tells Heather that the dinosaur keeps the "mean old man with claws" from grabbing his toes.

While Chase drives home in his pick-up truck, he grows sleepy. He nods off for a split second but the Freddy glove attacks and kills him in his dreams. At home, Heather awakens with a start, aware that something horrible has happened. The police arrive and notify her of Chase's death. Afraid that there is more going on than meets the eye, Heather insists on seeing the corpse. She travels to the morgue and the coroner lifts the sheet to reveal Chase's ruined body. There are four gashes down the center of the chest, as if he were stricken by Krueger. Heather asks about this but the coroner says that it just looks that way: Chase actually died in a wreck. Disgusted, Heather vomits. The coroner consoles her and tells her that "sometimes it's what we don't see that gets us through the night."

At Chase's funeral, all of Heather's friends have gathered: Julie, Wes Craven, Sara Risher, Bob Shaye and *Elm Street* co-stars Nick Corri, John Saxon and Robert Englund join her in her time of grief. During a brief tremor, Heather falls and hits her head on the ground. When she looks up, Dylan is missing and Chase's coffin has become unhinged. The door flies open and the coffin crashes into the grave. Heather looks down to see Dylan being pulled underground by a demonic creature that resembles Freddy. Now a zombie, Chase begs Heather to stay with him. Heather awakens back at the funeral and everything seems fine. At the end of the service, Craven stands solemnly in the background, looking concerned. He seems aware of something dreadful...

That night, Dylan sleepwalks downstairs and sees *A Nightmare on Elm Street* on TV again. Riveted, he is determined to see it through, but Heather awakens him and turns off the tube. Dylan then sings the jump rope song to his mother. Heather asks where Dylan heard that song and Dylan reveals that children were singing it to him in his bed. Then, suddenly, Dylan's nose starts to bleed. She lets the boy sleep with her that night but he is consumed by questions his mother cannot answer. Why does God allow bad things? Does one have to die to see God?

The next day at the park, Dylan plays while Heather talks to John Saxon, the actor who portrayed her father ten years earlier in *Elm Street*. She confides to John that there is a history of mental illness in her family and that she fears she has passed it along to Dylan. Unnoticed, Dylan climbs a towering jungle gym spaceship and reaches skyward, trying to touch God. He loses his balance and falls, and Heather just manages to catch him. Later in the afternoon, Heather calls Robert Englund at home and asks him what he knows about Craven's new script. Englund says he knows little, except that Craven has gotten as far as Dylan trying to "touch God." Heather and Robert are both alarmed that her little boy has ended up in Craven's script! Heather reveals to Robert that she is being harassed by a phone caller who sounds like Freddy. She also informs him of her nightmares. Englund is all too aware of the nightmares, however: He is suffering from them too! Alone in his home, he paints a picture of a frightening Freddy demon, a creature infinitely more dark and terrifying than the creature he portrayed.

After another sleepwalking incident and a close encounter with the phone caller, Heather takes Dylan to the hospital. Dr. Heffner fears the onset of childhood schizophrenia and insists that Dylan stay overnight for tests. When the physician asks if Dylan has seen Heather's films, she lies and says no. Heather knows the only way to solve Dylan's problem is to meet with the originator of Freddy, Wes Craven.

Heather Langenkamp (herself) and John Saxon (himself) have grave concerns about Fred Krueger in *Wes Craven's New Nightmare*.

Heather drives through the wreckage wrought by the last earthquake and visits Craven's hilltop home. She asks how the script is going and Craven responds that he dreams a little, writes it down and goes from there. He tells her that the new *Nightmare* film will be an unconventional one. It is a "nightmare in progress" about an ancient entity that lives for the murder of innocence. This demonic being can sometimes be caught, captured by, of all things, storytellers. A good story can capture the essence of evil for a while and hold it like a djinn in a bottle. But if the story dies for whatever reason, evil is set free. Sometimes a story gets watered down, becomes an easy sell, or is just too upsetting to society so it is banned outright. Craven believes that Freddy Krueger is this once-trapped demonic being. Now that the *Elm Street* movies are over and the Pandora's box is open, the demon is free. The problem is that the monster likes being Freddy and wants to cross over from movies into reality. Only one person, a gatekeeper, can stop Freddy. Craven reveals that the gatekeeper is Heather herself. Freddy still remembers her as Nancy Thompson, the heroine of *Elm Street*. She was the first to defeat him, the first to humiliate him. Heather gave Nancy her strength and so now Freddy is trying to get to her through her weakest link, Dylan. Craven assures Heather that there is only one way to stop Freddy: They must make a new movie and capture the evil in a story again. Heather just has to be courageous enough to play Nancy one last time.

As Heather returns home, she contemplates Craven's words and sets about diagnosing Dylan's condition herself. She realizes he is suffering not from schizophrenia but from severe sleep deprivation. There is another earthquake and suddenly Freddy strikes. He slashes at Heather's arm and calls her "Nancy." After he disappears, Heather realizes that Krueger is getting closer to reality and she rushes to the hospital to rescue her son. Julie is already waiting there to help. Heather meets with Dr. Heffner and learns that Dylan has been put into an oxygen tent. Dr. Heffner treats Heather's arm and asks if Dylan is being terrorized by the man in her films. Heather reveals that Dylan has seen some of the movie, but that (to Dylan) Freddy is like Santa Claus or King Kong. Dr. Heffner thinks Heather is a terrible parent and soon suggests that they remove Dylan to foster care since Heather is obviously incompetent. Heffner also suggests that perhaps there is a history of mental illness in the Langenkamp family and that Heather has passed it onto Dylan or may be suffering from it herself.

While Heather is held by security, Freddy enters the world of the sedated Dylan. He kills Julie, skinning her like a cat and dragging her across the ceiling. Dylan escapes from Krueger's grasp and sleepwalks out of the hospital, onto the freeway and towards home. Heather learns of Julie's death and realizes she must find Dylan before he is killed on the road. She calls John Saxon and asks him to meet her at the house. Spurred onward by a specter of a giant Freddy, Dylan sleepwalks through an eight-lane highway. Cars stop, swerve and crash to avoid the child but Freddy prolongs the terror by scooping the boy up like a rag doll and dangling him in front of oncoming traffic. Heather rushes to defend her son but is struck by a speeding car. Heather lays on the ground wounded but spots her son walking safely home. She forces herself to get up and she follows him. Once she arrives at her house, she meets Saxon, who informs her that Dylan is safe inside.

However, everything is not right. Saxon begins to call Heather "Nancy." His clothes change and suddenly he is wearing a police uniform. Heather looks down at herself and realizes she is back in the pajamas she wore in *A Nightmare on Elm Street*. She exits the house and her home is transformed into the haunted house of the Freddy Krueger films. When Heather finally accepts her role as Nancy Thompson, Freddy breaks out of Dylan's bed and pulls the young boy into his world. Following a trail of sedatives left like a "trail of bread crumbs" by Dylan, Heather follows her son into sedation and into the world of Freddy. Heather arrives in a dark, dank underworld with Greek columns and fiery furnaces. She discovers Wes Craven's script laying among the filth and realizes that the script is not just a script, it is full of her thoughts and experiences … the script is her life!

Dylan and Heather are briefly reunited before Freddy attacks and throws Heather into a vase of snakes. She rips one out of the muck and jams it into Freddy's eye, causing him to release her. Dylan runs for safety as Krueger and Heather fight it out. When Heather is in danger of losing the clash, Dylan returns to stab Krueger in the leg. Krueger is furious and he knocks Heather out. He pursues Dylan into a flaming oven. Dylan hides inside and closes the oven doors. Freddy cannot squeeze in, but his arms stretch and grope blindly for his quarry. Heather wakes up and tries to reach Dylan, but the stairs to the oven turn to mush and she can barely move. As Freddy opens his mouth wide to swallow Dylan, Heather arrives and stabs the killer in the back. Freddy turns his attention back to Langenkamp and his tongue stretches around her head. Dylan stabs at the end of the tongue and it rips open, leaving Krueger with a forked tongue. Together, Heather and Dylan push Freddy into the furnace. The monster dies inside, just like the witch in *Hansel and Gretel*. Krueger's domain goes up in flames and Heather and Dylan return to reality. In a flash, they roll out of Dylan's bed and onto the floor, where they discover Craven's script! Heather opens it to the first page and finds a personal note from Craven, thanking her for having the courage to play Nancy for the last time. Dylan wonders if the script is a story and Heather begins to read it to him, beginning at the start of the tale...

COMMENTARY: *Wes Craven's New Nightmare* is a great film that succeeds on a variety of thematic levels. It is part horror film, part self-reflexive view into the world of filmmaking, part savvy sequel, part meditation on the role of horror films in society, and also an anniversary celebration of the first *Nightmare on Elm Street*.

Above all perhaps, *New Nightmare* is a parent's personal journey. As the film opens, a grown-up Heather Langenkamp (playing herself) rigorously guards her son Dylan against the perceived "danger" of horror films. She admits she wouldn't let Dylan see her motion pictures (i.e., Wes Craven's *A Nightmare on Elm Street*) and that she is "not sure about doing horror" roles because of their impact on him and other children. Furthermore, she does not understand why Dylan, representing all America's children, is drawn to scary stories at all. About *Hansel and Gretel*, Heather states, "It's so violent. I don't know why you like it." As a result of her repression of horror films and stories, however, Dylan becomes partially possessed by the demons he has only half-glimpsed in these stories. Because he has not seen the "whole" picture, the whole film *A Nightmare on Elm Street*, he has not seen his mother defeat evil. He is therefore left open to evil influences and feelings. To illustrate this point, Craven's script has Dylan awaken as if from a trance each time Heather turns off the television to censor his viewing. His need for security shattered, Dylan screams in horror, frightened *not* by the images of terror on the screen but because his mother has robbed him of closure.

As Heather reads *Hansel and Gretel* to Dylan for the umpteenth time, he orders her to finish the story before calling it a night. "Say how they find their way home. It's important," he declares. Craven's implication is that children *like* to be scared and that horror stories/films serve as an outlet. By seeing a scary story all the way through, children learn that they too can beat scary influences in their life. Horror lets them know that they will survive. It is cathartic and it is fun.

As the picture develops, Heather realizes that, as Craven states so eloquently, an evil repressed can sometimes break through into reality. A woman who has refused to let her child see horror films is then thrust unexpectedly into the position of defending them. "I'm convinced that those films can send an unstable child over the edge!" the well-meaning Dr. Heffner declares, but the horror Dylan faces is *not* imagined but real, ironically, because the Freddy films are no longer being made. When they were being produced in the 1980s, the series served as a healthy outlet for teenage fears and anxieties. Since they have stopped, evil has escaped into the "real" world and is doing massive damage because of this cessation, this repression of the national catharsis.

Craven explores the theme of horror as acceptable outlet of fear by crafting an ongoing parallel between his *Elm Street* universe and the grim childhood story *Hansel and Gretel*. Since *Hansel and Gretel* is deemed acceptable "bedtime reading" by most parents, *A Nightmare on Elm Street* is by extension/parallel also acceptable. Like the witch in the scary story, Freddy Krueger tries to shove Dylan in an oven, and in the denouement is cooked himself. In stalking the young boy, Freddy declares, "I'm gonna eat you up!" and that he has some "gingerbread" for the boy. Furthering the parallel, Dylan leaves a symbolic trail of "bread crumbs" (sedatives) so Heather can find her way "home" to him. By associating *Elm Street* with *Hansel and Gretel*, Craven states that horror movies, like fairy tales, can be shared with children because they are cathartic exercises and altogether healthy. The end of the film is the final reiteration of this theme as Heather and Dylan sit together and read the *New Nightmare* script from start to finish. This gives them both closure, and vanquishes Freddy forever to the world of imagination ... or at least until people stop making horror movies again.

Clearly, *Wes Craven's New Nightmare* is a thematically rich film. Not only does it examine parental responsibility and the healthy aspects of horror films, it is also profoundly self-referential and an ironic commentary on the world of filmmaking. The "Freddy" phenomenon is roasted rather thoroughly. Freddy masks, costumes, gloves and fan signs are all seen on the talk show stage, memorabilia from the *Elm Street* line, (including reference books, action figures and paintings) are seen in Bob Shaye's office, and fans like the creepy limo driver keep popping up everywhere and startling Heather.

Interestingly, Craven contrasts the fanaticism of the fans with the blasé attitude of those who profit from horror films. "That thing puts bread on our table," Chase tells Heather nonchalantly when she objects to Freddy's new glove. "The fans, god bless 'em, they're clamoring for more," Bob Shaye laughs, realizing he has a money-making bonanza on his hands. Indeed, the very fact that the tenth

Trapped in Freddy's domain, Heather Langenkamp prepares for battle in the finale of *Wes Craven's New Nightmare*.

anniversary of *A Nightmare on Elm Street* is a plot point here speaks to both fan devotion and executive greed. Craven, never a man or artist of facile views, sees filmmaking as both art and business. Ironically, at the same time that he makes a horror film for New Line Cinema, he criticizes the company for literally running Freddy into the ground. Freddy has returned to the real world not just because of repression, but because his story has become too familiar, too watered down. It is quite unusual for a sequel to criticize its predecessors, but that is exactly what *New Nightmare* does.

Even as *New Nightmare* slams past sequels, it is filled with references to earlier entries in the seven-part *Elm Street* film series. It is a movie about transformation and alternate realities, so by the climax Heather's "real" world has turned into the world of the first *Nightmare on Elm Street*. Stairs turn to goo, earthquakes are shaking California, and a beautiful blonde friend is dragged across a ceiling and skinned by Freddy. There is even the obligatory funeral sequence included in *New Nightmare*. More significantly, Heather in *New Nightmare* cuts her arm in the same place as Nancy did in *Elm Street*. Her hair goes gray as well, and she finds herself repeating lines from the original film such as "Screw your pass!" and "Whatever you do, don't fall asleep."

The final transformation occurs when John Saxon begins to call Heather "Nancy," and her chic L.A. home turns into Freddy's house at 1428 Elm. Reality has folded upon itself and Heather has, for lack of a better phrase, entered *The Twilight Zone*.

The first *Nightmare on Elm Street* is not the only series entry referenced in *New Nightmare*. Dr. Heffner, the disbelieving professional, echoes Dr. Elizabeth Sims in *A Nightmare on Elm Street III: Dream Warriors*, who felt that Freddy was a byproduct of rampant sexuality. The roadside death of a male protagonist (Chase) is reminiscent of the death of Alice's boyfriend Dan in *A Nightmare on Elm Street V: The Dream Child*, down to the inclusion of a pick-up truck. Another repetition from the fifth film is the subplot that a child can be a vessel of evil through which Freddy can operate. Finally, Heather's comment to Dylan that people can only enter other people's dreams in the movies is a sly put-down of the premise of *Dream Warriors*.

By re-interpreting the standards of the *Nightmare on Elm Street* series, *New Nightmare* becomes strangely unpredictable. Viewers think they have seen these touches before, but as in *Scream* and *Scream 2*, all the clichés are twisted and given new meaning and power by their revision.

It was a daring move for Craven to create a horror film with as much brains as guts, but the result is one of labyrinthian realities and ever-spiralling fantasy aspects. In *New Nightmare*, the audience is watching a horror movie concerning an actress planning to play herself in a horror movie. The notion of fictional and real worlds overlapping is buttressed by the presence of Nick Corri, Robert Englund, Bob Shaye, Sara Risher and Craven, all of them playing themselves. And Craven's warning that only storytellers can catch evil and trap it in a story connects the world of reality and film in a way that had not been done before in cinema. For these reasons, *Wes Craven's New Nightmare* has often been referred to as a film of Pirandellian proportions.

Luigi Pirandello (1867–1936) was an Italian nobel laureate and author of *Six Characters in Search of an Author* (1922). His primary thesis was that an individual has many different personalities depending on how he appears to the people he relates to. The characters in Pirandello's work find true reality only in their conscious mind, but ultimately realize that they are wavering and inexplicable things ... and therefore that there is no concrete reality. *Wes Craven's New Nightmare* is indeed reminiscent of Pirandello since in the final moments of the film, Heather Langenkamp realizes that there is more going on than meets the eye. She is not just an actress in a horror film, she is not just a character on screen, she is not just a mother fighting for her son, and she is not merely Nancy Thompson. She is simultaneously all and none of these things. As she prepares for her final battle with Freddy, Heather discovers Wes Craven's script and reads aloud:

> The more she read, the more she realized that what she had in her hands was nothing more or less than her life itself, that everything she had experienced and thought was bound within these pages ... [T]here was no movie, there was only ... her life.

Seen in this light, *New Nightmare* is a blend of many worlds and realities. It is a film within a film within a film and it continues to add dimensions and thematic density the further one examines it. It is no wonder that critics responded with great enthusiasm. It is also quite obviously the spiritual predecessor to the similarly inclined *Scream* series.

The film works for other reasons too. It plays on fear of the dark, worries about "what's under the bed" and anxieties about hospitals. Like *The Exorcist*, it is about a child possessed and a parent's struggle to cope. It also deftly blends humor with these fears. "Every kid knows who Freddy is. He's like Santa Claus or King Kong!" Heather says, succinctly summarizing American pop culture.

Even horror film tradition is touched upon when Craven stages an elaborate shot of Freddy Krueger as he breaks into Dylan's world. His hand a twisted claw, Freddy is seen in shadow along the wall of a bedroom, precisely mimicking a shot of the vampire in Murnau's *Nosferatu* (1922). This is not just homage, this is a further example of self-reflexivity. The film is aware of its roots and forebearers, and it makes the audience aware of them too. In *Scream 2*, the very scene Craven mimics here would be shown on TV during the death of Sarah Michelle Gellar's Cici.

Whether it is taken as straight horror film, *Nightmare on Elm Street* sequel, social commentary or ironic, *The Player*-like satire, *Wes Craven's New Nightmare* is the director's most rewarding film. It only gets better on repeat viewing, and it is genuinely scary and self-assured. For these reasons, *Wes Craven's New Nightmare* is this author's favorite Craven film.

Vampire in Brooklyn (1995)

What makes *Vampire in Brooklyn* work in a way no Eddie Murphy movie has really managed since the first *Beverly Hills Cop* (1984) is the director Wes Craven. Like his contemporaries David Cronenberg and George Romero, Craven is a master of movie horror. But, unlike either of them, he also has a strange, dark sense of humor. That gives his movies ... an extra edge.—Michael Wilmington, (*Chicago Tribune: "Vampire in Brooklyn* Is One Eddie Murphy Movie Viewers Can Sink Their Teeth Into," October 27, 1995)

[Wes Craven and Eddie Murphy] stretch a little here with satisfying results. Craven shows unusual restraint... Murphy shows his sexy side. ...The script by Charles Murphy (Eddie's brother) and the team of Michael Lucker and Chris Parker is serviceable, though it goes mildly wrong in a couple of ways. It hasn't found any fresh angle for the familiar tale and it leaves questions unanswered.—Lawrence Toppman (*The Charlotte Observer: "Vampire*: Smiles, but few shivers," October 27, 1995)

Directed by Wes Craven, who hasn't made a good movie since 1988's *The Serpent and the Rainbow, Vampire in Brooklyn* is a horror comedy that mixes lame blood-pellet effects with lame gags, and it clunks along on a series of interchangeably deserted streets that manage to look dank and overlit at the same time.— Owen Gleiberman: (*Entertainment Weekly*: "Eddie Murphy is down for the count in *Vampire*, November 3, 1995, page 46)

It turns out to be an Eddie Murphy-Wes Craven movie that is not funny or scary. Now that's a nightmare... [I]t would have helped if Craven had been able to leave his fingerprints anywhere at all. His eye and wit are nowhere around.— Caryn James (*The New York Times:* "Single Black Vampire, New in Town," October 27, 1995)

Hardcore schlock director Wes Craven heads straight for what *Mad* might call humorlessness in a jugular vein. They cram more pointless obscenity than wit into the script and insist on all the vampire-genre conventions. ...[William] Marshall's 1972 *Blacula* seems like a masterpiece of intellectual humor by comparison.—Ralph Novak (*People Weekly*, November 13, 1995, page 26)

Considering it was directed by *Elm Street* creator Wes Craven, *Vampire* isn't stunningly scary or particularly atmospheric... The movie's pleasures are fairly minor... [L]ittle more than a Murphy potboiler.—Desson Howe (*The Washington Post*, October 27, 1995)

CAST: Eddie Murphy (Maximillian); Angela Bassett (Rita); Allen Payne (Justice); Kadeem Hardison (Julius Jones); John Witherspoon (Silas); Zakes Mokae (Dr. Zeko); Joanna Cassidy (Capt. Dewey); Simba Khali (Nikki); Missiri Freeman (Eva); Kelly Cinnane (Officer); Nick Corri (Anthony); Mitch Pileggi (Tony); W. Earl Brown (Thrasher); Adu Adeyemi (Bartender); Troy Curvey, Jr. (Choir Leader); Vickilyn Reynolds (Mrs. Brown); William Blount (Deacon Brown); Joe Costanza (Bear); John LaMotta (Lizzy); Marcelo Tubert (Waiter); Nick DeMauro (Caprisi); Jerry Hall (Woman in Park); Mark Haining (Man in

Park); Wendy Robie (Zealot at Police Station); Alyse Mondel (Cop); Larry Paul Marshall (Man at Church); Vince Micelli (Checker Player); Oren Waters, Carlton Davis, Clive Ross, Michael Hyde, Maxine Waters Willard, Josef Powell, Roy Galloway, Carmen Carter, Julie Walters Tillman, Carmen Twilly (Singers); Ray Combs (Game Show Host)

CREDITS: A Paramount Pictures Release. *Casting:* Eileen Mack Knight. *Music:* J. Peter Robinson. *Costume Designer:* Ha Nguyen. *Co-Producers:* Ray Murphy, Jr., Dixie J. Capp. *Editor:* Patrick Lussier. *Art Directors:* Gary Diamond, Cynthia Charette. *Director of Photography:* Mark Irwin, A.S.C. *Executive Producers:* Marianne Maddalena, Stuart M. Besser. *Story:* Eddie Murphy, Vernon Lynch, Charles Murphy. *Screenplay:* Charles Murphy, Michael Lucker, Chris Parker. *Producers:* Eddie Murphy, Mark Lipsky, *Director:* Wes Craven. *Stunt Coordinator:* Alan Oliney. *Stunt Performers:* LaFaye Baker, Alex Brown, Olisaun Elam, Dane Farwell, Mark Hicks, Al Lee Jr., Irving Lewis, Gary Littlejohn, Dennis Madalone, Rusty McClennon, Buck McDancer, Robert McGovern, Wayne Montano, Benny Moore, Charlie Picerni, Gary K. Price, Ronnie Rondell, Thomas Rosales Jr., Sharon Schaffer, Kim Washington. *Choreographer:* Eartha Robinson. *Unit Production Manager:* Stuart M. Besser. *First Assistant Director:* Nicholas C. Mastandrea. *Second Assistant Director:* Hayley Hsu. *Associate Producer:* Jeffrey Fenner. *Second Second Assistant Director:* Evan I. Gilner. *Script Supervisor:* Dawn Gilliam. *"A" Camera Operator:* Robert D. Tomer. *First Assistant Photographer:* Gary K. Ushino. *Second Assistant Photographer:* Jeffrey M. Civa. *"B" Camera Operator:* Michael Wheeler. *"B" Camera First Assistant Photographer:* Jeffrey L. Greene. *"B" Camera Second Assistant Photographer:* Eric Dyson. *Camera Loader:* Egor Davidoff. *Sound Mixer:* Jim Stoebe. *Boom Operator:* Moe Chamberlain. *Cableperson:* David B. Diamond. *Steadicam Operator:* Kirk Gardner. *Costume Supervisor:* Perri Kimono, Amy Stofsky. *Costumers:* Matthew A. Hooey, Molly C. Mitchell. *Costumer to Mr. Murphy:* Fetteroff F. Colen. *Assistant Art Director:* Troy Sizemore. *Set Designers:* Philip Dargent, Henri Alberti. *Illustrator:* David Russell. *Fine Artist:* Jerry Bingham. *Art Department Coordinator:* Donna Coxon. *Art Department Production Assistant:* Howard Miller. *Set Decorator:* Robert Kensinger. *Leadperson:* David C. Potter. *Property Buyer:* Lisa Denker. *Prop Persons:* Michael L. Holowach, John Bush, Alice Baker, Patrik Alvin. *Prop Master:* Will Blount. *Assistant Prop Master:* Monica Ragan. *Propmaker:* Michael P. Barnett. *Hair Department Supervisor:* Bill Howard. *Hairstylist:* Erma Kent. *Mr. Murphy Makeup Artist:* Toy Russell Van-Lierop. *Makeup Artist:* Marie Carter. *Additional Editor:* Edward R. Abroms. *First Assistant Editor:* Peter Devaney Flanagan. *Second Assistant Editor:* Yvonne Valdez. *Sound Design Supervision:* Paul Clay. *ADR Editors:* Lauren Stephens, Allan Bromberg, Michael Cook, Paul Benedict. *Effects Editors:* Victor Iorillo, Dan Tripoli, Vic Radulich, Jeff Sandler. *Sound Assistants:* Joe Schwartz, Kenneth Miller, Patricia Conaway, Nick Clay. *ADR Mixer:* Bob Baron. *ADR Voice Casting:* Barbara Harris. *Foley Mixer:* Randy Singer. *Foley Artists:* David Lee

Fine, Ken Dueva. *Re-Recording Mixers:* Peter Reale, Roberta Dohany, Tim Philbin. *Sound Editorial:* Clay Digital Sound. *Special Makeup Effects:* Kurtzman, Nicoreto, Berger EFX Group. *Special Makeup Effects:* Shannon Shea, Evan Campbell, Mark Tavares, Wayne Toth, Jeff Edwards, John Bisson, Brian Rae, Bob Hinderstein, Henrik Van Ryzin, Doug Noe, Robert Maverick. *Contact Lenses:* Richard Snell, Jean-Pierre Durand. *Special Makeup Effects On-Set Application:* Howard Berger, Robert Kurtzman. *Puppeteers:* Robert Kurtzman, Greg Nicoreto, Jeffrey Charles Edwards, Shannon Shea. *Special Make-up Effects Coordinator:* Erin Hagerty Karen Aubuchon. *First Company Grip:* Charles M. Smallwood. *Second Company Grip:* Dharmarata G. Dhiensuwana. *Rigging Grip:* Chris Reason. *Grips:* Gregory Wong, Sandy Bloom, Kevin Hall, Mike Foster, David P. Stein. *Dolly Grip:* Loren R. Hillebrand. *Chief Lighting Technician:* Eddie Taylor. *Lighting Technicians:* Troy Webb, Donald J. Sutherland. *Visual Effects Consultant:* Julia Gibson. *Visual Effects Coordinator:* Jessica L. Huebner. *Visual Effects Director of Photography:* Paul Gentry. *Visual Effects Camera Assistant:* Rick Taylor. *Special Visual Effects, Animation and Compositing:* Available Light, Ltd. *Animation Design and Supervision:* John T. Van-Vliet. *Visual Effects Producer:* Katherine Kean. *Digital Supervisor:* Laurel Klick. *Animators:* Michael Gagne, Conan Fitzpatrick, Bill Arance, January Nordmann, Randy Weeks. *Optical Printing:* Beverly Bernacki, Mona B. Howell. *Effects Editor:* Diana Desselle. *Animation Camera and Scanning:* Joseph Thomas. *Systems Manager:* Larry Stanton. *Production Assistant:* Martin Hilke. *Special Visual Effects:* Fantasy Film Effects, Inc. *Visual Effects Supervisor:* Gene Warren. *Visual Effects Producer:* Leslie Huntley. *Motion Control Camera:* Christopher Warren. *Optical Supervisor:* Betzy Bromberg. *Line-up:* Lindy Henry, Dan Emerson. *Camera Operators:* Dave Tucker, Don Ferglis. *Roto Scoping:* Bret Mixon. *Production Assistant:* Malina Kolan. *Digital Animation:* Hammerhead Productions, Inc., James Dixon, Daniel Chuba, Thad Bieier, Rebecca Marie, Larry Weiss. *Additional Digital Services:* TODD-AO Glenn Glenn Studios, Ilad Mamikunian, Brian Jennings. *Special Mechanical Effects:* Image Engineering. *Second Unit Director/Special Effects Designer:* Peter Chesney. *Special Effects Liason:* Katherina A. Steinberg. *Special Effects Foreperson:* Robert L. Olmstead. *Special Effects Technicians:* Gary D. Bierand, Roderic Duff, Don Markel, James D. Streett, Edward T. Reiff, Jr., James Nagle. *Special Effects Fabrication:* Don W. Miller, Chuck R. Schulthies, Jr., Chuck R. Schulthies, Sr., Tom Chesney, Katherine Duff. *Video Playback:* Mark Suveg. *Production Office Coordinator:* Andrew Francis Fenady. *Production Secretary:* Bob Vaupel. *Production Assistants:* Daniel Arrendando, Elizabeth Mersky, Montez A. Monroe, Helen Ruiz, James S. Gondek, James Manke, Amy Ho. *Production Auditor:* Crystal Hawkins. *Assistant Production Auditor:* David Rodriguez. *Assistant Production Accountant/Payroll:* Daniel Myers Boone. *Executive Assistant to Mr. Murphy:* Charisse M. Hewitt. *Executive Assistant to Ms. Bassett:* Andrew T. Rothmond. *Executive Assistant to Mr. Lipshaw:* Tiffany McLinn Lore. *Assistant to Ms. Bassett:* Darlene Jackson-Hall. *Assistant to Mr. Craven:* Lisa Harrison, Julie Plec. *Assistant to Ms. Maddalena:*

Angela Lussier. *Personal Assistants to Mr. Murphy:* Jemal Gullery, Donna Johnson, Roger Reid, Randy L. Webster. *Casting Assistant:* Meredith Behrend, Toby Sperber. *Location Manager:* Eric Klosterman. *Extras Casting:* Jim Green, Central Casting. *Assistant Location Manager:* James V. Selzer. *DGA Trainee:* Carlos Ramirez. *Unit Publicist:* Stanley Brossette. *Still Photographer:* Bruce W. Talamon. *Craft Service:* Chris Winn. *Caterer:* Deluxe Motion Picture. *Construction Coordinators:* Steven Rigamat, Javier Carrillo, Greg Villalva, Keith Kropf, Earl Brendlinger. *Production Painter:* Michael Gates. *Transportation Coordinator:* John "Dusty" Saunders. *Transportation Captain:* Daniel Briggs. *Color Timer:* Mike Stenwick. *Negative Cutter:* Theresa Repola Mohammed. *Title Design:* Dolly Swofford. *Music Supervisor:* Edward Gerrard. *Orchestra Conducted by:* J. Peter Robinson. *Orchestrations:* Michael McCuiston, Larry Rench. *Music Preparation:* Rob Bornstein. *Orchestra Contractor:* Carl Fortina. *Orchestra Scoring Mixer:* Robert Fernandez. *Orchestra Recorded at:* Paramount Pictures, Scoring Stage M. *Music Editor:* Steve McCroskey. *Color:* Deluxe. *Printed:* Eastman Kodak Film. *Camera equipment provided by:* Clairmont. *Special Thanks to:* The Charter Connection, Vincent Van Gogh Foundation, *Family Feud* footage courtesy of Mark Goodson Productions. "Whatta Man" by Herby Azor, Cheryl James and David Crawford and Performed by Salt N'Pepa courtesy of Polygram Records, "Pray" by Hammer and Prince, performed by Hammer, Courtesy of Capitol Records, and "Superstition" written by Stevie Wonder, performed by UB40 courtesy of Virgin Records. *Running Time:* 103 minutes. *MPAA Rating:* R

SYNOPSIS: Generations ago, a race of vampires known as Nosferatu was driven from Egypt. Many vampires fled to the Carpathian Mountains and Transylvania, but those with better taste, including the suave undead gentleman Maximillian, traveled over the Atlantic to an island deep in the Bermuda Triangle. The Nosferatu lived there happily for centuries, feasting on unwary travelers, until one day they were discovered again by vampire hunters. Soon, vampire blood was spilled and only Maximillian escaped unscathed. Now, his only chance to survive is to find the one known offspring of his people who was born in a foreign land ... a woman living somewhere in Brooklyn.

At the Port of Brooklyn, an unmanned cargo ship races into the harbor, crushing and destroying everything in its path. Inside the harbormaster's office, two black men watch *Family Feud* on television and argue about the Knicks. Outside, the boat races ever closer to them, out of control. The boat smashes through the dock house and finally stops, just inches from Julius and Silas. The two men look at the ship and it is a complete wreck, with no people visible on board. Scared, Julius runs off leaving the older man, Silas, to investigate. Silas finds the crew dead, their necks ripped apart. He then runs into a vicious wolf who leaps over him and runs away. Silas watches astonished as the wolf's shadow changes into a man's and walks inland.

Julius Jones is later thrown out of his girl's apartment because he was snoring while they were making love. He is spotted by "Pizza Man," an Italian mafioso to whom he owes money. Julius runs down an alley but is trapped there by two gangsters Tony and Anthony. They pull a gun on him but the vampire Maximillian materializes out of the mist. Tony shoots Maximillian in the heart, knocking him over. But Maximillian bolts back up, his wound healed. Maximillian then rips Tony's heart out and dispatches Anthony by ripping him limb from limb. Julius hides in a nearby warehouse, but is soon found by Maximillian. Maximillian chokes Julius and forces him to taste a drop of his vampire blood. This turns Julius into an undead slave called a "ghoul." He will be Maximillian's eyes by day and his servant by night. Maximillian informs his new slave that the first order of business is to find a woman, a half-vampire woman, before the next full moon. Maximillian tells Julius that the woman "sleepwalks" in humanity but he can change her into a vampire with one passionate dance.

The police arrive at the dock to investigate Maximillan's death ship. Eighteen corpses are found on the vessel, all drained of blood. The ship's log is written in some foreign language and has been sent to NYU for translation. Two of the officers on the scene, Rita and Justice, have just begun working together. Rita's mother recently passed away in an asylum. She investigates the ship's hold and finds Maximillian's coffin. She opens it and is confronted by a nightmare vision of herself sleeping inside. When she recovers from this image, the coffin is gone, taken away by Maximillian himself. Rita sees Max's shadow and tries to pursue him, but she loses his trail. Investigating further, Rita and Justice find a severed human ear in the hold. The ear belongs to Julius, who is quickly decomposing now that he is an undead ghoul.

Julius leads Maximillian to the tenement where Silas is the landlord. Maximillian provides Silas with enough gold coins to last a lifetime and Silas rents him an apartment. Together, Julius and Maximillian carry in the coffin and set about their quest to find Maximillian's woman. Maximillian is now quite sure that the woman he encountered on the boat is the object of his quest. The trick will be to seduce her. Rita can only become Max's bride if she gives herself willingly to him.

Justice and Rita continue to investigate the crime scene. They go to the nightclub of Dr. Zeko, the only man in the city who can translate the log of the strange cargo ship. Zeko informs them that the boat originated inside the Bermuda Triangle and that the crew believed there was "evil" aboard. Now, Zeko warns, the evil known as Nosferatu is in Brooklyn. Justice is reluctant to believe the story but Rita listens with rapt attention as Zeko tells her that vampires are more dangerous than anything the Brooklyn police have ever encountered. Zeko himself once fought one for a woman and was scarred in the battle.

Maximillian arrives in the club and sets about seducing Rita on the dance floor after saving her from an escaped snake. They dance together briefly but are interrupted by the decaying Julius, who offends Rita. Rita leaves the scene with Justice and Maximillian is furious. He pulls out Julius' tongue and threatens to hang him by it.

Rita and Justice stop at Rita's apartment and Justice meets her roommate Nicki. Nicki is obviously sweet on Justice, but he has eyes only for Rita. Maximillian watches the events unfold from the window, and once Justice has left he seduces Nicki himself. She invites him into her bedroom and they make passionate, violent love. Rita hears the lovemaking from her own room and is furious. She believes Justice is sleeping with Nicki. After finishing up with Nicki, Maximillian kills her and drains her body of blood. The next morning, Rita enters Nicki's room to confront her roommate but there is a note there stating that she has moved out. Max's plan to take everything from Rita and then offer himself to her seems to be working perfectly.

Confused by Justice's betrayal and Nicki's disappearance, Rita goes to church to talk with Preacher Pauley. Little does she know that Maximillian has killed Pauley and taken his form. The conversation is interrupted when Pauley is called inside the church to preach. Unable to stay on sanctified ground, Pauley/Maximillian suggests a sermon on the lawn. Once his congregation is there, Pauley preaches about necessary evil, telling his flock that without bad there can be no good, without dark there can be no light. He also says, "Ass is good, but evil ass is great." While the churchgoers blindly repeat Maximillian's sacrilegious phrases, Justice arrives and Rita accuses him of having sex with Nicki. It is clear to Justice that he and Rita are in love with each other even if they are unable to admit it. But there is more important business to consider: The corpses of the two Mafia thugs have been found in a dumpster.

Justice and Rita visit Mafia boss Caprisi at his restaurant to learn about the deaths. Maximillian is also there, now transformed into the inept white hitman Guido. Caprisi informs the cops that Julius, a numbers-runner, was the target of the two thugs when they disappeared. Before any more can be said, Guido holds up the restaurant and abducts Rita. Rita fights back and collars the criminal. She and Justice take him back to the police station, but Guido/Max escapes by making a religious zealot go crazy. When all eyes are diverted to the crazy woman, Guido shape-shifts back to his true form and leaves the precinct. Capt. Dewey is unhappy with Rita's performance on this case and suspends her from duty. Angry, Rita returns home and is intercepted on the street outside her apartment by Maximillian. He invites her to dinner at his place. Struck by Maximillian's animal magnetism, Rita accepts the invitation. As Julius' limo takes Rita to Max's newly refurbished (by magic spell) apartment, Justice watches with jealousy.

Maximillian and Rita dance together and the vampire tempts the beautiful woman with the promise of a brighter, better existence where she does not have to worry about Nicki, Justice or the police. All she has do is say that she wants that life. In a moment of weakness, Rita admits that she does want that life and Maximillian bites deep into her neck, drinking her blood. She is now a vampire, one of the undead who shall accompany Maximillian through all of time.

The next morning, Justice meets Silas and asks the whereabouts of Julius

Jones. Silas tells Justice about Maximillian and that he saw Rita go up to his apartment the night before. He also lets it slip that Rita spent the night. Justice is angry, but instead of confronting Rita he goes to another crime scene. To his horror, Justice discovers Nicki's body at the crime scene, strapped atop a building ... crucified. He rushes to Rita's apartment to see her, but she is asleep. Justice informs her of Nicki's death and that she was killed exactly in the pose painted by Rita earlier! As the two talk, they realize they love each other. They become intimate, but Rita is now a vampire and cannot resist the temptation to bite Justice's neck. As Rita is about to kill Justice, she looks into a mirror and sees her reflection, her humanity, vanishing before her eyes. Realizing that Maximillian is responsible for her transformation and all the murders in Brooklyn, Rita runs out of the apartment. Maximillian tells her that Rita's father sent him here. She is the daughter of a vampire and humans killed her father. Her father sacrificed herself so her mother might live. Rita is touched by this story and starts to accept her destiny as a vampire.

Justice visits Dr. Zeko and also learns the truth about Rita's heritage. Zeko was once in love with Rita's mother but she succumbed to dark forces. Zeko is aware that Maximillian needs Rita because he is the last of his kind. Their only chance of saving Rita is to kill Max before she feeds on human blood.

In Central Park, Maximillian and Rita prepare to feed. Maximillian pursues a rich woman and her poodle and drains the woman of blood. Rita is disgusted by the violence and cannot bring herself to kill a human being. She runs to a cemetery and cries on her mother's grave. She screams for deliverance from God, but Maximillian arrives and takes her back to the apartment. Rita is starving; she must have blood. Maximillian captures Silas and offers the old man to Rita. Justice and Zeko arrive just in time. After defeating Julius, Justice fights with Maximillian, but is defeated. Zeko plunges a ceremonial spear through Maximillian's stomach, missing the heart by several inches, and is knocked unconscious.

Maximillian and Rita retreat to the coffin room and Justice follows. He opens a coffin and finds a sleeping Rita. Maximillian materializes and warns Justice that it is too late: Rita is becoming a vampire. While Maximillian and Justice fight, Rita becomes a full-fledged vampire and grabs the ceremonial knife from Justice. She seems ready to kill her former partner, but instead plunges the blade through Maximillian's heart. Surprised, Maximillian tumbles into his coffin and disintegrates. The room starts to shake, windows shatter and a spirit flies across the sky. Rita is free of the evil influence and Maximillian is gone at last.

Downstairs, Julius and Silas steal Maximillian's limo and Julius recovers Max's ring. He puts it on and changes suddenly into a well-dressed, chic gangster. There is a new vampire in Brooklyn...

COMMENTARY: *A Vampire in Brooklyn* is an entertaining picture that sports an uneven mix of laugh and scares. It dutifully trots out all the time-honored vampire film clichés and features some great moments from familiar Wes Craven performers, yet nonetheless emerges as only a mild pleasure. The searing power of *Wes Craven's New Nightmare* has been supplanted by a joke-ridden atmosphere which undercuts the horror scenario. Since the film is an Eddie Murphy/Wes Craven collaboration, the film (not unlike *Deadly Friend*) is somewhat schizophrenic in tone. At times funny, at times scary, *A Vampire in Brooklyn* is neither funny nor scary enough to satisfy either the hardcore horror camp or the Eddie Murphy aficionados.

Still, *A Vampire in Brooklyn* has its moments. With its delightfully overblown musical score from J. Peter Robinson and its emphasis on Maximillian's romantic courtship of Rita, the picture emerges as a modern version of the 1930s or '40s vampire films cranked out by Universal Studios. Murphy is an elegant and romantic vampire along the lines of the regal Bela Lugosi rather than a feral one like Christopher Lee or a sultry one like Gary Oldman. Dressed to the nines in variations of black, Murphy delivers his lines with a convincing Caribbean accent and definitely emerges as a charmer. Murphy is restrained, too; he does not leap overtly into comedy terrain except when he shapeshifts into Preacher Pauley and the Italian hitman, Guido. On the contrary, Murphy holds back enough to maintain Maximillian's menace, allowing Kadeem Harrison's Julius Jones to crackwise and even steal a few scenes.

Eddie Murphy offers some delightful variations on stereotypical undead dialogue. "Listen ... it's the sound of the night calling," he declares to Angela Bassett at one point, reminding viewers of his cinematic lineage and the famous "children of the night—what music they make" dialogue of Bela Lugosi. When Murphy kisses Bassett's outstretched hand, his eyes are alive with charm. In these moments evocative of an earlier, kinder and gentler vampire era, *A Vampire in Brooklyn* is a truly charming film. The Murphy-Bassett courtship consumes much of the film's running time, and it is a delightful scenario that reminds one of the old-fashioned horror films that were about people rather than special effects. As the stars dance, with Craven's camera spinning around them, the film works well as romance.

Unfortunately, *A Vampire in Brooklyn*'s screenplay is not nearly sharp or original enough to maintain the feeling of an old-fashioned vampire film updated in modern Brooklyn. Instead, the writers apparently felt obligated to go through every vampire tradition in the modest running time, as if these sequences would be a revelation to fans. As a result, viewers are treated to vampire as wolf, vampire as fog, vampire as bat, plus an assortment of other setpieces of the sub-genre such as a mirror displaying no reflection and the undead menaced by a crucifix and garlic.

Much time is also consumed by Rita's unwillingness to "feed" on a human and become a vampire. This theme was central to the plots of *Near Dark* (1987), *The Lost Boys* (1987), *Fright Night* (1985) and *Interview With the Vampire* (1994).

Its presence here is crucial to Rita's conflicted nature (she is part-human and part-vampire), but this nonetheless feels like an element borrowed from the other modern vampire pictures.

The Julius Jones subplot is also derivative. It is amusing to watch Kadeem Harrison joke around as his undead body goes to pieces, and the actor certainly makes the most of the material ... but the same gag was handled better in John Landis' *An American Werewolf in London* (1981), an acknowledged classic. In that film, it was David Naughton's friend Griffin Dunne who kept reappearing in further states of decay. *A Vampire in Brooklyn* adds nothing new to this gag except some goopy special effects. Additionally, the Mafia angle and Italian-American settings that appear at the midpoint feel like a rehash of another Landis film, *Innocent Blood* (1992), which found a vampire in modern America and featured jokes about "Italian food." It is highly unusual for a Craven-directed film to appear derivative because the director is usually far ahead of the curve, rather than behind it. But then, it would be difficult for any vampire film made in 1995 to seem original. The dictates of the sub genre are now so well known that a lot of the "horror" has been removed from Bram Stoker's once-novel idea.

Today, vampire films tend to be as predictable as the latest entry in the James Bond film series, with only the actors differentiating one adventure from another. Perhaps it is for this reason that Craven has never before directed a vampire film. He usually finds horror in families and in "real life" scenarios, not in the traditional venues of the supernatural. Even Freddy and the Peytraud were supernatural avengers of unusual capabilities rather than traditional ghouls such as vampires, werewolves or mummies.

Despite the similarities to other vampire pictures, *A Vampire in Brooklyn* does update some of the oldest, less-seen *Dracula* clichés in interesting ways. The opening sequence, with a runaway boat crashing through a dockyard, is sensational. CGI effects are used believably here and the out-of-control "ghost ship" recalls the arrival of Maximillian Schreck's Count Orlok on the *Empusa* in Murnau's silent film *Nosferatu* (1922). Interestingly, *Nosferatu* was also the source of one of the most dramatic images in *Craven's New Nightmare*: the arrival of Freddy in the real world, his grotesque profile creating a devilish shadow on the wall, again in honor of Schreck's rat-like, clawed Orlock. In *A Vampire in Brooklyn*, the runaway boat sequence is a spectacular action piece that opens the film on a high note.

Also interesting are the well-staged shots of Maximillian crawling down the outside wall of Rita's apartment. This was also Dracula's mode of travel in Stoker's book, and an image that has not appeared frequently in the filmed versions of *Dracula* (although John Badham's 1979 picture and Francis Ford Coppola's 1992 version remembered to feature it). These touches, as well as the modification of the vampire hunter into a Caribbean night club owner, serve *A Vampire in Brooklyn* better than some of the vampire clichés.

What tends to sink *A Vampire in Brooklyn* is the obvious lowbrow humor.

2. The Feature Films 195

Kadeem Harrison (as Julius) and John Witherspoon (as Silas) are very funny together, and much of their work in *A Vampire in Brooklyn* is funny too. The script provides them with some droll lines, but also some real groaners. On the plus side, Julius complains about the coffin and asks Maximillian if he has "ever heard of a futon" and Silas wonders if "Stevie Wonder" is piloting the boat that crashed into his harbor house. On the down side, the script also provides some scatological dialogue like "ahoy, mother fucker!" and references to a "pussy surplus." This "lowest common denominator" style of humor clashes with the horror scenario and the more literate self-referential laughs ("Put a little heart into it," "Don't pull that *Blacula* shit," et cetera) that make the film witty instead of crass.

Eddie Murphy's two opportunities to shape-shift are also out of place in *A Vampire in Brooklyn*, as if they were edited into the picture from *Coming to America* (1987). In the first shape-shift, Murphy turns into an Al Sharpton-like preacher. He is very funny as he lectures his flock that "evil is good," "ass is good" and "evil ass" is the best. Craven, who has never had much fondness for Christianity, uses this sequence to expose organized religion to some pretty heavy ribbing. The interlude is undeniably funny and well performed, but it stops the plot's forward momentum and diminishes the horrific aspects.

The second shape-shift into the Italian hitman is *not* funny. Murphy has no good material in this sequence and so it just falls flat and again slows down the plot. There is no doubt that Murphy is highly versatile, but at times *A Vampire in Brooklyn* seems like his audition portfolio or outtakes from *Saturday Night Live*. He puts on several comedic hats successfully, but none of them fit *A Vampire in Brooklyn*. His performance as Maximillian is good enough to carry the film. The side shows are just that, circus distractions.

Craven populates *A Vampire in Brooklyn* with many familiar faces. Nick Corri (*A Nightmare on Elm Street*), Mitch Pileggi (*Shocker*), Joanna Cassidy (*Invitation to Hell*), W. Earl Brown (*Wes Craven's New Nightmare*), Angela Bassett (*Nightmare Cafe*), Zakes Mokae (*The Serpent and the Rainbow*) and Wendie Robie (*The People Under the Stairs*) all appear, to the delight of Craven fans. As central characters, Bassett and Mokae fare the best, and Pileggi and Robie have the most amusing cameos. The script also features standard Craven touches such as snakes gone wild, a mention of Sigmund Freud and a dream sequence to reveal a character's true identity. Although these are surface strokes, they remind the audience that this collaboration is indeed a Craven film.

Craven's cinematic techniques have lost none of their punch in *A Vampire in Brooklyn*, despite the soft nature of the script. High angles, rapid-fire editing, extreme close ups, spinning cameras and bloody special effects are employed to effectively dramatize the horror story. Despite the formalistic touches, Craven still knows when to back off and allow his performers to carry the day. As a result, Angela Bassett and Allen Payne create two very believable characters, even though Payne is saddled with the name "Justice"…a rather obvious moniker for a police detective.

Given the fact that *A Vampire in Brooklyn* is an entry in an over-exposed horror genre (the vampire film) and an uneasy mix of humor and horror, it is amazing that it is successful at all. It is no Craven masterpiece, but it is fun and involving throughout. The chemistry between Bassett and Murphy is strong, Kadeem Harrison and John Witherspoon are adept at comedy, the special effect sequences and transformations are startling, and the overall 1930s-'40s mood is charming.

Above all, *A Vampire in Brooklyn* shows that Craven is interested in more than just horror. As a director, he handles comedy, romance and horror well here, but is undone by a script which never finds a consistent tone. Certain questions remain unanswered as well. Why must Maximillian change Rita into a vampire before the next full moon? Is there a time limit on her half-breed heritage? And why, after Maximillian is staked through the heart, does a bat fly out through the window? Does the presence of this creature indicate that Maximillian has survived for a sequel? These questions are never answered.

Despite the modest values of *A Vampire in Brooklyn*, Craven and Eddie Murphy both went on to bigger and better things. Murphy found success with *The Nutty Professor* in 1996 and in the same year, Craven hit it big with *Scream*.

Scream (1996)

It's sensational in both senses of the word: a bravura, provocative send-up of horror pictures that's also scary and gruesome yet too swift-moving to lapse into morbidity. It risks going way over the top, deliberately generating considerable laughter in the process. It ends up a terrific entertainment that also explores the relationship between movies and their audiences, specifically — but hardly exclusively — teenagers who love the kind of horror pictures Craven specializes in.— Kevin Thomas (*The Los Angeles Times*: "Craven's *Scream* a Bravura Sendup of Horror Pictures")

As a film critic, I liked it. I liked the in-jokes and the self-aware characters. At the same time, I was aware of the incredible level of gore in this film. It is really violent.— Roger Ebert (*The Chicago Sun-Times*, December, 1996)

The best horror movie I've seen since *Halloween* and the added fun of trying to figure out who the killer is may make it even better than that 1978 classic that started all this "slasher" business in the first place.— Morgan Foehl (Internet review)

Pretty potent... [A]t times it's almost as nastily nihilistic as Craven's early, unsparing movies like *The Last House on the Left* and *The Hills Have Eyes*.— Glenn Kenny (*Premiere*, Summer 1997)

Scream, which has won some unaccountably indulgent reviews, is like [Wes Craven's] self-reverential *Wes Craven's New Nightmare* (1994): an idiot-savant movie, knowing but not smart. For viewers who are not scholars of the slasher genre, the latest Craven will seem one more exercise in voyeuristic sadism...—Richard Corliss (*Time*, December 30, 1996)

A kitsch-heavy, post-ironic commentary on horror films... In trying so hard to make fun of itself, *Scream* merely becomes what it is making fun of. It's edgy and fun, but not brilliant. And it's no better than it would have been as just a straight horror film... It's one too many winks away from being coherent.—Beth Pinkser (*The Dallas Morning News*: "Biggest foe in *Scream* is attempt at self-parody," December 20, 1996)

Having established himself as the best and most mischievous filmmaker currently working in the dead-babysitter horror genre, Wes Craven is in the mood for parody... In *Scream*, he wants things both ways, capitalizing on lurid material while undermining it with mocking humor. Not even horror fans who can answer all this film's knowing trivia questions may be fully comfortable with such an exploitative mix.—Janet Maslin (*The New York Times*: "*Scream*: Tricks of the Gory Trade," December 20, 1996)

CAST: David Arquette (Deputy Dewey Riley); Neve Campbell (Sidney Prescott); Courteney Cox (Gale Weathers); Matthew Lillard (Stu); Rose McGowan (Tatum Riley); Skeet Ulrich (Billy Loomis); Jamie Kennedy (Randy); W. Earl Brown (Kenny); Joseph Whipp (Sheriff Burke); Liev Schrieber (Cotton Weary); Drew Barrymore (Casey Becker); Roger Jackson (Phone Voice); David Booth (Casey's Father); Carla Hatley (Casey's Mother) Lawrence Hecht (Mr. Neil Prescott); Lois Sanders (Ms. Tate); Linda Blair (TV Reporter); Lisa Beach (TV Reporter #1); Tony Kilbert (TV Reporter #2); C.W. Morgan (Hank Loomis); Francis Lee McCain (Mrs. Riley); Troy Bishop (Expelled Teen #1); Ryan Kennedy (Expelled Teen #2); Leonara Scelfo (Cheerleader in Bathroom); Nancy Ann Ridder (Girl in Bathroom); Lisa Canning (Reporter With Mask); Bonnie Wood (Young Girl in Video Store); Aurora Draper (Party Teen #1); Kenny Kwony (Party Teen #2); Justin Sullivan (Teen on Couch); Kurtis Bedford (Bored Teen); Angela Miller (Girl on Couch).

CREDITS: A Woods Entertainment Production. A Dimensions Film Presentation. A Wes Craven Film. *Director:* Wes Craven. *Writer:* Kevin Williamson. *Producers:* Cary Woods, Cathy Konrad. *Executive Producers:* Bob Weinstein, Harvey Weinstein, Marianne Maddalena. *Co-Executive Producer:* Stuart M. Besser. *Co-Producer:* Dixie J. Capp. *Director of Photography:* Mark Irwin. *Production Designer:* Bruce Ann Miller. *Editor:* Patrick Lussier. *Music:* Marco Beltrami. *Costume Designer:* Cynthia Bergstrom. *Casting:* Lisa Beach. *Stunt Performers:* Dane Farwell, Noby Arden, Clay Boss, Frank Lloyd, Lynn Salvatori, Kathryn Marshall, Christine Baur, Christopher Doyle, Allen Robinson, Lee Waddel. *Unit Production Manager:* Stuart M. Besser. *First Assistant Director:* Nicholas Mastandrea. *Second Assistant Director:* Lucille Ouyang. *Additional Director of Photography:* Peter Deming. *Executives in Charge of Production:* Cary Granat, Richard Potter. *Music Supervisor:* Jeffrey Rabham. *Assistant Producer:* Nicholas Mastandrea. *Second Second Assistant Director:* Daniel K. Arrendando. *Script Supervisor:* Annie Wells. *Art Director:* David Lubin. *Set Decorator:* Michele Poulik. *Additional Set Decorator:*

Debra Echard. *Lead Person:* Richard Lambert. *Local Lead Person:* Ken Montante. *Set Designer:* Nanci Noblette. *Set Dresser/Buyer:* Lori Harrison. *On-Set Dresser:* Josh Elliott. *Standby Greensperson:* James Burke. *Standby Painter:* Victoria Carlson. *Prop Master:* John J.P. Jones. *Assistant Prop Master:* John "Skip" Weaver. *Assistant Department Coordinator:* Gerard Lehtola. *Art Department Production Assistant:* Charlene Barr. *"A" Camera Operator:* Robert Tomer, Paul Hughen. *First Assistant Camera:* Gary Ushino, Scott Ressler. *Second Assistant Director:* Jeffrey N. Civa, Renee Treyball. *Camera Loaders:* Egor Davidoff, Lisa Ferguson. *Steadicam Operators:* Kirk Gardner, Mark Van Loon, Dan Kneece. *Steadicam Assistant:* Marie Pederson, Penny Sprague, Steve Mann. *Chief Lighting Technician:* Jay W. Yowler. *Rigging Light Technicians:* Mark Lewis. *Lighting Technicians:* Steven Strong, Terry Sullivan, Kelsey Smith, Jason Boccaleoni. *First Company Grip:* Charles Smallwood. *Second Company Grip:* Kevin Ball. *Dolly Grip:* Charles J. Schray. *Rigging Grip:* Ron Diggory. *Grips:* Joe Allan, Nicholas Marks, Richard Span, Mark Shankel, James Ronnei, Dick Dova, Norris Fony. *First Assistant Editor:* Peter Devaney Flanagan. *Second Assistant Director:* Yvonne Valdinez. *Assistant Editor:* Paul Kiernan. *Apprentice Editor:* Lynn Dupre. *Costume Supervisors:* Matthew Clayton Hooey, Gary J. Saldutt. *Costumers:* Ricki Fournier, Patricia Kazmierowski. *Sound Mixer:* Richard Goodman. *Boom Operator:* Sean Rush. *Cable Person:* James Distefano. *Key Hairstylist:* Barbara Olvera. *Hairstylist:* Lynn Marie Curreri, Christina Raye *Key-Makeup Artist:* Carol Schwartz. *Makeup Artists:* Karen Bradley, Kris Ravetto, Melanie Levitt. *Special Makeup Effects:* Robert Kurtzman, Greg Nicoreto, Howard Berger. *Special Makeup Effects Crew:* Garret Immel, Theodore J. Haines, Robert Maverick, William Hunt, Christine Stahl, Ramon Velazco. *Special Effects Makeup Coordinator:* Kamar Bitar. *Stunt Coordinator:* Tony Cecere. *Special Effects Supervisor:* Frank Ceglia. *Special Effects Foreman:* Mark Byers. *Video Playback 24 Frames:* Marty Brenneis, Bernie Druckman. *Video Assist:* Doug Hunt. *Assistant to Mr. Craven:* Julie Plec. *Assistant to Ms. Maddalena:* Lisa McCampbell. *Assistants to Mr. Woods:* Lizzie Schwartz, Kristen March. *Assistant to Ms. Konrad:* Mo Milligan. *Production Office Coordinator:* Dean Wright. *Assistant Production Office Coordinator:* Andrew Durham. *Production Secretary:* Katherine Zilavy. *Production Assistants:* Lauren Feige, David Denison, Chad Maxwell, James Capp, Ivy K. Lukas, Sam Shank, John D. Embry, Brian Dettor, Christian Evol Waldman, Paul Boetigger, Jessica Clussen. *DGA Trainee:* Heather French. *Production Accountant:* David Crockett. *Assistant Production Accountant/Payroll:* Ivan Genit II. *Accounting Assistant:* Robert Cable. *Accounting Production Assistant:* Michelle Stevens. *Casting Assistant:* Sarah Katzman. *Local/Extra Casting:* Nancy Hayes, Merv Ladd, Hayes and Van Horne Casting. *Location Manager:* Eric Klosterman. *Additional Location Manager:* David Thornsberry. *Assistant Location Manager:* Thomas Harrigan. *Location Assistant:* Michael O. Gillis. *Unit Publicist:* Claire Rasking. *Still Photographer:* David Moir. *Craft Service:* Mary Ellen Leonard. *Caterer:* Tomkats Catering. *Construction Coordinator:* Robert Carlyle. *Construction General Foreman:* William A. Fobert. *Local*

Construction Coordinator: Dwight Williams. *Paint Foreperson:* Teresa Nielson. *Carpenters:* Art Williams, Braxton Bragg, Scott Newell, Katsuhiko Okuda. *Painters:* Wendy Gayner, Robert Burg, Leslie Turnball, Bernie Honigman, Carrie Nardello, David Erickson. *Transportation Coordinator:* Derek Raser. *Transportation Captain:* J.T. Thayer II. *Drivers:* Don Feeney, Earl Thielen, David Joseph, Glenn Midcap, Rick Suggett, Brian Moore, Mike Sawyer, John Peters, Rose Malley, Susan Rice, Ben Davis, Pete Brocco, Tracey Thielen, Steve Earle, Bruce Callahan, Jeff Coffman, Chuck Visconte, Dan Porteous, Henry Travers, Mike Ford, Jill Walters, Ken Skinner, Carsten Robehl, John Mattson, John Martin, Kevin Carstenson. *Post Production Supervisor:* Daniel Arrendando. *Post Production Assistant:* Ryan "The Kid" Krayser. *Sound Editorial:* Clay Digital Sound. *Sound Supervisor:* Paul Clay. *Dialogue Editors:* Vic Radulich, John Wilde, Bob Gold, Martha McGuire. *Effects Editors:* Scott Tinsley, Sam Gemette. *ADR Supervisor:* John Adams. *ADR Editor:* Patrick Somerset. *Sound Assistants:* Tom Ketterer, Vanessa Lapatto, Jean-Marie Mitchell. *Stunt Coordinator:* Tony Cecere. *Foley Artists:* Stan Fiferman, Roy Baker. *Foley Mixer:* Lee Tinkham, Beau Biggard. *ADR Voice Casting:* Barbara Harris. *ADR Loop Group:* Jeremy Miller, Tara Boger, Doris Hess, Noreen Rheardon, Steve Alterman, Jed Rhein, David McCharen, Greg Finley, Laura Galt, Casey Bishop, Justin Shenkarow, Alice Livingston. *Background Vocals:* Rose Thompson. *Re-Recording Mixers:* Rick Alexander, Leslie Schatz, Tom Dahl. *Re-Recorded at:* Buena Vista Sound. *Recordist:* Steve Kohler. *PDL:* Chris Sparks. *Music Editor:* E. Gedney Webb. *Orchestra Conducted by:* Marco Beltrami. *Orchestrations:* Peter Anthony, William Boston. *Orchestra Contractor:* Ken A. Watson. *Musical Preparation:* Julian Bratolyobov. *Scoring Mixer:* Tim Boyle. *Music Supervisor:* Ed Gerrard. *Negative Cutting:* RD Negative Cutting, Inc. *Color Timer:* Michael Mertens. *Camera Dailies:* Chapman/Leonard Studio Equipment. *Titles and Opticals:* CFI: The Image Company. *Insurance:* Great Northern/Reiff and Associates. *Legal Services:* Alexander, Halloran, Nau and Rose. *Halloween Footage courtesy of* Compass International Pictures. *Frankenstein Footage courtesy of:* MCA/Universal. *Ghost mask courtesy of:* Funworld Division of Easter Unlimited. *Special thanks to:* The City of Healdsburg, Frank Okun, Santa Rosa Doubletree Hotel, Sheree Green, Sonoma County Film Commission, Film Finances, Inc., Sonoma Community Center, Marco, Karin and Nicholas Ca'Biena, Les Perry. *No thanks whatsoever* to Santa Rose City School District Governing Board. From Dimension Films. *Running Time*: 100 minutes. *Rating:* R

SYNOPSIS: Casey Becker is home alone one evening when the phone rings. The stranger on the other end of the line has a smooth friendly voice, and he persists in calling back. Casey is mildly irritated at first as she makes popcorn and prepares to watch a scary movie on videocassette. Things take an ugly turn when the caller persists in ringing and asking probing questions. At one point, the mystery caller demands to know who he is looking at. This frightens Casey and she runs to all the doors in her home and locks them. The mystery caller continues to taunt her and he reveals that her boyfriend is out on the patio, tied to a chair. Casey has to answer a question correctly about a scary movie or Steve will die. Casey answers incorrectly about the identity of the killer in *Friday the 13th* and Steve is ripped apart before her eyes. Soon Casey is hunted in her home by a masked, cloaked killer. Casey's parents arrive home but are blind to her situation. Just feet from them, Casey is stabbed to death by her vicious assailant. After entering their home, Casey's parents realize something has happened. They exit the house only to see their daughter's perforated corpse swinging from a tree!

In another part of town, Billy Loomis sneaks through the window into the bedroom of his girlfriend, Sidney Prescott. His entrance frightens Sidney and she screams. Her father Neil knocks on the bedroom door and asks if there is a problem. Sidney assures him nothing is wrong, and Neil tells her about his next business trip. He will be gone all weekend at an expo, and will be registered at the Hilton Hotel if she needs him. After the father leaves, Billy (who was hiding under the bed), comes out and talks to Sidney about their relationship. He has come to feel that they are "edited for television," that all the fire in their relationship has disappeared. Sidney asks if he would settle for a PG-13 relationship and flashes her breasts at Billy for a split second. The visit ends on good terms and Billy disappears back into the night.

The next day at school, the press and police are there in force. Sidney's friend Tatum reveals that Casey and Steve were murdered the previous night. The authorities think the crime may be school-related and are interrogating students, faculty and custodial staff. This double murder is the worst crime to occur in Woodsboro since Sidney's mother was murdered and raped nearly a year ago. Sidney experiences *deja vu* and remembers all the gory details. She fingered a man named Cotton Weary as her mother's killer, and he now awaits execution. But reporter Gale Weathers, in town to report on the new double murder, feels that Weary was framed and that Sidney fingered the wrong man.

In school, Sidney and other students are interviewed by Principal Himbry, Sheriff Burke and Tatum's brother, Deputy Dwight "Dewey" Riley. After the interview, Sidney shares lunch with her boyfriend Billy, Tatum, and friends Stu and Randy. The subject of conversation is the killings. Stu insists that it takes a man to gut somebody, but Tatum points out that a woman could be the killer too. Randy suggests Stu is the killer since he once dated Casey, but Stu thinks that Randy, a movie freak who works at the video store, is a better suspect. Sidney is disturbed by all the talk of gutting and murder. She later calls Tatum and asks if she can spend the night at her house. Tatum agrees, but Sidney will have to wait until after dark until Tatum can pick her up.

That night, Sidney naps on the sofa and awaits Tatum. The phone rings and Sidney is taunted by the mellow-voiced killer. Sidney thinks it is just a prank call and so is surprised when the masked killer jumps out of a hall closet and nearly kills her. Sidney runs into her room, slams the door and the killer vanishes. An instant later, Billy climbs in through Sidney's bedroom window. Sidney tells him about the killer, and is horrified when a cellular phone falls out of Billy's shirt! Convinced that her boyfriend is the telephone stalker, she runs out to the front porch, where she runs into Dewey and the police. They arrest Billy and take Sidney to the police station.

At the station house, Billy insists that he did not make the calls and that he is innocent. Sheriff Burke counters that Billy will be held in custody while his cellular phone bill is pulled. Meanwhile, Deputy Dewey informs Sidney that he has been unable to locate her father. He is apparently not registered at the Hilton as he told Sid he would be. While the police continue to investigate, Sidney, Tatum and Dewey slip out a side exit and run into Gale Weathers and her cameraman, Kenny. Gale has written a book about Cotton Weary and Sidney's mother, so the reporter is not high on Sidney's list of favorite people. When Gale offers to send Sidney a copy of her book, Sidney punches the obnoxious reporter in the face and heads home with the Rileys. Later that night, the killer calls Sidney at Tatum's house and says that she has fingered the wrong person ... again. As a result of this call and a clean cellular bill, Billy is released from prison.

The next day at school, the students are wild with excitement over the killings. Two students dress as the killer and roam the hallways scaring people. Billy and Sidney talk about their relationship, and Billy says that Sidney has not been the same since her mother died. Billy does not understand Sidney's grief because he also lost his mother when his father had an affair and his mom abandoned the family. Sidney insists the situations are different and runs off. Elsewhere, the students caught wearing the costume and mask similar to the killer's are expelled by an angry Principal Himbry.

In the bathroom, Sidney is again stalked by the killer but manages another quick escape. This close call causes the police to act. All classes are suspended and a nine o'clock curfew is imposed. The students are jubilant about the unexpected holiday and Stu invites Tatum and Sidney to a party at his house. Meanwhile, Principal Himbry is stalked by the white-faced killer and murdered in his office.

Gale Weathers and Dewey strike up a friendship and Dewey inadvertently reveals to the nosy reporter that Neil Prescott has still not been located. He is now the prime suspect in the case, especially after it is revealed by Sheriff Burke that calls to Casey and Sidney were both made from Neil's cellular. The sheriff instructs Dewey to stay close to Sidney in case Neil Prescott attempts to kill his daughter on the one-year anniversary of his wife's death.

In preparation for the party at his house, Stu stops by the video store with Billy. He talks to Randy about the murders and Randy suggests that the cops are wasting time. They would know who the killer is if they just watched *Prom Night* or other horror films. Randy suggests that Billy is the killer but when Stu asks for a motive, he cannot provide one. Still, it is the millennium and Randy insists motives are "incidental." Billy overhears the conversation and suggests that Randy has seen one too many movies and that perhaps he is the killer. Frightened, Randy agrees that if this were a scary movie, he would be the prime suspect.

Dewey drives Sidney and Tatum to the party at Stu's house. Gale and Kenny also follow in their news van. Hiding a secret camera under her jacket, Gale accompanies Dewey inside to check things out. When no one is looking, she positions the camera next to the VCR in Stu's TV room so Kenny can watch the party on the van TV monitors (there is a 30-second delay on the camera). Meanwhile, Tatum goes out to fetch more beer from the garage and comes face to face with the Woodsboro Killer. She puts up a valiant struggle, then tries to escape through the doggie door in the garage door. The killer activates the garage door and Tatum's skull is crushed as it is pushed against the ceiling.

When the nine o'clock curfew arrives, and all but a few teens leave the party. Sidney is surprised when Billy shows up. She has been feeling guilty about being such a frigid girlfriend and takes him upstairs, where they make love. Downstairs, Randy and the remaining teens watch *Halloween* on the VCR. Randy pauses the movie and explains the rules of horror movies to his pals. (Rule #1: don't have sex! Rule #2: No drinking or drugs, it's the sin factor. Rule #3: Never say "I'll be right back!") In the news van, Dewey invites Gale to check out a report of a car parked in the nearby bushes. Gale agrees to go with him and tells Kenny that she'll "be right back." Back inside, Randy gets a call revealing that Principal Himbry has been murdered and hanged on a football goal post. The teens are ecstatic and race to the football field, leaving Randy and Stu alone downstairs.

Dewey and Gale discover the hidden car and are shocked when they realize it belongs to Neil Prescott. Apparently he has returned home on the eve of the anniversary of his wife's murder, this time to kill Sidney. Dewey and Gale race back to the house. Inside, Sidney and Billy dress after making love. Sidney wonders who Billy called from jail. She notes that if he were the killer, it would have been clever of him to call her to throw her off-track. Billy asks what he has to do to convince Sidney that he is not the killer. Before she can answer, Billy is attacked from behind and fatally stabbed by the masked psychopath. Sidney runs from the bedroom, the fiend in hot pursuit. She escapes into the attic and falls out a window onto a boat parked below. Shaken, Sidney looks up to see Tatum's corpse hanging from the garage door. She screams and runs off to find help. She makes it to the news van and finds Kenny. They watch the video monitor and see the killer standing in the living room behind Randy. Randy, watching *Halloween*, is oblivious to the devilish presence just feet away. Kenny panics and opens the van door to warn Randy. Unfortunately, he has forgotten the 30-second delay: When he opens the door, the killer is already waiting for him. As the murderer slashes Kenny's throat, Sidney escapes through the rear of the van.

At the same time, Dewey enters Stu's house. Gale runs to the van and finds a pool of blood. She starts the vehicle and Kenny's corpse falls on the windshield. Gale panics and starts driving crazily. She swerves to avoid Sidney and crashes the van into a tree. Sidney's last chance is to find Dewey. She

"It takes a man to do something like that." Stu (Matthew Lillard) and Tatum (Rose McGowan) discuss how to gut a human being in *Scream*.

runs back to the house just as Dewey staggers out onto the porch, a knife lodged in his back. Dewey collapses and Sidney runs into his car and hides. The killer, however, has the keys to the car and slips in through the hatchback, nearly killing his prey at last. Sidney escapes again and runs for the house. She picks up Dewey's gun and is confronted by Randy and Stu. Each one of them insists that the other one is the killer. Unable to make a choice, Sidney enters the house and locks them out. Before she can sort out the confusion, Billy falls down the stairs, bleeding. He offers to help her and takes the gun from her. Then he opens the door and shoots Randy at point-blank range. Sidney is shocked but Billy now reveals all. He was never stabbed, he just has corn syrup all over his shirt. He is the killer, and Stu is his accomplice. They have been taking turns telephoning victims and stalking them. They have worked in unison to trick Sidney.

The two psychotic teens reveal to Sidney that they actually murdered her mother and framed Cotton Weary. Sid's mother was having an affair with Billy's father, and that was the reason his mother abandoned him. Now the boys intend to kill Sidney and frame her father for her murder! To prove their point, Stu and Billy pull a badly beaten Neil Prescott out of a closet. They have cloned his cellular phone so he would appear guilty, and now they plan to stab Sidney and make it look as if Neil shot himself in the head after killing his daughter. Of course, for the plan to succeed, Stu and Billy will have to be wounded as well. To make the effect look real, Billy and Stu take turns stabbing each other with a hunting knife. Unfortunately, Billy has been too zealous and he cuts Stu deeply.

As Stu starts to feel woozy, he fails to notice Gale Weathers pick up his gun. She aims it at them and orders them to surrender immediately. Billy realizes she does not have the safety off and kicks Gale onto the porch, where she is knocked unconscious. During the scuffle, Sidney and her father have escaped. Billy and Stu panic and then the phone rings. It is Sidney, informing the boys she has called the police.

While Billy hunts for Sidney and her dad, Stu continues to bleed. Talking to Sidney on the phone, he confesses that he was only a part of this plan because of "peer pressure" and that his mother and father are going to be *really* mad at him. Billy continues searching the house and when he opens a closet door, Sidney spears him with an umbrella. After Billy goes down, Stu attacks Sid and they wrestle on the floor violently. Sidney gets the upper hand and dumps the television set, still playing *Halloween*, onto Stu's head. As he is electrocuted, Stu lets out a final whimper.

The horror is not yet over. Billy jumps up one last time, only to be shot by Gale Weathers, who this time remembers the safety on the gun. When Billy jumps up yet again, Sidney shoots him in the head, ending the reign of terror.

COMMENTARY: *Scream* is undeniably a modern horror masterpiece. It brilliantly combines Craven's intelligent direction and a literate and dramatic screenplay from newcomer Kevin Williamson. In his quarter-century career, Craven has proven time and again that with a solid script buttressing his efforts, he can work wonders (*The Serpent and the Rainbow, A Nightmare on Elm Street*). *Scream* ably demonstrates what this talented director is capable of achieving within a genre that is renowned neither for its intelligence nor wit. *Scream* is exceptional because it is so very intelligent, witty ... and, most importantly scary.

Scream is the ultimate tale of America's VCR generation. The teenagers portrayed in *Scream*, with their cellular phones, Pentium computers, pagers and extreme cynicism, are a perfect reflection of the mid-1990s. Like many young adults today, these fictional kids are acutely conscious that their technological toys are not really helping anyone, making things better or saving the world. Despite fax machines, MRIs and the Hubble telescope, the world is still fraught with dangers. AIDS runs rampant, the national deficit is tremendous and Generation X'ers are not leaving college to begin $40,000 a-year careers. On the contrary, they have discovered first-hand that the artificially inflated prosperity of the Reagan era is over and that they will be paying for the '80s for the rest of their adult lives. The result of this insight is that today's kids, and the high schoolers profiled in *Scream*, are often cynical or callous in the extreme.

Take for instance Tatum's comment when Sidney remarks that the murdered Casey Becker sits next to her English class. "Not any more," she comments straight-faced, more interested in a one-liner than a fallen comrade. There are other notable examples of callousness in *Scream*. Two students dress up as the killer and thoughtlessly parade around the school, not considering the effect their actions have. All they care about is their own entertainment, not the feelings of other people. When Principal Himbry is murdered, it is amusing to the teenagers. They do not think of the principal as a human being, only a nemesis. They do not consider his children, his wife or his parents at a terrible time like this. All they care about is having a good time.

The moment of greatest cynicism is a short scene in the girl's high school rest room. A beautiful blonde cheerleader with a super-model figure suggests to her friend that Sidney Prescott is the Woodsboro murderer. She knowledgeably rattles off a complicated psychological argument for this revelation and then ironically reveals that her source of information is *The Ricki Lake Show.* In scenes like these and others, *Scream* suggests that, because of intense exposure to television, movies and music videos, today's teens are not only callous and cynical, they are also unbelievably smart. It is a defense mechanism. They *have* to be smart to understand the Internet and other technological tools of modern society. Although Craven usually sees the next generation as representing a better future (as in *A Nightmare on Elm Street*), *Scream* is not so positive. It is suggested that VCRs, movies, the Internet and the like have actually made some young adults psychotic.

Exposure to sanitized movie violence has left them with no concept of real pain and suffering. Perhaps the best moment in the film occurs when Stu and Billy stab each other to make it appear that they were victims of the maniac. They are shocked when they realize it *hurts* to be stabbed. It certainly is not that way in *Rambo* or *The Running Man* or *The A-Team*! For the first time, Stu and Billy are able to sympathize with their victims.

Scream is perfect not only in its dramatization of today's high school set, but also in its self-aware attitude. The film is smart, like the kids it concerns. The teens endlessly wonder about who will play them in the movie version of these events ("With my luck, they'll cast Tori Spelling"), or comment that their lives are just like a movie ("This is like *Silence of the Lambs* when Jodie Foster kept having dreams of her dead father"). More than that, these kids are so familiar with movie lingo that they define their "real life" relationships based on movie terms. Billy comments that because Sidney will not have sex with him, their relationship has become "edited for television." Sidney flashes her breasts and replies that he will have to settle for a "PG-13" relationship. *Scream* is littered with references to movies of all varieties, from *Basic Instinct* and *Halloween* to *Clueless* and *The Town That Dreaded Sundown.*

These references have a purpose in the screenplay: They form a picture of kids who were not really raised by their parents (who seem to be constantly going away on business). Instead, they were raised by Blockbuster Video and the VCR. To them, Jamie Lee Curtis might as well be the girl next door as a movie star. They are that familiar with the actress and her work.

Craven expresses the importance of television in teenage life by positioning TV sets in places of importance throughout *Scream.* When Casey Becker is tormented by the killer, she seeks refuge between a wall and her TV set. Questioned about *Halloween* and *Friday the 13th* movies she has repeatedly seen on video, she is literally trapped between the TV and a hard place. When Randy stops to enlighten his friends about the "rules" of horror movies, he is positioned next to a giant-screen TV which has freeze-framed an image from *Halloween*. As Randy talks, Michael Myers' knife (on the TV) points right at him, suggesting that he too will be a victim of the TV-conscious villains. And, of course, in the ultimate use of a TV set, Sidney drops a TV smack onto Stu's head. Parents always warn that watching too much TV, or sitting too close to it, is bad for a kid, and in Stu's case that is absolutely true.

Additionally, all the action of the final party sequence is shown on Kenny and Gale Weathers' video monitor. So while the partygoers watch TV, there is a camera *watching them watching TV*. Going a step further, the audience is also watching characters watching other characters, and so on. Craven's world is one of an endless circle of television watching! Kenny's van video-monitor also sets up a nice gag that Craven exploits. Kenny's screen has a 30-second delay, so his TV sends him images that are not quite live. He forgets this fact and steps out of the van only to have his throat slit by the killer, who was just on his TV set! Like Stu, Kenny is a victim of video.

Virtually every character in *Scream* is in some way related to TV. Gale Weathers is a celebrity because she is a TV news reporter, and even Sidney is forced to watch incidents from her life unfold on the television set. There is no aspect of these characters' lives that does not relate in some way to the world of video. Craven is documenting something new in American culture here. The TV generation has come of age only to discover (especially in Stu, Billy and Kenny's case) that TV really is harmful to one's health.

It is also noteworthy that in *Scream* there are no healthy, traditional families in evidence. Billy Loomis (Skeet Ulrich) comes from a broken home. His mother left him after his father had an affair. Sidney also comes from a broken home, but her mother died after having an affair. Tatum and Dewey's father is never seen, and both of Stu's parents are missing in action. Thus Craven is back in familiar territory at the same time that he explores the flaws of a new generation. His subtext in *Scream* is that parental absenteeism has left a generation of children to be raised by TV. This generation thinks in terms of sitcom one-liners, movie references and TV-style ethics rather than traditional American values.

Like *The People Under the Stairs, A Nightmare on Elm Street*, or *The Hills Have Eyes, Scream* is an indictment of the middle-class family. At least in *The People Under the Stairs* and *A Nightmare on Elm Street*, there was hope that the next generation would escape from the repression and denial of the Baby Boomers, but *Scream* suggests that parents have poisoned the next generation by leaving them at the mercy of 240 channels, cable TV, video movie rentals and the like. Thanks, folks!

"Helllllo Sidney!" The killer telephones Sidney (Neve Campbell) while Tatum (McGowan) looks on in *Scream*.

The cast of *Scream* plays up these social aspects beautifully. This is a tremendously likable and talented group of young actors and they successfully transform *Scream* into something even better than an effective horror movie. They make it the *Halloween* of the 1990s. Both horror films take a group of teenagers and transform them into real people by accurately reflecting the mood of a decade. *Halloween* echoed the sweetness and innocence of the '70s with its free-wheeling attitudes. Kids smoked pot and the sheriff did not seem to care. Teens drank beer openly and had casual sex without worry. There was no AIDS to worry about and teenage alcoholism was an issue still in the closet. Nancy Loomis, Jamie Lee Curtis and P.J. Soles played innocent kids growing up in a world of hedonism and infinite possibilities. That world was shattered by a maniac, but the teenagers in no way precipitated the events that led to Michael Myers' killing spree.

A product of the '90s, *Scream* reflects a world where teenagers are aware of *everything*. They have seen teen addicts on *Ricki Lake* and are aware that drunk driving and AIDS can kill them. Unlike the kids in the '70s, the kids in the '90s live with the fact that experimentation, a normal thing for a teenager, can lead to death. The generation shown in *Scream* has reacted to this ongoing pressure by becoming sarcastic and cynical.

Most stalker movies are dumb because the characters they highlight are dumb. They disrobe in the strangest places at the strangest times, and generally behave stupidly. The teenagers in *Scream*, and in Kevin Williamson's later *I Know What You Did Last Summer*, are well drawn because they are smart just like today's teenagers are. Twenty years from now, people will watch *Scream* and be reminded of the '90s just as we now associate *Halloween* with the '70s.

Scream is a great film not only because it reflects the young generation and is genuinely smart. Its structure is brilliant because it shares the audience's ennui with formulaic horror pictures. It trots out all the same clichés that kids have seen in the *Hellraiser*, *Child's Play*, *Friday the 13th*, *Halloween*, *A Nightmare on Elm Street* (and other) film franchises. Then, it spins them around. A character named Randy is a movie buff, and he dutifully recounts all the rules of horror movies: no sex, no drugs, and don't say "I'll be right back." *Scream* establishes these paradigms, then faces each one of these clichés ... and overturns them.

Sidney gives up her virginity (a death warrant in any horror film) yet survives! The killer appears supernatural (like Jason Voorhees or Michael Myers) but the murderer of *Scream* is not a bogeyman, just two clever kids working in tandem. Also, the smart girl rails against horror films. She argues that they are insulting because some stupid girl who "can't act" is always running up the stairs instead of out the front door. In the very next scene, she is pursued upstairs by the killer! *Scream* relentlessly puts characters in situations where they must act as if they are themselves in a bad horror film. "Who's there?" Drew Barrymore asks at the opening of *Scream*, and the killer immediately admonishes her for asking a dumb question. "Never ask who's there! It's a death wish! You might as well go outside to investigate a strange noise or something," he barks.

The parody and horror movie references add to *Scream*'s ability to scare. Audience members are acutely aware that *Scream* is more intelligent and knowledgeable than they are. *Scream* knows the clichés inside and out. It is so confident of its manipulation of these clichés that it trots them out and dares the audience not to be scared. The overall impression is that anything is possible because the filmmakers have an encyclopedic knowledge of horror movies. Because of this vast fund of knowledge, *Scream* is the perfect blending of form and content. Frame for frame, it is the scariest movie Craven has ever made.

It has often been said that the first ten minutes of a film are the most crucial. In those important starting moments, an audience will either be hooked or bored. In *Scream*, Craven makes an incredible first impression by staging the ultimate scare set piece. It plays on horror clichés, but is terrifying nonetheless. A girl is home alone at night in a house dominated by large windows. A stranger calls and there is a killer outside. Horribly, he is one step ahead of her throughout the scene. It is a ruthless set-up brilliantly directed, and the scariest opening segment of any movie in recent history. Going one step further than *Psycho*, Craven and Williamson kill off their star, Drew Barrymore, not in the first third of the picture but in the first ten minutes. This scene is well paced, well directed and terrifying. It is the hook that captures the audience.

Friends star Courteney Fox finally found film success as Gale Weathers in *Scream*.

Scream also succeeds because it is dominated by a tantalizing and irresistable mystery. As Randy so insightfully declares, literally "everyone is a suspect." Stu, Dewey, Billy, Randy, the sheriff and Neil Prescott are viable suspects right up until the climax of the picture. Along the way, Cotton Weary, Principal Himbry and even Sidney herself are fingered as possible suspects. Craven does a brilliant job of keeping certain characters off-screen at precisely the right moment. When they return, their whereabouts during the critical time is left unaddressed, but not in an obvious fashion. The result is that *Scream* has an unrelenting atmosphere of uncertainty. There is never a "safe" moment, and one's mind is constantly engaged trying to solve the mystery. It is a beautifully written and executed "audience participation" picture. Viewers are engaged by it throughout as they try to solve the mystery.

It is often difficult to pinpoint the qualities which make a movie a hit. A reviewer's job is to dissect movies into their component pieces and see if the sum equals more than the parts. In *Scream*, every piece of the puzzle buttresses the rest. It has a great young cast, a terrific script, wonderful direction, a surprising plot and the all-important quality of "scariness." Is it a combination of these things, or just a magic synergy that made this picture an instant classic?

It is no surprise that audiences responded so enthusiastically to *Scream*. Kevin Williamson and Craven proved that the best way to succeed in horror is not to play to the lowest common denominator, but to challenge an audience instead. These talents have made a smart film in a lowbrow sub-genre (what Roger Ebert refers to as "The Dead Teenager Picture") and they should be commended for reviving what every newspaper, magazine and reviewer once called a "moribund" genre.

Scream 2 (1997)

Wes Craven and writer Kevin Williamson have raised the ante to the degree that contrivance and a horrendous body count combine to yield a morbid effect for discriminating filmgoers, despite a comic tone. Still, there's enough ingenuity and scariness to please plenty of fans... [*Scream 2*] abounds in confident stylistic and technical flourishes that are the result of Craven's long experience as a horrormeister.— Kevin Thomas (*The L.A. Times*: "Well, You'd *Scream* Too!")

[*Scream* 2] has so much tongue-in-cheek trickery that it virtually escapes the horror genre... It's so sharp ... that no pretty young things absolutely had to die... [Y]ou might enjoy helping *Scream 2* laugh all the way to the bank.— Janet Maslin (*The New York Times*: "Help, He's Back! Run! Shriek! Tempt Fate!")

It's just as sarcastically glib, funny and shrewd in commenting on horror-film conventions, which it gleefully skewers... At the same time, it falls prey to those conventions, including the most deadly of all: repeating itself when it runs out of fresh ideas.— Lawrence Toppman, (*The Charlotte Observer*: "Cutting commentary, *Scream* sequel makes a good stab at living up to the clever original")

Scream 2 doesn't suck. That's the ultimate compliment... Wes Craven and writer Kevin Williamson have sharpened the focus along with their killer's knives. They've smartly allowed their know-it-all horror yarn to grow up... [T]he satire is more sophisticated, the slayings more byzantine.— Susan Wloszczyna, (*USA Today*: "*Scream 2* takes a stab at sophistication")

CAST: Neve Campbell (Sidney Prescott); Jamie Kennedy (Randy Meeks); Courteney Cox (Gale Weathers); David Arquette (Dewey Riley); Liev Schreiber (Cotton Weary); Jerry O'Connell (Derek); Sarah Michelle Gellar (Casey "Cici"

Cooper); Jada Pinkett (Maureen Evans); Tori Spelling (Herself); Elise Neal (Hallie); Omar Epps (Phil Stevens); Duane Martin (Joel); Laurie Metcalf (Debbie Salt/Mrs. Loomis); Lewis Arquette (Chief Lewis Hartley); Timothy Olyphant (Mickey); David Warner (Gus); Heather Graham (*Stab* Casey Becker); Craig Shoemaker; Stephanie Belt; Lucy Linn; Luke Wilson; Jack Baun.

CREDITS: Dimension Films Presents a Konrad Pictures Production in Association with Craven/Maddalena Film. A Film by Wes Craven. *Director:* Wes Craven. *Writer:* Kevin Williamson. *Music:* Marco Beltrami. *Director of Photography:* Peter Deming. *Editor:* Patrick Lussier. *Production Designer:* Bob Ziembicki. *Producers:* Cathy Konrad, Marianne Maddalena. *Executive Producers:* Bob Weinstein, Harvey Weinstein, Kevin Wilson. *Co-Producer:* Daniel Lupi. *Costumes:* Kathleen DeToro. *Art Director:* Ted Berner. *Set Decorator:* Bob Kensinger. *First Assistant Director:* Nicholas Mastandrea. *Music Supervisor:* Ed Gerrard. *Cassandra Aria Composed by* Danny Elfman. *Casting:* Lisa Beach. *Stunt Coordinator:* Tony Cecere. *Unit Production Manager:* Daniel Lupi. *Choreographer:* Adam Shankman. *Graphic Art Supervisor:* Jason Sweers. *Sound Mixer:* Jim Stuebe. *Makeup:* Jane Galli. *Special Effects:* Class A Effects. *Casting Assistant:* Sarah Katzman. *Prop Maker:* Roy Dickson. *Post Production Manager:* Tina Anderson. *ADR Director:* Tina Anderson. *ADR Mixer:* Doc Kane. *Opticals and End Titles:* Pacific Title *Running Time*: 122 minutes. *MPAA Rating:* R

SYNOPSIS: In a small midwestern town near picturesque Windsor College, the movie *Stab* premieres at the Rialto Theater. Filmed in glorious "Stab-o-Vision," the picture is a graphic adaptation of Gale Weathers' best-selling book *The Woodsboro Murders*. As part of a promotional gimmick, all patrons on *Stab*'s opening night are given Munch-like fright masks and costumes (resembling the killer's in the film) and glow-in-the-dark "toy" knives.

Windsor high school seniors Phil Stevens and Maureen Evans arrive at the overcrowded movie premiere. Maureen is not happy to be there; she would rather be viewing the new Sandra Bullock movie instead of some stupid horror film. An African-American, Maureen is offended by what she calls a "lily white" genre. Why does she want to waste her time watching dumb white chicks baring their breasts and getting murdered? To prove her point, she reminds Phil that the killer's mask in *Stab* is *white*.

In the theater, Maureen becomes apprehensive. The auditorium is filled with people in the killer's costume and the film itself is scary. On-screen, a "home alone" Casey Becker is terrorized first by a strange telephone caller and then by the Woodsboro killer. Agitated and affected by the intensity of the film, Maureen escapes to the auditorium for some candy. On her way back to her seat, she is startled by Phil, who jumps at her from a dark corner. He is headed to the men's room, and she goes back inside. As Maureen watches the movie, Phil enters the lavatory to find himself surrounded by patrons resembling the killer. Since the urinals are occupied, he uses a stall. After finishing up, he hears strange sounds in the stall next to him. Curious, he puts his ear to the wall and a thick knife slices into it with fury! Phil dies in a pool of blood.

Maureen is oblivious when a masked figure she believes to be Phil sits down beside her. They watch together as the girl on screen is caught and brutally murdered. Maureen clings to her companion in fear, only to discover that he is bloody! Revealed, the killer stabs Maureen viciously. The audience, believing it is all part of the game, watches as Maureen bleeds to death and the killer escapes.

The next morning, Sidney Prescott wakes up in her dorm at Windsor College to a strange phone call. But it is just freshman Corey Gillis pulling a prank. This is such a routine gag on campus that Sidney has purchased caller I.D. to thwart tormenters! Sidney turns on the TV and sees Cotton Weary on *Current Edition*. He served a year in prison for killing Sidney's mother before it was learned that he was innocent, and society is still treating him badly. Sidney watches the interview until pulled away by her friend Hallie, who informs her that there is a big party planned at the sorority house that evening. Hallie wants Sidney (who in Hallie's opinion is suffering from "self-induced isolation") to get out and enjoy life. As it turns out, that will be a lot harder than either imagined. Soon the police are on campus to report the death of Maureen and Phil. Sidney is horrified by the copycat Woodsboro murder and runs to find Randy, who is also at Windsor in film school. On the way, she is swarmed by reporters.

In film class, students Randy, Mickey and Cici share a discussion about sequels. "Sequels suck," Randy insists, but Mickey points to several films including *Aliens*, *Terminator 2* and *House II*(?!) that were better than the original. Randy does not buy the argument ("Ridley Scott is God") and Cici just thinks Mickey has a "hard-on" for James Cameron movies. The group finally settles on *The Godfather II* as a sequel as good as or better than the original. The movie talk is interrupted by Sidney's arrival. She and Randy reflect on the Woodsboro case together until Sidney's new boyfriend Derek arrives on the scene to comfort her.

As Police Chief Lewis Hartley presides over a press conference about the killings, a bevy of familiar and new faces swarm the campus. Gale Weathers shows up, convinced that this new murder spree will make the box office for *Stab* go through the roof. She tries to learn the details of the murders but is impeded by a local reporter, Debbie Salt of the *Post Telegram*. Debbie claims to be a fan and asks Weathers how she feels about "violence in cinema" issues. Gale ignores the question and finds herself a new cameraman, the tentative Joel. Joel and Gale then descend on Sidney with a surprise, a face-to-face confrontation with Cotton Weary. Sidney refuses to talk on-camera; when Gale presses, Sidney decks her.

Gale is not the only Woodsboro veteran to show up. Deputy Dewey Riley has flown in after hearing about the murders and is there to protect Sidney. Dewey asks her who in her college life might want to kill her. Sidney cannot hazard a guess.

That night, the sorority party takes place as planned. A reluctant Sidney is dragged around by Hallie to meet the girls in charge. Not surprisingly, the sorority chicks are a vapid bunch thrilled to meet a celebrity. "Hi," one girl enthuses to Sidney. "No, I really mean it, hi!" As Sidney navigates through the pool of superficial compliments, lovely Cici Cooper stays home at the Omega Beta Zeta sorority house as a "sober sister." She watches *Nosferatu* on TV and is surprised to receive a strange phone call. "Do you want to die tonight, Cici?" the caller asks. Cici is frightened and runs outside to call the police, but there is interference on the line and she can't get through. The killer slips into the house unnoticed and chases her upstairs. Cici runs for her life but is stabbed in the back and then thrown from the roof.

The sorority party teens merrily run to the crime scene. Derek is worried and offers to take Sidney home. As he waits outside, Sidney picks up her coat ... and the phone rings. She answers and recognizes the voice of her onetime tormenter. She tells him to show his face, and the killer obliges, lunging at her with a knife! Sidney escapes and Derek chases the killer. Dewey shows up and helps Sidney. Derek has been stabbed in the arm.

Dewey, Sidney and Hallie wait in the hospital while Derek's wounds are treated. Both the cops and Dewey are a bit suspicious that Derek received only a flesh wound from such a vicious, bloodthirsty killer. Sidney refuses to believe Derek is involved.

Gale, Dewey and Randy set about investigating the crime and learn some important facts. First, there is a similarity between the names of the new victims and the Woodsboro dead. Maureen Prescott was killed, as was senior Maureen Evans. Cici's name was Casey, as in Casey Becker, and Phil Stevens shared the name "Steven" with Becker's boyfriend. Randy realizes that a copycat is trying to pull off a real-life sequel to the Woodsboro murders.

Sidney and Derek reach an impasse in their relationship. She claims she doesn't want him to get hurt, but Derek suspects she is actually distrusting of his motives and identity. To prove his intentions, he breaks into song at the campus cafeteria and gives her a necklace with his fraternity letters emblazoned on it.

Randy and Dewey share lunch and talk about the rules of sequels. They suggest several suspects. Derek is too obvious, Randy insists, because the whole boyfriend thing is "old." He suggests Mickey, the Tarantino-like film student, as a possible candidate, and Hallie, a black version of "Candyman." Gale, a ruthless opportunist, is not above suspicion. Randy and Dewey aren't the only ones worried about the murders. Gale's new cameraman Joel has learned what happened to Kenny in Woodsboro, and (being a black man) he realizes that "brothers don't last long" in these kinds of situations.

While Sidney rehearses for a lead role in an elaborate Greek stage drama about Cassandra, she has a panic attack and sees herself surrounded by the killer instead of her masked fellow actors. She runs off-stage and Derek shows up mysteriously to help her recover. Her guard up, Sidney cuts off the romantic relationship and informs her boyfriend that she needs "distance." Derek wants to do the right thing for Sidney, so he acquiesces to her wish. Outside the drama building, the killer telephones and taunts Gale, Randy and Dewey about his identity. As they search the campus square for the killer, Randy is isolated and then brutally murdered in a TV van.

For security reasons, Sidney is accompanied everywhere by two police detectives. At the school library, she receives an e-mail informing her that she is going to die that night. While the cops search the library for the sender of the message, Sidney runs into Cotton Weary. He wants her to go on TV with him for a Diane Sawyer interview. He already has a "900 number" but he also wants his 15 minutes of fame on TV. When Sidney refuses, Cotton grows violent and the police apprehend him.

Dewey and Gale, who have had a nasty falling-out over her cruel depiction of him in her book, reconcile and agree to hunt the killer together. They think Joel's videotape footage may reveal the identity of the killer, who apparently wants attention very badly. They travel to the film school building and review the footage there. As they watch themselves on TV, they realize they love each other and begin to make love. Suddenly, another TV screen comes to life and shows footage of each victim before the murder. Maureen Evans, Cici and even poor Randy are all captured on videotape just seconds before their murders! Most frightening, the tape ends with a shot of Dewey and Gale together in that very room! They are being watched! After Dewey goes to investigate the projection room, the killer pursues Gale into a sound studio. Dewey arrives to save her but is stabbed in the back by the psycho. Locked in a small closet, Gale escapes the killer's grasp, but mourns the death of Dewey. As she escapes, she runs into Cotton Weary. His hands are bloody, but he claims not to be the killer. Uncertain, Gale runs away from him and teams up with local reporter Debbie Salt to report him to the authorities.

Elsewhere on campus, Sidney and Hallie leave campus with a police escort. Derek says goodbye to his girlfriend and watches them leave. As they depart, Derek is stalked by his fraternity mates. They are upset with him for giving Sidney his letters and they spirit him away to the theater, tie him to the Greek stage and leave him there all night. Meanwhile, the police stop at a red light and are attacked by the masked killer at the intersection. One cop is thrown out of the vehicle and the other's throat is slit. The slasher takes the girls on a wild ride. The surviving cop jumps on the hood to stop him, but the killer purposely rams the car and the cop's skull is impaled by a metal rod. The impact also knocks out the killer, and Hallie and Sidney are trapped in the car with him. To escape, the young women crawl over the murderer. They escape intact but Sidney goes back to the car to remove the killer's mask. But when she returns to the vehicle, the killer is gone. She looks behind her and sees the ghost-faced monster kill Hallie!

Terrified, Sidney runs to the campus. She flees to the stage but is tracked there by her opponent. Shocked, she discovers Derek hanging from the stage roof, alive and well, but trapped as part of the fraternity stunt. She is about to release him from his prison when the killer enters the auditorium and unmasks himself. It is Mickey, the film student! More disturbingly, Mickey claims Derek is his partner! Sidney feels betrayed and shocked that another boyfriend would treat her this cruel way. As Derek asserts his innocence, Mickey shoots him in the heart. Mickey then tells Sidney that Derek *wasn't* in on it. Furthermore, Mickey informs Sidney that he is doing all this so he will get caught. He wants to go to trial and blame violence in films for his actions. He is sure the Christian Coalition will pay his bills, since they support the censorship of objectionable films. Before he kills Sidney, Mickey introduces his real partner...

From off-stage, Gale Weathers appears. Sidney is shocked by another betrayal, but Gale is not really the secret partner. She is being held at gunpoint by Debbie Salt ... who is actually Billy Loomis' mother! Mickey and Mrs. Loomis found each other on a "psycho" internet website and planned the whole thing. Mrs. Loomis gets revenge for the murder of her son and Mickey gets his shot at stardom. When Gale tries to save Sidney's life, she is shot. Then Mrs. Loomis *really* begins to dispose of the loose ends. She shoots Mickey so he can't reveal anything to the authorities, and turns her gun on Sidney. Just as Sidney is about to die, Cotton Weary arrives and saves the day, shooting the crazed mother. The villains defeated, Cotton and Sidney tend to Gale, who is not badly injured. When Mickey jumps up for one final scare, Sidney and Gale blow him away in a volley of gunfire. Then, Sidney plants a pre-emptive bullet in Mrs. Loomis' skull.

Sidney tries to re-build her life while Cotton finds himself at the center of the press attention he has so long desired. Gale is offered the opportunity to go on the air "live" to cover the scene, but she discovers that Dewey has survived and opts to ride with him to the hospital instead.

COMMENTARY: *Scream 2* is a kick-ass sequel that doesn't play favorites. Old friends and new characters alike are dispatched with equal vigor and the first movie is lovingly roasted in a "cheesy" re-staging called *Stab* (starring Tori Spelling as Sidney and *Boogie Night*s' Heather Graham as Drew Barrymore's character). Like its predecessor, *Scream 2* is also filled with references to other films, but in this case the references are situation-specific. Since the movie is obsessed with sequels, most of the films alluded to by Williamson's clever script are also sequels. The other category of reference is "college horror picture," which is another perfect touch since *Scream 2* unfolds on a college campus.

What elevates *Scream 2* above most sequels is its consistent *leitmotif* concerning the world of drama. Nearly every death (or near-death) in the picture is staged in an arena related to the world of the performing arts, and an interesting connection is forged. *Scream 2* is not just a sequel, Craven's direction and choice of locales asserts, it follows in a noble and age-old tradition of human storytelling. This link between *Scream 2* and the world of respectable literature/Greek drama, etc., is a clever way of deflecting moral criticism that Williamson's script identifies as "violence-in-cinema issues."

To wit: Jada Pinkett's character is murdered in a movie theater, and her last act is to crawl onto a movie stage showing *Stab*, symbolically joining the bloody action on-screen behind her. Randy is dispatched in a news van, with technical video equipment in evidence, and Dewey nearly meets his death in a sound studio (in a film school!). Tellingly, the final battle also occurs on stage, in front of a scenic backdrop from Greek drama. Sidney, who claims she knew that the terror would begin again and who plays the character Cassandra (an unheeded seer), defeats her opponents against the backdrop of stage lights, deadly props and storm sound effects. The implication is, as Shakespeare wrote, that "all the world's a stage," and it is not surprising that the motivation of two characters (Cotton Weary and the crazed Mickey) is to find attention on a national "center stage" through either a Diane Sawyer interview or the trial of the century.

The decision to stage *Scream 2*'s most dynamic moments around props of the performing arts world is Craven's latest post-modern Pirandellian touch. The audience (as in *Wes Craven's New Nightmare*) is constantly reminded of the world of drama/literature/film at the same time that it witnesses a new adventure. With the inclusion of *Stab*, this notion of a film-within-a-film-within-a-film is reinforced and carried to an extreme yet entertaining level. Sidney Prescott is not just Neve Campbell playing the role she made famous in *Scream*. She is also Cassandra and the fodder for Tori Spelling's thespian interpretation in *Stab*. Jada Pinkett is not just an actress playing Maureen, she is a character deploring the role of African-Americans in the genre. When she is killed, she defeats her own argument (simultaneously starring in *Scream 2*, and blending with the fictional action of *Stab* onscreen). The thematic complexities of this film would not have been possible if *New Nightmare* and *Scream* hadn't paved the way for a new generation of smart genre pictures. Now, Craven and Williamson's level of extraordinary wit and self-awareness is almost *de rigueur* (and visible in pictures such as *I Know What You Did Last Summer* and *Starship Troopers*). Pity the horror flicks like *Alien Resurrection* ... dumb old things that are part of a dying breed.

Further heightening the duality of actors/characters in *Scream 2* is the fact that everyone has multiple identities in the film and is obsessed with their larger-than-life counterparts. Randy laments that he is played by an unknown in *Stab*, whereas Dewey is played by the well-known David Schwimmer of *Friends*. Gale Weathers is disturbed because a nude picture of her was transmittted on the internet ... but she claims it was just her head on "Jennifer Aniston's body." Joel, the new cameraman, is upset by his real-life casting in the role of Kenny ... the dead cameraman from *Scream*. Each character sees him/herself on more than one level of reality; drama coach Gus (David Warner) tells Sidney to use that knowledge of "the other" identity to defeat her fears. Sidney is Cassandra, so Gus tells her to use her real-life pain to make Cassandra "real," and to be a fighter in reality. In all, the connection to drama and multiple identities is a complicated trick to pull off, but it keeps *Scream 2* from falling into a pattern of repetition. The film can never be accused of sucking blood from the original *Scream* because its own internal logic is quite separate from the first picture. Not surprisingly, many reviews reflected that. There is an overwhelming feeling in many of *Scream 2*'s reviews of grudging respect. The reviewer wolf pack *really* wanted to dismiss the film as a stupid sequel, but found it was unable to do so because of the complex issues *Scream 2* expertly explores.

Scream 2 is a very good film and it is filled with clever touches. In an early sequence, Kevin Williamson's screenplay brings up the specter of lousy sequels. This conversation not only allows for references to *Terminator 2* (1991), *Aliens* (1986), *The Godfather II* (1974), *The Empire Strikes Back* (1987) and, perversely, *House II: The Second Story* (1987), but further disarms the salivating critics who are looking for *Scream 2* to be an inferior clone of *Scream*. As a rule, critics are suckers for self-reflexivity in films (as the glowing reviews for *New Nightmare* attest) and Williamson's technique immediately inserts into *Scream 2* a knowing and intellectual argument about films and their sequels. Although the very fact that it is brought up and faced head-on is admirable, *Scream 2* does not win its own debate about sequels.

As Craven and Williamson have stated on numerous occasions, *Scream 2* is the second story in a trilogy. In *Scream 2*, Randy makes a distinction concerning *The Empire Strikes Back*. It is not just a sequel, he insists, but a second movement in a grand trilogy. By inference, the audience is supposed to intuit the same thing about *Scream 2*, that it is the second piece in a larger story. If that is the case, the film really does not work because it gives no hint where the third film will lead. There is never a feeling of being left in suspense in *Scream 2*.

In *The Empire Strikes Back*, Han Solo was frozen in carbonite and carted off to Jabba the Hutt while Luke discovered Ben Kenobi had lied and that Darth Vader was his father. In *Back to the Future II* (1990), Marty McFly was trapped in time and Doc Brown was feared dead, obliterated by a bolt of lightning. In both "second" stories, the suspense was unbearable at the end of the picture. Audiences left each motion picture with more questions than answers and the burning need for a third picture. There is no such need at the conclusion of *Scream 2*. There are survivors of a second massacre, but generally a feeling that everything is once again okay (as in the end of *Scream*). In other words, *Scream 2* could exist very well without a third and final picture. It really is just a sequel, and not a second part of a grand movement. Still, it is always dangerous to analyze a work in progress, so perhaps *Scream 3* will be a multiplication of the terror in *Scream 2*.

Scream 2 is also undone to a certain extent by the rules of sequels. Sequel Rule #1, according to Randy, is "carnage candy"...there is always a bigger body count in the sequel to a hit film. Considering *Aliens, Damien: Omen II* (1979), *Terminator 2, The Road Warrior, Halloween II* and a bevy of other sequels, that is an astute observation, and *Scream 2* follows that lead. As a result, however, there is an overall flattening of suspense regarding the new characters. Derek, Joel, Cici, Hallie, the sorority girls and Mickey never attain the depth of personality displayed by Tatum, Billy, Stu or even Principal Himbry in *Scream*. In *Scream*, any one of those characters could have been the murderer, and there were legitimate reasons for believing each character guilty. In *Scream 2*, it is a roll of the dice, a crap shoot, pure and simple. Any of the newcomers could be the copycat killer simply because the audience does not know any one of them well enough to form an opinion.

To its credit, the script tries to play Derek as a likely suspect. Is he a sweet hero or malicious bad boy (like Billy Loomis?). Unfortunately, the answer seems to have come from a coin flip rather than logic or character development. Same thing for Mickey. Olyphant has precious few scenes in this sequel to establish the character of Mickey. Certainly, the audience is not nearly as familiar with him as they were with Loomis or Stu. Sure, his motiviation at the end of the film is believable, but that exact same motivation could have been pinned on Derek, Hallie, Joel, Cici or anyone else the script demanded. Individualism has been replaced by the carnage candy.

On the other hand, *Scream 2* is remarkably effective for deepening the characters from the first film. Gale, Dewey, Sidney and Randy have all reached the status of beloved characters, and it is to the film's credit that it repeatedly puts each of them in jeopardy and does not pull back from that stance. The most devastating moment in the film occurs when Randy is unexpectedly killed. It is a shocking, unexpected and daring move. An unspoken rule of sequels (which Randy almost says, but thinks better of) is that all the survivors of the first film survive the second film and suspense is therefore lessened. Williamson and Craven daringly overturn that rule and kill Randy early on. This is a striking move that calls everything into question. If the beloved Randy can die, so can Dewey, Gale and even Sidney. The carpet is pulled out from under the viewers and they feel rudderless.

Still, no matter how daring, killing Randy is also a bad call. Randy is the unquestioned mouthpiece of the *Scream* saga, the character who offers viewers the road maps to survival. Who is going to tell us the rules in *Scream 3*? In killing off Randy, an admittedly ballsy move, the creators of *Scream 2* have done a disservice to *Scream 3*. Unless, of course they have a great joke in store for all of us. If *Scream 3* really wanted to play with conventions, Randy would show up alive and well (with a few scars) in *Scream 3*, saying how lucky he was to survive the Windsor College massacre. Why? Well, a rule of sequels is that nobody important really died in the previous installment.

Donald Pleasence's Dr. Loomis died in a fire in *Halloween II* (1981) but returned for action in *Halloween IV* (but with some bad burns). He died again in *Halloween V* (1989) but showed up healthy and retired in *Halloween VI*. Mr. Spock bought the farm in *Star Trek II: The Wrath of Khan* (1982) only to be reborn in *Star Trek III: The Search for Spock* (1984). Sigourney Weaver's Ripley died in *Alien 3* (1992) only to be cloned in 1997's *Alien Resurrection*. Hopefully, Randy will go the same (ridiculous) route and return in *Scream 3*, thus making the ultimate point about the silliness and paucity of creativity in movie sequels.

Scream 2 is undoubtedly a clever film. The final revelation, that Billy's mother is the copycat killer out for revenge, echoes a film referenced in *Scream*: *Friday the 13th* (1980). In that picture, Mrs. Voorhees went on a killing spree to avenge the death of her son years earlier.

Also, in what has to be a first in cinema, Williamson's script builds a character almost exclusively through film references, a kind of Information Age shorthand for viewers. Mickey is mostly undeveloped by scenes in the actual film, but through his film references his identity is revealed. His love for James Cameron films is obvious from his quotes about *Aliens* and *T2*; it is demonstrated again in the finale when he informs Sidney that she has a "Linda Hamilton" kind of thing going on. Also, in the spirit of Cameron sequels, there is a multiplicaton of terror and suspense in *Scream 2* so Mickey is like Billy Loomis and Stu on acid, and he racks up a considerably larger body count than the Woodsboro boys. Also, and most importantly, he believes there are many sequels that are better than the original films ... *because he is the character orchestrating the killings in the sequel!* His point-of-view subtly tips off the audience to his identity as the copycat. Brilliant!

The more times one watches *Scream 2*, the more one realizes how well the details fit together, even if the film takes unnecessary detours (like the murder of Cici). Early in the film, Gale recognizes Mrs. Loomis, claiming she looks familiar. Loomis chalks it off to a seminar she went to with Gale, but of course, Gale recognizes her from her *Woodsboro Murders* research! Randy also references a whole slew of appropriate college horror films including *The House on Sorority Row* (1983), *The Dorm that Dripped Blood* (1981) and *Splatter University* (1984). *Scream* was a high school film that referenced high school horror such as *Prom Night* and *Halloween*, so it is a logical development that *Scream 2* would grow up and feature references to these campus-bound cinematic terrors. The *Stab* sequences, which re-stage scenes from *Scream*, are also very funny, and the opening scene in a cinema filled with fans in masks recalls the Freddy Krueger talk show sequence in *Wes Craven's New Nightmare*. *Scream*'s thesis about teen apathy is also carried over to the sequel. When the sorority chicks discover that "sister" Cici has been killed, they are thrilled about the publicity and run to the crime scene. They also want Sidney to pledge their house because of the celebrity she would bring them.

A highlight of *Scream 2* is the sequence in which Sidney believes she is being attacked by the ghost-faced predator during a rehearsal of the Greek drama. Craven uses this opportunity to direct a surreal, almost byzantine horror sequence that plays with the boundaries of reality in a terrifying manner and also forges that connection betweeen literary history and the horror film. Indeed, Craven's skill in film directing has never been more evident than in the virtuoso *Scream 2*. At some points (especially in the crane shots gliding down on the campus and finding reporters, cop and students), he mimics the *modus operandi* of *Scream*, and at other moments (the car chase, the hunt through the sound studio) he elevates the suspense far beyond anything evident in the first picture. When Sidney and Hallie crawl over an unconscious slasher, the viewer's heart pounds with terror.

As mentioned earlier, some of the returning characters are deepened. Sidney takes steps towards becoming an even more assertive fighter. Cotton Weary explodes from red herring to full-fledged human being, and Dewey and Gale fall in love. If *Scream 2* really belongs to any character it is probably Courteney Cox's Gale. At the start of the film, she is even more opportunistic and manipulative than she was in *Scream*. By the end of the picture, she has changed completely. Her final act, choosing Dewey over fame, is quite a change in her personality. If anything, *Scream 2* goes almost too far in this regard; there is nowhere left for Dewey and Gale to go in *Scream 3*. Perhaps that was the plan, as Courteney Cox demanded (and received) a large salary increase for this sequel. *Scream 3* could be made without her and/or Arquette now, since their characters have reached a new apex.

Scream 2 is an accomplished film and one well worth seeing. However, perhaps unfairly, it does not make this author's list of the top five Craven pictures despite its overall high quality. Even though some of Craven's earlier films have rough spots, many (*The Serpent and the Rainbow*, *A Nightmare on Elm Street*, *New Nightmare*, *Scream*) are stronger than this perfectly produced picture because they really explore some deep aspect of human nature in a provocative or new manner. *Scream 2* follows in Craven's *New Nightmare* and *Scream* "Generation X"/Pirandellian horror genre, but as the third venture in the tradition it is not as consistently interesting as the others. It is scary and funny and suspenseful, but ultimately not involving enough because of the inclusion of peripheral and mostly undeveloped characters (Cici, Derek, Hallie, Joel) who serve the plot but don't ever come to life as real people. This is not to say *Scream 2* is not an excellent entertainment filled with enjoyable and heart-stopping moments. It is just that no matter how hard the clever script tries to surpass *Scream*'s tricky combination of smarts, scares and smiles, that damn rule about carnage candy and a higher body count sinks it. The feeling that *Scream 2* is really just a sequel (and a good one) and not the middle piece of a trilogy also undermines the ending, which plays as sort of lackluster.

One looks forward to *Scream 3*, however, and hopes that Craven will again be at the helm.

Chapter 3

The Television Movies

A Stranger in Our House (1978) (a.k.a. Summer of Fear)

CAST: Linda Blair (Rachel Bryant); Lee Purcell (Julia/Sarah); Jeremy Slate (Tom Bryant); Jeff McCracken (Mike Gallagher); Jeff East (Peter Bryant); Carol Lawrence (Leslie Bryant); Macdonald Carey (Prof. Jarvis); Fran Drescher (Carolyn Baker); James Jarnagin (Bobby); Sierra Pecheur (Nurse Duncan); Billy Beck (Sheriff); Patricia Wilson (Mrs. Gallagher); Gwil Richards (Dr. Morgan); Frederick Rule (Mailman); Helena Mackela (Beverly Hills Lady); Nicole Keller (Elizabeth); John Steadman (Veterinarian); Kerry Arquette (Anne); Kim Wells (Female Rider); Beatrice Manley (Marge Trent).

CREDIT: *Director of Photography:* William M. Jurgenson. *Executive Producers:* Max A. Keller, Michaeline H. Keller. *Producers:* Pat and Bill Finnegan. *Teleplay:* Glenn M. Benest, Max A. Keller. *Based on the Novel* Summer of Fear *by* Lois Duncan. *Director:* Wes Craven. *Music:* Michael Lloyd, John D'Andrea. *Film Editor:* Howard A. Smith, A.C.E. *Associate Producer/Art Director:* Joe Aubel. *Production Manager:* Steve Nicolaides. *Casting:* Ellison/Gartzman Company. *Associate Executive Producer:* Wade G. Davis II. *Assistant Director:* Charles Ziarko. *Second Assistant Directors:* Kevin Finnegan, M.E. Canniff. *Set Decorator:* Anthony Mordell. *Production Sound:* William Randall. *Music Editor:* Dan Carlin. *Sound Editing:* Echo Film Services, Michael Hilkene. *Script Supervisor:* Marjorie Mullen. *Auditor:* Paul D. Roedl. *Producton Coordinator:* Margaret Fannin. *Costumes:* Kathy O'Read. *Makeup:* Stephen Gautier. *Hairstylist:* Carolyn Elias. *Assistant Editor:* George Talley. *Re-recording Mixer:* Don MacDougall. *Construction:* Woodrow Willis. *Stunt Coordinator:* Mickey Gilbert. *Wrangler:* Jim Medearis. *Special Effects:* John Frazier. *Key Grip:* Jay Johnson. *Gaffer:* Ron Knox. *Property:* Craig Raiche. *Transportation:* Bob Hendrix.

SYNOPSIS: Albuquerque teenager Rachel Bryant awakens one summer morning to learn that a car accident has claimed the life of her Uncle Ryan and Aunt Marge. Even though it has been ten years since Rachel and her family saw them, their death is still a terrible shock. As her parents, Leslie and Tom, make arrangements to fly to Little Rock for the funeral, Rachel learns that Aunt Marge's babysitter, Sarah, was also killed in the wreck. Marge and Ryan also had a daughter (Julia) a little older than Rachel. Leslie and Tom plan to bring her to Albuquerque for the summer to help her through the grieving process. Rachel looks forward to the return of her parents and the arrival of Julia.

While her parents are flying to Little Rock, Rachel continues to hone her equestrian skills for an upcoming horse show. She owns a beautiful white horse named Sundance, and her boyfriend Mike Gallagher is Sundance's trainer.

The Bryants return home with Julia, a quiet girl with an unusual accent. Sundance reacts strangely to the girl, and it is clear that the horse does not like Julia and that Julia does not like the horse. Later, Julia seems fascinated by a photograph of Mike on Rachel's nightstand. At dinner that night, Julia makes a comment about the Ozark hill folk and tells the Bryants that her father was writing a book about them. He had hired a local girl named Sarah so as to examine a hill-person up close. When Mike arrives there seems to be a connection between him and Julia. When Rachel goes back to her room and accidentally knocks over Julia's suitcase, she finds a bottle with a human tooth inside. Later, when she tells Mike about this oddity, he accuses her of snooping.

Rachel does her best to become friends with the new arrival in her house. One day, Rachel, Julia and Rachel's friend Carolyn, a nurse, run into Prof. Jarvis, an anthropologist and occult expert. He notices that Julia has the same facial features and bone structure that the people from the Ozarks do. Julia makes light of this comment and heads home. On the way in, Sundance breaks out of the stable and attacks her. The horse is finally restrained, and the family blames Sundance and Rachel for the attack. Rachel defends Sundance's behavior, which further irritates the family. Rachel's dad bandages Julia's leg and Rachel gets the distinct impression of an "interest" between them. Soon Mr. Bryant and Julia begin to grow closer: They start to play chess together, and Julia even takes to rubbing her uncle's sore back.

One morning, Rachel wakes up with ugly red blotches all over her face and body. The doctor treats her and tells her that she should not go to the big dance that night. Rachel's brother Peter asks a favor: He has a crush on Julia and wants to know if Mike can take Julia to the dance so she can hear Peter play the guitar there. Rachel agrees and asks Mike, who is only too happy to take Julia to the dance. Julia has nothing to wear, so Rachel lets her borrow the dress she had made for the dance. It looks fabulous on her. Rachel is jealous as Julia preens in front of her mother, and for a split-second she thinks Julia casts no reflection in the mirror! As Mike arrives to take Julia out for the evening, Mr. Bryant seems jealous.

Late that night, Rachel dreams of being on a winding mountain road with

Mike. He says that he sees her mother's car in the distance, speeding toward them. Rachel awakens suddenly and begins to suspect that there is more to Julia than meets the eye. She searches her room and finds strands of her own hair and burned matches in the garbage can. In a bureau drawer, she finds a wax sculpture of Sundance. A few moments later, an angry Peter arrives home. Julia is not with him. According to Peter, Julia and Mike were together the whole evening. They left the dance at an intermission, totally wrapped up in each other. Rachel is heartbroken by Mike's betrayal and she confronts him the next morning at the horse show. He apologizes but says that he is madly in love with Julia.

Mad at Mike and Julia, Rachel rides Sundance in the show. During the performance, Sundance explodes into a rage and runs wild. He breaks through a fence and falls down over a hill. Rachel is shattered when she learns that Sundance's leg is broken and that he must be killed. Rachel suffers terribly but her family seems not to notice. Julia's hold on the family and Mike has deepened. She and Mike are now lovers and Julia and Mr. Bryant are becoming uncomfortably close. Even Julia and Mrs. Bryant are bonding, cleaning silver together and joking. Rachel and Julia become bitter enemies. Soon, even Carolyn has become Julia's best friend.

When Rachel meets with Prof. Jarvis and asks him about witchcraft, he gives her several books to read. Rachel reads *The Encyclopedia of Witchcraft* and *Witchcraft: Then and Now* and learns that the one animal immune to witchcraft is the horse, which explains Sundance's immediate dislike of Julia. Rachel suggests to her parents that Julia is a witch who has enchanted them, but her father counters that Rachel is the one acting like a witch. When Rachel confronts Julia with her accusations, Julia denies everything and claims that she tried to be friends with Rachel. Rachel insists Julia is a witch and tells her that Prof. Jarvis can prove it. Julia replies that Rachel should not count on him. Soon Rachel understands the meaning of that remark when she learns that Jarvis has suffered a stroke!

The Bryants call an ambulance and the old professor is taken to the hospital. Rachel is more convinced than ever that Julia is somehow behind all of the evil goings-on. When a letter arrives for Julia, Rachel opens it and sees it is from Mary Cairncross, a girl in Boston. After another nightmare, in which a car races straight towards her, Rachel continues her research into witchcraft and learns that witches are powerless when they sleep. Julia's college roommate Rachel calls Mary Cairncross while Julia sleeps and learns that Julia was the president at the Glee Club in college. Later Carolyn, working on the graveyard shift at the hospital, calls and says the professor is conscious and demanding to see Rachel.

Rachel rushes to the hospital to confer with Jarvis. He tells her that the evidence against Julia is becoming overwhelming. He suggests that a witch cannot be photographed because witches do not reflect light. Now Rachel has a way to trap her enemy. The next morning, she suggests to her mother, a professional photographer, that she take shots of Julia. Mrs. Bryant thinks this is a wonderful idea and pressures Julia into posing for her. Unfortunately, Mrs. Bryant cannot develop the pictures for a few days because she has to go on a trip. Mrs. Bryant asks Rachel to go with her on the long drive, and Rachel again tries to convince her mother that Julia is a witch. Mrs. Bryant slaps Rachel and runs to the kitchen, only to find her husband and Julia in a compromising position. Later that night, Mrs. Bryant tries to talk to her husband about Julia. He tells her that she is being ridiculous.

The next morning, after a despondent Mrs. Bryant has left on her trip. Rachel searches Julia's room. She finds a photograph of herself marked up with red magic marker, proving that Julia cast a spell and caused her bout of hives. More troubling is the fact that Julia has taken a map, burned a certain area and attached a dead fly to it. Rachel realizes that Julia is planning an accident for her mother. As Mr. Bryant and Julia make love, Rachel develops her mother's photographs. As Prof. Jarvis predicted, there is no sign of Julia in the shots. Julia suddenly attacks Rachel and burns the photographs. She reveals to Rachel that she is not Julia but Sarah, the Ozark housekeeper of her aunt and uncle. She also tells Rachel that she plans to kill both her and her mother and take over the family. Rachel locks Julia in the darkroom, then must evade her own deranged father. Julia breaks through a wall using her dark powers, and Rachel runs to Mike. She asks him to drive her away from the house as fast as possible. Mike is confused but he agrees.

On the road, Mike and Rachel are pursued by Julia in another car. Mike is shocked when his car windows roll up by themselves and the hood pops open. Then he loses control of the car and it goes over the side of a cliff! Mike and Rachel survive the wreck and climb the hill just in time to see Mrs. Bryant's car rapidly approaching. It is out of control, just like in Rachel's dream. Julia's car and Mrs. Bryant's car nearly collide, Julia's, forced off the road, explodes. Later, the Bryant family thanks Rachel for saving them from Julia. Mr. Bryant claims to remember "nothing" about the last few weeks and tells Rachel that he is sorry he doubted her. Mike gives Rachel a new pony and all is well again. Rachel has her life back.

In Beverly Hills, a taxi cab pulls up a in front of mansion. Julia steps out of the car and introduces herself to a young mother and her baby. She is the new governess...

COMMENTARY: *A Stranger in Our House* is a fairly faithful adaptation of Lois Duncan's 1976 novel *Summer of Fear*. There are some interesting differences between the novel and the teleplay, but much of the book's dialogue is delivered, word-for-word on the screen.

Summer of Fear begins differently than the script by Glenn M. Benest and Max A. Keller. Four years after the events portrayed in the film, a mature Rachel Bryant picks up a newspaper and reads a frightening passage about the disappearance of a family on a camping trip. Included in the piece is a reference to an unidentified girlfriend who is actually Julia/Sarah. The book then flashes back to the events four summers earlier when Julia, really Sarah Blane, arrived in the Bryant home and nearly destroyed Rachel's life. Duncan's novel is written in the first person to increase audience identification with Rachel, who sees each segment of her life (pet, room, family, friends) stolen or destroyed by the interloper. This is a technique the telefilm does not mimic, but Craven always keeps his camera on star Linda Blair (Rachel), making her the protagonist of the production.

Point-for-point, the plot of the telefilm follows the book. Lee Purcell perfectly captures the shifts of Julia's accent highlighted in the book. Just as in the novel, she pronounces the word "tired" as "tarred" and slips into Ozark slang when riled, talking about "varmints" and the like. The dream sequences, which take place on a winding mountain road, are also translated directly from novel to screen with no variations.

A major difference in the two versions of the story, however, is that Rachel is obsessed with horses in the telefilm. She owns a white stallion named Sundance which is trained by her boyfriend, Mike Gallagher. This development is a fabrication of the screenwriters (in the book, Mike is a lifeguard). There is no horse in *Summer of Fear*, only a dog named Trickle. Interestingly, Trickle and Sundance do play the same role: Each animal is the first to be aware of Julia's dark side. In the film, Rachel reads a book stating that of all animals, only horses cannot abide witches. In the book, when the same passage is read, only a *dog* cannot abide the evil creatures. It is hard to deny that a horse is a more dramatic and interesting animal than the family dog.

The most significant differences from book to film occur in the conclusion. In the novel, Julia pauses to explain to Rachel why she is planning to kill her mother. She intends to replace Mrs. Bryant as the woman of the household. She had to kill Aunt Marge's family because the real Julia came home from school and replaced her. The family let it be known that they would soon be leaving Pine Crest and the Ozarks. Sarah, who had grown to love life with a "civilized" family, was already 22 years old and did not want to start all over again. She assumed Julia's identity so she could infiltrate another family and win it over. She never really had any interest in Mike Gallagher, she was just "practicing" so it would be easier to snare Mr. Bryant. Her reasons for wanting an older man had to do with materialistic desires:

> What would I want with a boy still wet behind the ears?. ...The next time I make a man love me, it's going to count. I will marry a man who is older and working at a good job, a man who has money and a place in the town, who can give me a nice home, my own car, clothes, all the things I need.[1]

Although none of this exposition appears in the film, Julia's purpose remains plain and the picture, like *The Hills Have Eyes*, walks on the familiar landscape of Craven's perennial theme: the "haves" versus the "have-nots." In the novel, Ozark girl Sarah Blane reveals through expositional dialogue her plan to replace

Rachel's mother. In the film, this plan is dramatized visually instead. There is actually physical affection (neck massages, hands-on-knees), and even an affair between Mr. Bryant and the beautiful interloper, something which was never detailed in Duncan's novel. In the book, Rachel saved her parents before the adultery could occur. In Craven's film, the father succumbs to the wiles of the girl and then claims rather lamely to remember "nothing" about it.

Duncan's *Summer of Fear* is also a bit more ambiguous than *A Stranger in Our House*. It leaves open the possibility that Julia is not a witch at all, that she just believes she is a witch and others are manipulated by her strong will. This is a door that *A Stranger in Our House* walks straight through. In the film, special effects, weird contact lenses and slow-motion photography accompany Julia's on-screen transformation into a supernatural force. Importantly, she *does not* cast a reflection when photographed in the telemovie. In the book, Julia destroys the photographs before they can be developed. She considers herself a witch and therefore *fears* that she will not cast a reflection. Therefore, there is no acknowledgment in the book that a supernatural force is at work, only the realization that Sarah believes herself to be a witch. After the climax, Rachel's father goes on at some length about how everything (failed brakes, car accident, Rachel's hives, Trickle's death, etc.) could have merely been a collection of coincidences. The movie leaves no doubt whatsoever: Sarah is definitely a witch!

The final confrontation in *A Stranger in Our House* is also different from that of *Summer of Fear*. In the novel, Rachel's mother is saved because of her "love" of Rachel. On the way home from a meeting, she stops to purchase a new dog for her daughter and is therefore not where Julia expects her to be in order to orchestrate an "accident." In the film, Julia (with nostrils flaring, hair blowing and eyes glowing) hops in a car and chases Rachel and Mike on a windy mountain road. Her car spins out of control and goes over a cliff just as Mrs. Bryant is entering the fray in her own vehicle. In this case, the message of the book has been lost in the transition. In *Summer of Fear*, Julia cannot conquer Mrs. Bryant's love for Rachel, and is defeated. In the film, a car accident resolves the crisis at the Bryant home.

In *Summer of Fear*, however, the conclusion is a bit anti-climactic. Rachel and Mrs. Bryant return home to find that Julia has simply "disappeared." They never see her again, and Rachel wonders about her for years to come. This is an eerie pay-off which offers some chills, but it is not very intense or rewarding from a visual or dramatic standpoint. In the film, there is a final confrontation between Rachel and Sarah, a fiery explosion, and then the revelation that Julia has moved on to infiltrate another family.

Despite these changes, the intent of Duncan's novel is captured well by Craven and his screenwriters. Both *Summer of Fear* and *A Stranger in Our House* capture the universal fear of being "replaced" by someone "better." Who among us has not felt jealousy when confronted with someone better-looking, smarter or funnier than we are? Jealousy is the crux of the issue in Duncan's story (book and film). Rachel is jealous of Julia/Sarah and loses her life, piece by piece, to an interloper whom her family adores.

Since *A Stranger in Our House* was made for television, it is not scary in the same visceral manner as *A Nightmare on Elm Street*, *The Hills Have Eyes* or *The Serpent and the Rainbow*. Instead, it is merely suspenseful. Viewers are hooked by this universal fear of being the only one who knows something horrible while others are seemingly incapable of seeing the truth for themselves.

Linda Blair makes an excellent Rachel Bryant. She plays Rachel as a selfish and slightly spoiled girl who has gotten everything she has always wanted. She lives a spectacular life complete with beautiful horses, a gorgeous boyfriend and doting parents. As these things are taken from her, she becomes petulant and her resourcefulness and strength comes to the fore. Audiences sympathize with her because they know she is right about Julia (the audience and Rachel alone are privy to "evidence" supporting witchcraft, such as the wax figure of Sundance,) but they are also frustrated because her spoiled nature makes it easy for her parents to discount her accusations. Although some people may find Blair's whining heroine annoying, the actress nicely captures Rachel's typical "teenager" essence. She does not really realize how lucky she is until everything is taken away from her.

Lee Purcell is the perfect foil for Blair's Rachel and a character who travels exactly the opposite trajectory. Julia started with nothing and realizes how dreadful that state is, so she will stop at nothing to gain everything Rachel has. Purcell takes the character Julia/Sarah through distinct personality stages, which Duncan's book refers to as the "three faces" of Julia. At first, she is shy and self-deprecating as she learns about the family. Then she becomes confident after she has bought the right clothes and learned the Albuquerque lingo. Finally, Purcell's Sarah is downright arrogant and openly admits to Rachel that she is a witch. Nicely dramatizing the transformation from meek to mighty, Purcell's makeup, wardrobe and hair style change with each ascending "stage" of power. At first Julia is a plain Jane who wears ill-fitting dresses and seems out-of-place. As she grows more confident and powerful, Julia becomes beautiful and seductive. Her hair becomes more elegant and her clothes become skimpier and tighter-fitting. Together, Purcell and Blair create a powerful animosity towards one another and they make the final battle of *A Stranger in Our House* an involving one.

In a unique way, Craven explores Lois Duncan's implicit subject matter more fully than the book actually does. Instead of merely hinting that Mr. Bryant is attracted to Julia and the target of all her plans, the film depicts a full-fledged affair. Thus Mr. Bryant becomes another of Craven's famous "bad fathers," something the character was definitely *not* in *Summer of Fear*. In the novel, the patriarch of the Bryant clan was merely influenced by a witch's brew called *milfoil*. In the film, there is never an indication that the witch has used any substance to win Bryant's affections. To the contrary, it is merely the physical presence of a beautiful young thing that stirs his libido. The impression in the film is that Mr.

Bryant considers Julia preferable to his wife because of her youthful looks and seductive attitudes, not because she has "bewitched" him with a chemical. In the film, Bryant actually becomes a slave to Julia. After they have sex in the Bryant bedroom (off-screen but hinted at), Bryant becomes a zombie to her will, even trying to kill Rachel outside the darkroom. His transformation from head of the household to sex-slave is something the book never indicated, but it is a development in keeping with Craven's feelings about middle-class families. Just under the surface, repressed lust dwells, even in an ostensibly "perfect" household such as the Bryants'.

A Stranger in Our House is definitely a product of the '70s. The presence of '70s icon Linda Blair, an underrated actress, and the campy "witch" appearance of Julia with wind-blown hair and flowing black gown rippling in slow motion reduce some of the telefilm's visual impact today. Still, it is a solid translation of Duncan's novel and very suspenseful in the manner of an old-fashioned *Twilight Zone* episode. At its heart, it is about a girl who has everything, and loses everything, only to learn about herself and her family. An air of paranoia creeps into the proceedings since her opponent is so powerful and everyone refuses to believe her. When one considers the lame quality of recent TV movies such as the *Rosemary's Baby* rip-off *The Devil's Child* (starring *Scream*'s Matthew Lillard), *A Stranger in Our House* seems all the more potent. If one can get past the '70s trimmings, it is a telefilm worth seeing because it so deftly fits in with Craven's film canon. Like *The Last House on the Left*, *The Hills Have Eyes* and other Craven projects, *A Stranger in Our House* dramatizes the destruction of an American middle-class family and a duel between the "haves" and a particularly ruthless "have-not."

A Stranger in Our House is also the forerunner of a whole slew of "evil" seductress movies including *The Babysitter* (1980), another telefilm in which possible Devil's spawn Stephanie Zimbalist seduced patriarch William Shatner, and *The Hand That Rocks the Cradle* starring Rebecca DeMornay.

There are a couple of interesting trivia notes related to *A Stranger in Our House*. In 1981's *Deadly Blessing*, two characters went to a local theater. The film being shown there was *Summer of Fear*! Secondly, Linda Blair worked with Craven again almost 20 years after this NBC telemovie. She can be briefly seen as an abrasive newswoman asking questions about the occult in *Scream*. She asks Neve Campbell's Sidney how it feels to almost be killed. "People have a right to know!" she shouts. It is a funny moment, and a welcome cameo from the beloved star of *The Exorcist*.

Invitation to Hell (1984)

CAST: Robert Urich (Matt Winslow); Joanna Cassidy (Pat Winslow); Susan Lucci (Jessica Jones); Joe Regalbuto (Tom Peterson); Kevin McCarthy (Harry

Thompson); Patricia McCormack (Mrs. Mary Peterson); Bill Erwin (Dr. Walt Henderson); Soleil Moon Frye (Chrissy Winslow); Barret Oliver (Robby Winslow); Nicholas Worth (Sheriff); Virginia Vincent (Grace Henderson); Greg Monaghan (Pete); Lois Hamilton (Ms. Winters); Cal Bartlett (Stepson); Annemarie McEvoy (Jamie); Bruce Gray (Larry Ferris); Gino De Mauro (Jimmy); Jason Presson (Billy Ferris); John Zenda (Doorman); Billy Beck (Mover); Michael Berryman (Valet); Frank Von Zerneck, Jr. (Newsboy)

CREDITS: *Presented by ITC. Music:* Sylvester Levay. *Editors:* George Prange, Ann Mills. *Art Director:* Hub Braden. *Director of Photography:* Dean Cundey. *Executive Producer:* Frank Von Zerneck. *Producer:* Robert M. Sertner. *Writer:* Richard Rothstein. *Director:* Wes Craven. *Casting:* The Dinman Company. *Production Manager:* Phillips Wylly, Sr. *First Assistant Director:* John Poer. *Second Assistant Director:* John Whittle. *Set Decorator:* Bill Harp. *Women's Wardrobe:* Roberta Newman. *Men's Wardrobe:* Sandy Slepak. *Makeup:* Les Berns. *Hairstylist:* Steve Robinette. *Property Master:* Vic Petrotta. *Script Supervisor:* Stuart Lippman. *Assistant to Executive Producer:* Marilyn R. Berro. *Production Coordinator:* Susan Weber-Gold. *Production Controller:* Norm Webster. *Production Secretary:* Jayne Bieber. *Transportation:* Jeri Kelley. *Location Manager:* Tony Saenz. *Sound:* Dick Church. *Production Services:* Orion TV Productions, Inc. *Music Supervisor:* Terri Fricon. *Second Unit Director:* Greg Prange. *Stunt Coordinator:* Tony Cecere. *Sound Effects:* Rich Harrison. *Laser Effects:* Laser Images, Inc. *Hell Sequence:* Introvision. *Illustrator:* Petro Kadiev. *Laboratory:* CFI. *Post Production Supervisor:* Mick and Roni McAffe. *Assistant Editors:* Thomas Jarvis, Bert Glatstein. *Music Editor:* John Mick. *Negative Cutter:* Susanne Gervay. *Sound Rerecording:* The Burbank Stuios. *Locations Equipped by* Filmtrucks. *Lens and Panaflex Camera:* Panavision. *Executive in Charge of Production:* Phillips Wylly, Sr. Moonlight Productions

SYNOPSIS: At the Steaming Springs Country Club, many club members enjoy a beautiful day playing tennis, swimming or just tanning themselves. As a club-owned car races onto the premises, the driver is momentarily distracted by two bikini-clad beauties. In that instant, he strikes and runs over the club coordinator, Jessica Jones. Amazingly, she stands up and points an accusing finger at him. Suddenly, he melts and dies. Jessica Jones smiles hideously.

Not far away, the Winslows are driving their old station wagon to their new home. Matt Winslow has just been promoted to executive in charge of special projects at a corporation called Micro-Digitech. He promises his wife Patricia that the lean years are over and that finally the family can enjoy the good life. In the back seat, Robby and Chrissy, their two children, bicker. Chrissy wants to go back home to the midwest because she likes the snow.

The Winslows pull up to their new tract home in upper-class suburbia. Matt carries Pat across the threshold and they unpack. Pat raves about the house and the kitchen. That night, the Winslows sing songs together by their fireplace and enjoy their new place. Suddenly, a rattling is heard from one of the windows. Matt checks it out and is surprised by neighbors wearing Halloween masks! The neighbors are old friends from the midwest, the Petersons. They welcome the Winslows to "paradise" and share a huge bucket of fried chicken. Tom Peterson, an old college buddy, also works at Micro-Digitech as a sales and marketing representative. As they sing songs around the piano, Tom and his wife Mary assure the Winslows that the days of "out-of-tune pianos and beat-up furniture" are over for them. This remark hurts Patricia's feelings but she tries not to let it spoil the celebration.

After the impromptu party, Matt says good night to his children. Robby is upset because Tom's son Jimmy told him of a big Halloween party coming up, and Robby will not be allowed to go because his family does not have a membership at Steaming Springs Country Club. Robby says that "everybody who is anybody in this town" belongs to the organization. Matt tells his son to keep an open mind and returns to his bedroom. He and Patricia reflect on their love and on the Petersons' rude comment about old pianos and beat-up furniture, and then make love.

The next morning, Matt and Tom car-pool to work. In the backseat is Larry Ferris, Tom's sponsor at Steaming Springs. He is a cruel person and he insults Tom. Later, Matt calls him reptilian. Once at the Micro-Digitech office, Tom introduces Matt to Grace Henderson, the firm receptionist. Then they go to the lab to see the spacesuit that Digitech is developing. The U.S. government has made it known that it wants to put a man on the surface of Venus within three years and Digitech wants the contract to build the suit. Matt has been hired to perfect it. Since it is extremely hot on Venus, the suit has been padded to make sure that no astronauts become "human French fries." The suit has a built-in laser weapon, a flame thrower and a radio. Matt begins work adapting his revolutionary new sensors and computers to the suit. His devices will be able to sense temperature changes, atmospheric conditions and even the presence of "other beings."

At the Winslow house, Robby is visited by Jimmy Peterson and Billy Ferris, a boy as cruel as his father. Billy remarks thoughtlessly that the furniture in the house "sure is old." Later, after Billy loses a videogame to Robby, Billy destroys the videogame. This odd behavior goes unreported by the children even when Matt and Patricia take them out for a ride. While driving around town, the Winslow station wagon is nearly run off the road by a Steaming Springs car. Matt demands an apology and meets Jessica Jones, the club director. The local sheriff arrives and supports Jessica, instructing Matt to forget the incident. Matt is flabbergasted, but Patricia (afraid he is making a scene) demands they continue their drive.

When Jessica enters the club, she proceeds immediately to the club initiation of the Peterson family. She tells them that they are about to gain entrance

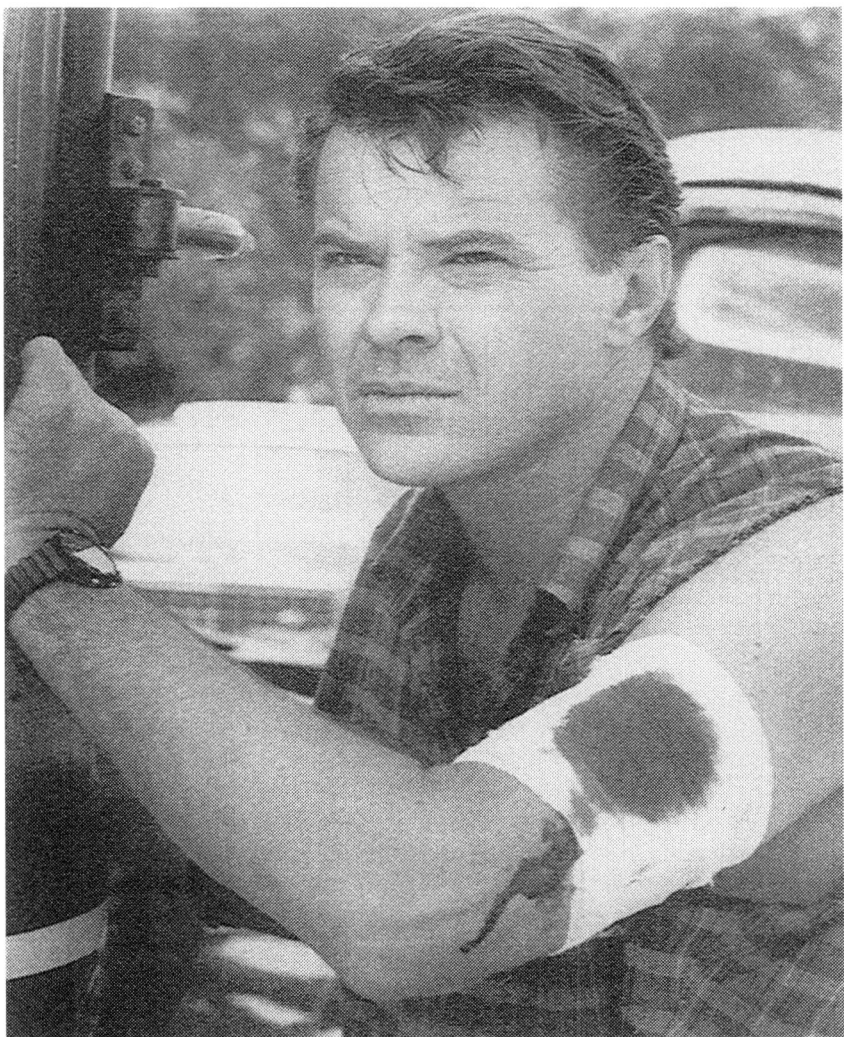

Matt Winslow (Robert Urich) saves his family from a demonic Susan Lucci, damnation, and encroaching yuppie values in *Invitation to Hell*.

to an ancient spring. She asks them if they will "forsake all for the club" and they nod. She smiles and leads them through a heavy vault into a steaming room. The door slams shut behind them.

Back at Micro-Digitech, Matt tests the helmet. The thermal sensors come on-line first and then Matt tests the "life form scanner." It scans Matt as a "human terrestrial, benign." Then it scans a plant (non-human terrestrial, benign). Matt is thrilled and he wants to tell Tom Peterson the news. He is intercepted by Grace Henderson, who tells him that she has something important she needs to discuss with him. Matt is not able to pursue the matter because he is called into the office of Harry Thompson, president of Micro-Digitech. Thompson introduces Matt to Jessica and asks him to give her a demonstration of the top secret suit. Matt is reluctant, but he does so after Thompson says she is like family. While they are alone in the lab, Jessica comes onto Matt and compliments his physique. She also tells him that there are "lots of pleasurable" things at the club and that it is full of "people on their way up." Matt begs off and Jessica leaves. Unbeknownst to Matt, the suit scanner has scanned Jessica and categorized her as a "non-human, malignant."

Matt finally catches up with Tom Peterson and discovers that he has been promoted and given a luxurious new office in the executive wing. Tom says he owes all his success to the "club" and that he would be willing to sponsor Matt and the Winslows for immediate membership. Matt resists, saying he is not much of a joiner, but Tom pushes the matter, ordering Matt to "rub shoulders with people at that club!"

Patricia is also being pressured to join the club but, unlike Matt, she does not see anything threatening in the notion. She sees that Mary Peterson has a brand new town-car and her jealousy increases. She tells Matt that she wants her "piece of the pie." Matt is disgusted. He tells her that all he sees are people climbing over each other at any cost, and he wants no part of the club. Pat and Matt quarrel into the night and finally he goes downstairs. He finds Billy Ferris sitting in front of the television, watching footage of Nazi war atrocities. The boy thinks the acts are funny! He smiles at the TV ghoulishly until Matt turns it off. Later, the TV turns itself back on and plays the same grotesque war footage.

The next day at work, Grace Henderson has been replaced by Miss Winters. Matt demands to know why Grace was let go and Harry Thompson replies that she just was not "company timber." Matt and Patricia meet with Tom Peterson at the club. They confer with Jessica, who takes them on a tour. She walks them through the gym and informs them of the initiation process. Matt wanders off by himself and hears screaming. He finds his way to a restricted area and arrives at the door to the sacred spring. He hears moaning and crying from behind it and then touches it. The door is so hot that it burns his hand. He looks at a nearby control panel and is about to push a button when he is intercepted by Jessica. She tells him that pleasure is important to him and that she will personally see to it that his membership at the club is as pleasurable as possible. He begs off and returns to Patricia. Jessica invites them both to lunch, but Matt refuses to join "the in-crowd." Patricia is angry and goes to lunch with Jessica alone.

That evening, Matt comes home with wine and flowers and apologizes to Patricia for his behavior. Patricia accepts his apology but behind his back she meets again with Jessica. Jessica suggests that Pat and the children join without

Matt. Pat and the children are led to the initiation. With steam beating against their faces, they enter the spring to taste its power. Chrissy is frightened but Jessica pushes her inside the gates of Hell.

The next morning at breakfast, Matt realizes his family has changed. Albert the dog will not stop barking at them, as if he does not recognize Chrissy, Robby or Patricia. Pat throws him out of the house. Later that day, Matt gets a call from Dr. Walt Henderson, Grace's husband, who tells him that Patricia has brought the dog to him and instructed him to kill it! Walt assured her he would, but once Patricia left the office, he saved Albert's life. Matt is confused by this behavior and rushes home to confront Patricia. He is surprised to find that the interior of the house has been re-painted. It is now dark and cold inside. Pat herself has changed. She works in the kitchen in a sultry black evening dress and heavy, sexy makeup. When Matt asks where the dog is, Pat tries to lay a guilt-trip on him, saying that he loves the dog more than her and the children. Matt gives in and they reconcile. Later, Pat attacks Matt. Acting like a wild woman, she claws his back and makes fierce love to him. Afterwards, Matt realizes that Pat has joined the club without him and changed. He calls Walt to tell him about the odd behavior and learns from the kindly old vet that Grace is dead — killed in a car accident.

When Matt returns home, Pat is playing a brand new grand piano, a gift from Jessica Jones. All the furniture in the house is different. It is chic but cold, and with a strong emphasis on black. Matt comments that Patricia has changed, that she is not the gentle woman he married. Patricia lashes out him and asks where being gentle ever got her. She wants power! Matt is astonished by her greed and leaves the house. He sneaks into Micro-Digitech and tries to recover the information that Grace once asked him to read. He loads a tape into a computer and asks about key employee movements in Micro-Digitech. He learns that all the promotions in the last two years have come after initiations into Steaming Springs Country Club.

Matt Winslow breaks into the club and goes to the initiation room. He uses a small computer to open the door and then scans the temperature of the spring. It is 800 degrees inside! As Matt ponders the significance of this, he is attacked by the sheriff. They fight it out, and Matt manages to electrocute him. He drives home and finds Chrissy sitting on the floor. She has torn the stuffing out of her rabbit doll with a tire iron! She attacks him and he realizes that she is not his daughter any more. He locks her in a closet but is then attacked by Robby. After wrestling his son to the ground, Matt throws him in the closet too. Finally he faces down Patricia, who tries to crack his skull with a golf club. Matt knocks his wife unconscious and promises her that he will save her. He rushes to Micro-Digitech and dons the Venus spacesuit and helmet. The suit is the only thing that can survive the heat inside the steaming spring. He is stopped by Tom Peterson, who challenges him with a pistol. Matt utilizes the suit laser to blast Peterson, and then drives Tom's car to the club. Fortunately, it is the night of the

Halloween ball and the Club members mistake Matt for a space-suited Peterson. Matt makes his way into the initiation room and opens the door.

Jessica tries to stop Matt from entering the evil domain, but he sprays fire at her with the suit's flame thrower. Immune to the heat, Jessica walks through the fire and pursues Matt as he enters the spring. Matt finds himself in a fiery underground cavern. It is the route to Hell itself. He walks down to a precipice and sees thousands of feet below a simulacrum of his town. He can hear his family screaming in torment down there!

Mustering all of his courage, Matt jumps off the precipice and arrives in the Hell version of his town. He runs to his home to free his family and finds his gentle Patricia trapped in a force field. She is eternally playing the piano, eternally suffering. Jessica arrives and orders Matt to submit to her. He refuses and she tempts him again with power and sex. She tells him that his suit cannot protect him any more. Matt acknowledges this fact and removes the suit to pierce the force field. He saves Patricia and makes her remember where they were when they loved each other. His love breaks the force field, and Patricia and Matt rush to save their children from the torments of Hell. Their actions cause an imbalance in this dimension and a blue vortex opens up behind Jessica. The dimension of Hell is destroyed and the family wakes up to find themselves back at home, safe. Outside, Steaming Springs Country Club burns to the ground.

COMMENTARY: As written by Richard Rothstein and directed by Wes Craven, *Invitation to Hell* unfolds like a 90-minute excursion into Rod Serling's *The Twilight Zone*. Protagonist Matt Winslow awakens one morning to discover that his family, friends, job and even world have changed suddenly. His values and ethics remain the same, but he is the only person who still has them! Like the best of *The Twilight Zone* or *The Outer Limits*, *Invitation to Hell* also offers an important social comment: that material wealth and greed can never replace simple human love and caring. As each of Winslow's friends and family members are replaced by yuppie doppelgangers, *Invitation to Hell* also comes to resemble a 1980s version of *Invasion of the Body Snatchers*. It even features actor Kevin McCarthy, survivor of the original Don Siegel film, in a supporting role. Instead of serving as a warning about encroaching Communism or McCarthyism, however, Craven's telefilm warns that corporate America and Reagan-era values will steal your soul if you're not vigilant.

Beyond this moral point, *Invitation to Hell* also sports a fascinating "what if" sci-fi premise, What if modern man could don a protective spacesuit and stroll into Hell unharmed? What would he find there? Or, more to the point, who would he find there? These fascinating premises make *Invitation to Hell* a surprisingly compelling TV movie that is a fine addition to Craven's teleography.

Like Craven's *A Stranger in Our House*, *Invitation to Hell* focuses almost exclusively on one individual, a family member who *just knows* that something is wrong even though the rest of the family blindly endures an evil situation. In this case it is the patriarch, actor Robert Urich, who is aware that things have changed for the worse. Beyond the personal struggle of one person to save the family, both stories are similar in structural approach: "Evil" subverts a modern suburban family one step at a time, virtually unnoticed, until finally someone must go beyond denial and repression to confront the changes. In this case, there is not just one evil individual attempting to gain a foothold on a middle-class family, it is Hell itself! Hell grabs hold of even good people like the Winslows not through demons, witchcraft or nightmares but through greed, particularly Patricia Winslow's. It is clear that Rothstein and Craven feel her avaricious nature is typical of America's middle class. Why else populate an entire town with soulless creatures who are occupied only with the accumulation of wealth?

At first, Patricia Winslow (Joanna Cassidy) is thrilled to move into a brand new house in suburbia, a roomy tract home like the one featured in *Poltergeist*. When she moves into the house, Patricia finds that everything is "perfect" and raves about finally having a "taste of the good life." As soon as the neighbors arrive, however, the house is no longer good enough for Pat. One neighbor thoughtlessly remarks about "out-of-tune pianos and beat-up furniture" and Pat suddenly wants more than what she has. Because she perceives that she no longer has "the best things," she feels bad about herself and her family. The very next morning, she complains that the new home, which yesterday was "gorgeous" and "perfect," now resembles "a fraternity house." She is worried that people will "laugh at the place." From there, her materialistic demands escalate rapidly. She watches in jealousy as her neighbors join a club and buy an extravagant new car. Frustrated, she informs her husband that she too wants "a piece of the pie." Next comes repainted walls, new furnishings and a grand piano.

In a matter of days, Pat changes from a loving wife who sings with her children and flirts with Matt to every husband's worst nightmare: a manipulative social climber who coldly wields sex as a weapon. Transformed into a minion of Hell, Pat cooks dinner in a sultry nightgown, teased hair and heavy makeup accentuating her sexy features. Later, she ferociously jumps Matt in the bedroom and makes love to him to get what she wants. She also uses that old stand-by: guilt. When Matt confronts her about her lies, she runs a guilt trip on him. "I try to be a perfect wife, mother and lover. Do I ask very much in return?" she asks. Later, she insists that she only wants Matt to join the country club so she can get the power and the possessions she claims she "deserves."

Fortunately, Matt is not nearly as susceptible to greed and materialistic thoughts as his wife is. He is disgusted by what he sees at work and shakes his head in disbelief that he is "joining a corporation." He confides in Patricia that "everyone at work is climbing all over each other...no matter the cost." He does not like the cutthroat mentality that dominates Micro-Digitech. The picture of corporate America that *Invitation to Hell* paints is a negative one where all decisions are made not just by greedy businessmen, but literally by the soulless minions of Hell. The president of Matt's company callously refers to people as "timber" and he ominously informs Matt that he is looking forward to Winslow "becoming one of us." The message conveyed is one of total conformity. If Matt will just "learn how to play the game...step over a few bodies," he can have all the material wealth that his wife and children so desperately desire. If he will change his ways, become a member of the club and submit to a humiliating "initiation" process that depends on "how quickly" he "can fit in," then new cars, new homes and money, money, money will all be his. Of course, the price for all this wealth is his soul. *Invitation to Hell* suggests that those who willingly conform, who step over the bodies of others, who only want new things, are damned to Hell.

It is highly unusual for a telefilm of 1984 vintage to take such a negative view of the '80s yuppie mentality, but Craven has proven time and again his ability to think outside societal norms and trends, and here he has selected an excellent script to highlight his philosophy about the middle class.

The Steaming Springs Club is not only the gateway to Hell, it is the physical embodiment of the shallow yuppie values which dominate the businessmen and manipulative housewives of *Invitation to Hell*. It boasts a world-class golf course (the game of the wealthy) and everyone there is "encouraged to work out, to stay trim and attractive." Thus Craven's target is not just material wealth and cutthroat business, but America's obsession with surface values such as physical beauty (remember the importance of surface appearances in *Shocker* and *A Nightmare on Elm Street*)? What could be a more appropriate comment to a country caught in Jane Fonda's aerobic and fitness craze? Everything from pop music such as Olivia Newton-John's song *Physical* to the motion picture *Perfect* were pushing physical perfection. Craven suggests in *Invitation to Hell* that the worship of "surface" qualities such as wealth, success and beauty come at the cost of one's humanity.

Significantly, Pat is freed from her personal trap in Hell only when Matt forces her to remember where they were when they loved each other, when they cared about "each other more than anything else." Matt can only touch her, only break through to her, with his naked hands. Rothstein's teleplay indicates that a simple human touch, uncluttered by technology or materialism, is the greatest connection between people. Country clubs are not necessary to create a sense of community, but love certainly is.

When the evil yuppies of *Invitation to Hell* are confronted by Matt and forced to look at their shallow values, they respond with hostility and fear because he reminds them that he is better than they are. "You're not one of us," Matt's "friend" snickers. "You're a loser. We are the winners. We have to get rid of the losers." To many of those who have no love, only careers, beautiful homes and money, others must conform to their way or get lost. America, Craven and Rothstein hint, does not tolerate those who will not conform to the capitalist values of the nation.

The climax of *Invitation to Hell* is augmented by a visually interesting descent into Hell. Matt Winslow dons his spacesuit and steps into the evil domain. An excellent matte painting depicts a beautiful suburban town far below the caverns. This is a perfect analogy for the plot. On the surface is a society of supposedly "happy" people who claim that suburbia is "paradise." They have money, new cars, club membership and great careers. Yet below the surface, under all the material wealth, is a sort of "anti"-town where the people dwell in spiritual torment. This is an acknowledgment that those people who appear happy because they "have" material things are in fact suffering because of their spiritual emptiness. To further highlight the differences between what is on the surface and what lays buried and repressed beneath it, the "anti"-town is filmed in a negative and colorized image. The image is negative, of course, because it is the opposite of the town above.

Like *A Stranger in Our House*, *Invitation to Hell* is not so much a "scary" movie as it is a compelling one. Because the protagonist is so well drawn by Robert Urich and Rothstein's script, and because Winslow is up against a massive conspiracy of evil, audience identification with his plight is instant. Who among us has not wished for more money, newer furniture or a better home? *Invitation to Hell* grabs attention by taking these desires and showing how they can lead to a spiritual crisis. Perhaps the scariest moment in *Invitation to Hell* is the one in which Susan Lucci declares that "everyone who joined the club did so willingly." In other words, no one was forced to give up their soul for a promotion, a big car or popularity...they all went willingly because *things* were more important to them than feelings. It is an intense moment and a telling comment about human nature.

Invitation to Hell has one major failing that prevents it from reaching a plateau of high quality. It opens with a ludicrous sequence in which a limo driver runs over Susan Lucci. She stands up and points a finger at him, and he melts in a burst of smoke. This sequence immediately establishes that there is *definitely* a supernatural danger in town, a very real force of evil from another dimension. The picture would have been far more effective without this prologue because the true nature of Steaming Springs Club would have been a mystery until the conclusion. Then the audience would have been put in the situation where they were not sure if there was "real" evil involved, or if Matt was just being stubborn about accepting his wife's new values and joining "the in-crowd." One of the reasons *Rosemary's Baby* was such an effective film was its ambiguity. Viewers were not sure if there really was a conspiracy of evil in Rosemary's apartment building or merely one frightened pregnant woman. *Invitation to Hell* could have walked that same line and generated the same amount of tension had audiences wondered if there was a really a threat from beyond. The over-the-top horror opening immediately and artlessly declares that evil is not just within (the ultimate point of the film), but also from an outside non-human source.

Also mildly unsatisfying is the all-too-fast wrap-up. It is perfectly acceptable and dramatically sound that Winslow should be able to rescue his family by reminding them how much they care about each other. What is not so believable is that one family's love would topple the entire hellish domain. Once Matt has freed Patricia and the kids, a blue vortex opens and Hell is soon no more. It is hard to believe that Hell, a franchise which has ostensibly been in operation a long time, would fall apart because one family escapes it. A more satisfying conclusion might have seen the Winslows escape but the other townspeople, still trapped by their materialism, remaining slaves to the evil. Such an ending could have also added to the cautionary tone of *Invitation to Hell*: If there is no love, there is no escape.

Invitation to Hell is still compelling for a TV movie. Good performances and a taut teleplay make it an exceptional product. Of interest to Craven fans is the fact that several Craven "stars" make appearances in the film. Virginia Vincent, the matriarch of *The Hills Have Eyes,* is back as the company secretary, Mrs. Henderson. Nicholas Worth, one of Arcane's goons in *Swamp Thing,* and even Michael Berryman also show up in (appropriately enough) the devil's country club. The family dog also plays a familiar role. Just as the family pet was the first to sense evil in *The Last House on the Left, The Hills Have Eyes,* and *A Stranger in Our House,* so does little Albert here prove to be the first to realize that Pat and the kids have transformed. In this regard and in Matt's open-eyes sojourn into the dark dimension, *Invitation to Hell* lives up to a line from *The Twilight Zone* episode called "The Hunt" by Earl Hammer, Jr.: "A man, well, he'll walk right into Hell with both eyes open—but even the Devil can't fool a dog."

Chiller (1984)

CAST: Michael Beck (Miles Creighton); Beatrice Straight (Marion Creighton); Laura Johnson (Leigh Canyon); Jill Schoelen (Stacey); Paul Sorvino (Reverend Felix Penny); Dick O'Neill (Clarence M. Beeson); Kenneth White (Technician #1); Ned Wertimer (Mr. Hanna); Wendy Goldman (Secretary); Joseph Whipp (Detective); Karen Hue (Nurse #1); Melanie E. Williams (Nurse #2); Paula Walter (Night Nurse); Mimi Meyer-Craven (Nurse Cooper); Bill Dearth (Officer #1); Roger Hampton (Officer #2); William Forward (Anesthesiologist); Alan Fudge; Charles Richard Nelson; Anne Seymour; Jerry Lacy; Edward Brackoff; Brian Libby; Russ Marin; Starletta Dupois

CREDITS: *Music:* Dana Kaproff. *Special Effects Makeup:* Stan Winston. *Film Editor:* Duane Hartzell. *Art Director:* Charles Hughes. *Director of Photography:* Frank Thackery. *Writer/Producer:* J.D. Feigelson. *Director:* Wes Craven. *Exective Producer:* Richard Kobritz. *Casting:* Karen Rea. *Production Executive:* James Thornsberry. *Associate Producer and Unit Production Manager:* Anderson

G. House. *First Assistant Director:* Stephen Lofaro. *Second Assistant Director:* Ian Bryce. *Set Decorator:* James Hassinger. *Makeup Artist:* Mark Reedall. *Hairstylist:* Connie Nichols. *Men's Costumes:* Darryl Athons. *Women's Costumes:* Deborah Hopper. *Script Supervisor:* Larry K. Johnson. *Property Master:* Guy Bushman. *Camera Operator:* Jiggs Garcia. *Key Grip:* Brian Smith. *Chief Lighting Technicians:* Joseph E. Garcia. *Stunt Coordinator:* Tony Cecere. *Special Effects Coordinator:* Ken Pepiot. *Location Manager:* Richard Davis. *Production Coordinator:* Jacqueline Roberts. *Production Auditor:* Sam Bernstein. *Assistant to Mr. Kobritz:* Shirley Bonner. *Assistant Auditor:* Eileen McGuire. *Casting Associate:* Joanne Zaluski. *Production Assistant:* Steve Keller. *DGA Trainee:* Scott Printz. *Special Effects Makeup Crew:* Shane Mahan, Tom Woodruff, John Rosengrant, Richard Landon. *Sound Mixer:* Tom Causey. *Re-recording Mixers:* Don MacDougall, John Mack C.A.S., Dick Tyler C.A.S. *Assistant Film Editor:* Barbara J. Boguski. *Sound Editing:* Earl Watson. *Music Editing:* Ted Roberts. *Post Production:* Gomillion Studios. *Negative Cutter:* Vivian Hengsteller. *Titles, Opticals:* CFI. *Camera Equipment By:* Interface Market. *Main Title Design:* Cimarron Productions. Frozen Man Productions. From Polar Films. In Association with J.D. Feigelson Productions, Inc. Lorimar Telepictures.

> Cryonics is the science that places a body in a frozen state until such time as the illness that terminated its lifeforce can be medically treated. Thus far, no human being has returned from a cryonic suspension ... until tonight.
> —Opening narration of *Chiller*.

SYNOPSIS: On the wall of a Cryonic Repository hangs a logo which reads "They Shall See Tomorrow." Beyond the framed slogan are rows and rows of cryonic suspension chambers which hold the bodies of people who have passed away due to incurable diseases but who have been frozen in the hope that someday they may be thawed, cured and restored to life. Hayes, a security guard, monitors the sleepers and notes that one container seems to be dripping water. It is thawing. He runs to the main computer and confirms the temperature drop. The thawing process has proceeded too far and cannot be stopped. A red siren which should have indicated the crisis earlier has malfunctioned; only now does it begin to blink. Hayes immediately calls his supervisor and reports that there is an emergency concerning container number 59.

Marion Creighton, a regular financial contributor to the local church, awakens Reverend Penny with an urgent phone call and asks him to meet her at the hospital as soon as possible. Once there, Mrs. Creighton tells him that a miracle is occurring: Her "dead" son is coming back. Young Miles never actually died, he was put to sleep in cryonic suspension. Now, the doctors are going to attempt to cure and awaken him. Drs. Strickland and Collier realize they have to replace Miles' liver, something they could not do ten years earlier, before cyclosporin. They already have a transplant liver waiting so they begin surgery as soon as Mrs.

Creighton signs the consent forms. The doctors warn her that the procedure is dangerous but she has faith. Reverend Penny is worried. Can man now restore life? What will that life look like? The doctor to whom he asks these questions can provide no answers.

Surgery begins. The doctors cut through the aluminum foil-like wrappings around Miles' body. The operation stretches well into the night and the doctors finally close at 5:25 a.m. At 5:37, they restart his heart. The doctors report to Reverend Penny and Mrs. Creighton that Miles is alive. Mrs. Creighton calls the 20th century "the age of miracles." Unfortunately, Mrs. Creighton's optimism is brief. For six weeks after the operation, Miles remains in a deep coma. Marion sits by his bedside every day with Stacey, her adopted daughter. Finally, the hospital administrator meets with Mrs. Creighton and suggests the termination of life support systems. Miles is functioning but not living. Mrs. Creighton refuses to give up on her son. She says that the doctors have performed a miracle but they counter that the miracle was "not enough" and that they are not "God." They cannot imbue Miles with the will to live. Mrs. Creighton refuses to order the termination of life support and says she wants to hold onto Miles for a while longer.

When Nurse Cooper gives Miles a body massage, his body starts to convulse violently with life. Veins momentarily enlarge and his muscles twitch uncontrollably. His body stabilizes and Miles opens his eyes to reveal two evil-looking golden orbs. Cooper screams in shock and asks an orderly to check the patient. He does so and reports that Miles' eyes are normal. Later, Mrs. Creighton and the doctors celebrate as Miles makes a healthy return to the land of the living. Still, something is not right. Miles seems cold and distant. All he says upon awaking is that he is hungry. Also, he stares at Stacey lasciviously and she is uncomfortable under his gaze.

Mrs. Creighton and Stacey prepare their estate for Miles' homecoming. The ambulance arrives, and after ten years, Miles is home. Strangely, his dog Happy does not recognize him. Furthermore, the dog actually seems frightened of him! That night, Mrs. Creighton invites a friend, Clarence Beeson, over for dinner. He has been running the family company for a decade. Mrs. Creighton breaks the news that she feels Miles should take over the company. Clarence graciously offers to stay on to keep an eye on things for the family. He goes upstairs to welcome Miles to the firm, but Miles ignores him. Clarence makes further attempts to welcome the revived man to the company, but Miles rudely asks what Clarence is still doing there. Indignant, Clarence responds that he has been looking out for the family's interests. Ominously, Miles assures Clarence that he is back and can look out for the family himself. Clarence leaves the Creighton home in a worried state of mind.

In the middle of the night, Miles tries to sleep but finds that he is unable to stay warm. Furthermore, Happy's incessant barking is bothering him. Happy runs up to Miles' room, but Miles has laid a trap for the dog and he kills it without mercy. When Stacey looks for Happy the next day, she discovers from the groundkeeper, Mr. Hanna, that the dog has been murdered. He says that some kind of "wild animal" must have gotten to it. When Stacey goes to Miles' room, she finds a photograph of Miles and Happy torn up in the garbage can.

At the company, Miles conducts a board meeting and listens while Clarence gives the annual report. Clarence believes the stats are good but Miles thinks the company's performance is pathetic. He hates donations and contributions and believes they should be cut out of the budget to make room for more profits. Advertising representative Leigh Canyon stands up to him and says that the company has an obligation to the community. Miles disagrees and says that his administration will stress efficiency. He plans to take a cold, hard look at everything and ruthlessly cut out the fat. To start, he fires Clarence Beeson! Clarence, dumbstruck, calls Mrs. Creighton to complain. She promises to get him his job back, but Miles has other plans. Late in the evening, Miles encounters a drunken Beeson and accuses him of incompetence. Clarence begs Miles to let him maintain his dignity and stay with the company for one more year, until he earns his retirement. Miles refuses and goads the older man into pursuing him up a staircase. Beeson has a heart attack and dies. Miles returns home and promises Marion that he will re-hire Clarence in the morning. When Stacey retires to her room and disrobes, Miles peers at her through a peephole.

From his office, Miles tells his mother the next morning that Clarence has died. Mrs. Creighton is flabbergasted and saddened but she does not suspect foul play. Miles meets with Leigh Canyon, who delivers her sales and marketing report. Miles offers to discuss it with her over drinks. She agrees and they meet at a hotel bar. He informs Leigh that he is making changes in the company and wants her to fill Clarence's position. He describes the job, which includes stock options and a better office. Then he tells her he has a room in the hotel if she really wants to work for him. Leigh reacts indignantly to the proposal and refuses to join him. Miles replies that even she has a price. He tells her he will be waiting for her in room 817. Sure enough, Leigh makes her way to the hotel room and joins Miles for a nightcap. He informs the beautiful woman that he likes his pleasure "cold" and he begins to hurt her.

The next day, Reverend Penny visits Leigh at the firm because the company has stopped donating to the church. Leigh reports that all donations have been terminated by Miles' orders. When she faces the Reverend, he sees that she is badly bruised and has a black eye. She reveals she is quitting the company and breaks down crying. Penny asks her who has done this to her and she says that Miles is responsible! The Reverend visits Mrs. Creighton and tells her that people at the office are terrified of Miles. He also tells her that Miles beat Leigh. Mrs. Creighton refuses to believe it, and says that the Reverend is trying to get money out of her.

Dismayed, Reverend Penny returns to the Rectory. He plays cards with his secretary that evening but he is visibly distracted. He wonders what happens to a man's soul when he dies. Does the soul go off to a spiritual life as per Scripture? Or does something else occur? A man is a combination of body, mind and spirit. Suppose a man dies, really dies, is buried for ten years, and then revived? The body and the mind may function again, but what of the soul? Would it be required to rejoin the body, or would it stay on the other side? And, if the soul does not return, what does that leave inside the body? These are the questions that consume the Reverend as he contemplates the possibility that Miles has become a soulless monster. He goes out to the park to take a walk under the full moon and hears some disturbing noises. As he turns a corner, he is confronted by Miles. He maintains his composure and asks Miles who "he really is." Miles, amused, offers to tell the Reverend the truth about death. He informs Penny that there is no afterlife, simply darkness and nothingness. Then he says that he never cares to see the Reverend at his home again.

Infuriated, Reverend Penny pursues Miles to his car. He tells him that he has faith in his beliefs and that Miles is a liar. As he shouts that his beliefs are true, the Reverend's jacket becomes caught in the door of Miles' car. Miles drives away and purposely drags the Reverend down the road. The reverend finally breaks free and tumbles to the ground. When he looks up, Miles is speeding towards him, coming back to finish the job.

Mrs. Creighton rushes to the hospital when she hears of Reverend Penny's condition. He awakens and tells Mrs. Creighton that Miles is responsible. He tells her that Miles' body has been revived but he has no soul. Marion rushes to a pay phone to warn Stacey to get out of the house, but the line is busy. Mrs. Creighton leaves County General and rushes for home.

Returning home after a workout, Stacey finds the house dark and the phone off the hook. Miles offers her cognac and she refuses. He starts to caress her hair and shoulders, but she resists. He presses her down to the sofa and begins kissing her roughly. Before he can go any further, Mrs. Creighton arrives home and orders Stacey to her bedroom. Then she confronts Miles and tells him that she knows what he has done. Furthermore, she has called the police and they are on their way! Miles is enraged. He chases his mother through the house with a metal hunting hook. She runs into the basement and traps Miles in the walk-in freezer. She locks the door and activates the unit, hoping to freeze her crazed son. Then she runs upstairs and tells Stacey everything is all right. She says that she has been living in the past and that the person she really loves is Stacey, not Miles.

The police arrive and are led to the freezer by Mrs. Creighton. They enter the frozen chamber, but find no sign of Miles. They check the corners and find him frozen. One officer leaves to call the coroner. As soon as he is gone, Miles jumps to life and strangles the other cop. Mrs. Creighton picks up the officer's pistol and shoots Miles twice. He falls to the ground and then makes one more attempt to kill his mother, his eyes glowing with inhuman ferocity. Finally, Miles dies.

Days later, Mrs. Creighton tends to the dying Reverend Penny. She begs

Dr. Strickland to save him, and the doctor replies that Mrs. Creighton should "pray." She sees the value in this comment and promises to pray for the life of her dear friend.

At the Cryonics facility, another body suddenly begins to defrost. The security guard watches in horror as the process continues. One canister starts to thaw, then another, then another...

COMMENTARY: When Robert Englund suggested during a brief interview with the Sci-Fi Channel that friend Craven was the "heir apparent" to the visionary Rod Serling, the actor was not far from the mark. In his choice of television material (from the new *Twilight Zone* to his various TV movies), Craven has consistently shown a preference for thought-provoking genre scenarios that spur not only terror, but which also bring to light some significant social commentary. In their ironic lessons about materialism, family dynamics and even the fabric of reality itself, *Invitation to Hell*, *A Stranger in Our House* and *Nightmare Cafe* all inspire goosebumps in the manner of Serling's ironic series. *Chiller* is no exception to this trend and its author, J.D. Feigelson, even wrote several episodes of the new *Twilight Zone* including "The Burning Man," "Dealer's Choice" (directed by Craven) and "The Little People of Killany Woods." Although *Chiller* highlights fewer special effects and less graphic violence than Craven's earlier TV films, it is by far the creepiest and darkest of the bunch, in large part due to Michael Beck's "cold" performance as reanimated sociopath Miles Creighton.

On the surface, *Chiller* explores another fascinating "what if?" premise. This time, the central question is one concerning the human soul. If a man dies and is frozen through an advanced technology, will he return with his soul intact? Or has his soul already departed to some nether region with no obligation to return to the host body? Paul Sorvino as Reverend Penny obsesses on this issue throughout *Chiller,* and it is a worthy science fiction premise that plays into a natural human fear of progress. Twentieth century man lives in the age of miracles, so much so that a so-called "miracle" technology can revive the dead. *Chiller* suggests that such a technological breakthrough is not only dangerous but evil as well.

Thematically, *Chiller* focuses on other issues beyond its "what if?" genre premise. In typical Craven fashion, the movie has a distinct stance on life, and an ironic one to boot. When Miles returns from the grave, he immediately becomes a highly successful businessman. By inference, one can conclude that to prosper in corporate America, one must separate oneself from one's soul. At his first board meeting, Miles complains about the company's policy of donating money to the church and other charities. Without a soul to guide him, he sees no reason to help others. On the contrary, he suggests that charity money could be extra profit for himself. Callously he fires Clarence Beeson, an old friend, because he has "no further use" for him. Like the people of Micro-Digitech in *Invitation to Hell*, Miles is the ultimate capitalist. People are not to be empathized with, they are merely "timber" to be manipulated so more money can be made.

Miles is not the only person to be overcome with the desire for success in *Chiller*. When Leigh Canyon senses that Miles is interested in her, she willingly romances him. When Miles' proposal comes to include stock options and a better office, Leigh becomes a prostitute. She sells herself and has intercourse with Miles. Just as in *Invitation to Hell*, *Chiller* suggests that people will sell their souls for material gains. Sadly, Leigh pays the price for her prostitution. Miles beats her ferociously and she ends up disgraced — all because she did not know when to stop "playing the game."

Craven's belief that it takes a soulless creature to succeed in corporate America is further enunciated by a comparison of two generations. Clarence Beeson is of the World War II generation, a man who has guided the company through ten years of mild prosperity. Under his guidance, the company is a family which is part of a larger community. Profit is important, but so is the community. Under Miles, a soulless yuppie, modest profits are no longer deemed sufficient, and a sense of community is the last thing on Creighton's mind. Miles is only interested in the pleasures and riches he can attain for himself. He likes his pleasures "cold," and so turns the once-friendly company into a place where people will climb over each other for a better office, a promotion or stock options. *Chiller* demonstrates how even a single shift in generational leadership can change the values of an organization.

As has come to be expected with Craven-directed material, the American family is never far from the heart of *Chiller*. Once again a picture focuses on a mother-figure who is heavily into denial. Beatrice Straight (*Poltergeist*) plays Marion Creighton, a woman who is unwilling to accept reality. When Miles is close to death, Mrs. Creighton denies fate and freezes him in cryonic suspension. When he is revived, she denies that he is a vegetable and refuses to take him off life support. The price for this denial is that Miles does return, but as a heartless, empty creature. All along, Marion Creighton turns her head and claims that there is nothing wrong with *her* son. She is confronted by Penny and others about his true nature, yet she represses and denies the truth. The result is catastrophic for many of Miles' associates.

Like Mrs. Carter in *The Hills Have Eyes*, Mrs. Creighton depends on tradition and ritualized religion to get her through travails. She "prays" that things will get better, but her prayers do not stop Miles from committing murder. Finally, she summons the courage to confront Miles, but Clarence is already dead, Leigh is injured, Penny is in the hospital dying and Stacey is in mortal danger. Mrs. Creighton is complicit in this violence because she sat back, "prayed" and denied the truth about Miles rather than facing it like Nancy Thompson did in *A Nightmare on Elm Street*.

Chiller shares with *Invitation to Hell* the notion that a dog can ferret out the truth about a person. The pup in *Chiller* is Miles' first victim because the dog is not fooled by the soulless creature. The insightful "family" dog is a recurring image in Craven films. Typically, it is the one family member who does not repress, deny or obfuscate the truth. Unlike the deluded Mrs. Creighton in *Chiller*, Happy *knows* immediately what Miles is.

Chiller is filmed mostly in shadowy light. The cryonics chamber, the Creighton living room and the park where Penny is attacked are all seen in degrees of blackness. This shadowy approach gives *Chiller* a very different look from *A Stranger in Our House* and *Invitation to Hell*, both of which take place mostly in broad daylight. The focus on blackness lends an oppressive air to *Chiller*, and the mood created is a frightening one. The mood is also enhanced by the central performer, Michael Beck. He is quite good as the conscienceless creature who inherits Miles' body. Beck never overacts, never overstates his malevolence. Though it may sound like a left-handed compliment, Beck is really the perfect sociopath. As if internalizing the "frozen" motif, Beck makes Miles the most icy and cold of Craven villains.

The character of Miles is an interesting one. Because of his family connections, he has power and is quite content to use it to get what he wants. He finds joy only in causing others pain, and is one of the most terrifying of Craven's television monsters. Unlike Julia in *A Stranger in Our House*, Miles does not really bother with "integration" into his family. He does not attempt to be accepted or to usurp another's position. Why should he, when his mother already puts him up on a pedestal? In its mother-child dynamic, *Chiller* suggests that love is blind even when it should not be.

Like *Invitation to Hell*, *Chiller* might also be more ambiguous (and scary) if one scene had been altered. When Miles awakens in the hospital, his body ripples and his muscles coruscate strangely. A Stan Winston-created special effects head (like the one used in *The Terminator*) substitutes for Michael Beck's at points during this strange transformation. Along with gold contact lenses, these effects clearly establish that Miles is an entity beyond the norm. *Chiller* could have been more effective if, again, the audience had doubts about the character's true nature. If they had been unsure Miles was a cold-blooded s.o.b. or a supernatural entity, the horror of the scenario would have been a bit more effective. As it stands, audiences know early on that Miles is not just a "bad" guy, he is a force of evil.

Chiller remains a "chilling" film. It boasts what is perhaps the best cast of all of Craven's telefilms: Paul Sorvino, Michael Beck, Beatrice Straight and new horror scream queen Jill Schoelen. It is also the darkest and most cutthroat of the group; Miles' reign of terror is a real horror show. He does not just select victims at random (or wholesale, like the Steaming Springs Club of *Invitation to Hell*), he kills people who are not usually so callously knocked-off in genre pictures. Miles wipes out a helpless old man, bruises a beautiful woman (typically the heroine) and relentlessly tortures a man of God. These figures all represent important pillars of American culture (wisdom, beauty and religion, respectively), so Miles' spree seems doubly brutal (and purposeful).

Ironically, *Chiller* has been aired repeatedly on the Lifetime network. Lifetime airs films/dramas about women's issues, and *Chiller* does not view women in a particularly positive light. Leigh Canyon is a whore for stock options and Marion Creighton is deluded and slow to act. Though Stacey is a positive character, her primary role is to be put into jeopardy. Still, it is refreshing that a major cable channel has the rights to the film and is showing it on a regular basis. If only the same were true of Craven's last telefilm...

Night Visions (1990)

CAST: Loryn Locklin (Dr. Sally Powers); Penny Johnson (Luanne); Mitch Pileggi (Keller); John Tenney (Martin); Francis McCarthy (Dowd); Timothy Leary, Bruce MacVittie, James Remar

CREDITS: *Writers:* Wes Craven and Thomas Baum. *Cinematographer:* Peter Stein. *Music:* Brad Fiedel. *Production Designer:* Vincent M. Crescima. *Editors:* James Coblentz, Mark Melnick. *Producers:* Marianne Maddalena, Rick Nathanson. *Executive Producer/Director:* Wes Craven

SYNOPSIS: Psychologist Sally Powers has the ability to see into the minds of psychotic killers, and joins with a Los Angeles police officer to catch the serial murderer known as the "Spread Eagle Killer." As a relationship develops between the two partners, Powers is forced to confront not only her dark abilities but haunting elements of her own past as well.

COMMENTARY: Wes Craven's *Night Vision* (not to be confused with the 1987 film about a demonic VCR) is not currently available on videocassette and was not rerun on network or local television during the writing of this text. The picture was written by Craven and his *Nightmare Cafe* co-creator Thomas Baum, and it starred several alumni of his previous pictures. Penny Johnson of *The Hills Have Eyes Part II*, Mitch Pileggi of *Shocker* and *A Vampire in Brooklyn* and Timothy Leary of *Shocker* all contributed to the two-hour NBC pilot which aired November 30, 1990.

In concept, *Night Vision* is interesting because it appears to be the predecessor of such successful series as *Millennium* and *Profiler*, both of which feature tortured main characters with an unexplained ability to "get" into the minds of psychotic killers. In *Millennium*, Henriksen's character is partnered with cop Bill Smitrovitch; in *Night Vision*, Locklyn's disturbed psychologist is partnered with James Remar. Of all Craven's TV films, *Night Vision* is the only one in the "buddy-cop" sub-genre.

Night Vision never went to series. Craven and partner Baum returned to television with *Nightmare Cafe* in 1992.

Chapter 4

Craven as Executive Producer

As Craven solidified a reputation in Hollywood for expertly creating horror visions, he also expanded his repertoire. He has not only written, edited and directed movies, TV episodes and television films, he has also executive-produced a series of films. In 1987, Craven wrote the story, co-wrote the screenplay and was executive producer on *Dream Warriors*, the third film in the New Line Cinema *Nightmare on Elm Street* franchise. In 1995, the first *Wes Craven Presents* picture was unveiled on HBO. Entitled *Wes Craven Presents Mind Ripper*, this first anthology picture under the title umbrella "Wes Craven Presents" was produced and co-written by Craven's son Jonathan. Filmed on location in Bulgaria, the low-budget picture starred Lance Henriksen (*Aliens, Alien³*) and Natasha Wagner (*Lost Highway*). A weak movie, it was not released in theaters. Following the videocassette release of *Scream*, *Mind Ripper* was released on the home video market.

On September 19, 1997, the second *Wes Craven Presents* picture, *Wishmaster*, was released in theaters nationwide through Alive Films. It was a step above *Mind Ripper* but a throwback to the formula '80s-style horror sequels like *Dream Warriors* or *Hellbound: Hellraiser 2*.

All three of the pictures managed by Craven in an "executive" capacity have been substantially less interesting than the projects he has chosen to direct. Still, *Wes Craven Presents* may very well represent the future of Craven's horror participation. Should he leave the genre as a director, he could still function as a high-level horror "brand name" and present films by burgeoning talents such as Robert Kurtzman, Joe Gayton, Jonathan Craven and others.

A Nightmare on Elm Street Part III: Dream Warriors

Wes Craven ... figured that to raise Freddy from the dead would take so much contrivance that the whole procedure should be treated as a joke... The morbid tone of the original has given way to horror comedy set off by quite spectacular and imaginative fantasy sequences.— Kevin Thomas (*The Los Angeles Times*, February 27, 1987)

...not scary ... [I]t is inartistic to the point of cynicism, exhibiting an unshakable confidence that its audience will go for anything it dishes out.— James Gardner (*New Leader*, March 23, 1987)

CAST: Heather Langenkamp (Nancy Thompson); Craig Wasson (Neil Gordon); Patricia Arquette (Kristen Parker); Robert Englund (Freddy Krueger); Ken Sagoes (Kincaid); Rodney Eastman (Joey); Jennifer Rubin (Taryn); Bradley Gregg (Phillip); Ira Heiden (Will); Larry Fishburne (Max); Penelope Sudrow (Jennifer); John Saxon (Thompson); Priscilla Pointer (Dr. Elizabeth Sims); Clayton Landey (Lorenzo); Brooke Bundy (Elaine Parker); Kristen Clayton (Little Girl); Sally Piper (Nurse #1); Rozyln Sorrell (Nurse #2); Nan Martin (Nun); Stacey Alden (Marcie); Dick Cavett (Himself); Zsa Zsa Gabor (Herself); Michael Rougas (Priest in Church); Jack Shea (Priest in Cemetery); Paul Kent (Dr. Carver); Mary Brown (Neurosurgeon); Melanie Doctors (Girl in Cemetery); Donna Durham (Girl in Crowd)

CREDITS: New Line Cinema, Heron Communications Inc., and Smart Egg Pictures Present a Robert Shaye Production. *Casting:* Annette Benson. *Art Directors:* Mick Strawn, C.J. Strawn. *Production Manager:* Gerald T. Olson. *First Assistant Director:* Dennis Maguire. *Second Assistant Director:* Robin Randal Oliver. *Mechanical Special Effects:* Peter Chesney, Image Engineering Inc. *Krueger Makeup and Effects:* Kevin Yagher. *Special Makeup Effects Sequences:* Greg Cannom, Mark Shostrum. *Special Visual Effects:* Dreamquest Images. *Visual Effects Supervisor:* Hoyt Yeatman. *Editors:* Terry Stokes, Chuck Weiss. *Associate Producer:* Niki Marvin. *Director of Photography:* Roy Wagner. *Executive Producers:* Wes Craven, Stephen Diener. *Music:* Angelo Badalamenti. *Line Producer:* Rachel Talalay. *Executive in Charge of Production:* Gerald T. Olson. *Co-Producer:* Sara Risher. *Screenplay:* Wes Craven, Bruce Wagner, Chuck Russell, Frank Darabont. *Story:* Wes Craven, Bruce Wagner. *Producer:* Robert Shaye. *Director:* Chuck Russell. *First Assistant Director:* Jim Behnke. *Second Assistant Director:* Carol Bonnefil. *Assistant Production Manager:* Rebecca Greeley. *Production Coordinator:* Patricia Frazier. *First Assistant Camera:* Ed Giovanni. *Second Assistant Camera:* Juliette King. *Loader:* Giles Dunny. *Gaffer:* Shane D. Kelly. *Best Boy Electrical:* John Doherty. *Electricians:* Larry Linsey, Nick Cline, Antar Adderrahaman Jr. *First Rigging Gaffer:* Martin J. Aguilar. *Rigging Electrician:* Brian Robert Shaw. *Key Grip:* J. Patrick Daily. *Best Boy Grip:* Tom West. *Dolly Grip:* Kent Jorgenson. *Grip Electric:* Bob Whitehead, Ismael Araujo. *Rigging Key Grip:* Charles Norcross. *Sound Mixer:* William Fiege. *Boom Operator:* William Shaffer. *Art Department Coordinator:* Timothy Gray. *Set Decoration:* James P. Barrows. *Lead Man*: Andrew Erasuchen. *Set Dresser:* Jane Whitehead. *Assistant Set Dresser:* John Jackinsen, Linda

Syupy. *Costume Designer:* Camile Schroeder. *Wardrobe Supervisor:* Donna R. Schultz. *Prop Master:* Batia Grafka. *Assistant Props:* Cesar D. Alava. *Key-Makeup:* Christa Reusch. *Assistant Makeup:* Carrie Lou Nanigan. *Key Hairdresser:* H. Wayne Coker. *Storyboard Artist/Visual Consultant:* Peter Von Sholly. *Location Manager:* David Cannon. *Transportation Coordinator:* Griff Ruggles. *Transportation Captain:* D.J. Gardner. *Drivers:* Steven Casey, David Hannah, Timothy Leitch, Terry Mack, Chaz Merriam, Brian Joseph Moore, Danny Naten, Larry Smith. *Construction Coordinator:* Thomas A. O'Connor. *Lead Carpenter:* Thomas E. Lee. *Special Effects Bone Ghouls:* Thomas Bellissimo, Bryan Moore. *Special Effects Carpenter:* Charles Belardinelli. *Set Carpenter:* Vincent Hammong. *Carpenters:* John Cazin, George Dunn, Dan Driscoll, Mark Hames, Andre Ellingson, Lewis McCoy. *Scenic Artist:* Mitch Simmons. *Painters:* Joseph Melore, Tony Montesion, Felisa Finn. *Art Department Production Assistant:* Rebecca Carriage, Bazak T.R. Shokrian. *Extras Casting:* Creative Casting. *Casting Assistant:* Nan Diacovo. *Production Accountant:* Debra Moore. *Assistant Accountant:* June Karz. *Production Assistants:* Tome Lowe, Ella Blaney, Scott Coder, Jordan Rudelson. *Assistant to Director:* Susan H. Graham. *Craft Services:* Lori Ball, Randy Haney. *First Aid:* Hank McGill. *Post Production Supervisor:* Joseph R. Fineman. *First Assistant Editor:* Maria Digiovanni. *Second Assistant Editor:* Carol Street. *Apprentice Editor:* Rolf Johnson, Ira McAliley. *Stunt Coordinator:* Rick Barker. *Stunts:* Alison Brown, Deborah Porte, Joe Gilbride, Gary Littlejohn, William R. Perry, Robert K. Cummings, Gregg Dandridge, Tony Snegoff, Charly Morgan, J.D. Silvester. **Second Unit Director:** Dan Perri. *First Assistant Director:* Robert Engelman. *Second Unit Director of Photography:* Glen Kershaw. *First Assistant Camera:* James L. Eaton. *Gaffer:* Paul W. McIlvaine. *Electric:* John Schwartzman, Joseph Mealey. *Key Grip:* Peter Van Eynde. *Set Dressery:* Linda Syufy. *Script Supervisor:* Ellen Evans, Susan Stribling. *Production Assistant:* Hayden Yates. **Sound Designer:** David Lewis Yewdall. *Supervising Sound Editor:* R.J. Palmer. *Sound Effects Editors:* P. Hudson Miller, Kelly Tartan, Ted Goodspeed, Willy R. Allen. *Dialogue Editor:* Steve Rice. *Music Editor:* Earl Gilaffari. *Re-Recording Mixers:* Dick Weaver, Allen Stone, Michael Jeron. *Stop Motion Skeleton and Marionette Special Effects:* Doug Beswick Productions. *Stop Motion Animation:* Doug Beswick. *Special Effects Photography Supervisor:* Jim Aupperle. *Stop-Motion Puppet Construction:* Yancy Calzada. *Marionette Construction:* Mark Wilson. *Miniatures:* James Belohoven. *Illustrator:* Larry Nikolai. *Special Visual Effects:* Dreamquest Images. *Visual Effects Superviser:* Hoye Yeatman. *Motion Control Supervisor:* Michael Bigelow. *Production Coordinator:* Craig Newman. *Effects Photography:* Justin Karrenbeck, James Green, Scott Beattie, Michael Shen. *Matte Artist:* Robert Scifo. *Effects Rigging:* Rick Johnson, Mark Hollister. *Optical Supervisor:* Robert Hall. *Optical Compositing:* Michael Ferriter. *Optical Line-up:* Richard Rippel. *Effects Editorial:* Clint Hutchison. *Animation Effects:* Jeff Burks. *Visual Effects Production Manager:* Keith Sharfle. *Makeup Effects Supervisor:* Greg Cannom. *Assistants to Mr. Cannom:* Larry Odiem, Earl Ellis, John Yulich, Keith

Edmier, Brent Barker. *Krueger Makeup:* Kevin Yagher. *Assistant to Mr. Yagher:* Jim Kagel, Mitch DeVane, Gino Grognale, Brian Peniras, Dave Kindlon, Steve James, Everett Burrell. *Makeup Effects Sequences:* Mark Shostrum. *Assistants to Mr. Shostrum:* Robert Kurtzman, Bryant Tauser, John Blake Dutro, Jim McLoughlin, Cathy Carpenter. *Additional Makeup Effects:* Matthew Mungel. *Assistant to Mr. Mungel:* Russell Seifert. *Mechanical Effects:* Image Engineering. *Special Effects Coordinator:* Peter Chesney. *Lead Technician:* Lenny Dalrymple. *Mechanical Designer:* Bruce Hayes, Joe Starr. *Effects Technicians:* Bernardo Munoz, Rod Schumacher, Bob Ammanson. *Effects Crew:* Scott Nesselrode, Tom Chesney, Kelly Mann, Phillip Hartman, Ralph Miller, Joel Fletcher, Brian McFadden, Sandy Stewart, Troy Mack, Elaine Converse, Brendan C. Quigley. *Camera Equipment:* Interface Marketing, Clairmont Camera. *Grip and Electrical Equipment:* Filmtrucks. *Catering:* Radical Catering. *Main Title Sequence Designed and Directed by* Dan Perri. *Color:* Deluxe. *Titles:* Cinema Research Group. *Musical Supervision:* Kevin Benson. *Based on Characters created by* Wes Craven. *The Third Elm Street Venture.* "Dream Warrior" Composed and performed by Dokken on Elektra/Asylum Records. "Into the Fire" Composed and performed by Dokken. *Additional Music:* Ken Harrison, Don Dokken. *Music From A Nightmare on Elm Street* composed and performed by Charles Bernstein.

SYNOPSIS: In Springwood, teenager Kristen Parker is haunted by nightmares of Freddy Krueger. This nefarious dream demon has grown more devious over the years and changed his method of attack. Now he makes the deaths of the Elm Street children appear to be suicides. Accordingly, Kristen inadvertently slits her wrist in her sleep. From her perspective, she is battling for her life against a bogeyman. From her mother's perspective, she is just trying to get attention.

Elsewhere in town, Dr. Neil Gordon works with a ward full of youngsters who have attempted to kill themselves. There has been a rash of teen suicides lately and neither Dr. Gordon nor the rigid Dr. Sims are able to explain the alarming trend. Neil conducts a group therapy session consisting of Kincaid, Jennifer, Taryn, Joey, Will and Phillip. Soon Kristen Parker is welcomed to the therapy session. The teens share what Neil and Dr. Sims believe to be a mass delusion: They fear that a horrible man is trying to kill them in their dreams. Dr. Sims insists this is just a by-product of guilt feelings, psychological scars and overt sexuality. The teens feel hopeless until Nancy Thompson enters their life. A grad-student doing groundbreaking research in pattern nightmares (and a former nemesis of Freddy Krueger), Thompson believes she holds the key to the survival of the Elm Street children. She wants to prescribe for the kids an experimental psychoactive drug, Hypnocil. She herself takes the medicine to suppress her own dreams. Neil is reluctant to prescribe an experimental drug for unstable kids.

One night, when Kristen experiences a nightmare, she calls to Nancy and pulls the grad-student into her dream with her. Nancy believes that with

Kristin (Patricia Arquette) approaches the house where Freddy dwells in *Dream Warriors*, executive produced by *Elm Street* creator Wes Craven.

Kristen's dream skill and the Hypnocil, Krueger can finally be defeated. Tragedy strikes, however. Phillip, a maker of puppets, is transformed into a marionette and pushed off the roof of the hospital tower. Jennifer, who wishes to be a movie star, is pushed head-first into a TV set and electrocuted. Neil finally realizes that these kids require immediate assistance and agrees to Nancy's plan. The students take the Hypnocil and then Nancy hypnotizes them. Together, they enter the dream world. In this fantasy existence, the crippled Will can walk, Kincaid has the strength of a superman and Taryn is a beautiful vixen. Things soon go dreadfully wrong, however, when Krueger (posing as a beautiful nurse) lures the mute Joey into a trap. The nurse spits out writhing tongues and uses them to suspend Joey over the mouth of Hell.

When Dr. Sims interrupts the hypnosis session, everyone is fine except for Joey, who is in a coma. Nancy and the others realize that Freddy has him. Unfortunately, Neil and Nancy are fired by the hospital administrator for prescribing a dangerous drug. Late that night, Neil runs into a strange nun. She takes him to an abandoned wing of the hospital and informs the psychologist that the hospital used to be an insane asylum. Once, in the '40s, a beautiful young nun was trapped in the ward during the holidays. She was raped repeatedly during a two-week period by the inmates. She later give birth to Freddy Krueger, "the bastard son of a hundred maniacs." Neil is shocked by this story but it confirms what Nancy and the teens have been telling him. Most importantly, the nun reveals that Krueger is haunting the dreams of children because his spirit is not at rest. His bones must be buried in hallowed ground.

Nancy realizes that only one person knows where Krueger's remains are hidden: her own father, Lt. Thompson. Donald has become an alcoholic and is reluctant to help his own daughter. Nancy returns to the hospital to help Kristen, who has been sedated and put in isolation, while Neil pressures her father into helping recover Freddy's bones. At the clinic, the survivors of the group are pulled into Kristen's dream. Working together as dream "warriors," they free Joey from his prison. Soon, however, Freddy divides and conquers. In the ensuing battle, Taryn and Will are killed.

While Nancy, Kristen, Kincaid and Joey face mortal danger in a dream, Neil and Thompson travel to an abandoned junkyard where Thompson finds the bag of Freddy's bones in the trunk of a ruined automobile. The bones jump together and form a skeleton: Incredibly powerful, the wraith kills Thompson and incapacitates Neil with a shovel.

Back in the dreamworld, Thompson appears to say farewell to his daughter. In fact, Thompson is Freddy and he uses his disguise to kill Nancy. Although it is too late for Nancy, Neil manages to splash holy water on Freddy's bones and he then gives the monster a proper burial. Kristen, Kincaid and Joey survive the massacre unscathed. At Nancy's funeral, Neil learns that the nun with whom he spoke was the ghost of Freddy's mother, Sister Amanda Krueger.

COMMENTARY: *A Nightmare on Elm Street III: Dream Warriors* is an entertaining enhancement of the "rubber reality" world defined by Craven's *A Nightmare on Elm Street*. With a story and screenplay straight from Craven's typewriter, the film succeeds in blending nightmares and reality. In that regard at least, the picture goes beyond the bounds of the original *A Nightmare on Elm Street*. Bathroom faucets sprout bony hands and come to life, TV sets unfurl robotic arms, and there are swift and unexpected location switches between shots. At one juncture, Kristen is sound asleep in her bedroom when the camera pulls back to reveal the front yard of Freddy's house instead of the confines of the bedroom the audience expects. At another point, Kristen closes her ward room door in the hospital to find herself slamming the front door of Freddy's house. As if in shock, the camera rockets backwards to note that Kristen has trapped herself in the worst place imaginable. The suggestion is that no matter how much this girl tries to escape Freddy, his nightmare world pulls her back in.

Delightfully, even time itself repeats near the climax when the film's opening passage is rerun with a slight modification: a deadly (and funny) special effects intrusion by Freddy Krueger. In its seamless blending of two worlds or realities, *Dream Warriors* is a visual feast filled with exciting special effects and camera gimmicks like those described above. Chuck Russell is a very capable director and he makes the most of the fantasy elements in Craven's story.

A Nightmare on Elm Street III also fulfills a rule of sequels: the body count is larger. In fact, everything is larger. Instead of going after four friends (as in the original *Nightmare*) or trying to co-opt the body of a sexually confused boy (as in *Freddy's Revenge*), Krueger in this picture haunts an entire ward of Elm Street teens. The special effects depict this haunting in some startling ways that the original (budgeted at $1.8 million) could simply not afford. Freddy transforms into a giant worm that devours Patricia Arquette, and stop motion photography is utilized in the marionette and skeleton sequences. There is even a special effects "chest of souls" which reveals where Freddy's victims finally end up.

This "big" approach to the sequel's set pieces and cast causes some problems. Because there is a bigger cast, there is also less time for individuality. The large cast is not well served by the final screenplay (rewritten by Darabont and Russell). Half the teens would have accomplished the same thing and been more identifiable for confused audiences. *Dream Warriors* offers half-a-dozen teenage "victims," a bevy of adult staff (Nancy, Neil, Dr. Sims and Max), two dysfunctional parental figures (Don Thompson and Mrs. Parker), and even two supernatural creations (Krueger and his dear old mom). Half the cast exists just to be killed and others are given just enough screen time to become interesting (Larry Fishburne's Max). John Saxon and Heather Langenkamp both return to *Elm Street* only to be rather unceremoniously knocked off.

The spectacular dream sequences which punctuated *A Nightmare on Elm Street* have lost their intimacy and personality in *Dream Warriors*. Instead of being scary personal visions of a frightened but determined teen like Nancy Thompson, they are pure phantasmagoria lensed in excellent light (so the great special effects can be seen). The result is that special effects and fantasy landscapes have replaced terror and genuine scares. Freddy is seen so commonly in *A Nightmare on Elm Street III: Dream Warriors* that he has lost his scariness. Though competently designed and applied by Kevin Yagher, his makeup is no more frightening than Odo's on *Deep Space Nine* or Worf's on *Star Trek: The Next Generation*. Familiarity has changed Freddy into just another special effects creation, a *Star Trek* alien, if you will. Since he no longer has the ability to scare audiences, Freddy in *Dream Warriors* is a transformed creature. No longer is society's guilty secret skulking in the boiler room and avenging his own death. Instead he is a demonic trickster full of puns and witticisms. Rather than trapping teens in his particular dream world (the boiler room), he torments them based on their one-line psychological/character hooks. Phillip builds marionettes, so Freddy turns him into one. Jennifer wants to be on TV, so Freddy jams her into a set. Joey likes chicks, so Freddy lures him to his doom with a foxy nurse. *Ad nauseam, ad infinitum.* The characters are developed only to the extent that a single character detail can be used by Freddy to kill them.

The comedy dialogue of *A Nightmare on Elm Street III: Dream Warriors* is witty at times. When Freddy ties Joey to a bed with human tongues, he gurgles, "What's the matter, Joey? Feeling tongue-tied?" When he shoves Jennifer head-first into a television set, he croaks, "Welcome to prime time, bitch." When he sucks the life out of Taryn with hypodermic needles, he oozes, "What a rush!" There is even a comic interlude featuring Zsa Zsa Gabor and Dick Cavett! Fulfilling audience desires, Cavett/Krueger silences the talkative Gabor with a slice of his glove and the exclamation, "I don't give a fuck what you think!"

All of these moments would have been virtually unthinkable in Craven's *A Nightmare on Elm Street*, which is an oppressively dark horror film that featured what *Entertainment Weekly*'s Owen Gleiberman called "a trance-like dread." *Dream Warriors'* modified tone is an indication of New Line's "new" approach to the franchise. Instead of scaring audiences with a bogeyman, they transformed him into an anti-James Bond for the '80s. True to the Bond format, Krueger is involved in amazing action sequences, he ably dispatches his victims and then he belts out a rib-tickling one-liner. It is a mundane approach for a horror film and one that completely destroys Freddy's ability to scare. For that reason, Craven had to thoroughly "reinvent" Freddy in 1994's *New Nightmare*. The old Freddy was just not scary any more, so Craven conjured up an ancient uberFreddy creature instead. To his credit, the revamp worked and *New Nightmare* is indeed a scary film.

Like its Jack Sholder-directed predecessor, *Dream Warriors* faces some rather large hurdles on the track to plausibility. An ongoing theme in the script is that the adult world believes the teens are attempting suicide. When Freddy offs the kids, he makes it appear as if they have killed themselves. However, it would be absolutely impossible for the teens to commit suicide in the manner depicted in the film. Take aspiring actress Jennifer, for example. Max finds her dead, with her head jammed into a TV set. Now, hold on a minute! The television is attached to a wall about eight feet off the floor. To jump into a TV that high with such force, Jennifer would have had to take a running start, jump off a trampoline, and aim (head-first) at the TV set. There is no way that anyone with even a modicum of intelligence could believe that her very, very peculiar death was a suicide. There is not even a table or chair nearby that she could have used as a springboard!

At another point, Freddy carves into Joey's chest the words, "Come and get him, bitch." Not a single nurse or physician seems to think that this scar is anything out of the ordinary. How did he cut himself up like that while in a coma? And if he did cut himself, why did he refer to himself as "him" instead of "me" in his carving?

Finally, Phillip is transformed into a marionette and led to his death by Freddy. As he walks down a hallway, he walks right *through* a locked doorway. He de-materializes and re-materializes on the far side of the locked barrier. How is this possible? Freddy can make the boy think anything in his dreams, but unless Freddy is far more powerful than the audience believes, he cannot deconstruct and reconstruct matter in our reality!

When viewed in the context of later sequels, *Dream Warriors* also seems like a dead end. Nancy and Don Thompson are killed while putting Freddy to rest in this film. They die to stop him, giving him a decent burial at last. Yet in the opening scenes of *A Nightmare on Elm Street IV: The Dream Master*, a dog urinates on Freddy's bones and revives him. This silly resurrection undercuts the climax of *Dream Warriors* and Nancy's final battle with Freddy. *The Dream Master*, in the time-honored tradition of very bad sequels, also immediately kills off Kristen, Joey and Kincaid ... the last survivors of *Dream Warriors*. Ironically, Dr. Gordon is nowhere to be seen. Since he is not an Elm Street child himself, he should not be susceptible to Freddy's powers. On the contrary, he should be the one man in *Dream Master* who can help these kids. Of course, Craig Wasson and Dr. Gordon are not in the sequels. Adding insult to injury, in *Nightmare V: The Dream Child*, the hospital where the events of *Dream Warriors* takes place is described as being abandoned since the 1940s ... thus negating all the action there in the third film anyway! As these gaffes make clear, without Craven's input the *Elm Street* film series is one woefully lacking in continuity.

Despite these flaws, *Dream Warriors* does boast some strong points. The moment in which Nancy meets Freddy in Kristen's dream makes the blood run cold. The Freddy worm groans the word "*You ... "* in a sort of low howl, and his recognition of Nancy is frightening. Nancy recognizes her opponent as well, and the look that crosses Langenkamp's face is one of pure terror. In moments like this one, the meaningful relationship between Freddy and potential victim is powerfully re-established. Freddy's origin is also detailed for the first time, leading up to that great line about Krueger being "the bastard son of a hundred maniacs." *A Nightmare on Elm Street V: The Dream Child* would later show the events recounted here by Amanda Krueger in the most gruesome and frightening detail.

The screenplay also finds time to continue the underlying themes pioneered by Craven in *A Nightmare on Elm Street*. The parents responsible for Freddy's death are even more despicable than before. Don Thompson (Saxon) has become an alcoholic and Mrs. Parker is a horrible woman who makes no attempt to understand her suffering child. After Kristen attempts to kill herself, Mrs. Parker tells the doctors that her daughter is "just trying to get attention." Of course, if Parker would give her any attention, there would be no need for Kristen to do such things. Parker's comment is an admission that she has no time for her own child. She later tells Nancy that Kristen's nightmares started when she "took away her credit cards." Unlike the Lantzes or Tina's mother in *Elm Street*, Mrs. Parker is not even well meaning. She is a cold-hearted person who cares nothing about her own daughter.

That Freddy's bones need to be buried is also an indictment of the Elm Street parents. It was their failure to provide a proper, Christian burial that allowed Freddy to enter the minds of their children. From original to *Dream Warriors*, the *Nightmare on Elm Street* series remains consistent in its indictment of middle-class parents.

Dream Warriors also has a positive message somewhere amidst its special effects sequences. Each of the children has a unique "gift," a dream skill that allows them to overcome their worst fears and survive in a cruel world dominated by the ultimate bad father. The film thus demonstrates to today's youth that anything is possible if teenagers "believe" in themselves. This message, delivered through Craven's notion of "dream skills," is sadly undercut by *The Dream Master*, in which not even these gifts can save the children. In that film, there is no hope.

Despite these strengths, *Dream Warriors* is very much indicative of New Line's MTV approach to the *Elm Street* franchise. Freddy Krueger serves as a sort of evil veejay, entering music-video-like dreams and dispatching children with a joke and wink. The film seems tailor-made for someone weaned on music videos, someone with an attention span of five minutes. This makes it a stark contrast to Craven's terrifying original which was compelling throughout. That film was challenging. In its commentary on America and pontification about the nature of dreams, it demanded to be watched from the first frame until the ambiguous conclusion. After ten years, 1987's *Elm Street* sequel seems particularly empty. Since the special effects have aged and later sequels have killed off the characters and undercut the film's message, *Dream Warriors* looks and feels painfully obsolete. One can be certain that things would have been different had Craven directed this picture.

Wes Craven Presents Mind Ripper (1995)

Hardcore horror fans will not be disappointed with this gory fast-paced TV movie... If you like 'em graphic, satisfaction is guaranteed thanks to Joe Gayton's direction.—John Stanley, *Creature Features: The Science Fiction, Fantasy and Horror Movie Guide* (Boulevard Books, 1997, page 557)

CAST: Lance Henriksen (Dr. Jim Stockton); John Diehl (Alex Hunter);

Natasha Wagner (Wendy Stockton); Giovanni Ribisi (Scott Stockton); Gregory Sporleder (Rob); Dan Blom (Thor); Adam Solomon (Mark); John Apicella (Larry); Peter Shepherd (Frank); Claire Stansfield (Joanne)

CREDITS: A Kushner-Locke Company. An Outpost Production. *Costume Designer:* Elizabeth Jett. *Special Makeup Effects:* Image Animation. *Music:* J. Peter Robinson. *Editor:* Harry Hitner. *Production Design:* Jeremy Levine. *Director of Photography:* Fernando Arguelles. *Co-producer:* Peter Shepherd. *Executive Producer:* Wes Craven. *Writers:* Jonathan Craven, Phil Mittleman. *Producer:* Jonathan Craven. *Director:* Joe Gayton. *Production Services:* Interfilm, Sofia, Bulgaria. *Managing Director:* Sashko Velichkov. *Production Manager:* Rumen Alexandrov Obraztov. *Unit Manager:* Nikolai Vasiliev Tzvetkov. *First Assistant Director:* Paul Martin. *Script Supervisor:* Kathy Mulligan. *Location Manager:* Peicho Peichev, Keril Borisov Konstantinonov. *Second Assistant Director:* Zlatina Philopova Kushtinvova. *Production Accountant:* Chris Elkins. *Accountant (Interfilm):* Toma Tomov. *Additional Photography:* Roberto Forges Davanzati. *Operator:* Dimitar Gorchev. *Focus Pullers:* Luigi Andrei, Dimitrov Lubomir. *Steadicam:* Jukka Talikka, Alessandro Borgheses. *Leader:* Atanas Atanasov. *Gaffer:* Mario Palermi. *Best Boy:* Franco Caporale. *Electrician:* Veselini Vesco Antonov, Ivan Andriev. *Key Grip:* Sergio Fabriani. *Best Boy:* Ivan Christoshkor. *Grip:* Plamen "Paco" Folev. *Second Unit Director/Stunt Coordinator:* Tony Cecere. *Second Unit Operator:* Toma Tomav. *Bulgarian Stunts:* Emil Videv. *Art Director:* Prolet Spasova Georgivia. *Construction Supervisor:* Zoravko Hristor. *Set Dresser:* Aneta Petrova Jotova. *Props:* Manuel Wilhelm. *Prop Buyers:* Luka Bistrekova, Todorka Bistrekova. *On-Set Construction:* Stefan Batchvasov, Metodi Mihailov. *Storyboard Artist:* Andrew Baron. *Special Effects Makeup Director:* Paul Jones. *Artists:* Shaune Harrison, James Barr, Valentin Genov Volov. *Makeup:* Anastasia "Sia" Satrora, Hristo Naidenov. *Hairstylist:* Nellie Marinova Naidenova. *Seamstress:* Ivanka Dimitrova. *Sound Mixer:* Roberto Alberghini. *Boom Operator:* Jordan "Dancho" Tzinzarski. *Video Assistant:* Ivan Jotov. *Mechanical Effects:* Ivan Angelov, Georgi Mladenov. *Production Secretary:* Nadejda Dimitrova. *Rome Liaison:* Francesco Martina De Carles. *Assistant to Mr. Shepherd:* Peter Kirilov Popor. *Production Assistant:* Suetlio Svetoslav, Doichan Hristar Margoevsky, Denitza Alexandrova Alexova. *Unit Publicist:* Stephen Jones. *Publicity Assistant:* Jo Fletcher. *Still Photographer:* Peter Kernot. *Interpreters:* Sylvia Tzintzarska, Reni Marcheyska, Milena Tzintzarska, Elina Blagoeva Pesheva. *Caterers:* Valio and Mimi's Restaurant. *Craft Services:* Alexander Youlievi. *On-Set Craft Services:* Dimitar Moskov. *Drivers:* Nikola Damainov Denev, Ivan Petrov Pashalitski, Peter Injov, Rogoi Joanov, Peter Violtor Kostov, Java Kotov, Ivan Konev, Pancho Milhailov, Krasimir Georgiev. **Canadian Crew:** *Production Manager:* George Chapman. *Location Manager:* Will Fearn. *Production Accountant:* Wendy Ladret. *Production Coordinator:* Jo-Anne Barry. *Script Supervisor:* Jean Christopher. *First Assistant Director:* Dan Tohill. *Second Assistant Director:* Dan Munro. *DGC Trainee:* Wayne McDonell. *Stunt Coordinator:*

John Wardlow. *Stunts:* Darryl Scheelan, Schott Nicholson, Ailette Falle, Michael Desabrais, Dorothy Ferr, Garvin Cross, Scott Walden. *Production Designer:* Ricardo Spinace. *Construction Coordinator:* Michael Caluori. *Prop Master:* Cher Lewis. *On-Set Props:* John Johnston. *Set Decorator:* Kevin Mosley. *Assistant Decorator:* Demian Gordon. *Head Carpenter:* Matthew Versteeg. *Stand-by Carpenter:* Jonathan Kiekish. *Head Painter:* D. Morris. *Scenic Painter:* Rene Dow. *Camera/Steadicam Operator:* Alan Lennox. *First Assistant Camera:* Jeff Hohener, Bradd Whitlock. *Second Assistant Camera:* Kimber Lee Ritz. *Second Unit Director of Photography:* Peter Rausche. *Video Playback:* Bill Kitchen. *Second Unit Assistant Camera:* Michael Horner-O'Leary. *Sound Mixer:* David Husby. *Boom Operator:* Rick Bold, Bob Holbrook. *Gaffer:* Steve Miko. *Best Boy Electric:* Dave Hamm. *Electricians:* Derek Soong, Michael Trawiek. *Generator Operators:* Peter Denham, Geoff Brown. *Key Grip:* Stephen berg. *Best Boy Grip:* Guy Williamson. *Dolly Grip:* Jason Robbins. *Makeup:* Donna Rutherford. *Grips:* Steve Noah, Ting Henson, Paul Marcus, James Vinblad. *Hair:* Eileen A. Dezouche. *Wardrobe Supervisor:* Sam Turkis. *On-Set Wardrobe:* Sylvie Gendron. *Special Effects:* Ray Roedyk. *Nuclear Barrel Effect:* Peter Salmon. *Armorer:* Felcan Enterprises, Inc. *Effects Trainee:* Ali Nurse. *Animal Handler:* Debra Coe. *Transportation Coordinator:* Ben Derrick. *Transportation Captain:* Darryll Archibald. *Special Equipment Driver:* Laurie Morriss. *Cast Driver:* Brent Hill. *Driver:* Albert Franz. *Assistant Locations:* Tish Heaven. *Location Production Assistant:* Adam Hogarth, Darcy Wild, Cindy Dainard. *Production Trainee:* Leanne Chapman. *Assistant Accountant:* Alan Homma. *Catering:* Studio Bistro. *First Aid:* Ken Lemon. *Security Captain:* John Curran. *Security Coordinator:* Gerry Baker. *Canadian Dailies Developed By:* Alpha Cine Services. *Sound Transfer/Synch:* Sharpe Sound Studios. *Camera Rental:* Laslo George, Inc. *Electric Equipment:* William F. White, Ltd. *Grip Equipment:* Grip Tou, Inc. *Star Wagons:* Tahoe R.V. Rentals. *Post Production Supervisor:* Anais Sturgess. *Assistant Editors:* Bill Strousse, Maria Katzeva. *Apprentice Editors:* Doug Sherin, Margaritz Katzeva. *Post Production Assistant:* Patrick Bonaventura. *Audio Post Production:* Sharpe Sound Studios. *Sound Supervisor:* Jacqueline Christinani. *Dialogue Editor:* Marc Chiasson. *ADR Editor:* Sheena Macrae. *Special Effects Editors:* Ken Cade, Isaac Strozberg. *Background Editor:* Ken Cade. *Foley Recordist:* Sina Oroomchi. *Foley Artists:* Boardwalk Foley. *Re-Recording Mixers:* Paul Sharpe, Bill Sheppard, Kelly Cole. **Digital Visual Effects:** OCS/Freeze Frame/Pixel Magic. *Digital Supervisor:* Ray McIntyre, Jr. *Digital Artist:* Jim Gorman. *Negative Cutter:* Magic Film and Video Works. *Color Timer:* Mike Milliken. *Title Design:* Melissa Limmer. *Titles and Opticals:* Title House. *Camera Rental:* Arodue, s.r.l., Rome. *Equipment Rental:* Interfilm, Sofia. *Insurance:* RHW/Alberg G. Ruben. *Production Counsel:* Law Office of Alan Abrams. *Computer Graphics:* UBLIK, s.r.l., Milan. *Special Effect Contact Lenses:* Bodytech. *Secuurity System and Intercom Devices:* Plinko Password, s.r.l., Milan. *Robotcam and Electron Microscope:* Franco Varorio. *Sound Recorded at:* Rebrush Music Studios, Los Angeles. *Orchestrations:* J. Peter Robinson. *Assistant to Mr. Robinson:* Demelza Rylance.

Music Score Published and Administered by: Rebrush Music, Inc./ASCAP. *Additional Music Coordinator:* Mickey Petralia. *Additional Music:* "Mammals" written and performed by Lucifer Wong (Wong Song/BMI), "Blacknailed Fingers" written by S. Franklin and M. Petralia and performed by Terrordactyl (Ratchet Blade/BMI), "Back Down" written by S. Franklin and S. Wheelere, performed by Charley Horse (Ratchet Blade/BMI), and "Bodies Piled up" written by S. Franklin and performed by Charley Horse (Ratchet Blade/BMI). All Musical Performances Courtesy of Hellnote Recordings. *Film Lab Dailies:* Telecolor-Rome. *Dolby Stereo Consultant:* Brad Hohle. *Special Thanks to:* National Palace of Culture, Sofia, Novotel Europa Hotel, Sofia, Bulgaria Foreign Trade Bank, Ltd., Bulgarian Academy of Sciences-Physical Institute, Nelli's Business Club Restaurant in Sofia, The Novotel Fatimas, Cecchetti Speed Coop, s.r.l, Rome, Uanchi Corporation, Rome, British Columbia Film Commission, The Coast Plaza at Stanley Park, CA Creative Lighting, Inc., Payments Plus, Union of B.C. Performers, Association of Canadian Film Craftspeople, West, Director's Guild of Canada, Jerry Stahl, Jonathan Reiss, Peter Chesney, Scott Cymbala, Meredith Chinn, Lisa Harrison, Marianne Maddalena, Jeff Fenner, Derek Power, Bonnie Chapin. Filmed Entirely on Location in Bulgaria and Vancouver, British Columbia. The Kushner-Locke Company. *MPAA Rating:* R

SYNOPSIS: Three people garbed in gray overalls march up the side of a desert mountain to recover the body of a wounded man. The dying man is sprawled among the rocks, bloodied. His rescuers lift him gently onto a stretcher and carry him to a black van at the foot of the mountain. Later that night, they work desperately to save his life in the blackness of a lab. Their patient has lost massive amounts of blood, his brain is dead and only seconds remain before he dies. One of the doctors, Alex Hunter, suggests to his companions that they give the patient "the virus" immediately. Joanne, a beautiful brunette physician, argues that the patient is not a guinea pig, but Jim Stockton makes the final decision. The patient will die without the virus, so Jim administers it via a hypodermic needle.

Six months later, the scientists monitor the progress of their patient in an abandoned nuclear outpost. Now the compound is reserved for the use of Gentec. Jim Stockton has left the experiment because he did not like the direction the research was going; the cruel-hearted Alex is now in charge. For the most part, the scientists who live in the underground compound live a life of boredom. A bearded scientist, Frank, informs colleagues, Joanne, Alex, Larry and Rob that their patient is dying. Alex says that the man's body is merely accepting the virus.

In California, Jim Stockton gathers his family for a camping trip. Daughter Wendy and her boyfriend Mark are perpetually involved in foreplay and son Scott is a detached punk who is hooked on cigarettes and heavy metal music. Scott would rather not accompany his family on the camping trip, but Jim forces him to. The family packs.

At the Gentec outpost, Alex grows worried about Thor, his patient, has begun to convulse. He calls Jim and begs him to return to the compound to save the patient's life. Jim reminds Alex that he no longer works there, but Alex pressures him. He also reminds Jim that it was he (Jim) who invented and administered the virus, so he shares the responsibility. Jim hangs up angrily but cannot stop thinking about the project. He informs his family that he has to go back to work just to check things out, and that they are welcome to come. Wendy, Mark and Scott agree and they all set out for their father's private plane.

Inside the compound, Frank and Joanne discover that Alex has been pumping Thor with the virus at ten times the normal rate. They think this acceleration of the experiment is responsible for his convulsions. With Alex leading the team, the scientists try to restart Thor's heart after a cardiac arrest. Thor bursts to life just as the power goes out. When the lights flicker back on, Thor attacks. He breaks Frank's neck and pulls Larry apart. Joanne and Alex escape and meet up with Rob, who was monitoring from the network room. Joanne and Rob want to evacuate, but Alex's hand-print is the only one which can open the outer door to the outpost. But Alex refuses to leave: He wants to sell Thor, a biologically enhanced super soldier, to the highest bidder and make a fortune. With a shotgun in hand, Alex forces Rob and Joanne to help him locate the deranged Thor. Joanne and Rob rig tranquilizer guns but have little hope of stopping a monster that was designed to be invincible. Joanne surveys an overhead duct and discovers rats chewing on a human eyeball, but no sign of Thor.

Thor is in another overhead duct, transforming into something inhuman. After he vomits up a strange bulbous thing, he uses his heightened sense of hearing and realizes the scientists are tracking him. As Alex erases his hand-print from the computer so no one can leave, Thor strikes again. He grabs Alex and pulls him up into the duct.

Jim pilots his small plane to the compound. Shortly before landing, he asks Scott if the young man remembers his flying lessons. Still bitter after his parents' recent divorce, Scott ignores Jim's attempt at bonding. The plane lands at the foot of the mountain and the family proceeds to the main outpost door. While Mark and Wendy have a moment alone, Jim and Scott argue again. Jim says he wants to be a better father but that he needs Scott's help. Scott ignores him and Jim demands that he grow up. Jim utilizes his hand-print to open the door and his family enters the Gentec laboratory.

Alex awakens in a cocoon of wires and cables. He has been abducted by Thor! The mutating creature recognizes Alex as the person who made him hurt. Alex tries to make an alliance with Thor, but Thor is starving. Thor's only source of nourishment is the human brain, which contains a large amount of a particular cholesterol. Thor opens his mouth and a fleshy spike protrudes from a vagina-like opening in his throat. It stretches and an outer layer of skin unfolds to reveal a glistening white tusk. Thor inserts the spike into Alex's eye and sucks out his brain.

On his way to repair the computers, Rob is attacked by Thor. He escapes, but a toenail is ripped off during the scuffle. He limps to safety and begins working. He is caught unaware when Thor attacks him again. Thor drains the life from the victim's brain, inserting his fleshy tube up Rob's nostril. After feasting on Rob's brain, Thor continues his transformation. His hair starts to fall out.

The Stocktons are unaware of the danger they face inside the lab. Wendy sees some horrible monstrosities through a laboratory window and wonders if her father was creating a monster. Jim explains it was because of those mutations that he quit, but Wendy is upset and she runs off. While Mark and Jim search for Wendy, Scott sits down and listens to more heavy metal music on his headphones. The sound of the music is conducted through a pipe, and Thor detects it. He follows Scott to a kitchen and prepares to kill him, but the microwave alarm goes off and paralyzes the beast. Jim returns to find his son in danger and plunges a butcher knife into Thor's back. Thor heals instantaneously and his muscles squeeze the knife out rapidly. Jim fights Thor while Scott escapes down a corridor. Scott meets up with Mark and Wendy, who by now have encountered Joanne. They run to help their father, but Thor drags him up an incline and disappears with him into an airduct. Wendy and Scott are heartbroken by the loss of their father and Joanne shares the truth of the research with them. Their father had developed a powerful virus that regenerates human tissue. He wanted to use it to save people around the world, but the Army intervened in Gentec's work and demanded that the corporation create a super-soldier. Jim found out about the new goal and resigned in disgust. Wendy listens, but is resentful. She believes that Joanne and Jim had an affair that broke up her parents' marriage.

Jim awakens to find himself near the dead body of Alex Hunter. Thor is still changing, his face bulging and mutating. The mutant remembers that Stockton once brought him back from the dead. He asks Jim if he's God and Jim says no. He tells Thor how the scientific team found him out in the desert, brain dead. He tells Thor how the virus was injected into him to regenerate his cells. The monster remembers Jim feeding him chicken noodle soup and reading *The Hardy Boys* to him. He wants to die, but Jim tells him that is impossible—Thor could live for a thousand years. Thor becomes enraged and rips out the rest of his hair. He approaches Jim and opens his mouth. The fleshy, organic spike protrudes...

Joanne works feverishly in the lab to analyze a sample of Thor's blood obtained from the butcher knife. She understands that if he does not get a dose of cholesterol, he will die. She decides they can use a trail of frozen human brains to lure Thor into a walk-in freezer, where he will be trapped. The attempt fails: Thor detects the trap and does not go into the freezer. Instead he kills Mark, twisting his head and breaking his neck. Joanne fires her shotgun and the blast propels Thor into the freezer. Scott, Wendy and Joanne lock the door and plan to escape. Unfortunately, they cannot leave the base without the appropriate hand-print reading. Joanne formulates a grim plan: They will find Jim's body, cut off his hand and use it to open the door. Wendy and Scott are naturally resistant to this morbid plan, but Thor is growing stronger and will soon escape from his prison.

The survivors locate Jim and discover he is not dead. For some reason, Thor did not feast on his mind. Jim awakens and his family and Joanne carry him to the main door. Meanwhile, Thor breaks out of the freezer and pursues. He surprises the humans and carries Wendy away to mate with her. Scott remembers that the high-pitched alarm of the microwave hurt Thor, and with Jim and Joanne he runs to the control room to use the intercom. They transmit a high-pitched squeal which immobilizes Thor just as he is making sexual advances on Wendy with his oral tusk. She runs away and meets her family. Thor pursues, but Scott electrocutes the monster in the control room. Still, that is not enough to kill the beast. The humans run for the exit and Jim opens the outer door with his hand-print. They escape into the desert and drive away in the research team's van. Before long, Thor is on top of the van attacking. Jim points his gun upward and shoots Thor through the roof. Thor falls off, then jumps through the back window. He grabs Scott by the throat, but the young man uses a shard of broken glass to lop off Thor's organic tusk. Then Wendy shoots the beast in the stomach, causing him to fall off the truck.

The family and Joanne run to the plane. Jim cannot push the pedals and operate the controls because his leg is broken. He says that Scott will have to fly them home. Scott remembers the lessons his father once gave him and takes off successfully. High in the sky, Thor attacks again. He breaks a window and grabs Joanne. She breaks free and uses the shotgun to blast him in the head. Thor falls hundreds of feet to the ground and the plane heads home triumphantly. On the rocks far below, Thor is motionless for a moment before he twitches...

COMMENTARY: *Wes Craven Presents Mind Ripper* is as weak a motion picture as one is likely to find with Craven's name attached to it. Since he did not direct, edit or write the film, he can hardly be considered responsible for its lack of quality, but since he is "presenting" it to his faithful audience, one has to wonder why it is such a trite collection of horror clichés.

Originally titled *Outpost*, *Mind Ripper* plays like a compilation film of all the best bits from the incredible *Alien* franchise. Like *Aliens* (1986), *Mind Ripper* is set in a hi-tech installation with dark corridors and dead ends. Like Sigourney Weaver's Ripley in *Aliens*, the heroine in *Mind Ripper* is a resourceful, gun-toting, beautiful woman who is the voice of reason and sanity. The monster of the film, in this case a genetically engineered human, cocoons people (Alex) just as the aliens do in the Cameron picture, and Thor even sports a similar biological killing mechanism. While the famous xenomorph of *Aliens* has a ferocious silver jaw tucked inside another jaw which often protrudes and smashes the faces of its victims, the creature in *Mind Ripper* has not an inner jaw but an inner tusk which also smashes the faces of victims. The character of Alex in *Mind Ripper* is also an *Aliens* retread. Like Paul Reiser's space yuppie Carter Burke, Alex is a selfish and ambitious capitalist acting on his own agenda in order to attain wealth. Even the fact that the creature is being developed for an agency the (U.S. army) mimics the first *Alien* picture.

Mind Ripper opens in the installation cafeteria with small talk among the crew, and one scientist complains about the "bonuses," mimicking almost word-for-word Yaphet Kotto's remarks about the "bonus situation" in an early scene in *Alien*. Later, Joanne (Claire Stansfield) sticks her head up a vent shaft and (in close up) points a flashlight around in search of the monster, a shot-by-shot rerun of a sequence in *Aliens* wherein Corp. Hicks (Michael Biehn) uses a flashlight in an overhead compartment to search out the bad guys. Damningly, the *Mind Ripper* scientists also hunt Thor with a portable tracking device which bleeps at appropriate moments ... again like the devices used by the colonial marines in *Aliens*. Even the failed attempt to lure Thor into a vault and lock him there is reminiscent of Ripley's plan to trap the xenomorph inside the Fury 161 installation in *Alien³*. Just as the obnoxious warden is pulled up through the ceiling in that David Fincher film, so is the obnoxious Alex carried away in *Mind Ripper*. Even the nicely shot and composed opening sequence of *Mind Ripper*, which scans the dingy corridors of the nuclear waste dump, is repetitive of Ridley Scott's first pan through the vacant *Nostromo* in the opening of *Alien*.

Mind Ripper's regurgitation of the *Alien* saga and *Alien* clichés is quite thorough. Casting is a problem too: Star Lance Henriksen is an *Aliens* and *Alien³* veteran himself! Recognizing the *Alien* templates in *Mind Ripper* is not difficult; this author has used them all himself in a 1993 amateur film titled *Intruder*, shot in the winding basement of the University of Richmond's Biology Department in 1992-1993. That film is no more original than *Mind Ripper*; unfortunately, *Mind Ripper* also appears to have been shot in a basement, although the crew had to trek all the way to Bulgaria to find it!

Perhaps if *Mind Ripper* were the first film to follow the templates set down by *Alien*, its lack of originality would not be bothersome. One must consider, however, that *Wes Craven Presents Mind Ripper* also follows *Deepstar Six* (1989), *Leviathan* (1989), *Predator 2* (1990), *Dark Universe* (1992), *Deep Space* (1987), *Galaxy of Terror* (1981), *Forbidden World* (1982) and innumerable others. By 1995 and *Mind Ripper*, the concepts of *Alien* and its progeny had been exploited and re-worked by every filmmaker from B-grade schlockmeister Fred Olen Ray to prestige director George Cosmatos. The tough-talking female lead, the diverse ensemble, the traitor of the group, the alien bug hunt, the duplicitous outside organization and the transforming monster are concepts that have been worn threadbare in modern cinema.

Way back in 1972, Craven directed *The Last House on the Left*, a picture that was a remake of *The Virgin Spring*. It re-interpreted the story of Bergman's film and changed the context of the tale from a religious one to an existentialist one. It was therefore much more than a derivative clone of another work. Contrarily, *Mind Ripper* is content to simply trot out the same *Alien* clichés that audiences had been familiar with for over a decade; it introduces no new spin on the old material.

The *Alien* saga is not the only source which *Mind Ripper* references. In some senses, it also explores the same territory as *The Hills Have Eyes*: A dysfunctional family with an alienated son goes on a camping trip but is waylaid in the desert. Once there, lives are threatened and the siblings are forced to overcome society's conventions and use their father's corpse (for his hand-print) to escape the installation. Unlike *The Hills Have Eyes*, however, *Mind Ripper* cops out in its finale. The father is not dead after all, and his children need not resort to such gruesome measures to survive. In *Mind Ripper*, the Stocktons only lose boyfriend Mark ... which the father was eager to do since the start of the film anyway! By the end of *Mind Ripper*, Scott's feelings of alienation have subsided and the family is miraculously healed even though the son's feelings have not really been confronted. This facile reconciliation would never occur in a film constructed personally by psychology expert Wes Craven who, love him or hate him, always strives for honesty in the pictures he directs. Even *A Stranger in Our House*, which saw the Bryant family happily reunited, ended on a sour note with the patriarch claiming to remember "nothing" of his infidelity, and with the menace of the picture (Julia) living to torment another middle-class family. *Mind Ripper*'s conclusion hints rather unbelievably that an external crisis can heal real internal pain.

Besides the *Alien* riffs and hard-to-swallow family dynamics, *Mind Ripper* is dominated by other problems. The central monster portrayed by Dan Blom is unabashedly lame. Thor is simply a long-haired body-builder in tight blue gym pants and a T-shirt! Although he wears yellow contact lenses and a modified head appliance at times, Thor is a very low-budget villain all the way. A low budget need not be a handicap, as *The Last House on the Left*, *The Hills Have Eyes* and *Deadly Blessing* dramatically proved, but those films never promised more than they could deliver. They avoided supernatural makeups and other expensive gimmicks that the budget could not afford, concentrating instead on "human" horror. *Mind Ripper*, which is about a genetically engineered superman, offers a creation less imaginative than virtually any low-budget pictures of the 1950s. *It! The Terror from Beyond Space* was a low-budget picture, too, but it created an interesting monster instead of a buff Fabio look-alike.

Mind Ripper's screenplay, which Craven did *not* write, is pretty weak, and all the characters are cardboard figures who speak in the peculiar movie language known as "exposition speak." "Does anyone remember we're out here in this abandoned nuclear dump?" one character asks, alerting the audience to the movie's locale. "He quit because of how we were using his research. Do you think he's gonna come back?" another character asks, awkwardly filling the audience in on some important character back-history. Unlike Craven's artful dialogue (remember the "Willow" and "Agatha Greenwood" interludes in *The Last House on the Left* and the Pirandellian speech in *Wes Craven's New Nightmare*?), *Mind Ripper* is resolute in its artlessness. The script is filled with sketchy dialogue like the dreadful lines listed above, including Ribisi's unfortunate joke to Solomon that he "couldn't get a piece of ass" if he were "a toilet seat." It is no surprise that even the best performers in *Mind Ripper* stumble with this lackluster material. Natasha Wagner, Giovanni Ribisi (who would later suffer through another bad script together in *Lost Highway*) and Adam Solomon play stereotypical "stupid" teens. Unlike the kids in *Scream*, these teenagers are spectacularly *un*-self-aware and overly preoccupied with those old *Friday the 13th* clichés: sex, drugs and rock and roll.

Amidst all of its missteps in originality, execution, writing and performance, *Mind Ripper* has some good moments worthy of mention. Director Joe Gayton effectively opens the picture with a high angle shot, far above the craggy terrain of a desert. The locale is instantly established from this distance as a forbidding and isolating one, the perfect setting for a horror picture. Then Gayton cuts to P.O.V. shots from Thor's perspective as the scientists administer the virus to him. Faces are lit against a black backdrop and there are closeups of the hypodermic syringe. Throughout this interlude, the camera sways back and forth ever so slowly, suggesting Thor's groggy and disoriented state. After eerie tracking shots of his basement complex, Gayton rapidly creates a link between Thor's hearing and the day-to-day noises of the research group. Closeups of Thor's ears are cut with the sound effects of Joanne showering, Alex boxing and two other scientists talking. This juxtaposition of sound effects and images adeptly illustrate that Jim's creation has superhuman auditory capabilities. To Gayton's credit, this opening is well directed, and the first ten minutes of *Mind Ripper* are stylish and interesting. But the camera soon becomes mired in one basement corridor after the other.

Unfortunately, *Mind Ripper*'s climax is also a botch job. Once the survivors have left the complex in the black van, the music grinds to a dead halt. In *Aliens*, James Horner's pulse-pounding score maintained the momentum of climax upon climax until viewers were left breathless. Without effective music accompanying the action in *Mind Ripper*, Thor's subsequent two attacks on the van and final assault on the airplane are totally lacking in suspense or excitement. *Mind Ripper*'s denouement sits blandly on the screen without generating any feeling other than indifference. As Randy knowingly warns Sidney in *Scream*, this is the point "where the supposedly dead killer comes back from the dead for one last scare." That "last scare" is attempted 3 times in *Mind Ripper*'s finale, and not one of them is jolting. As far back as 1991 and *The People Under the Stairs*, Craven had the good sense not to succumb to clichés and offer up the final "jolt." He purposely cut out Everett McGill's ascension from the slime pit from the final version of *The People Under the Stairs*, ended *New Nightmare* on a peaceful note and closed *A Vampire in Brooklyn* with a comedy sequence instead of the requisite "jump." *Scream 2* did feature a final jump, but it was a surprise where the jolt originated from. *Mind Ripper* has not learned from its executive producer's fine example.

Mind Ripper does succeed for one brief moment in creating sympathy for Thor. The best scene in the film is one between creator and child, Jim Stockton and Thor. Thor remembers a father who was kind to him, and so he spares Stockton's life. Thor's questions about his existence, God and his own mortality elevate this picture above its derivative roots. For a few moments, the picture seems to be going for a *King Kong* or *Frankenstein* feeling of sympathy and, for the most part, attains that. Jim is obviously an absentee father not only to his biological children but to Thor as well.

Like *Frankenstein*, *Mind Ripper* can easily be read as an indictment of bad fathers. Like Victor Frankenstein, Jim assumes no responsibility for his creation, and death and murder ensues. Unfortunately, this aspect of *Mind Ripper* is an aborted one and, by the end of the film, everyone (including "daddy" Jim) is committed to killing the tragic Thor. Yet it is rewarding that even for a minute, *Mind Ripper* sought to overcome two-dimensional thinking and give its starring monster a point-of-view. Had it continued thoughtfully on those lines, it might have found a place outside of its *Alien* trappings.

Mind Ripper is a weak motion picture which succinctly explains why the horror genre was considered dead in the mid-'90s. It recycles old material without invention, fails to create interesting characters, and is not scary in the slightest. Joe Gayton can obviously direct capably and Jonathan Craven can certainly write a good screenplay, so one can only hope that these talents will work on more original material soon.

Wes Craven Presents Wishmaster (1997)

... a washout in its painfully obvious attempt to launch a new horror franchise... Kurtzman clumsily apes the *Elm Street* mix of mass carnage, smart-alecky wisecracks and bizarre make-up effects.— Joe Leydon (*Variety:* "*Wishmaster:* A Bloody Mess," September 22, 1997)

Though the name of Wes Craven, director of *A Nightmare on Elm Street*, is draped over the film's advertising, the fact is that this tedious excursion into ancient legend and gory modern special effects credits him only as executive producer. The director of *Wishmaster*, which is notable for its weak acting and lack of suspense, is Robert Kurtzman, who arrives by way of makeup of such films as *Alien*.— Lawrence Van Gelder (*The New York Times*, September 20, 1997)

CAST: Tammy Lauren (Alex Amberson); Andrew Divoff (Djinn); Tony Crane (Josh); Nick Merritt (Chris Lemmon); Jenny O'Hary (Prof. Wendy Derleth); Wendy Benson (Shannon Amberson); Robert Englund (Raymond

Beaumont); Tony Todd (Johnny Valentine); Kane Hodder (Merritt's Guard); Theodore Raimi (Ed Finney); Reggie Bannister (Pharmacy Owner); George "Buck" Flower (Street Bum).

CREDITS: Live Film and Mediaworks, Inc. A Pierre David Production. *Writer:* Peter Atkins. *Director:* Robert Kurtzman. *Casting:* Cathy Henderson-Martin, Dori Zuckerman. *Special Makeup Effects:* Robert Kurtzman, Greg Nicotero, Howard Berger. *Visual Effects Supervisor:* Thomas C. Rainone. *Costume Designer:* Karyn Wagner. *Music:* Harry Manfredini. *Editor:* David Handman. *Production Designer:* Deborah Raymond, Dorian Dernacchio. *Director of Photography:* Jacques Haitkin. *Line Producer:* Russ Markowitz. *Executive Producer:* Wes Craven. *Co-Producer:* David Tripet. *Producers:* Pierre David, Clark Peterson, Noela Zonitzch. *Assistant Producer:* Erik Satzgan. *Set Designer:* Jackson Bishop. *Video Playback:* Mark Hindle. *Script Supervisor:* Licia Wolf. *Key Grip:* Stephen B. Martinez. *Sound Mixer:* James Hilton. *Sound Design:* Philip Seretti. *Costume Designer:* Heather Pain. *Musical Supervision:* Ed Gerrard. *First Assistant Director:* Dave Tanaka. *Additional Visual Effects:* Gary J. Tunnicliffe, Imagine Animations, Inc. *Digital Visual Effects:* Digital Magic Co., Computer Cafe, Inc. Area 51, Inc., 2G Effects. *Running Time:* 91 minutes. *MPAA Rating:* R

SYNOPSIS: In the Kingdom of Persia, circa 1127 A.D., a curious King asks a Djinn to show him wonders. The Djinn, an individual of an evil race that dwells between worlds and was created from fire, grants the ruler's naive wish and wreaks havoc upon the King's audience. One unfortunate man is hurled across the great hall and turned to stone. Another is transformed into a living skeleton. A woman becomes a human tree and one poor soul is reshaped into a lizard/human hybrid. The Djinn then informs the King that only by asking for his last of three wishes can the people of Persia be freed. The King almost acquiesces, but a resourceful sorcerer intervenes. The wise sorcerer warns his majesty that if his third wish is granted, the Djinn will be permitted to open the gates between worlds. Once the gate is open, the Djinn's people will swarm upon the Earth and enslave humanity. The sorcerer then uses a beautiful opal to expel the Djinn back to the netherworld.

In present-day America, Raymond Beaumont and his assistant Ed Finney wait on a loading dock and watch anxiously as a priceless statue is unloaded from a recently docked cargo ship. Beaumont is a wealthy collector who has paid a fortune to own the prized statue of the pre-Islamic God called Ahura Mazda. The crane operator aboard the ship has been drinking and the crate sways dangerously as it is lowered to the dock. Finney panics and screams at the crane operator. The drunken worker panics too and accidentally releases the crate. It crushes Finney and the priceless statue is destroyed. As several dock workers gather the pieces, one man finds a jewel amidst the stones of the shattered statue. He pockets it and nobody notices.

Not long after the dock incident, a pawnbroker arrives at Regal Auctioneers and asks to have the rare jewel appraised. He has purchased it from the dishonest dock worker for a few hundred dollars, but suspects it is worth far more. Nick, the boss at Regal Auctioneers, promises to get his best gemologist, Alex Amberson, right on it. But Alex is not working in the office that morning; she is at a nearby park playing tennis with her friend Josh, who works at a local university. He is her best friend and wants to become more than that.

Alex later heads back to Regal Auctioneers and is asked to appraise the fire opal. She studies the gem and notes its unique qualities and excellent translucence. She blows air on it to polish the stone and something stirs within it. Alex hears a voice whisper, "You woke me." She takes it to Josh and asks him to conduct a laser analysis. While Josh works on the stone, Alex heads off to coach a girl's basketball team. Her team is not performing well and Alex reminds the players that to succeed in competition, they must find the "stillness" inside. Time should not exist; they should only see the basket!

When Josh performs a laser analysis, there is an explosion in the lab. Josh is badly wounded and the lab erupts in fire. Far away, Alex senses he is in danger and calls the lab, but there is no answer. A badly injured Josh watches as a monster materializes beside him. A slimy and disgusting thing, it approaches the dying man. It confides that it can ease Josh's suffering if only Josh will ask. Josh does ask and the beast kills him, ending his anguish. Alex has a vision of Josh's death and rushes to the university. By the time she arrives, the police are already there, and Detective Nathanson informs Alex that Josh is dead. The cause of death is listed as an equipment malfunction.

Elsewhere in the city, a starving bum follows customers into a pharmacy, begging for money. A pharmacist argues with the derelict and demands that he leave at once. As the bum heads back into his alley, he is confronted by the now-grown Djinn, who offers to make a deal with him. He will kill the arrogant pharmacist in exchange for the bum's soul. The bum thinks this strange hooded creature is a lunatic and agrees to his terms. He says he "wishes" the pharmacist would contract cancer and die. The Djinn grants the bum his wish and Alex sees the results in her mind as the pharmacist convulses and dies, his face and body bubbling with cancerous lesions. "Was it worth it?" the Djinn wonders as the bum runs away, frightened.

At Alex's apartment, she tells her sister Shannon that she blames herself for Josh's death. She thinks there was something weird in the opal that caused the explosion. Shannon sees how seriously Alex is taking the death of her friend and wonders if she needs to see a therapist again. (Alex had a recent nervous breakdown following a family tragedy. Her house caught on fire and Alex was able to pull Shannon from the flames, but her parents died in the blaze.) Alex assures Shannon that she is fine, but later that night, she has a terrible nightmare about the fire and the Djinn communicates with her again. He tells her that he can smell her fear.

The next morning, Alex visits the docks and confronts the worker who stole the opal. She has traced him from the pawnshop and threatens to involve the police if he does not tell her where he found the unusual stone. He tells her about the dock accident and Beaumont's statue. While Alex heads for the Beaumont mansion, the Djinn travels to the School of Medicine. He peels off Josh's dead face and transforms into a devilishly handsome young man. This will be his new face while he is on Earth. He is confronted in the morgue by a young anatomy student. The student says that he wishes not to see what the Djinn is doing, so the Djinn accommodates him by causing skin to fold up over the student's eyes!

At Beaumont's estate, Alex learns the details of the dock accident. She asks him about the Ahura Mazda statue and learns that Ahura was an ancient deity who was both good and bad. Then Beaumont gives Alex a tour of his gallery, where he has a room devoted to ancient gods. After suggesting that Alex meet with an antiquities professor at the university, Beaumont invites Alex to an upcoming party. Still curious about the gem, Alex meets Dr. Derleth, a professor in the Folklore Department. In ancient Persia, Dr. Derleth reveals, a sorcerer imprisoned a Djinn with a sacred stone like the one Alex describes. The professor asserts that Djinn are not cute or funny like Barbara Eden on *I Dream of Jeannie*. They are the "face of fear" themselves. The Djinn were created by God after the angels but before mankind. Although they are obliged to grant wishes, their evil desire is to usurp our world and leave their nether region. They are driven by ancient and unending malevolence.

While Alex learns about her enemy, the Djinn works his mischief. He buys himself a new wardrobe at a department store and meets a young cashier who wishes to remain beautiful forever. The Djinn grants her wish and she is transformed into a mannequin. Then he visits Detective Nathanson at the police department. The detective refuses to give the stranger Alex's address, but he says he would do anything just to nail a wily suspect for murder. The wishmaster takes him at his wish and causes the suspect to go on a killing spree in the precinct house. The detective shoots him dead and his wish to nail his opponent is fulfilled. While the detective is busy, cleaning up the mess, the Djinn learns that Alex is employed at Regal Auctioneers.

Reading further about the Djinn, Alex learns that the opal is actually a powerful talisman called the Stone of Sacred Fire. It is both a curse and a blessing because it opens doorways to other worlds. The Djinn must charge the stone with human souls to whom he has granted one wish. However, he must grant three wishes to the person who brought him into this world if he plans to open the door to his world and allow his people to conquer the Earth. Alex realizes that she is the person the Djinn seeks. As she makes this realization, the Djinn kills a Regal Auctioneers security guard. At first, Nick refuses to give the Djinn Alex's home address, but then the Djinn grants his wish for a million dollars. Nick does not know it but his mother dies in a plane crash and he is the beneficiary of her life insurance policy!

Tracking Alex to basketball practice, the Djinn watches as she tries to contact Prof. Derleth again. He borrows her cellular phone and hits the redial button. He then proceeds to Derleth's house and kills her. He sits down on her sofa and claims that which he is owed, the souls of those unfortunate people he has made "deals" with. The stone is charged and Alex feels terrible pain as the bum, the anatomy student, the department store cashier, the detective, the guard and Nick are all drained of their souls.

Disguised as Prof. Derleth, the Djinn tells Alex that all the sorcerers are dead and that all the spells Alex seeks are lost to time. The Djinn is the only magical thing left in a world of reason. Hence, there is no way to stop him. Alex soon realizes she is talking to her mortal enemy and the Djinn changes back to his demonic form. He says it is time for her to be granted her three wishes. Alex refuses to comply, but the Djinn offers to give her one "free" wish. Alex agrees and wishes the Djinn would blow his brains out. The Djinn complies but since he is eternal, he cannot die. Hoping to learn more, Alex makes her first wish. She wants to know what the Djinn is.

Alex and the Djinn are suddenly transported to a realm of red-hot terror where the Djinn tortures human souls from his perch on a magnificent throne. Alex runs from a terrifying dog-like monster and finally makes her second wish: She wants to be returned home to her apartment. Before he grants this wish, the Djinn warns Alex that the next soul he steals will be Shannon's! Once Alex is returned home, she discovers that her sister is at Beaumont's party. She rushes to intercept Shannon before the Djinn traps her. The Djinn pursues Alex to the Beaumont home but is prevented from entering the party by Johnny Valentine, the macho doorman. The Djinn tempts him with a more exciting job and asks Valentine if he would like to escape. When Valentine admits that he would, he ends up in a glass container, drowning underwater with his hands tied behind his back ... a situation only Houdini could escape from.

Inside the party, Alex looks for Shannon while the Djinn meets with Beaumont. The Djinn tells him of the party in ancient Persia where a djinn showed the king wonders beyond human imagination. Beaumont remarks that he would "like to host a party like that" and the Djinn grants his wish. The party is turned into a literal hell as people are tortured. One woman turns to glass and is shattered. The piano plays by itself and then piano wire is stretched around a man's head. Watching as another man catches fire, the Djinn comments that he loves the music of human agony. He then tells Alex that all she has to do is wish it all away. Knowing that would enable the Djinn to cross over to Earth and torture humanity for all of time, Alex refuses. She escapes down a dark corridor as Beaumont's priceless statues come to life. Beaumont's guards shoot at the creatures but it is no use. Alex runs through a vault of horrors and is finally cornered in the room of the ancient gods. She looks for Shannon there, but the Djinn has already trapped Alex's sister inside a painting! Even worse, the Djinn has caused the artwork to burn. Shannon will soon die unless Alex makes her final wish.

Alex remembers her own coaching advice and finds the "still spot" inside her heart. Steeled, she finally makes her third wish. She wishes that the dock worker who dropped the Ahura Mazda crate two days ago was not drinking on the job! This wish is granted and time is undone. The Djinn realizes he has lost the battle and time is reversed. Because the dock worker was not inebriated, the statue was not shattered and the troublesome opal is never found. Thus Josh and all the rest are never killed by the Djinn!

Realizing how precious time really is, Alex agrees to start a romantic relationship with her friend Josh. In another realm, the wishmaster awaits another opportunity to escape eternal imprisonment between dimensions.

COMMENTARY: Although *Wes Craven Presents Wishmaster* met with savage reviews from mainstream critics, it is not a terrible horror film at all. To the contrary, it is an above-average picture and a tremendous improvement over *Wes Craven Presents Mind Ripper*. It looks and feels like a variation on the *A Nightmare on Elm Street* and *Hellraiser* franchises, and like those horror "epics," *Wishmaster* deals in Craven-esque "rubber reality." It also spotlights the efforts of a charismatic anti-hero (like Freddy Krueger) to destroy the forces of good. As is the standard now for the genre, the devilish creature is opposed in his plans by a feisty independent (and beautiful) woman. What makes *Wishmaster* slightly better than average is the spectacular special effects work, the cameos by horror-icons, and the hellish party scenes which book-end the film.

If *Wishmaster* has any obvious antecedent, it is probably 1992's *Hellraiser III: Hell on Earth*, a film which saw *Star Trek: Deep Space Nine*'s Terry Farrell attempt to prevent the villainous Cenobite called Pinhead (Doug Bradley) from opening the gateway to Hell in New York City. The plucky Farrell, not unlike the plucky Tammy Lauren in *Wishmaster*, sought to prevent this blending of worlds by evading the monster. Unfortunately, he made this difficult by killing those who were close to her, including a friendly cameraman and a likable young waif. If one substitutes a gem expert and Alex's sister for those supporting characters, the plots of *Hell on Earth* and *Wishmaster* are virtually identical, down to shifts into terrifying dimensions and grisly party scenes in which innocent people are slaughtered wholesale. The mass murders, set at a night club in *Hellraiser III* and at an extravagant party in *Wishmaster*, are the special effects centerpieces of both films. Also quite similar is the villain's "personal" relationship with the protagonist. The despicable Pinhead and the evil Djinn gain a sort of respect for their female opponents and share a cat-and-mouse relationship with them after being released from their respective prisons/statues. These plot similarities are hardly coincidental since *Wishmaster* scribe Tony Atkins also wrote *Hellraiser III* and its follow-up *Hellraiser IV: Bloodline*.

The Djinn, like Pinhead or Freddy Krueger, also utilizes the psychological weaknesses of his victims against them. Just as Freddy lured poor Joey to his death in *Nightmare III* by taking on the guise of a pretty nurse, and sucked the air out of an asthmatic teenager in *Nightmare IV*, so does the Djinn exploit the souls he requires to charge the all-powerful opal stone. As Pinhead expertly manipulates victims to open the lament configuration puzzle box in various *Hellraisers*, the Djinn coaxes his victims into making wishes that actually work against them. These wishes, like the dream sequences in the *Nightmare on Elm Street* series or the hooks and chains scenes of the *Hellraiser* pictures, are the major set pieces of *Wishmaster*. Fortunately, they are pretty amazing in their hellish imagery. With KNB effects director Robert Kurtzman directing *Wishmaster*, the special effects are never anything less than amazing and mind-bending. Extraordinary and grotesque, the wishes run the gamut from sublime (the life insurance policy on Nick's mother) to over-the-top (Reggie Bannister's sudden bout with cancer). For that reason, *Wishmaster* is never dull to watch as visual fantasy. The film even has a modicum of wit as it nicely exploits its ad line "Be careful what you wish for... " Since it follows a consistent motif, Kurtzman's film is also more linear and action-packed than *Freddy's Dead: The Final Nightmare*, the late *Friday the 13th* sequels or even *Hellraiser IV*. Still, even such a comparison is not much of a compliment considering the low quality of those productions. The formula of bloody set piece followed by wisecrack quickly wears out its welcome in *Wishmaster* and again reminds one of Freddy Krueger's juicy *bon mots*. And although Andrew Divoff is slick as the chain-smoking Djinn and Tammy Lauren is just fine as Alex, their performances are a notch below recent high genre standards set by pictures such as *I Know What You Did Last Summer*, *Event Horizon*, *Breakdown*, *Mimic* and Craven's own *Scream*. The characters never seem real (or intelligent), especially after the fine efforts made by performers in those other pictures.

It is hard to be attentive to *Wishmaster* for long because it feels so disturbingly "retro," very much like the two-dimensional product which nearly killed the genre in the late '80s. Because it resembles a *Nightmare on Elm Street* film of the 1987-89 vintage, *Wishmaster* seems stale, as if it has been sitting on a shelf somewhere for almost a decade.

Although there is little suspense or true terror in *Wishmaster* (trademarks of the films directed by Craven), there is much horror and a plethora of "gross out" moments throughout. For many horror fans looking for a Freddy or Pinhead sequel, those elements are more than enough to satisfy them, but sadly *Wishmaster* is not the fourth or fifth film in a continuing horror story; it is the first. If it were compared to the real terror evident in Craven's original *A Nightmare on Elm Street* or in Clive Barker's grisly, blood-drenched *Hellraiser* (1987), it would come up short. Still, the picture is competent and Robert Kurtzman can definitely direct horror ably. For his next project, he should eschew special effects and concentrate on a really good, scary story. *Wishmaster* proves he is skilled enough to work with superior dramatic material.

Beyond its fantastic special effects, *Wishmaster* remains interesting by throwing modern horror icons into its brew of gross-out special effects and devilish wisecracks. Robert Englund ("Freddy Krueger"), Tony Todd ("Candyman"),

Kane Hodder ("Jason Voorhees"), Reggie Bannister ("Reggie") and familiar faces such as Theodore Raimi (*Shocker, SeaQuest DSV*) and George Buck Flower (*They Live*) make the picture a sort of "who's who" of horror movies and it is delightful to see all of them. Unfortunately, they each have only a few minutes of screen time and merely play victims of the Djinn. Of all the legends, Englund probably fares best as Beaumont as he is afforded the most screen time. Although *Wishmaster* will go down in history because it joined all these horror stars together for some gruesome partying, people may also recall that their presence is mostly wasted. After all, what self-respecting horror fan wants to watch Tammy Lauren and Andrew Divoff when they could be seeing Englund, Todd, Hodder or Bannister doing their thing? The presence of so many prominent genre stars (as well as Craven's name over the title) actually diminishes *Wishmaster*'s chances of success. With Craven's name and the involvement of so many stars, expectations for the picture are understandably high. Had the picture come out without trumpeting Craven's moniker and the cast presence of the horror legends, people might have been more willing to overlook the film's flaws. Still, it is great to see Hodder (gone since 1993), Todd (gone since 1995), Englund (gone since 1995) and Bannister (gone since 1995) back in a genre setting.

Despite some flaws, *Wishmaster* has a nice dramatic structure. Disgusting but spectacular party scenes begin and end the film and give it a nice unity that is lacking in later *Hellraiser* or *Elm Street* ventures. These scenes provide not only literate cohesion, but show-stopping special effects that serve to rattle audiences. Statues come to life, piano wire decapitates victims, people are turned to stone and glass, etc. It is a showcase for virtuoso special effects work, and Kurtzman captures it all on film with finesse. If the industry were not prejudiced against low-budget horror films, *Wishmaster* would surely earn an Academy Award nomination for best special effects in 1997.

With *Wes Craven Presents Wishmaster*, the *Wes Craven Presents* umbrella series shows signs of noticeable improvement. It is better than *Mind Ripper* and it gives one hope that the next film in the umbrella series will be better still. It would be nice to see Kurtzman directing a third picture, one with more concentration on characterization and terror and less on the fantastic special effects. As for the evil Djinn of *Wishmaster*, he may yet be back. The film opened on September 19, 1997, and made $10.3 million. By the week of September 26, its earnings dropped down to $6 million. By Halloween of 1997, the picture was mostly gone from first-run theaters, a victim of blockbusters such as *In & Out*, *The Peacemaker* and the better-acted and scarier *I Know What You Did Last Summer*. Still, it was judged a success by many. A third *Wes Craven Presents* picture has also been accounced: *Wes Craven Presents Carnival of Souls*.

Chapter 5

The Television Series

The Twilight Zone (1985)

Writer/producer Rod Serling is an icon in modern American pop culture and *The Twilight Zone* (1959–64) is his greatest legacy. That well-loved TV series, which has aired non-stop in syndication around the world for almost 40 years and inspired comic books, magazines and even a 1983 feature film, is his inspired vision; Serling penned more episodes of the series (over 90 of the almost 160 stories) than any other scribe. In the 1985 TV season, 20 years after *The Twilight Zone*'s demise, anthologies were the flavor of the month again on American network TV: In one season, viewers were treated not only to Steven Spielberg's *Amazing Stories* and *Alfred Hitchcock Presents* but a CBS revival of *The Twilight Zone*.

Since Serling passed away in 1975 (after the cancellation of his second anthology series, *Night Gallery*), the *Twilight Zone* revival was peopled by a new staff of executives, writers and directors. Executive producer Philip DeGuere (*Otherworld* [1985], *Simon and Simon* [1984–1991]), executive story consultant Alan Brennert (*Wonder Woman* [1978–80], *Buck Rogers in the 25th Century* [1979–81]), story editor Rockne O'Bannon and creative consultant Harlan Ellison provided the core of this new team and dedicated the new series to defining what they called "the mortal dreads ... the things we fear on a day-to-day basis translated into fantasy terms."[1]

Also present during the genesis of this TV resurrection was Wes Craven, a long-time friend of Phil DeGuere. Fresh off the success of *A Nightmare on Elm Street*, Craven was anxious to prove on *The Twilight Zone* that he could tell compelling human stories outside the confines of the horror genre.

On Stage Eight at CBS/Studio City on Monday, March 11, 1985, the revival began lensing.[2] Although the series would weather rugged times, including the departure of Ellison in November 1985 after network interference, it still managed to run for two years on CBS during the eight P.M. timeslot before running for another year in syndication under the guidance of J. Michael Straczynski.

Craven was involved primarily during *The Twilight Zone*'s first season and he directed seven segments of the hour-long series, each shot over a period of four 10–15 hour days. The general format was different from the original *Twilight Zone*. Although the CBS revival show ran for an hour, it would sometimes have as many as three segments per hour, all of varying lengths. Craven directed the segments which served as the series premiere of September 27, 1985: "Shatterday" (by Harlan Ellison, starring Bruce Willis) and "A Little Peace and Quiet" (written by James Crocker, starring Melinda Dillon).

The remainder of the series was equally well cast with many talented actors entering the *Twilight Zone*. Among the more notable were Meg Foster (*Leviathan, They Live*) in "Dreams for Sale," Dee Wallace (*The Hills Have Eyes*) in "Wish Bank," Adrienne Barbeau (*Swamp Thing*) in "Teacher's Aide," Martin Kove (*The Last House on the Left*) in "Opening Day," Martin Landau (*Space: 1999*) in "The Beacon," Anne Twomey (*Deadly Friend*) in "Her Pilgrim Soul," Jonathan Frakes (*Star Trek: The Next Generation*) in "But Can She Type?", John Glover (*Gremlins II: The New Batch*) and Jeff Yagher (*V*) in "The Once and Future King," Tom Skerritt (*Picket Fences*) in "What Are Friends For?", Mimi Meyer-Craven (*Swamp Thing, Chiller*) in "Wordplay" with Joseph Whipp (*Chiller, A Nightmare on Elm Street, Scream*) and even Craven himself in "Children's Zoo."

Craven was not the only director of merit involved in the production. Sigmund Neufeld, Jr. (*Battlestar Galactica*), William Friedkin (*The Exorcist*), Peter Medak (*Space: 1999, Species 2*), Joe Dante (*Gremlins*), John Milius (*Conan the Barbarian*), Gerd Oswald (*Star Trek, The Outer Limits*), Martha Coolidge (*Real Genius*) and Jeannot Szwarc (*Somewhere in Time*) all steered various segments. All in all, *The Twilight Zone* was a prestigious gig all around, with good stories coming from Harlan Ellison, David Gerrold, Jim McBride, George R.R. Martin, Alan Brennert, Stephen King and even from the shelf of Rod Serling.

The Twilight Zone was a good forum for Craven. He skillfully directed suspenseful stories ("Shatterday," "Chameleon"), ironic ones ("Dealer's Choice," "A Little Peace and Quiet") and, best of all, a tender love story called "Her Pilgrim Soul." For those fans who think Craven is a one-note horror man, this addition to his portfolio proves otherwise in dramatic and entertaining fashion. Fans of his work are encouraged to search out the reruns and find "Her Pilgrim Soul," a story that quotes from William Butler Yeats and understands that real love is not between two bodies or two minds, but between two spirits.

The credits for CBS revival of *The Twilight Zone* are included below, as well as a brief description of each episode which Craven directed.

CREDITS: *The Twilight Zone Creator:* Rod Serling. *Executive Producer:* Phil DeGuere. *Producer:* Harvey Frand. *New Twilight Zone Theme Music:* The Grateful Dead and Merl Saunders. *Original Twilight Zone Theme Music:* Marius Constant. *Creative Consultant:* Harlan Ellison. *Story Editor:* Rockne O'Bannon. *Art*

Director: Jeffrey L. Goldstein, John Mansbridge. *Narrator:* Robin Ward. *Director of Photography:* Bradford May. *Editor:* Gary Blair. *Music:* William Goldstein. *Executive in Charge of Casting:* Bob Weiner. *Casting:* Gary M. Zuckerbrod. *Production Manager and Associate Producer:* Ken Swor. *Unit Production Manager:* Paul Wurtzel. *Associate Producer:* Mark Michaels. *Set Dressers:* Robert Zilliox, Rochelle Moser. *Property Master:* Jim Zemansky. *Script Supervisor:* Kenneth Gilbert. *Costume Designer:* Robert Moore. *Costume Supervisor:* Judith Grant. *Sound Design:* Mickey Hart. *Acoustic Consultant:* Betsy Cohen. *Production Sound Mixer:* Lowell Harris. *Re-Recording Mixer:* Phillip Seretti. *Sound Editor:* Jeremy Hoenack. *Music Editor:* Robert Y. Takagi. *Music Supervision:* Robert Drasnin. *Lenses and Panaflex Camera:* Panavision. *Visual Effects:* Don Lee, Price Pethel, Kevin Cox, Maury Rosenfield, Peter Sternlight, Rich Thorne. *Main Title Designed and Produced by:* Colossal Pictures. *Production Executive:* Paul Tucker. *Post Production Executive:* Cosmas P. Bolger. CBS Entertainment Productions; In Association with London Films; In Cooperation with Persistence Of Vision; Distributed by MGM/UA Telecommunications.

Episodes Directed by Wes Craven

1A. "Shatterday" (by Harlan Ellison; Airdate: September 27, 1985)

SYNOPSIS: Know-it-all, arrogant Peter Jay Novins is stunned to discover that a well-mannered doppelganger is systematically taking over his life.

CAST: Bruce Willis (Peter Jay Novins); Dan Gilvezan (Bartender); Anthony Gumbach (Bellboy)

1B. "A Little Peace and Quiet" (by James Crocker; Airdate: September 27, 1985)

SYNOPSIS: Frazzled mother and wife Penny is able to stop time and find a little peace and quiet for herself thanks to a magical piece of jewelry. A nuclear assault is launched and Penny finds that she must remain alone in a "frozen" moment lest the world be destroyed by an atomic holocaust.

CAST: Melinda Dillon (Penny); Greg Mullavey (Russell)

2A. "Wordplay" (by Rockne S. O'Bannon; Airdate: October 4, 1985)

SYNOPSIS: Businessman Bill Lowery is in danger of becoming obsolete when his sales agency unveils a vast new line of merchandise. He studies his inventory list all night and awakens the next day to discover to his alarm that the rest of the world has developed a sort of aphasia. Lowery cannot understand anything his family, his neighbors or his co-workers say to him, and he finds himself in

"A Little Peace and Quiet?" Melinda Dillon enters *The Twilight Zone* in an episode directed by Craven.

danger of becoming obsolete again. Defeated, Lowery begins to study the "new" language of his world, lest he be left behind.

CAST: Robert Klein (Bill Lowery); Annie Potts (Mrs. Lowery); Brian Bradley (Salesman); Adam Raber (Donnie Lowery); Mimi Meyer-Craven (Front Desk Secretary); Joseph Whipp (Doug).

2B. "Chameleon" (by James Crocker; Airdate: October 4, 1985)

SYNOPSIS: An alien makes trouble for space shuttle astronauts by mimicking members of the crew.

CAST: Terry O'Quinn (Lochridge); John Ashton (Chief); Ben Piaza (Dr. Hillman); Iona Morris (Annie).

3. "Dealer's Choice" (by J.D. Feigelson; Airdate: November 15, 1985)

SYNOPSIS: A man who repeatedly draws a "six" card in poker is suspected of being the Devil. This suspicion is confirmed and the Devil informs the circle of gamblers that the winner of the game will be given a terrifying prize: a one-way trip to Hell!

CAST: Morgan Freeman (Marty); Garret Morris (Jake); Dan Hedaya (Nick); M. Emmet Walsh (Peter)

4. **"Her Pilgrim Soul"** (by Alan Brennert; Airdate: December 13, 1985)

SYNOPSIS: When a human fetus appears inside a holographic generator, a scientist having marital difficulty becomes obsessed with the phenomenon. The fetus grows into the spirit of a beautiful woman named Nola who died many years ago in childbirth. She has returned from the spiritual plane to help the reincarnation of her husband find peace in his life. That reincarnation is the very scientist who has discovered her. In a tender conclusion, Nola asks her soulmate to find peace in his life and cherish the relationship he now shares with a new wife.

CAST: Kristoffer Tabori (Kevin); Anne Twomey (Nola); Gary Cole (Dan); Wendy Girard (Carol); Richard McGonagle (Lester); Nelson Welch (Ruskin); Betsy Jane Licon (Nola, age five); Dana McKellar (Nola, age ten)

5. **"The Road Less Traveled"** (by George R.R. Martin; Airdate: December 18, 1986)

SYNOPSIS: Jeff McDowell experiences terrifying visions of jungle combat in the Vietnam War ... visions that make no sense to him since he dodged the draft and missed the war altogether!

CAST: Cliff De Young (Jeff); Margaret Klenck (Denise); Jaclyn Lester (Megan); Christopher Brown (Soldier)

Nightmare Cafe (1992)

Several years after *The Twilight Zone* faded to black, Craven developed a horror property for NBC called *Nightmare Cafe*. Robert Englund starred as the owner of a peculiar cafe where regulars Jack Coleman and Lindsay Frost, along with various guest stars familiar to Craven fans (such as Angela Bassett and Brandon Adams), experienced alternate realities that forced them to examine their own lives. Though the series died after six episodes, it was later rerun on the Sci Fi Channel.

CAST: Robert Englund (Blackie); Jack Coleman (Frank Nolan); Lindsay Frost (Faye Perronovic)

CREDITS: *Creators:* Wes Craven and Thomas Baum. *Developed by* Jonathan

Craven, Peter Spears. *Senior Producer:* Marianne Maddalena. *Producers:* Bruce A. Pobjoy, Thomas Baum. *Executive Producer:* Wes Craven. *Line Producer:* Ron Colby. *Creative Consultants:* Jonathan Craven, Peter Spears. *Executive Consultant:* Phillip Noyce. *Director of Photography:* Mark Irwin. *Production Designer:* Richard Kent Wilcox. *Editors:* Richard Francis Bruce, Patrick Lussier. *Unit Production Manager:* Joseph Patrick Finn. *First Assistant Director:* Anthony Atkins. *Second Assistant Director:* Morgan James Beggs. *Music:* J. Peter Robinson. *Special Visual Effects:* Bill Millar. *Casting:* Gary M. Zuckerbrod. *Costume Designer:* Susan DeLaval. *Set Decorator:* Marti Wright. *Property Master:* Bryan D. Korenberg. *Chief Lighting Technician:* Stephen Jackson. *Key Grip:* Dillard Brinson. *Sound Mixer:* Lars Ekstrom. *Construction Coordinator:* Douglas Hardwick. *Camera Operator:* Roderick J. Pridy. *Video Playback Coordinator:* Klaus Melchoir. *Location Manager:* Todd Pittson. *Stunt Coordinator:* Jacob Rupp. *Wardrobe Supervisor:* Susan Stella. *Costume Supervisor:* Donna M. Cristiano. *Makeup Artist:* Connie Parker. *Hairstylist:* Julie McHaffie. *Special Effects:* Bill Orr. *Script Supervisor:* Jean Bereziuk. *Production Coordinator:* Carol Schafer, Wendy Lavis. *Assistants to the producers:* Jeffrey Fenner, Chris Parker. *Canadian Casting:* Trish Robinson. *Assistant Editors:* Ron Yoshida, Stein Myhrstad. *Music-Editing:* Bunny Andrews. *Re-Recording:* Gregory Watkins, John Stephens, Bill W. Benton. *Music Supervision:* Richard Kaufman. *Main Title Design:* Bill Millar, Deena Burkett. *Lab Services:* Gastown Film Labs. *Post Production Services:* Gastown Post and Transfer; Filmed at North Shore Studios, British Vancouver; Wes Craven Films in association with MGM/UA Television Productions.

> Lost somewhere between life and death, time and eternity, there are places which ... leave you forever changed. This is one such place ... each door leads ... someone to that second chance that will turn their life around and to others that reckoning that will end their sleep forever. Welcome ... to the Nightmare Cafe.

Episodes

1. "Nightmare Cafe"/"Pilot" (by Wes Craven and Thomas Baum; Directed by Phillip Noyce; Airdate: January 29, 1992)

> Good or bad, dead or alive, we get 'em all ... never suspecting this place is anything out of the ordinary, never knowing what secrets lie beyond the doors. And you have been selected to help them, and maybe learn something about yourselves along the way.
> — Blackie explains the premise of *Nightmare Cafe* to his bewildered associates

SYNOPSIS: On a dark night, Faye Perronovic drives to the bay, contemplates suicide and then jumps into the bay. As she drowns, she spots another man in the drink, Frank Nolan. Both of them disappear beneath the water, and later find themselves back on dry land. They make their way to an abandoned all-night cafe, and strange things start to occur. While changing into a dry waitress uniform in the ladies room, Faye hears someone crying. She opens a medicine cabinet and is confronted by an image of herself in despair. She slams the cabinet shut in fear.

Meanwhile, Frank turns on the cafe's television and watches as familiar images unfold. Frank is the night watchman at a nearby chemical plant and he watches on the TV as the owners of the plant plot to dump toxic chemicals in the bay. Frank

Blackie (Robert Englund) lives between dimensions in the last chance diner called *The Nightmare Cafe*.

remembers these events. In fact, he witnessed this conspiracy but did nothing to stop the dumpers. Faye watches with shock as Frank disappears into the TV. He now has an opportunity to replay the events of that night. He interferes with the dumping operation and is subsequently killed by two thugs when a truck full of toxic materials explodes. Amazingly, Frank returns to the cafe unharmed.

Faye must also replay events from that night. Her boyfriend Al is the man who runs the chemical company. Faye discovers that Al is cheating on her, and she steals a report that details the toxic dumping. Al and his goons chase Faye to the bay, but this time she jumps into the water to save her life instead of in despair. Faye and Frank are understandably confused by these events, but they soon encounter Blackie, a man who lives in the cafe. He informs them that the all-night cafe is a place for second chances. Both Frank and Fay died that night under disturbing circumstances. Faye committed suicide and Frank was murdered when he attempted to stop the dumpers. The cafe gave each tortured soul a second chance, a chance to die with dignity instead of despair. Blackie informs his two guests that they will now be employees of the cafe. Their job will be to help others receive a second chance as well.

Soon Al enters the cafe and Blackie, Frank and Faye use the mystical powers of the establishment to scare him. He walks into the bathroom and finds himself on trial for dumping toxic wastes. He runs through the kitchen and drops a hundred feet into a vat of acid. Then he wakes up, only to find himself trapped in a jail cell. As well as giving people a second chance, the cafe can deliver "justice." After ridding the world of Al, Frank and Faye receive the cafe's first new customer.

CAST: Joan Chen (First Customer); John DiAquino (Al); Philip Hayes (Driver); Carrie-Anne Moss (Amanda); Bill Croft (Thug)

COMMENTARY: The first episodes of science-fiction/fantasy series are usually the most difficult for reviewers to assess. Oftentimes, concepts and characters will change from pilot to series, as will overall story thrust. None of that happens to be true with Craven's *Nightmare Cafe*. The first episode lays down the groundwork for the series' direction, and develops the characters who will become the stars of the show.

In many science-fiction productions, story is of paramount importance, as is drawing the audience into a compelling initial adventure; viewers will usually learn about characters in bits and pieces in later stories. *Nightmare Cafe* intentionally takes the opposite route by focusing the entire debut episode on the two main characters, Frank and Faye. It also defines these people in a unique style for television. Faye is shown to be a pill-popping, suicidal loser and Frank is dramatized as a coward who would rather keep his job than rock the boat! These traits are hardly typical of the cardboard superheroes of *Star Trek: The Next Generation* or *Babylon 5,* but indicative of real people with foibles and flaws. Faye and Frank come to realize what their flaws are, and in this episode get a second chance to better their lives (or deaths). This episode promises that the series will be not only about new adventures in the cafe, but about Faye's and Frank's ongoing process of "learning about themselves." This is a wonderful idea for a genre series, but in the six episodes produced of *Nightmare Cafe*, the promise of an inner quest remained partially unfulfilled. Almost immediately, Frank and Faye became dependable additions to the cafe, never relapsing into their earlier bad behavior. By the end of the short-lived series, they have learned no more about themselves than Gopher and Isaac have learned on *The Love Boat.* Still, it is rewarding that the writers and producers had an "arc" in mind when they created *Nightmare Cafe.*

The opening hour of *Nightmare Cafe* has some dynamic moments. Robert Englund's Blackie immediately breaks the "fourth wall" and converses with the TV audience, thus taking on a role as a Rod Serling-like narrator as well as story participant. The Blackie character represents Craven's further exploration of "rubber reality." He is a character who exists inside the drama as a player, outside the drama as a narrator, and who can even shape events and people to his way of thinking. Architect, writer and player, Blackie is the perfect resident of the otherworldly cafe, another arena of "rubber reality" where a kitchen sink can be a porthole from the bay, where a bathroom stall can lead to prison, where a TV can rerun a night's events...

The cafe is as versatile as Blackie is. It is a gateway not only to inner dimensions, but also to outer ones. Like *Doctor Who*'s TARDIS (Time And Relative Dimensions In Space), it can travel through space, land all across the world, or even go backwards and forwards in time. With such a dynamic host and vehicle for adventure, Craven created one of the most flexible formats in TV history. The nightmare cafe and its employees are like the stalwart crew of the starship *Enterprise*, but instead of navigating space and discovering other worlds, they travel exclusively within the borders of the twilight zone.

This is a good concept, but many of the individual stories in *Nightmare Cafe* are, alas, not so good. The series' potential to explore infinite realities or infinite quantum possibilities is never fulfilled ... but in fairness, that is to be expected. As a rule, science fiction or fantasy programs do not find their voice in the first season, a time of experimentation, and *Nightmare Cafe* did not have time in just six episodes to grow into what could have been a multi-season hit. If the terrain, operations and mechanisms of the cafe had been explored (as *Doctor Who* explored the TARDIS) and details about Blackie's mysterious past had been further explored, the series might have become a very compelling one.

As it must inform viewers about its lead characters as well as the mechanisms of the cafe, the pilot of *Nightmare Cafe* is not particularly complex. Two down-on-their luck losers are given a second chance at redemption and are drawn into a world beyond what they perceive to be reality. Not much else happens, except the bad are punished and there is a promise of greater wonders to come. In one magnificent moment, Lindsay Frost runs to the cafe door and swings it open to be unexpectedly confronted with the vastness of interstellar space. The special effects are fabulous, the image one of pure wonder. In this sequence (and the one in which Blackie opens the door to reveal that the cafe is hovering above Earth), the series promises to forget the laws of physics and explore the infinite possibilities of human existence in a multitude of dimensions and realities. If only the series had survived long enough to undertake such a noble exploration...

The *Nightmare Cafe* pilot is directed by Phillip Noyce, director of *Dead Calm* (1989), *Sliver* (1991) and *Patriot Games* (1993). Guest stars in this episode are also familiar to genre buffs. John D'Aquino (Al) went on to become a regular on the first season of *SeaQuest DSV* and the cafe's first customer is none other than beautiful Joan Chen, the star of the sleeper *The Blood of Heroes* (1989) and villainess of *Judge Dredd* (1995).

2. "Dying Well Is the Best Revenge" (by Barry Pullman; Directed by Armand Mastroianni; Airdate: March 6, 1992)

SYNOPSIS: Angela and Edward have a bad marriage riddled with infidelity and lies. This couple becomes entangled with the otherworldly cafe when Edward is beaten and stabbed on the docks near the cafe by a man named Darrin. Frank grows increasingly attracted to Angela, apparently an abused wife, but Faye and Blackie are not sure she is quite as innocent as she appears. Although for a time they suspect Edward is involved with the Mafia, they learn that Angela and Darrin are lovers, and that Frank is being set up as a patsy to murder Edward! To put things right they must harness all the resources of the cafe.

CAST: Beth Toussaint (Angela); Justin Deas (Edward); Jo-Anne Bates (Jan); Holly Chester (Tracy); Doug Stewart (Ambulance Driver); Andrew Airlie (Darryn)

COMMENTARY: "Dying Well Is the Best Revenge" is another *Nightmare Cafe* story that suffers because of audience expectations more than anything else. Put succinctly, this tale by Barry Pullman is not a horror or fantasy story, but a tale of double-crosses, false leads and unscrupulous personalities. As such, it is undeniably entertaining but audiences who tuned in because of Craven and Robert Englund were geared (rightly or wrongly) for a more fanciful tale than this episode. Although it was never the intent of Craven or his stars to make *A Nightmare on Elm Street* every week, the series suffered because NBC promoted it as such, and the solid reputations of Craven and Englund contributed to the notion that this series was horror, not a mind-bending exploration of humanity.

Beth Toussaint, who appears here as the duplicitous Angela, also played a double-crossing siren and sister to the deceased Tasha Yar (Denise Crosby) in the 1990 episode of *Star Trek: The Next Generation* entitled "Legacy."

3. "Faye and Ivy" (by Wes Craven, Thomas Baum and John Leekley; Directed by Chris Leitch; Airdate: March 13, 1992)

SYNOPSIS: For years, Faye has been sending letters to her younger sister Ivy detailing her life as the rich paramour of an important businessman. Believing her, Ivy and her delinquent boyfriend Jesse leave home in Oklahoma to find Faye and share in her wealth. Once in the big city, Ivy and Jesse quickly run out of money and Jesse resorts to robbing a local liquor store. The Korean owner dies from a heart attack during the incident and Jesse is wanted for murder. The two youngsters end up at the Cafe, but Ivy does not recognize her own sister because it has been so many years since they have seen one another. Faye left home when Ivy was only six, and though it is too late to repair her own life, Blackie suggests it is not yet too late to save Ivy.

Embarrassed to be caught as a waitress in a lowly cafe, Faye pretends to be a friend of Faye's while Frank promises to take Jesse and Ivy to Faye's apartment. Once outside, Ivy and Jesse are pursued by police for his role in the robbery/murder and Jesse knocks out Frank and switches jackets with him. The police chase Frank, believing he is the suspect. Blackie rescues Frank in the guise of a foreign cab driver. When Frank insults the Cafe, Blackie says that the cafe is touchy. Frank is cut off from its resources; he must apologize before he can return.

Worried about Ivy, Faye telephones her mother, with whom she has not communicated in a decade. While they talk, the cafe transports Faye to her mother's home so she can see her as they converse. Faye reveals Ivy is in trouble and her mother travels to the city to retrieve her. While Ivy and Jesse are branded with tattoos (with Blackie as the artist), Frank and Faye's mother meet and go to the Cafe together. When Jesse realizes that Faye filled her letters with lies and has no money which he can steal, he turns violent and attempts to kill Ivy. After much conflict, Ivy is freed from Jesse's nefarious influence, Frank reconciles with the cafe and Faye's family is reunited for a brief time.

CAST: Molly Parker (Ivy); Peter Outerbridge (Jesse); Penny Fuller (Victoria); Randall Wong (Liquor Store Owner)

COMMENTARY: Like the later episode, "Sanctuary for a Child," "Faye and Ivy" is a *Nightmare Cafe* story that attempts to fulfill the promise laid out by Blackie in the premiere: that the series would concern Frank and Faye learning about themselves. Here Lindsay Frost's character must come to terms with a family in disarray, and is finally able to accept her own fate. "Faye and Ivy" is an interesting story, but like the premiere and "Dying Well Is the Best Revenge," it is preoccupied with petty crime and small-time crooks. John D'Aquino was the lousy boyfriend in the premiere, Justin Deas played same in "Dying Well..." and Peter Outerbridge does so here. In a series that could go anywhere in any time and tell any kind of story, the repetition of stock melodrama characters disturbing.

Nightmare Cafe lore continues to be intertwined with the major story in a small subplot. Here Frank learns that the Cafe, like *Doctor Who*'s TARDIS or even the starship *Enterprise*, has a distinct personality, and that it can even get its feelings hurt. Typical of the series, it is these moments that center on the "rules" and powers of the Cafe that are the most interesting. "Faye and Ivy" though well acted is less science fiction, less view of alternate reality, than it is kitchen-sink drama with shattered family ties and hard-luck lessons about love and the big city. There is nothing wrong with that focus, but it undoubtedly left the more "genre"-oriented viewers somewhat confused. The series was never what they expected.

4. "The Heart of the Mystery" (by Christopher Stone and Bruce Cameron; Director: John Harrison; Airdate: March 20, 1992)

SYNOPSIS: Detective Stan Gates has been obsessed with the murder of

Charlotte Benning for a decade and a half. The heiress was killed in her mansion one night while her wheelchair bound husband lay unconscious on the floor. Stan has even turned his apartment into a shrine to the dead Charlotte.

One dark night, while investigating another case, Stan is shot by a perp and dies. His soul wanders to the Cafe and Blackie shows him an image on the TV. The set shows Stan with a bullet racing towards him. Blackie reveals that he has a few seconds left before he dies and gives the man a chance to solve the mystery that has plagued him.

As the bullet inches towards his body, Stan travels back in time to solve the mystery of Charlotte's death. He finds himself in the mansion, and shoots at a skittering figure in darkness. It is Charlotte! In shock, Stan realizes that he has killed Charlotte himself. This is devastating to Stan because he and Charlotte were secret lovers ... the real reason for his obsession.

Ballistics soon confirm that it was Stan's weapon which killed the heiress, but Frankie and Faye don't believe Stan is guilty. They focus their attention on the crippled Phillip Benning and solve the mystery which has plagued Gates. Benning is not wheelchair-bound at all, as the scuff marks on his shoes reveal. Now Faye and Frank must catch the real killer before he kills again. Unfortunately, his first target is Faye...

CAST: Timothy Carhart (Detective Stan Gates); Laura Mae Tate (Charlotte Benning); Denis Forest (Phil Benning); Alfonso Quijada (Kid)

COMMENTARY: Although "Heart of the Mystery" again focuses *Nightmare Cafe*'s attention on crime and a love affair gone wrong, this story works because of its fantasy premise. Although the mystery is paramount, the premise is a distinctly *Twilight Zone* one and therefore chilling.

A well-constructed paradox keeps "Heart of the Mystery" moving at a fast clip, and there is nothing more involving for viewers than a compelling mystery. Above all, "Heart of the Mystery" demonstrates *Nightmare Cafe*'s versatility. One week it tells a kitchen-sink drama about a shattered family, the next week it offers a fantastic mystery, and then later it boasts farce and *Twin Peaks*-style humor in "Aliens Ate My Lunch." If the series had lasted longer than six weeks, it might have added hardcore horror and science fiction to its repertoire as well, and satisfied those viewers who came to the show expecting something truly weird.

5. **"Sanctuary for a Child"** (by John Leekley; Directed by Armand Mastroianni; Airdate: March 27, 1992)

"What are you doing working in a dump like this?"
— Thomas, wondering why Frank is a cook in an all-night cafe

SYNOPSIS: The cafe materializes in a beautiful town at dawn. A young black boy enters the cafe, but has no money to buy breakfast. Frank takes the boy, Luke, under his wing and offers to let him help cook breakfast in exchange for food. Luke later disappears. When Frank searches for him in the cafe's men's room, he steps into a hospital ward. There in bed is Luke. The boy has been in a coma for a year, and is only hours away from death. Frank is confused by this but even more puzzled when he leaves the hospital and realizes that Blackie and the Cafe have brought him back to Zion, his hometown.

Frank encounters Luke's spirit again, and learns that the boy is holding onto life for some reason. He is unwilling to die until things are right again between his parents. Frank recognizes Luke's parents. Luke's dad is Thomas, a local hero and Frank's former best friend. His mother is Evelyn, Frank's ex-girlfriend. Frank re-connects with his old friends and tries to get them to reconcile. At the same time, he returns home to his dad's farm and relives some painful memories. He joined the Navy at 18 and left his father behind when his dad did not approve of Frank dating Evelyn, an African-American. While in South America, Frank learned that his father passed away. He never had the chance to make things right with his own dad, and he realizes he must help Luke so the tortured spirit can move on.

Thanks to the Cafe's influence, the selfish Thomas finds himself trapped in Pirate's Cave, an abandoned mine shaft, and he realizes he has similarly abandoned Luke. Like him, Luke is trapped immobile in a coma and he needs his help. When freed, Thomas returns to Evelyn and Luke and confesses his love to the dying boy. Satisfied that things are right again between his parents, Luke's soul travels onward to the afterlife. Mourning the loss of their son, Evelyn and Thomas give their marriage a second chance. Satisfied that one father-son relationship has been healed, Frank visits his father's grave and makes his own peace.

CAST: Brandon Adams (Luke); Angela Bassett (Evelyn); William B. Davis (Doctor); Vondie Curtis Hall (Thomas); Hillary Strang (Nurse); Walter Marsh (Mr. Cartwright)

COMMENTARY: "Sanctuary for a Child" may be the best installment of the *Nightmare Cafe*. For once, the promise that a series regular will learn about himself is fulfilled; this story is as much Frank's story as it is Luke's. The well-written story begins with Blackie's on-screen narration. He mentions that a person can't "go home again," but in the sentimental finale, the opposite has been revealed: No matter how far you travel, you never truly escape your home, your family and your memories.

"Sanctuary for a Child" adds much back-story to Jack Coleman's Frank. The viewer learns he is a former Navy officer, a runaway, and that this mother died when he was very young. The story also visits his home, reveals his old loves and old friends, and demonstrates the character's resourcefulness. Although at times the story has the "weepy" feeling of *Touched By an Angel*, it is a sincere adventure told without cynicism or gimmicks. Remarkably, it does not cop out either. The Cafe does not miraculously save Luke's life, and the boy finally dies. How often does TV have the guts to let something as tragic as a child's death occur?

Fortunately, "Sanctuary for a Child" is also very well performed. A pre-stardom Angela Bassett (*A Vampire in Brooklyn*) breathes life into a stereotypical soap opera role (the grieving mother) and Brandon Adams (*The People Under the Stairs*) is energetic and moving as the doomed child. Genre fans will recognize not only these two stars of Craven productions, but actor William B. Davis, who portrays Luke's doctor. Davis is none other than "Cancer/Cigarette Man," the ongoing villain of *The X-Files*. Interestingly, Davis shows little more warmth as a physician than he does as a government agent! Maybe it's a conspiracy. Also of note is the excellent performance by Vondie Curtis Hall, late of *Eve's Bayou* (1997).

6. "Aliens Ate My Lunch" (by Wes Craven; Directed by Wes Craven; Airdate: April 3, 1992)

"...the most scary aliens of all don't come from the stars above, but the darkness of space within."— Blackie waxes philosophic after a close encounter with the mob mentality in "Aliens Ate My Lunch."

SYNOPSIS: Blackie guides the cafe to a rural town in America's heartland so Frank can have a rendezvous with his hero, *National Conspirer* columnist Harry Tambor. Desperate to find a story, Tambor has come to town to investigate livestock disappearances. Instead of investigating the case, the reporter determines to perpetrate a massive hoax. With three mysterious dwarves whom he picked up hitchhiking on a rural highway, Tambor creates his own "alien" invasion. Using a makeshift UFO, and garbing the little men in green outfits and floppy antennae, Tambor stages his extraterrestrial landing.

The town responds with a bloodthirsty attitude and sets out immediately to kill the "aliens." Once they have killed in the name of "town security," the villagers hope to open an expensive tourist trap and make a great deal of money off their discovery. The angry mob is led by Sheriff Dan Filcher, a narrow-minded red-neck.

Faye and Frank jump into the fray to help the three dwarves escape the hunt. They all return to the Cafe but are tracked there by the mob. Sheriff Dan Filcher suspects that Faye, Frank and Blackie are aliens too, and that the Cafe is their "space pod." The three midgets escape into outer space while Faye, Frank and Blackie are put before a firing squad to be executed.

Suddenly, a massive spaceship arrives overhead and "beams" Harry up. The townspeople panic, and reflect that their behavior has been pretty inexcusable. Back in the Cafe, the three midgets return. They are not humans at all, but chicken-like aliens from another galaxy. They return the stolen livestock and arrest Sheriff Filcher for violations of interstellar law. The aliens return to outer space, leaving Harry Tambor (temporarily trapped in a giant hairball) with the greatest story of his career.

CAST: Bobby Slayton (Harry Tambor); Don S. Davis (Sheriff Dan Filcher); Arturo Gil (Winston/"Wind"); Kevin Thompson (Fred/"Fire"); Jimmy Briscoe (Earl/"Earth"); Scott Swanson (Editor); Stephen E. Miller (Deputy); Suzie Payne (Drugstore Mum); Adrien Dorval (Elmore); Smitty Smith (Hardware Codger); John R. Taylor (Station Farmer)

COMMENTARY: "Aliens Ate My Lunch" is a rollicking satire which attempts to humorously make the same point as the classic *Twilight Zone* episode "The Monsters Are Due on Maple Street," a story which saw suburban neighbors revealing their inner ugliness to one another because of paranoia about invading aliens. Strangely, this Craven morality play about the mob mentality comes to *Nightmare Cafe* not only by way of *The Twilight Zone*, but by way of David Lynch's *Twin Peaks* with three mysterious midgets playing a cryptic role in the proceedings. Written and directed by Craven, "Aliens Ate My Lunch" is a story that never takes itself seriously, jumping merrily from one bizarre incident to the next. The alien costume (a cosmic chicken) is purposely silly, as is the sequence of a bewildered cow ascending heavenward. If one realizes that this story is meant to be a humorous tale with a serious point, it works. If, however, one reads this episode as a horror show, it is confusing. "Aliens Ate My Lunch" determinedly plays against audience expectations and is neither scary nor horrific in the slightest. It is not even a "serious" drama, like the other episodes of the series. Instead, it is a bold attempt by Craven to do something utterly outlandish and bizarre.

Again, the rules of the Cafe are not clear and therefore there is little tension. Since the Cafe is basically omnipotent and omniscient, the characters never really seem to be in danger. Also, the subplot concerning Harry Tambor is confusing. Is Frank supposed to learn a lesson about tabloids? Is Harry supposed to learn something about himself, and realize that he is a terrible person? These questions are raised and never resolved, lending "Aliens Ate My Lunch" a distinctly muddled atmosphere at times.

Also notable is the very expensive-looking special effects finale. The massive, cigar-shaped alien ship that appears in the sky is not actually indigenous to *Nightmare Cafe*, it is stock footage from the 1983 science-fiction thriller *Strange Invaders* which starred Paul LeMat, Nancy Allen, Louise Fletcher, June Lockhart and Kenneth Tobey! Disturbingly, this footage from Michael Loughlin's film does not edit well with *Nightmare Cafe* material. The characters below are in total darkness, yet the spaceship is hovering in a brilliant orange sky! A more interesting special effects moment occurs at the end of the show. Piece by piece, the Cafe turns to static and then vanishes into nothingness. It is a good effect and an eerie mode of travel. It was seen in other episodes of the series, but against the backdrop of night, it is positively stunning.

As in the other episodes of *Nightmare Cafe*, a little is learned about Blackie's mysterious background in this story. At one point he jokes that the last time someone attempted to shoot him it was with crossbows, indicating that he has been alive and in service of the Cafe for a very long time. These kind of enigmatic references succeeded in making Englund's the most interesting character on the series.

Another notation about the Cafe is made in this story as well. Frank is shot in the arm, and Blackie confirms that both Frank and Faye could conceivably "die" again ... this time for good. This adds that element of danger to the series that had been missing because the audience merely assumed that these characters were now invincible spirits dwelling in an all-powerful arena.

With "Aliens Ate My Lunch," Craven was clearly exploring the boundaries of his anthology-like format. He wanted his series to sport all kinds of adventures (like *The Twilight Zone*), not just drama or horror. It is a noble notion, but Craven might have done well to remember that *The Twilight Zone* comedies such as "Cavender Is Coming" and "The Mighty Casey" were uniformly rotten, as were *Amazing Stories* shows with funny aspects such as the dreadful "Fine Tuning." "Aliens Ate My Lunch" is a bit more fun than any of those adventures because it is filled with snappy lines and odd ball behavior. But it still is not a very satisfying adventure in a universe where literally anything was possible.

Chapter 6

The Battle Over Censorship

On July 10, 1997, *The Charlotte Observer* ran an editorial entitled "Mortal Combat: The Battle Over Movies and Kids." It was an opinion piece written by Kathleen Parker, a regular columnist for the *Orlando Sentinel*. In a nutshell, the article concerned Parker's ongoing battle to keep "adult" (R-rated) movies from the eyes of her curious teenager John. The war was not an easy one for Parker since so many bloody movies were being released by Hollywood, but Parker stated firmly that this was one fight she was determined to win. As "exhibit A" in her battle against violent moviemaking, Parker cited *Scream*. She declared war on *Scream* and by extension, one supposes, on all movies of the horror genre. While it is certainly admirable of Parker to take an active stance in John's viewing habits, like many conservative forces in America, Parker has again chosen the wrong target for her animosity.

Scream is not only the wittiest, most thoughtful and best directed of recent horror films, it is also a movie which carries an important message. Although Parker most certainly did not "get it," *Scream* exposes the wicked underside of modern American suburbia. For the most part, the teens in the film are people without a lick of compassion. When lead Neve Campbell states that a recent murder victim "sits next to me in English class," her best friend responds callously, "Not any more." Even the murderers in the film are painted as sociopathic teens who have never experienced pain themselves ... they've only seen it on TV! When (during the climax of the film) the killers stab each other to establish an alibi, they experience real pain for the first time and finally understand, albeit briefly, what horrible injury they have inflicted on others. It is a powerful moment in film history; *Scream* is the first motion picture to address modern teen apathy in a substantive way.

By so ingeniously crafting a film that exposes the lack of moral values among our most affluent teens, Craven and writer Kevin Williamson offered a masterpiece of social commentary that speaks directly to a crisis of our time. In a world where middle-class teenagers blithely commit infanticide at the prom between dances, who can truthfully deny that *Scream* powerfully offers social commentary amidst its post-modern irony and rampant sarcasm? Parker should praise *Scream* for so effectively expressing the dangers of "peer pressure" in our society (a motive of one of the killers in *Scream*), not condemning the film because it highlights graphic acts of violence.

Unfortunately, Parker goes even further in her tirade against *Scream*. She states that anybody who enjoys a film such as *Scream* can't be possessed of a "heart and possibly a soul." And why is that? There is much to be enjoyed in *Scream*, including humor, scares, solid acting, good direction and a witty screenplay. Does an enjoyment of the finer points of cinema make one a sociopath, bereft of a soul and a heart? Have not other violent films, such as *Full Metal Jacket*, *Platoon* and *JFK*, been praised on the basis of their technical superiority, and the message they convey beneath the graphic violence? Perhaps one should ask Parker this pertinent question: Where should the line be drawn? Should John be permitted to see *Braveheart*, *Con Air*, *Starship Troopers* and *The Lost World*, four films which feature far more graphic violence and bloody death than *Scream* does? Or how about Roman Polanski's version of *Macbeth* or Kenneth Branagh's *Hamlet*, both of which are also quite violent in content? Are the works of Shakespeare to be censored too, since they also feature acts of wicked violence? Does an enjoyment of Shakespeare's timeless plays or of Mel Gibson's bloody *Braveheart* preclude the possibility that a person has a heart and a soul? Or does Parker just flatly dislike the horror genre?

Of course, a sophist might argue that *Braveheart* or the films based on Shakespeare utilize violence for a more noble dramatic purpose than *Scream*, but that is surely a bogus and subjective response. There is much social commentary in *Scream* if one watches it with an open mind. One wonders if Parker has allowed her son to see *Star Wars*, a film that features more violent death than all of Craven's horror films combined. After all, the entire population of the planet Alderaan is *wiped out* in one second in *Star Wars*: billions of lives gone forever in a holocaust of global proportions! And what about the adrenalin rush audiences feel when they see manned spaceships destroyed and storm troopers (human beings in armor) blasted to death by the hundreds? Yet the violence in *Star Wars* is candy-coated with beautiful Fourth of July explosions and rainbow-colored laser beams. *Star Wars* renders violence impersonal, and therefore inoffensive to society's censors. Not so in *Scream* or the other films of Wes Craven, where violence against human beings is shown to have *direct*, bloody consequences. What Parker really argues for is the ultimate de-humanization of violence in cinema. *Star Wars* and its ilk are presumably "okay" because they do not show the personal consequences of intense violence; they do not show the *truth*. By this manner of thinking, *Scream*—which shows how brutal violence really affects people—is a bad influence simply because it shows blood and guts. Yet humans are made of blood and guts, and violence *does* result in the spilling of blood. Is it better for violence to be glamorized than for it to be truthful?

For all her obvious dislike of horror films, Parker cannot deny that violence has been an intrinsic element of drama since Homer and *The Iliad* and *The Odyssey*. What is so troubling about Parker's column is that she seems to think that she has the right to keep these films not only from her children, but from everybody. Does America really need another self-righteous parent deciding what the rest of us should be allowed to watch? More to the point, why does Parker get to judge what determines who has a heart and a soul? It is a shame that instead of talking seriously to her son about the content of *Scream*, Parker ordered him from the room early in a viewing of the film on videocassette. Of course it is Parker's right to do as she will as a parent, as well as express her opinion in writing, but just imagine what effect her decision has had on poor John Parker! After seeing only a few minutes of *Scream*, he must have a multitude of questions running around in his head about what little he saw before being unceremoniously yanked from the TV, just as this author had many questions when he first saw *Dressed to Kill* on videotape at age 14.

After viewing that Brian DePalma film, my father took me aside and said to me, "If I had seen that movie when I was 14, I would have a lot of questions about it. Let's talk." We then proceeded to discuss the film and how it made me feel. I worry about children who do not have the benefit of such honest dialogue with their parents, who are instead left with a head full of unanswered questions. Craven's most frequent tenet in film is that repressed feelings do not vanish, but return instead as symptoms. What will be the final outgrowth of Kathleen Parker's repression of horror films in her home? How will this denial affect her son? One hopes she is prepared to handle the results of her actions.

Wes Craven's New Nightmare made a unique and telling point when a young child in the film begged his mother to finish the story of Hansel and Gretel before he went to sleep at night. He *had* to know that there would be a happy ending, and that the world was right again, before his own imagination took over in the darkness of the night, just as Parker's John needed to see the finale of *Scream*, in which the wicked are punished and good prevails, instead of being sent to his room with a head full of questions.

Parents have a responsibility not only to guard the eyes of their children, but to satisfy their questions about the dark side of human nature. If Parker maintains such a repressive atmosphere in her home, John is bound to go outside her jurisdiction and see *Scream* on the sly. Is it not preferable to watch the film all the way through with him and answer his questions about it in a sincere, open fashion? No one can tell anyone how to raise their children, just as no one has the right to censor *Scream* or horror movies, but I sincerely hope that John will continue to goad his mother into confronting the things that frighten her instead of ruthlessly censoring and repressing them.

Besides, horror movies are the most moral of films made today. Isn't the Devil defeated in *The Exorcist*? Isn't the alien vanquished in *Alien*? Isn't Freddy destroyed in *Wes Craven's New Nightmare*? Is not order restored in *Scream*? Horror movies are exhilarating and worthwhile because they are about people who face evil and come out on top. Horror movies offer a reinforcing message of hope, and it will be a sad day when Parker and her cohorts have their way. Our children will have no more stories like *Hansel and Gretel* to assure them that there is order in the world, even in the face of bad things and bad people. And without that harmless outlet of their fears, the real horror will begin...

Epilogue

Since 1972, Wes Craven has toiled in a film genre that, like Rodney Dangerfield, gets no respect. Virtually every interview conducted with the artist from 1978 to 1997 begins with a few jokey lines describing how Craven bears no resemblance whatsoever to Charles Manson or any other mass murderer of recent memory. One has to wonder why journalists consider that fact such a surprise. Such comments reveal more about the reporter's prejudices than they do about Craven as either a person or a director of merit.

Why is it that contemporary society is immediately wary of someone who explores the dark side of human existence? Why must he be branded a freak? As a people, are we so afraid of the power of the subconscious, of our own human nature, that we stand poised to condemn those pioneers who face it more boldly than the rest of us do? Craven's physical appearance is surely irrelevant; it is his contribution to that uniquely twentieth century technical art, filmmaking, that is the issue at hand. Do people expect Stanley Kubrick, Oliver Stone, George Lucas, Steven Spielberg or David Lynch to look like mass murderers, even though they too have been responsible for some pretty violent films during their careers? Or is the horror film just so misunderstood, so misrepresented in a society of conservative censors that people actually believe that *A Nightmare on Elm Street* and its cinematic brethren could only be created by someone harboring psychotic tendencies instead of someone merely in touch with dreams of darkness?

Considering horror's status as the black sheep of film genres, it is no wonder that Craven has for many years viewed himself as a frustrated artist. His films consistently deal with contemporary social problems in witty, intelligent and even subversive fashion. Teen apathy (*Scream*), dysfunctional families (*A Nightmare on Elm Street, The Hills Have Eyes*), the role of horror films in pop culture (*Wes Craven's New Nightmare*), child abuse (*The People Under the Stairs*), the boundaries of civilized behavior (*The Last House on the Left*), religious oppression (*Deadly Blessing*), parental infidelity (*A Stranger in Our House*) and even the role of TV in suburbia (*Shocker*) have been fodder for Craven's movies. Yet despite the commendable focus on social commentary, Craven is likened to a serial killer or purveyor of pornography wherever he goes. Sometimes, it seems as if the critics who despise his pictures the most, as well as the "concerned citizens" who want to repress them, have had their intellectual capacities lobotomized by the sight of blood and the rush of adrenalin his scary films invariably cause to course through their bodies. Rarely in recent years has an artist of Craven's caliber been so misunderstood and misrepresented by so many. Even Stephen King, the reigning king of horror, failed to mention Craven or his early films in his 1981 defense of horror films, *Danse Macabre*.

After the successful and engaging *Scream 2*, Craven will apparently have the opportunity to tell human stories outside the limitations of the horror milieu. One wonders if he will be accepted by critics for this jump to a different kind of film, or instead be made the butt of jokes based on his long career in horror. Once people have made up their minds, even a talent as rich and as smart as Craven's may not be able to alter that perception. If Craven does leave horror films behind for *Fiddlefest* and other films like it, it will be a switch that causes sadness among his loyal fans and admirers. As happy as his fans will be for Craven personally that he has escaped low-budget hell and stories filled with dismemberment and death, they will also mourn his ascendance from his position "under the stairs."

Even if he does become a "mainstream" Hollywood director, Craven's gifts to cinematic horror will be remembered and honored by those who have watched and admired his films for a quarter century. His massive body of work in film, series TV and telefilms, as well as his numerous re-inventions of horror style and content, assure that eventuality. In addition, what other director currently working in Hollywood can point to four successful film franchises (*Swamp Thing, The Hills Have Eyes, A Nightmare on Elm Street* and *Scream*)? Still, these successes can be considered relatively minor when one contemplates Craven's greatest gift: his directorial honesty.

In *A Nightmare on Elm Street*, Nancy Thompson's mother (Ronee Blakeley) apologizes to her daughter for repressing the horrid truth about Freddy Krueger. She tells Nancy, "You face things. That's your nature. That's your gift." The same can be said of Wes Craven and his quarter century of provocative horror filmmaking. As a forward-looking culture, we should be infinitely grateful for an honest look inside ourselves, when many other technicians in the film world, like the twisted mom and dad in *A People Under the Stairs*, would rather see, hear and speak no evil.

Appendix A

Movie References in *Scream*

Scream won rave reviews from movie critics and audiences not only for its effective scares, but for its many smart references to popular films. In fact, *Scream* is loaded with direct references (films mentioned/seen by name) as well as indirect references (character names, songs, situations) from cinematic forebearers. Below, for the trivia-minded, is a complete list of both types of references.

Direct References
(Films mentioned/seen by name in *Scream*)

All the Right Moves (1984)
The Bad Seed (1956)
Basic Instinct (1991)
Candyman (1992)
Carrie (1976)
Clerks (1995)
E.T. (1982)
The Evil Dead (1981)
The Exorcist (1973)
Friday the 13th (1980)
Friday the 13th Part II (1981)
Halloween (1978)
Hellraiser (1987)
The Howling (1981)
Mother's Boys (1993)
A Nightmare on Elm Street (1984)
Psycho (1960)
The Silence of the Lambs (1991)
Terror Train (1987)
The Town That Dreaded Sundown (1977)
Trading Places (1983)

Indirect References
(Names, situations alluded to in *Scream*)

Halloween (dialogue): "Drive down to the Mackenzies..."

When a Stranger Calls (1979) (situation): A killer uses the telephone to terrorize his prey.

A Nightmare on Elm Street (situation): The heroine's boyfriend climbs through her bedroom window and is nearly caught by a single parent.

Halloween (song): "Don't Fear the Reaper" was played early in the John Carpenter film, and early in *Scream*.

The Exorcist (situation): A reporter in *Scream* played by Linda Blair asks about occult activity in the high school.

Halloween/Psycho (name): Billy "Loomis" refers to the Loomis character in *Halloween*, who is actually a reference to the Sam Loomis character in *Psycho*.

Chiller/A Nightmare on Elm Street (actor): Joseph Whipp is the town sheriff in *Scream*, a role he played in two earlier Craven productions.

A Nightmare on Elm Street (costume): Craven appears in *Scream* as the school janitor. He wears Freddy's sweater and hat from the first *Elm Street* film.

The Texas Chainsaw Massacre (1974) (dialogue): Randy refers to Billy as "Leatherface," the killer in *Chainsaw*.

Clueless (1995) (dialogue): Randy refers to Stu as "Alicia," meaning Alicia Silverstone.

Wes Craven's New Nightmare/A Vampire in Brooklyn (actor): W. Earl Brown plays Kenny in *Scream*. He was a morgue attendant in *New Nightmare* and a cop in *Vampire in Brooklyn*.

Frankenstein (1931) (video): This film is playing on a TV in the video store.

A Vampire in Brooklyn (character name): The police captain in *Vampire* is named "Dewey"...the same name as the deputy in *Scream*.

Mother's Boys (1993) (poster): A poster for a Jamie Lee Curtis stalker film of recent vintage is on display in the video store in *Scream*, and the title provides the key to the identity of the killer in *Scream*. Billy is a mother's boy (Sidney even calls him a "momma's boy" in the finale!). Not coincidentally, *Mother's Boys* was released by *Scream*'s studio, Dimension Films.

Appendix B

The Family in Craven's Films

In one way or another, the majority of Craven's films focus on the collapse of the family in modern America. Causes of the disintegration of the family unit include "the generation gap" in *The Last House on the Left*, overbearing parental figures in *The Hills Have Eyes*, alcoholism and murder in *A Nightmare on Elm Street*, unfaithful family members in *A Stranger in Our House* and *Scream*, denial of reality in *Chiller, A Nightmare on Elm Street, Shocker* and *Scream*, incest in *The People Under the Stairs* and obsessive-compulsive disorder in *Deadly Friend*. Below is a complete list of the films, the families and their dysfunctions.

The Last House on the Left (1972)
Family: The Collingwoods
Dysfunction: The generation gap

Family: The Krugs
Dysfunction: Child abuse

The Hills Have Eyes (1977)
Family: The Carters
Dysfunction: Overbearing father; Mother in denial; Rampant dishonesty

Family: The Cannibals
Dysfunction: Cannibalism

A Stranger in Our House (1978)
Family: The Bryants
Dysfunction: Unfaithful father; Mother in denial; Passive-aggressive brother

Invitation to Hell (1984)
Family: The Winslows
Dysfunction: Yuppie, materialistic mother; Father in denial; Yuppie children

Chiller (1984)
Family: The Creightons
Dysfunction: Mother in denial; Son is sociopath/abusive

A Nightmare on Elm Street (1984)
Family: The Thompsons
Dysfunction: Alcoholic mother; Father in denial; Mom and Dad are murderers

Deadly Friend (1986)
Family: The Conways
Dysfunction: Absentee father; Obsessive-compulsive son; Mother in denial

Shocker (1989)
Family: The Pinkers
Dysfunction: Sociopathic/abusive father; Dad killed Mom; Foster son in denial
Family: The Parkers
Dysfunction: Father in denial

The People Under the Stairs (1991)
Family: The Robsons
Dysfunction: Incest; Rampant yuppieism; Child abuse; Sexual abuse

Scream (1996)
Family: The Prescotts
Dysfunction: Unfaithful mother; Absentee father; Sid is emotional traumatized and afraid of intimacy
Family: The Loomises
Dysfunction: Unfaithful father; Absentee mother; Psychotic/sociopathic son
Family: The Rileys
Dysfunction: Absentee father

Scream 2 (1997)
Family: The Loomises
Dysfunction: Mom is murderer/psychopath

Appendix C

Recurring Imagery

Many common threads appear throughout the films directed by Wes Craven. Images, incidences and objects recur with regularity but are often put to contrasting uses. For instance, "the family dog" appears in no fewer than six films, but it represents different things throughout Craven's career. In *The Hills Have Eyes, Chiller, Invitation to Hell* and *The Hills Have Eyes II*, the dog is seen as the family defender. It pays for the sins of the family in *The Hills Have Eyes* and *Chiller* by being the first family member killed by the villain(s). In *Invitation to Hell* and *The Hills Have Eyes*, the dog is the first family member to sense nearby evil. By contrast, the dog in *The Last House on the Left* senses evil but is unable to fulfill its role of "family defender" because it is tethered by the Collingwoods. The family dog in *The People Under the Stairs* defends the "evil" family instead of a good family.

Snakes, on the other hand, are symbols of evil throughout Craven's films. They are used as weapons of death in *The Hills Have Eyes, Deadly Blessing, Swamp Thing, The Hills Have Eyes II, The Serpent and the Rainbow* and *Wes Craven's New Nightmare*. In Craven films, snakes are invariably attached to the face of an attacking villain.

Nightmares, on the other hand, vex nearly all of Craven's characters, heroes and villains alike. Nancy (*A Nightmare on Elm Street*), Rachel (*A Stranger in Our House*), Lana (*Deadly Blessing*), Paul (*Deadly Friend*), Dennis Alan (*The Serpent and the Rainbow)*, Jonathan Parker (*Shocker*) and Heather Langenkamp (*Wes Craven's New Nightmare*) are tormented by nightmares, as is "The Weasel," the despicable sex criminal of *The Last House on the Left*.

Craven also finds that our faith in society's institutions are misplaced. Ineffective police officers who fail to save lives turn up with alarming regularity. And, on a personal note, Craven likes *Nosferatu* and Sigmund Freud.

The following are lists of subjects/objects/ideas repeated throughout Craven's work. Note that films not directed by Craven (such as *Mind Ripper* or *Wishmaster*) have not been included since they involve directors other than Craven.

Snakes

The Hills Have Eyes (1977)
Deadly Blessing (1981)
Swamp Thing (1982)
The Hills Have Eyes II (1983)
A Nightmare on Elm Street (1984)
The Serpent and the Rainbow (1988)
Wes Craven's New Nightmare
A Vampire in Brooklyn (1995)

The family dog

The Last House on the Left (1972)
The Hills Have Eyes (1977)
Chiller (1984)
The Hills Have Eyes II (1984)
Invitation to Hell (1984)
The People Under the Stairs (1991)

Nightmares

The Last House on the Left (1972)
A Stranger in Our House (1978)
Deadly Blessing (1981)
A Nightmare on Elm Street (1984)
Deadly Friend (1986)
The Serpent and the Rainbow (1988)
Shocker (1989)
Wes Craven's New Nightmare (1994)
A Vampire in Brooklyn (1995)

Ineffective cops

The Last House on the Left (1972)
Deadly Blessing (1981)
A Nightmare on Elm Street (1984)
Deadly Friend (1986)
Shocker (1989)
The People Under the Stairs (1991)
Scream (1996)
Scream 2 (1997)

The film Nosferatu

Wes Craven's New Nightmare (1994)
A Vampire in Brooklyn (1995)
Scream 2 (1997)

Sigmund Freud

The Last House on the Left (1972)
The Hills Have Eyes (1977)
The Hills Have Eyes Part II (1983)
A Vampire in Brooklyn (1995)

Appendix D

Rating the Films

Below is a list of this author's personal preferences in the Wes Craven film canon. Craven's films are ranked below from best to worst; the top five pictures would probably be the best place for a curious filmgoer to begin a study of this director. The first nine films are certainly in the range "very good" or "excellent." Films 10–12 are mediocre, and movies 13 and 14 are Craven's least satisfying. This author repeatedly viewed all of these films, except for *Scream 2*, which opened shortly before the deadline for this text. It is entirely possible that down the road, it will have moved (either up or down) on this list.

1. *Wes Craven's New Nightmare* (1994)
2. *A Nightmare on Elm Street* (1984)
3. *Scream* (1996)
4. *The Serpent and the Rainbow* (1987)
5. *The Last House on the Left* (1972)
6. *The Hills Have Eyes* (1977)
7. *The People Under the Stairs* (1991)
8. *Scream 2* (1997)
9. *Deadly Blessing* (1981)
10. *Shocker* (1989)
11. *A Vampire in Brooklyn* (1995)
12. *Swamp Thing* (1982)
13. *Deadly Friend* (1986)
14. *The Hills Have Eyes Part II* (1983)

Notes

Introduction

1. Roger Ebert, *Roger Ebert's Movie Home Companion, 1993 Edition* (Kansas City, Mo.: Andrews and McMeel, 1993), p. 361.
2. Tony Williams, *Hearths of Darkness: The Family in the American Horror Film* (Cranbury, N. J.: Associated University Presses, 1996), page 130.

Chapter 1. The Film Career

1. Robin Finn, "Wes Craven: Despite Its Charms, Horror Can Pale," *The New York Times*, January 2, 1997, page 34.
2. William Schoell and James Spencer, *The Nightmare Never Ends: The Official History of Freddy Krueger and the Nightmare on Elm Street Films* (New York: Citadel, 1992), p. 179.
3. Dann Gire, "Bye Bye, Freddy! Elm Street Creator Wes Craven Quits Series," *Cinefantastique* 18, no. 5 (July 1988), p. 10.
4. Gire, "Bye Bye, Freddy!" p. 10.
5. Tony Williams, "Wes Craven: An Interview," *The Journal of Popular Film and TV* 8, no. 3 (Fall 1980), p. 18.
6. Barry Forshaw, "The Films of Wes Craven," *Starburst* 7, no. 7 (April 1985), p. 29.
7. Danny Peary, *Cult Movies* (New York: Delacorte, 1981), p. 22.
8. Williams, "Wes Craven: An Interview," p. 18.
9. John Stanley, *The Creature Features Movie Guide Strikes Again* (Creatures At Large Press: 1994), p. 222.
10. Jack Harris, "*Swamp Thing*—From the Comics to the Silver Screen," *Fantastic Films* Collector's Edition # 27 (January 1982), p. 13.
11. David J. Hogan, *Dark Romance: Sexuality in the Horror Film* (Jefferson, N. C.: McFarland, 1986), page 246.
12. Forshaw, "The Films of Wes Craven," p. 29.
13. John McCarty, *Psychos: Eighty Years of Mad Movies, Maniacs, and Murderous Deeds* (New York: St. Martin's, 1986), pp. 155–156.
14. Will Murray, "The Long Awaited Return of *Swamp Thing*," *Fangoria* no. 82 (May 1989), p. 20.
15. Lee Goldberg, "The Year of Wes Craven," *The Bloody Best of Fangoria* 5 (1986), p. 27.

16. Tim Ferrante, "Meet Freddie Krueger!" *The Bloody Best of Fangoria* 5 (1986), p. 44.

17. Linda Badley, *Film, Horror, and the Body Fantastic* (Westport, Conn.: Greenwood, 1995), p. 51.

18. John Javna, *The Best of Science Fiction TV* (New York: Harmony, 1987), p. 33.

19. Goldberg, "The Year of Wes Craven," p. 27.

20. Dennis Fischer, "Deadly Friend: Wes Craven Shocker Stars Robot," *Cinefantastique* 16, no. 3 (July 1986), p. 14.

21. Lee Goldberg, "Visiting with a *Deadly Friend*," *Starlog* no. 109 (August 1986), p. 53.

22. Daniel Schweiger, "Climbing the Ladder of Success," *Fangoria* no. 98 (November 1990), p. 54.

23. Stanley Wiater, *Dark Vision: Conversation with the Masters of the Horror Film* (New York: Avon, 1992), p. 52.

24. Gire, "Bye Bye, Freddy!" p. 10.

25. Frederick S. Clarke, "New Line Cinema on Working with Wes Craven," *Cinefantastique* 18, no. 5 (July 1988), p. 11.

26. Frank Darabont, "Craven Comments," *Fangoria* no. 64 (July 1987), p. 8.

27. Marc Shapiro, "Craven's Latest," *Fangoria* no. 70 (January 1988), p. 10.

28. Steve Biodrowski, "*No More Mr. Nice Guy:* Wes Craven Plans to Knock Freddy Krueger off His Horror Roost." *Cinefantastique* 19, no. 4 (May 1989), p. 11.

29. Marc Shapiro, "The People Under the Stairs," *Fangoria* no. 107, p. 9.

30. Steve Biodrowski, "Director Wes Craven on the Politics of Horror," *Cinefantastique* 22, no. 5 (April 1992), p. 58.

31. Steve Biodrowski, "Wes Craven: Alive and Shocking!" *Cinefantastique* 22, no. 2 (October 1991), p. 11.

32. Steve Biodrowski, "*Body Bags*: John Carpenter Challenges *Tales from the Crypt*," *Cinefantastique* 24, no. 3/4 (October 1993), p. 113.

33. Gregg Kilday and Anne Thompson, "To Infinity and Below, the 1995 Box Office Report," *Entertainment Weekly* no. 312 (February 2, 1996), p. 32.

34. Chris Nashawaty, "Scream On," *Entertainment Weekly* no. 387 (July 11, 1997), pp. 6–7.

35. Glenn Lovell, "One More *Scream*, Then a Dream," *The Los Angeles Times*, June 11, 1997.

36. Lovell, "One More *Scream*."

37. Jancee Dunn, "Starring Neve Campbell," *Rolling Stone*, September 18, 1997, p. 116.

38. Janet Weeks, "*Scream* Movies Cultivate Special Audience: Girls," *U.S.A. Today*, December 12, 1997, p. 2A.

Chapter 2. The Feature Films

1. Gregory A. Waller, ed., *American Horrors: Essays on the Modern American Horror Film* (Champaign: University of Illinois Press, 1987), p. 168.

2. Carol J. Clover, *Men, Women and Chainsaws: Gender in the Modern Horror Film* (Princeton, N. J.: Princeton University Press, 1992), p. 125.

3. Dan Persons, "Wes Craven: Is Freddy's Father Scream-ing for More?" *Cinefantastique* 29, no. 4/5 (October 1997), p. 88.

4. Roy Kinnard, *The Comics Come Alive: A Guide to Comic-Strip Characters in Live Action Productions* (Metuchen, N. J.: Scarecrow, 1991), p. 196.

5. David J. Hogan, *Dark Romance: Sexuality in the Horror Film* (Jefferson, N. C.: McFarland, 1986), p. 113.

6. Tim Bywater and Thomas Sobchack, *Introduction to Film Criticism: Major Critical Approaches to Narrative Film* (Longman, 1989), p. 18.

Chapter 3. The Television Movies

1. Lois Duncan, *Summer of Fear* (Boston: Little, Brown, 1976), p. 202.

Chapter 5. The Television Series

1. Ben Herndon, "*The Twilight Zone*," *Cinefantastique* 16, no. 1 (March 1986), p. 22.
2. Max Rebeaux, "Twilight Zone: CBS TV Revives Everyone's Favorite Anthology Series of Fantasy and Science Fiction in September," *Cinefantastique* 15, no. 4 (October 1985), p. 22.

Bibliography

Badley, Linda. *Film, Horror, and the Body Fantastic.* Westport, Conn.: Greenwood, 1995.
Bywater, Tim, and Sobchack, Thomas. *Introduction to Film Criticism: Major Critical Approaches to Narrative Film.* Longman, 1989.
Clover, Carol J. *Men, Women and Chainsaws: Gender in the Modern Horror Film.* Princeton, N. J.: Princeton University Press, 1992.
Davis, Wade. *The Serpent and the Rainbow.* New York: Simon & Schuster, 1985.
Duncan, Lois. *Summer of Fear.* Boston: Little, Brown, 1974.
Ebert, Roger. *Roger Ebert's Movie Home Companion, 1993 Edition.* Kansas City, Mo.: Andrews and McMeel, 1993.
Hogan, David J. *Dark Romance: Sexuality in the Horror Film.* Jefferson, N. C.: McFarland, 1986.
Javna, John. *The Best of Science Fiction TV.* New York: Harmony, 1987.
King, Stephen. *Danse Macabre.* New York: Berkley, 1981.
Kinnard, Roy. *The Comics Come Alive: A Guide to Comic-Strip Characters in Live Action Productions.* Metuchen, N. J.: Scarecrow, 1991.
McCarty, John. *Psychos: Eighty Years of Mad Movies, Maniacs, and Murderous Deeds.* New York: St. Martin's, 1986.
Menville, Douglas, Reginald, R. *Future Visions: The New Golden Age of the Science Fiction Film.* North Hollywood, Calif.: Newcastle, 1985.
Moore, Darrell. *The Best, Worst and Most Unusual: Horror Films.* Publication International, 1983.
Peary, Danny. *Cult Movies.* New York: Delacorte, 1981.
Schoell, William, and Spencer, James. *The Nightmare Never Ends: The Official History of Freddy Krueger and the Nightmare on Elm Street Films.* New York: Citadel, 1992.
Stanley, John. *The Creature Features Movie Guide Strikes Again.* Creatures At Large Press, 1994.
Waller, Gregory A., ed. *American Horrors: Essays on the Modern American Horror Film.* Champaign: University of Illinois Press, 1987.
Wiater, Stanley. *Dark Vision: Conversation with the Masters of the Horror Film.* New York: Avon, 1992.
Williams, Tony. *Hearths of Darkness: The Family in the American Horror Film.* Cranbury, N. J.: Associated University Presses, 1996.
Zicree, Marc Scott. *The Twilight Zone Companion.* New York: Bantam, 1982.

Index

*Numbers in **boldface** refer to pages with photographs.*

The A-Team (TV series) 205
Adams, Brandon 29, 30, 159, 167, 279, 287
Agar, John 31
The Alamo (film) 64
Alfred Hitchcock Presents (TV series) 22, 275
Alien (film) 262–264, 266
Alien Resurrection 38, 216, 219, 266, 293
Alien³ 219, 247, 263
Aliens (film) 33, 154, 212, 217, 219, 247, 262, 263, 265
"Aliens Ate My Lunch" (*Nightmare Cafe* episode) 31, 286–290
Alive films 28, 29, 146, 159, 247
"All Shook Up" (song) 11
Allen, Nancy 289
Alone in the Dark (film) 20
Altman, Robert 3
The Amazing Spiderman (TV series) 31
Amazing Stories (TV series) 20, 21, 22, 275, 290
American Horrors: Essay on the Modern American Horror Film (book) 68
An American Werewolf in London (film) 194
Amistad (film) 38
Andrews, Dave 106
Andrews, V.C. 23
Angel, Dan 31
Angel Heart (film) 27
Angels in the Outfield (film) 32
Aniston, Jennifer 216

Anker, Marshall 40
Apicelli, John 257
Apocalypse Now (film) 67
Arnold, Tom 21, 31
Arquette, David 34–36, 197, 210
Arquette, Patricia 248, **251**, 253
Ashton, John 278
Assault on Precinct 13 (film) 64
Atkins, Tony 36, 267, 271
Automan (TV series) 31
Avco-Embassy 16

The Babysitter (telefilm) 228
Babylon 5 (TV series) 22, 282
Back to the Future (film) 126
Back to the Future II (film) 217
Bad Dreams (film) 2, 158
Bad Moon Rising (film) 34, 38
The Bad Seed (film) 154
Badham, John 194
Bannister, Reggie 36, 267, 273
Barbeau, Adrienne 16, 22, **86**, 91, 92, 95, 104, 276
Barish, Keith 132
Barker, Clive 33
Barr, Douglas 75
Barr, Matthew 75
Barr, Roseanne 21
Barrymore, Drew 26, 34, 35, 197, 208, 215
Basic Instinct (film) 205
Bassett, Angela 30, 186, 193, 195, 279, 287, 288

Bates, Ben 86
Batman (film) 16, 17, 20, 92
Batman (TV series) 16
Battlestar Galactica (TV series) 16, 276
Baum, Thomas 30, 246, 279, 280, 284
The Beast of Yucca Flats (film) 16
Beck, Michael 21, 238, 243, 245
The Bees (film) 19
Beetlejuice (film) 28
Behind the Green Door (film) 10
Beinhart, Larry 40
The Believers (film) 27
Beltrami, Marco 197, 211
Benest, Glenn 75, 221, 224
Benson, Annette 248
Berg, Peter 28, 145, **151**, **156**
Berger, Howard 160, 173, 267
Bergman, Ingmar 1, 11, 46–50
Bernstein, Charles 121, 250
Berryman, Michael 14, 16, 59, **71**, 72, 74, 75, 81, 95, **101**, 238
Besser, Stuart M. 159, 187, 197
Biehn, Michael 263
Big Foot (film) 1
Black Magic Woman (film) 31
Blacula (film) 195
Blade Runner (film) 17
Blair, Kevin 95, 105, 197

311

Index

Blair, Linda 15, 221, 225, 227
Blakeley, Ronee 20, 105, 296
Blay, Andre 28
The Blob (1988 remake) 20
Blom, Dan 33, 257, 264
Blom, John 95
Blood Beach (film) 19
The Blood of Heroes (film) 283
Bloom, Jeffrey 23
Blumenthal, Andy 146
Blythe, Janus 59, 74, 95
Bonnie and Clyde (film) 55
Boogie Nights (film) 154, 215
Borgnine, Ernest 16, 75, 82
Bracken, Richard 75, 86, 96
Bradley, Doug 271
Bram Stoker's Dracula (film) 3
Branagh, Kenneth 3, 292
Braveheart (film) 292
Brennert, Alan 22, 275, 279
Briscoe, Jimmy 259
Brown, Billy 31
Brown, Nannette 86
Brown, W. Earl 186, 195, 197
Bruno, Dominick 95
Buck Rogers in the 25th Century (TV series) 275
Buckner, Susan 75
Buffy the Vampire Slayer (film) 23, 31
Bug (film) 22
Bundy, Brooke 248
"The Burning Man" (new *Twilight Zone* episode) 243
Burton, Tim 17, 34
"But Can She Type" (new *Twilight Zone* episode) 276

Cagney and Lacey (TV series) 11
Cahn, Barry 96
Call, Ed 106
Cameron, James 35, 154
Camp Nowhere (film) 32
Campbell, Neve 34, 35, 37, 197, **207**, 210, 216, 228
Candyman II: Farewell to the Flesh (film) 33
Cannibals Are in the Streets (film) 19
Cannom, Greg 248

Capp, Dixie 159, 187, 197
Carey, Macdonald 15, 221
Carhart, Timothy 286
Carpenter, John 2, 3, 4, 17, 19, 28, 31, 33, 64, 81, 104, 119
Carr, Cynthia 40
Carrie (film) 114
Carter, Chris 29
Cassell, Sandra 11, 40, **43**
Cassidy, Joanna 21, 186, 195, 228, 235
Cates, Phoebe 126
"Cavender Is Coming" (*Twilight Zone* episode) 290
Cavett, Dick 248, 254
CBS 29, 275, 276
Cecere, Tony 17, 86, 107, 132, 146, 160, 211
Chambers, Marilyn 10
"Chameleon" (*Twilight Zone* revival episode) 22
The Changeling (film) 22
Chapin, Harry 9
Cheers (TV series) 30
Chen, Joan 282, 283
Chesney, Peter 250
"Children's Zoo" (new *Twilight Zone* episode) 276
Child's Play (film) 158, 208
Chiller (telefilm) 6, 17, 21, 29, 238–246, 276
Christian, Spencer 37
Cinefantastique (magazine) 25, 168
Clark, Cordy 59
Clarke, Arthur C. 22
Class of 1999 (film) 31
A Clockwork Orange (film) 57, 58
Clooney, George 36
Close Encounters of the Third Kind (film) 16
Clueless (film) 205
Cobbs, Bill 159
Coblentz, James 159, 246
Cohen, Rob 132
Cole, Gary 279
Coleman, Jack 30, 279, 287
Comedy Central 34
Con Air (film)
Conan the Barbarian (film) 276
"Conspiracy" (*Star Trek: The Next Generation* episode) 14

Coolidge, Martha 276
Cooper, Alice 28, 152
Cooper, Cami 145
Coppola, Francis Ford 3, 4, 194
Copycat (film) 3
Corman, Roger 23, 31
Corri, Nick 19, 106, 172, 186
Coscarelli, Don 115
Cox, Courteney 34, 35, 37, 197, **209**, 210, 220
Crane, Tony 266
Crash (film) 4
Craven, Jessica 9, 145
Craven, Jonathan 9, 33, 247, 257, 266, 2800
Craven, Mimi Meyer 106, 276, 278
Creepshow (film) 92
Crittendon, Diane 132
Crocker, James 276–278
Cronenberg, David 4
Crosby, Denise 284
The Crow (1994) 17
Cruise, Tom 34
Cult Movies (book) 11
Cundey, Dean 229
Cunningham, Sean 10, 13, 15, 40
Cunningham, Susan 40
Curtis, Jamie Lee 15, 37, 102, 104, 107, 119, 205, 207
Curtis Hall, Vondie 287, 288
Cushing, Peter 1, 2
Cutthroat Island (film) 20

D.A.R.Y.L. (film) 126
D.C. Comics 16, 90
The Daily Show (TV series) 34
Damiano, Gerard 10
Damien: Omen II (film) 217
Dangerous Minds (film) 35
Danse Macabre (book) 129, 295
Dante, Joe 14, 22, 276
Darabont, Frank 25, 253
Dark Universe (film) 263
Darkman (film) 4, 17
Darkroom (TV series) 31
Datcher, Alex 31
Davis, Wade 26, 132, 140, 142, 143

Index

Davis, William B. 287, 288
Dawn of the Dead (film) 19
A Day in the Country (film) 55
Dead Calm (film) 30, 283
Dead Poets Society (film)
Deadly Blessing (film) 8, 14–17, 74–85, 90, 112, 119, 128, 144, 228, 264, 295
Deadly Friend (film) 2, 5, 22, 23–25, 30, 119, 120–130, **130**, 131, 144, 154, 158, 298
"Dealer's Choice" (*Twilight Zone* revival episode) 22, 243
Death Wish (film) 1
Debin, Jonathan 95
Deep Space (film) 263
Deep Star Six (film) 263
Deep Throat (film) 10, 11
De Guere, Phil 21, 275, 276
Deliverance (film) 155
Demme, Jonathan 3
De Mornay, Rebecca 228
DePalma, Brian 4, 5, 15
Depp, Johnny 19, 35
Derry, Charles 68
Devil in Miss Jones (film) 10
The Devil's Advocate (film) 36
The Devil's Child (film) 228
The Devil's Rain (film) 16
De Young, Cliff, 279
Di Aquino, John 282, 283
Diehl, John 256
Dillon, Melinda 276, 277, **278**
Dimension Films 33, 197, 199
Divoff, Andrew 266, 273
Djola, Badja 131
Do the Right Thing (film) 57, 58
Doctor Who (TV series) 283, 285
Donner, Richard 16
Donovan, Dick 40
The Dorm That Dripped Blood (film) 219
Dracula (film) 194
Dream Demons (film) 2
Dreamaniac (film) **2**
Drescher, Fran 221
Dressed to Kill (film) 15
The Driller Killer (film) 15, 293
Duchovny, David 36

Dudelson, Stanley 106
Duncan, Lois 15, 221, 224, 226, 227
Duncan, Ted 86
Dune (film) 47
Dunne, Griffin 194
Durock, Dick 16, 17, 86, **93**
Dust Devil (film) 27
Duvall, Robert 8, 69
"Dying Well Is the Best Revenge" (*Nightmare Cafe* episode) 283–285

E.T. (film) 14, 17
East, Jeff 16, 75, 221
Easton, Sheena 31
Eastwood, Clint 17, 21
Easy Rider (film) 4, 10
Eaten Alive (film) 19
Ebert, Robert 1, 12, 17, 27, 210
Ed Wood (film) 19
Edwards, Ray 40
Edwards, Vince 32, 73
Elfman, Danny 211
Ellison, Harlan 22, 276, 277
Embassy Pictures 86
The Empire Strikes Back (film) 217
The English Patient (film) 155
Englund, Robert 2, 3, 19, 21, 22, 30, 32, 36, 37, 106, **116**, 120, 172–185, 243, 248, 266, 272, 279–281, **281**, 282–290
Enter the Dragon (film) 18
Entertainment Tonight (TV series) 28
Epps, Omar 211
Escape from L.A. (film) 5
Escape from New York (film) 5
Event Horizon (film) 4
Eve's Bayou (film) 287
The Evil Dead (film) 4
The Exorcist (film) 1, 22, 47, 155, 276
Explorers (film) 22, 126
Eyes of Laura Mars (film) 29

Fade to Black (film) 15
Fallen (film) 158
Family Feud (TV game show) 189
Fancey, Adrienne 95
Fangoria (magazine) 14, 25

The Fantastic Journey 31
Farrell, Terry 271
"Faye and Ivy" (*Nightmare Cafe* episode) 284, 285
The Fear (film) 32, 73
Feigelson, J.D. 238, 243, 278
Fellows, Edith 95
Fiddlefest (film) 34, 38, 296
Fiedel, Brad 132, 246
"Fine Tuning" (*Amazing Stories* episode) 290
Firefox (film) 17
Fishburne, Larry 248
Five Easy Pieces (film) 10
Flash Gordon (film) 47
Fleischer, Charles 106, 121, 127
Fletcher, Louise 23, 289
Flower, George "Buck" 31, 267, 273
Flowers in the Attic (book) 23
Flowers in the Attic (film) 23
Flubber (film, 1997) 38
Fog (film) 104
For Richer or Poorer (film) 38
Forbidden World (film) 263
Forest, Denis 286
Forrest Gump (film) 155, 158
The Fountain Society (novel) 34, 38
Frakes, Jonathan 276
Frand, Harvey 276
Frankenstein (1931 film) 92, 126, 152, 155, 266
Frankenstein and the Monster from Hell (film)
Frankenstein Must Be Destroyed (film)
Franklin, Richard 15
Frechette, Peter 95
Freddy's Dead: The Final Nightmare (film) 21, 31
Freddy's Nightmares (TV series) 21, 28
Freeman, Morgan 279
Friday the 13th (film) 2, 10, 14, 15, 18, 36, 52, 81, 102, 104, 105, 120, 200, 206, 208, 219
Friday the 13th V: A New Beginning (film) 13, 105
Friday the 13 VIII: Jason Takes Manhattan (film) 20
Friedkin, William 1, 22, 155, 276

Index

Friend (book) 23; see also *Deadly Friend*
Fright Night (film) 193
The Frighteners (film) 14
From Dusk Till Dawn (film) 19, 158
Frost, Lindsay 30, 279, 283
Full Metal Jacket (film) 292
Furie, Sidney J. 25

Gabor, Zsa Zsa 248, 254
Galaxy of Terror (film) 263
"The Gas Station" (vignette) 31; see also *John Carpenter Presents Body Bags*
Gayton, Joe 33, 247, 257, 265, 266
Gellar, Sarah Michelle 35, 37, 210
Gerrold, David 22, 276
Ghost (film) 23
Gibson, Charles 36
Gibson, Mel 292
Gil, Arturo 289
Glover, John 276
Godfather II (film) 212, 217
Gold Coast 37
Goldstein, William 146
Good Morning America (TV) 36
Goodwin, Robin 86
Gordon, Lance 59, 95
Gordon, Shep 28, 146, 159
Gough, Michael 132
Graham, Heather 211, 215
Grantham, Lucy 11, 40, **43**
The Green Berets (film) 69
Gremlins (film) 22, 126, 276
Gremlins II: The New Batch (film) 276
Grieve, Russ 59
Gross, Mary 28
Guilfoyle, Paul 132
The Guyver (film) 31

Haitkin, Jacques 106, 146
Halloween (film) 2, 14, 18, 19, 81, 102, 104, 119, 202, 204, 205–208, 219
Halloween II (film) 217
Halloween VI: The Curse of Michael Myers (film) 33
Hamill, Mark 31
Hamilton, Linda 219
Hamlet (film) 292
Hammer, Earl, Jr. 238
Hammer Studios **1**

The Hand That Rocks the Cradle (film) 228
Hanneman, Yvonne 40
Hansel and Gretel 175–181, 293, 294
Happy Birthday to Me (film) 2
Harlin, Renny 20
Harris, Danielle 155
Harrison, John 285
Harrison, Kadeem 186, 193, 195, 196
Harry, Deborah 31
Hartman, Lisa 75
Hartzell, Duane 238
Haunted (unmade film) 23
The Haunting (film) 34
HBO 33, 247
He Knows You're Alone (film) 2
Heads and Tales (album) 9
"Heart of the Mystery" (*Nightmare Cafe* episode) 285–286
Hearths of Darkness (book) 69
Hedaya, Dan 279
Hell Night (film) 2, 15
Hellbound: Hellraiser II (film) 36, 158, 247
Hellraiser (film) 36, 158, 208, 271, 272
Hellraiser III: Hell on Earth (film) 36, 271
Hellraiser IV: Blood Lines (film) 271
Henn, Carrie 154
Henriksen, Lance 33, 256, 263
Henstell, Diana 23, 121
"Her Pilgrim Soul" (*Twilight Zone* revival episode) 22, 276
Hess, David Alexander 11, 40, **44**, 54, 86, 91
The Hidden (film) 20
Hideaway (film) 33
The Hills Have Eyes (film) 2, 3, 5, 8, 10, 13–16, 18, 21, 29, 58–74, 81, 82, 85, 90, **101**, 102–104, 117, 119, 127, 128, 152, 158, 167, 168, 170, 206, 225, 227, 228, 244, 264, 295, 296
The Hills Have Eyes Part II (film) 14, 18, 95–105, 119, 158, 246

The Hills Have Eyes Part III (unmade film) 28
Hodder, Kane 36, 105, 267, 273
Holliday, Polly 126
Home Alone 3 (film) 38
Hooper, Tobe 1, 4, 17, 19, 21, 22, 31, 114
Hopkins, Stephen 20
Horner, James 75, 265
House on Sorority Row 219
House II: The Second Story 212, 217
Houston, Robert 59, 74, 95, 100
Howard the Duck (film) **28**
The Howling (film) 14
Hughes, Miko 32, 172, **177**
"The Hunt" (new *Twilight Zone* episode) 238
Hurwitz, Victor 40
Hyams, Peter 22

I Am Curious (Yellow) (film) 19
I Know What You Did Last Summer (film) 4, 35, 37, 208, 216, 273
I Spit on Your Grave (film) 1
I Was a Teenage Frankenstein (film) 24
In and Out (film) 36, **273**
In the Mouth of Madness (film) 33
Independence Day (film) 27, 34
Indiana Jones and the Last Crusade (film) 20
Innocent Blood (film) 194
Insatiable (film) 10
Interview with the Vampire (film) 3, 32, 193
Invaders from Mars (film) 4, 23
Invasion of the Body Snatchers (film) 234
Invitation to Hell (telefilm) 6, 21, 74, 195, 228–238, 243–245
Irving, Amy 114
Irwin, Mark 172, 187, 197, 280
Isaksson, Ulla 46
It! The Terror from Beyond Space (film) 264
It Happened in Hollywood (film) 10, 11, 13

Jackie Brown (film) 158
Jackson, Peter 14
Jacob's Ladder (film) 23
Jaeckin, Just 10
Jason Goes to Hell: The Final Friday (film) 3
Jaws (film) 119, 120
Jaws 2 (film) 22
Jennings, Brent 131
Jensen, Maren 16, 75, **80**, 81, 84
Jerry Maguire (film) 21, 34
Jessup, Robert 75
JFK (film) 292
Joe's Apartment (film) 35
John Carpenter Presents Body Bags (film) 31, 33
Johnson, Penny 95
Johnson, Tor 13
Jones, Jeffrey 28
Jordan, Neil 3
Jourdan, Louis 17, 86, 91, **94**
Judge Dredd (film) 283
Jungfrakallan (film) see *The Virgin Spring*
Jurgenson, William 221

Kaproff, Dana 235
Keach, Stacy 31
Keller, Max A. 221, 224
Keller, Michaeline 221
Kennedy, Jamie 34–36, 197, 210
Kidman, Nicole 36
King, Arthur 59
King, Robb Wilson 86
King, Sandy 31
King, Stephen 129, 276, 296
King, Zalman 10
King Kong (1933 film) 266
Klein, Robert 22, 278
Kline, Kevin 36
Konrad, Cathy 197, 211
Koontz, Dean 33
Kotto, Yaphet 263
Kove, Martin 11, 40, 276
Krug and Company (unused title) 11; see also *The Last House on the Left*
Kubrick, Stanley 295
Kumar, Barin 146
Kurosawa, Akira 47
Kurtzman, Robert 36, 160, 173, 247, 267, 272

Laborteaux, Matthew 24, 121, **123**, 127
Landau, Martin 276
Langenkamp, Heather 3, 19, 28, 32, 106, **112**, 115, **116**, 120, 145, 172–177, **177**, 178, 179–183, **179**, **183**, 184, 185, 248, 253, 255
Langer, A.J. 159
Lanier, Susan 59, **71**, 95
The Last House on the Left (film) 1–5, 10–15, 19, 38–58, 65, 68, 70, 72, 81, 82, 85, 103, 104, 117, 118, 127, 128, 152, 159, 170, 228, 238, 263, 274, 276, 295
The Last House to the Left II (film) 13
Lathrop, Philip 121
Laughlin, John 95
Lauren, Tammy 266, 273
Leary, Timothy 5, 28, 146, 157, 246
Leave It to Beaver (TV series) 28, 152, 155, 156
Lee, Brandon 17
Lee, Christopher 1, 2, **193**
Lee, Spike 33
Leekley, John 284, 286
The Legend of Boggy Creek (film) 1
Leigh, Janet 19
Leitch, Chris 284
Lethal Weapon 2 (film) 20
Levine, Jeffrey 106
Lewis, David 95
Licence to Kill (film) 20
Lifeforce (film) 4
Lifetime 245
Lillard, Matthew 34, 197, **203**, 228
Lincoln, Fred 40, **44**
Lindley, John 132
Lipton, Sandy 106
The Little Girl Who Lived Down the Lane (film) 1
"A Little Peace and Quiet" (new *Twilight Zone* episode) 276, 277, 278
"Little People of Killany Woods" (new *Twilight Zone* episode) 243
Lloyd, Michael 221
Locke, Peter 9, 13, 59, 96
Locklear, Heather **94**
Locklyn, Loryn 246
Lolita (film) 10
Lomino, Daniel 121

The Long Kiss Goodnight (film) 20
Lord of Illusions (film) 33
Lorimar 21
Lost Highway (film) 27, 247, 265
The Lost World (film) 292
The Love Boat (TV series) 252
Lucas, George 295
Lucci, Susan 37, 228, 237
Lugosi, Bela 193
Lussier, Patrick 172, 187, 197, 280
Lynch, David 4, 289, 295
Lynch, Richard 158
Lyne, Adrian 10

Maddalena, Marianne 145, 159, 172, 187, 197, 211, 246, 280
Madonna 35
Malice (film) 27
Manfredini, Harry 86, 96, 267
Mann and Machine (TV series) 31
Margol, Bill 37
Marin, Russ 121
Marinoff, Brenda 59, 95
Mars Attacks! (film) 34
Martin, George R.R. 276, 279
Mary Shelley's Frankenstein (film) 3, 25, 32
Maslin, Janet 16, 84
Mastandrea, Nicholas 187, 197, 211
Mastroianni, Armand 283, 286
Maxwell, Richard 27, 132
McBride, Jim 276
McCarthy, Kevin 228, 234
McFarlane, Tod 17
McGill, Everett 29, 159, 169, 170, 265
McGowan, Rose 34, 197, **203**, **207**
Medak, Peter 22, 276
Media Home Entertainment 106
Melnick, Mark 246
Melnicker, Benjamin 16, 86
Metcalf, Laurie 211
Meyer, Nicholas 17
Meyrink, Michelle 126

"The Mighty Casey" (*Twilight Zone* episode) 290
Milius, John 276
Millennium (TV series) 29, 246
Miller, David 173
Mimic (film) 4
Miner, David 40
Miner, Steve 40
Miramax 33, 35, 38
Mission: Impossible (film) 5
Mission: Impossible (TV series) 9
Mr. Holland's Opus (film) 35
Mittleman, Phil 33, 257
Mokae, Zakes 27, 132, 141, 186, 195
The Mole People (film) 31
Mom and Dad Save the World (film) 28
Mona Lisa (film)
Monster Mash (song) 34
"The Monsters Are Due on Maple Street" (*Twilight Zone* episode) 289
Morris, Garret 279
MTV 34, 38, 256
Murphy, Eddie 3, 33, 186, 193, 187, 195
Murphy, Michael 28, 145, 153, **156**
Musetto, V.A. 155
My Bloody Valentine (film) 2
My Friend Needs Killing (film) 1
My Science Project (film) 24

Napier, Charles
National Coalition on TV Violence 21
Natural Born Killers (film) 57, 58, 158
Naughton, David 31
NBC 279
Neal, Elise 211
Near Dark (film) 33, 193
Nettleton, Lois 75
The New Dark Shadows (TV series) 31
New Line Cinema 2, 3, 17, 19, 21, 24–26, 32, 106, 172–174, 248, 254
Nichols, David 86, 95
Nicoreto, Greg 160, 173, 267
Night Gallery (TV series) 275
Night of the Living Dead (film) 64

Night of Vengenace (unused film title) 11; see also *The Last House on the Left*
Night Vision (telefilm) 29, 30, 105, 246
"Nightmare at 20,000 Feet" (film) 118
Nightmare Cafe (TV series) 3, 23, 30, 31, 64, 243, 246, 279–290
A Nightmare on Elm Street (film) 2, 3, 4, 5, 8, 12, 17–26, 28, 30, 32, 34, 37, 74, 85, 90, 103–109, **109**, **110**, 111, **112**, 112–120, 127–129, 142, 144, 152, 153, 158, 169, 181, 186, 204–206, 227, 236, 253, 271, 284, 295, 296
A Nightmare on Elm Street II: Freddy's Revenge (film) 3, 20, 26, 253
A Nightmare on Elm Street III: Dream Warriors (film) **3**, 20, 25, 184, 247–256
A Nightmare on Elm Street IV: The Dream Master (film) 3, 20, 255, 256, 278
A Nightmare on Elm Street V: The Dream Child (film) 3, 20
"No More Mr. Nice Guy" (*Freddy's Nightmares* episode) 30
No More Mr. Nice Guy (alternate title) 30; see also *Shocker*
Nordgren, Erik 55
Nosferatu (film) 194, 213
Novak, Ralph 116, 128
Noyce, Phillip 30, 283
The Nutty Professor (film) 33

O'Bannon, Rockne 276, 277
O'Connell, Jerry 35, 37, 210
Oehler, Gretchen 172, 173
Old Fears (unmade film) 23
Oldman, Gary 193
Oliney, Alan 187
Olyphant, Timothy 211
One Flew Over the Cuckoo's Nest (1975) 23
O'Neill, Dick 238
"Opening Day" (*Twilight Zone* revival episode) 276; see also Kove, Martin

O'Quinn, Terry 278
Oswald, Gerd 22, 276
Otherworld (TV series) 275
The Outer Limits (TV series) 22, 234, 276
Outerbridge, Peter 285

Pacino, Al 36
Paperhouse (film) 2
Parker, Kathleen 291–294
Parker, Molly 285
Passage of Darkness: The Ethnobiology of the Haitian Zombie (book) 26
Passenger 57 (film) 31
Patriot Games (film) 30, 283
Paul, Anne 40
Payne, Allen 193, 195
The Peacemaker (film) 36, 273
Peake, Don 59, 159
Peary, Danny 11
Peck, Gregory 8
The People Next Door (TV series) 28
The People Under the Stairs (film) 3, 5, 21, 23, 29, 30, 37, 103, 104, 158–167, **167**, 168–171, 195, 206, 265, 295, 296
Perfect (film) 236
Phantasm (film) 36, 115
Phantasm II (film) 158
The Phantom (film)
Physical (song) 236
Pickette, Tom 59
Pileggi, Mitch 28, 145, 158, 187, 195
Pinkett, Jada 35, 37
Piranha (film) 22
Pirandello, Luigi 3, 184, 185
Planet of the Apes (TV series) 31
Platoon (film) 57, 58, 292
The Player (film) 185
Playing God (film) 36
Poltergeist (film) 17, 114, 157, 235, 244
Poltergeist III (film) 158
The Preacher's Wife (film) 34
Predator 2 (film) 20
Presley, Elvis 11
Price, Vincent 2
Prince of Darkness (film) 28
Profiler (TV series) 29
Prom Night (film) 14, 15, 84, 219, 246

Psycho (film) 19, 84, 119
Pugh, Willard 95
Pullman, Barry 283, 284
Pullman, Bill 27, 131, **135**
Pulp Fiction (film) 158
Pumpkinhead (film) 33
Purcell, Lee 221

Raimi, Sam 4, 17, 107
Raimi, Theodore 145, 267
Rain, Jeramie 40, **44**, 53
Rambo (film) 205
Ramsey, Ann 121, 126
Rea, Karen 238
Real Genius (film) 24, 25, 126
Reeves, Keanu 36
Regalbuto, Joe 228
Reiser, Paul 262
Remar, James 246
Renoir, Jean 55
The Resurrection of Eve (film) 10
Return of the Swamp Thing (film) 17, 18, 91, 94
Revenge of the Creature (film) 31
Rhames, Ving 159
Ribisi, Giovanni 257, 265
Rice, Anne 3
The Ricki Lake Show (TV series) 205, 207
Riley, Coleen 75
Risher, Sara 18, 25, 32, 106, 172
Road Games (film) 15, 31
"The Road Less Traveled" (*Twilight Zone* episode) 22, 279
The Road Warrior (film) 217
Roberts, Conrad 131
Robie, Wendie 29, 159, 169, 170, 187, 195
Robinson, J. Peter 172
Romero, George 4, 19, 64, 92
Roperto, Andrew 121
Rosemary's Baby (film) 228–237
Roshomon (film) 47
Rothstein, Richard 229, 234–236
Ruban, Al 86
Rubin, Bruce Joel 23, 127
Rubin, Jennifer 248
Russell, Chuck 20, 25, 26, 248, 253
Saarinen, Eric 59

Sagoes, Ken 248
St. James, Gaylord 40, 47
"Sanctuary for a Child" (*Nightmare Cafe* episode) 285, 286
Saturday Night Live 195
Saxon, John 18, 28, 32, 106, 172–185, **179**, 248, 253, 255
Scary Movie (alternate title) see *Scream*
Schindler's List (film) 57, 58
Schoelen, Jill 238, 245
Schreiber, Liev 35, 197, 210
Schwimmer, David 216
Sci-Fi Channel 31, 243
Scorsese, Martin 22
Scott, Ridley 17
Scream (film) 3–5, 15, 16, 26, 33–36, 85, 92, 102, 114, 119, 157, 185, 196–210, 216, 217, 219, 220, 228, 276, 291–296
Scream the Sequel (film) see *Scream 2*
Scream 2 (film) 34–38, 102, 104, 119, 210–218, 265, 296
Scrimm, Angus 1154
SeaQuest DSV (TV series) 273, 283
Secret of My Success (film) 21
Serling, Rod 21, **243, 275, 276, 282**
The Serpent and the Rainbow (book) 8, 26, 27, 132–145, 152, 158, 204, 220, 227
The Serpent and the Rainbow (film) 2, 8, 26, 27, 30, 104, 119, 130–145, 195, 227
Seven (film) 3
The Sex Crime of the Century (alternate film title) 11; see also *The Last House on the Left*
The Shadow (film)
Sharrett, Michael 121, 127
Shatner, William 228
"Shatterday" (new *Twilight Zone* episode) 276, 277
Shaye, Robert 3, 18, 20, 25, 32, 106, 172, 173, 175, 182
Shea, Jack 106, 248
Sheedy, Ally 126
Sheffler, Marc 40
Shelley, Mary 3
Shepherd, Peter 257

Shocker (film) 2, 5, 28–30, 82, 92, 103, 120, 144–159, 167, 195, 236, 245, 295
Sholder, Jack 20, 107, 254
Short Circuit (film) 24, 25, 126, 127
Showtime 31
Siegel, Don 234
Siegel, Joel 37
The Silence of the Lambs (film) 3, 205
Simon and Schuster 140
Simon and Simon (TV series) 275
Simoun, A.R. 132
Siskel, Gene 154
Six Characters in Search of an Author 185
Skerritt, Tom 276
Slate, Jeremy 221
Slaughter of the Innocent (film) 3
Slayton, Bobby 289
Sleepwalkers (film) 31
Sliders (TV series) 37
Sliver (film) 30, 283
Smith, Smitty 289
Soles, P.J. 207
Solomon, Adam 257, 265
Somewhere in Time (film) 22
Sorvino, Paul 238, 243, 245
Space: 1999 (TV series) 22, 276
Spaceballs (film) 24
Spacecamp (film) 27, **126**
Spawn (film) 17, 32, 92
Spears, Peter 280
The Specialist (film) 32
Speer, Martin 59, 95
Spelling, Tori 35, 37, 205, 211, 216
Spielberg, Steven 17, 21, 22, 275, 295
Splatter University (film) 219
Sporleder, Gregory 257
Stafford, Tamara 95, 104
Stansfield, Claire 257, 263
Star Trek (TV series) 22, 276
Star Trek: Deep Space Nine (TV series) 105, 253, 271
Star Trek: Generations (film) 32
Star Trek: The Next Generation (TV series) 253, 282, 284
Star Trek II: The Wrath of Khan (film) 17

Index

Star Trek III: The Search for Spock (film) 219
Star Trek IV: The Voyage Home (film) 14
Star Trek V: The Final Frontier (film) 20
Star Wars (film) 16, 31, 292
Stargate (film) 32
Starlog (magazine) 16
Starship Troopers (film) 38, 216, 292
Steadman, John 59, 74
Steinmann, Danny 13
Stoker, Bram 3, 194
Stone, Christopher 285
Stone, Oliver 295
Stone, Sharon 16, 75
Straczynski, J. Michael 22, 275
Straight, Beatrice 238, 244
Strange Invaders (film) 289
A Stranger in Our House (telefilm) 6, 15, 74, 82, 221–229, 234, 237, 238, 243, 245, 264, 295
Summer of Fear (alternate film title) see *A Stranger in Our House*
Summer of Fear (book) 15, 221–228
Superman (film) 16
Superman II (film) 16
Superman IV: The Quest for Peace (film) 25
Swamp Thing (comic book) 16
Swamp Thing (film) 16–18, 21, 22, 26, 38, 85–95, 144, 158, 238, 276, 296
Swanson, Kristy 121, **123, 126**, 127, 129
Swanson, Scott 289
Szwarc, Jeannot 22, 276

Tabori, Kristoffer 279
Tales from the Darkside (TV series) 21
Tapin, Mark 24
Tarentino, Quentin 158
Tartikoff, Brandon 22
Tate, Laura Mae 286
Taylor, John 289
"Teacher's Aide" (*Twilight Zone* revival episode) 22, 276; see also Barbeau, Adrienne
"Teliko" (*X-Files* episode) 27

Tennant, Victoria 23
The Terminator (film) 245
Terminator 2: Judgment Day (film) 212, 217, 219
Terror Train (film) 2, 84
Tesh, John 5, 145, 152
The Texas Chainsaw Massacre (film) 1, 4
They Live (film) 28, 31, 273, 276
The Thing (1982 film) 17
Thompson, Howard 12
Thompson, Kevin 298
Three on a Meathook (film) 1
Time After Time (film) 31
Time Bandits (film) 31
Tin Cup (film) 21
Titanic (1997 film) 35, 36
Tobey, Kenneth 289
Todd, Tony 36, 276, 272
To Kill a Mockingbird (film) 8
Together (film) 10, 11
Tomorrow Never Dies (film) 35, 36
Touched by an Angel (TV series) 287
Toussaint, Beth 284
The Town That Dreaded Sundown (film) 205
Twiggy 31
The Twilight Zone (TV series/original) 17, 30, 118, 184, 234, 238, 275–279, 290
The Twilight Zone (TV series/revival) 21–23, 30, 234, 275–279, 289
Twin Peaks (TV series) 286, 289
Twomey, Anne 22, 121, 127, 276, 279
Tyson, Cathy 27, 131, **135**, 141

Ulrich, Skeet 34, 35, 197
Unger, Brian 34
Unger, Joe 106
Universal Studios 1, 28, 146
Urich, Robert 74, 228, **231**, 235, 237
Uslan, Michael 16, 86

V (TV series) 276
A Vampire in Brooklyn (film) 3, 21, 27, 30, 33, 186–195, 246, 265, 288

Videodrome (film) 31
Village of the Damned (1995 film) 3, 33
Vincent, Virginia 59, 95, 238
The Virgin Spring (film) 46–50, 57, 58, 73, 263
Von Sydow, Max 47
Von Zerneck, Danielle 126

Wagner, Bruce 25, 28, 105, 248
Wagner, Natasha 247, 264
Wait Until Dark (film) 102
Wallace, Dee 14, 59, 276
Walsh, M. Emmet 279
War Games (film) 126
Warner, David 31, 211, 216
Warner Brothers 23, 24, 121
The Warriors (film) 21
Washington, Ada 40, 91
Washington, Denzel 34
Waxworks (film) 31, 158
Wayne, John 69
Weaver, Sigourney 262
Wein, Len 16, 91
Weinstein, Bob 197, 211
Weinstein, Harvey 197, 211
Weird Science (film) 24, 126
Wertimer, Ned 238
Wes Craven Presents Mind Ripper (film) 4, 33, 247, 256–266, 271, 273
Wes Craven Presents Wishmaster (film) 4, 31, 36, 105, 266–273
Wes Craven's New Nightmare (film) 3–5, 21, 32, 74, 119, 144, 171–185, 193, 195, 216, 219, 220, 254, 264, 265, 293, 295
Wes Craven's Principles of Fear (CD-ROM) 34
Whale, James 92
Whalen, Sean 159, **164**
"What Are Friends For?" (new *Twilight Zone* episode) 276
Whipp, Joseph 22, 106, 120, 197, 276, 278
Whitworth, James 59, **63**, 95
Whiz Kids (TV series) 126
Wild Orchid (film) 10
Williams, Tony 69

Williamson, Kevin 4, 26, 33, 37, 197, 204, 208, 210, 211, 215, 216, 291
Willis, Bruce 22, 276, 277
Winfield, Paul 131
Winston, Stan 238, 245
Wise, Ray 86, 95
Wise, Robert 33
Witherspoon, John 186, 195, 196
Wolf, Joseph 106
Wonder Woman (TV series) 275
Wong, Randall 285
Woodrum, Donna 106
"Wordplay" (new *Twilight Zone* episode) 22, 276, 277
Worth, Nicholas 86, 238
Wrightson, Berni 16
Wyndham, John **3**
Wynorski, Jim 17
Wyss, Amanda **19**, 106, **109**

The X-Files (TV series) 27, 36, 288

Yagher, Kevin 248, 253
Young, Dey 132
Young, Vernon 46
You've Got to Walk It Like You Talk It or You'll Lose That Beat (film) 10

Ziembicki, Bob 211
Zimbalist, Stephanie 22
Zuckerbrod, Gary M. 146, 172, 280